Values in Sustainable Development

To enhance sustainable development research and practice, the values of the researchers, project managers and participants must first be made explicit. *Values in Sustainable Development* introduces and compares worldviews and values from multiple countries and perspectives, providing a survey of empirical methods available to study environmental values as affected by sustainable development. Part I is methodological, looking at what values are, why they are important, and how to include values in sustainable development. Part II looks at how values differ across social contexts, religions and viewpoints, demonstrating how various individuals may value nature from a variety of cultural, social, and religious points of view. Part III presents case studies ordered by scale from the individual and community levels through to the national, regional and international levels. These examples show how values can motivate, be incorporated into and be an integral part of the success of a project.

This thought-provoking book gives researchers, students and practitioners in sustainable development a wealth of approaches to include values in their research.

Jack Appleton is a Research Fellow at the University of Malaysia Sabah, Borneo, and teaches "Principles of Sustainability" and "Research and Quantitative Methods" at Merlyhurst University, USA.

Routledge Studies in Sustainable Development

Values in Sustainable Development

Edited by
Jack Appleton

Routledge
Taylor & Francis Group

LONDON AND NEW YORK

First published 2014
by Routledge
2 Park Square, Milton Park, Abingdon, Oxon OX14 4RN

Simultaneously published in the USA and Canada
by Routledge
711 Third Avenue, New York, NY 10017

Routledge is an imprint of the Taylor & Francis Group, an informa business

British Library Cataloguing in Publication Data
A catalogue record for this book is available from the British Library

Library of Congress Cataloguing in Publication data
   Values in sustainable development / edited by Jack Appleton.
      pages   cm. – (Routledge studies in sustainable development ; 6)
   Includes bibliographical references and index.
   1. Sustainable development – Moral and ethical aspects.   2. Environmental ethics.   I. Appleton, Jack.
   HC79.E5V255 2013
   174′.4–dc23
   2013010773

ISBN13: 978-0-415-64350-4 (hbk)
ISBN13: 978-0-203-08017-7 (ebk)

Typeset in Goudy by Out of House Publishing

MIX
Paper from
responsible sources
FSC
www.fsc.org   FSC® C013604

Printed and bound in Great Britain by
CPI Group (UK) Ltd, Croydon, CR0 4YY

Contents

    KWEK YAN CHONG, MARCUS AIK HWEE CHUA, MEI LIN NEO,
    DANIEL JIA JUN NG, SITI MARYAM YAAKUB, TAI CHONG TOH,
    ALISON KIM SHAN WEE, AND DING LI YONG

29 Environmental law as a foundation for sustainable development   299
    AMBASSADOR AMADO S. TOLENTINO JR

    Further reading   306
    Index   309

Figures

Tables

Contributors

Jack Appleton is a Research Fellow at the University of Malaysia Sabah, Borneo, Institute of Tropical Biology and Conservation, and teaches "Principles of Sustainability" and "Research and Quantitative Methods" at Merlyhurst University, USA.

Marc Bekoff PhD is a former Professor of Ecology and Evolutionary Biology at the University of Colorado, Boulder, a Fellow of the Animal Behavior Society, and a past Guggenheim Fellow. He and Jane Goodall authored *The Emotional Lives of Animals: A Leading Scientist Explores Animal Joy, Sorrow, and Empathy – and Why They Matter*. (2008, New World Library).

David M. Boje PhD is a Professor of Management at New Mexico State University, Distinguished Achievement Professor, Honorary Doctorate from Aalborg University (Denmark) and author of *Handbook of Antenarrative* (2012, Routledge).

J. M. Bowker is a PhD Agricultural and Resource Economics Scientist with the United States Department of Agriculture (USDA) Forest Service, Southern Research Station.

W. Puck Brecher PhD is an Assistant Professor of Japanese at Washington State University. He is author of *The Aesthetics of Strangeness: Eccentricity and Madness in Early Modern Japan* (2013, University of Hawai'i Press), and *An Investigation of Japan's Relationship to Nature and Environment* (2000, Edwin Mellen Press).

Zinta S. Byrne PhD is a Professor of Industrial Organizational Psychology at Colorado State University.

Wallace P. H. Chang PhD is a Professor at the Chinese University Hong Kong School of Architecture; he is both an architectural practitioner and theorist on urban design, cultural conservation and community participation. His research focuses on the cultural identity and urban sustainability issues during the urban transformation process in Hong Kong and southern Chinese cities.

Kwek Yan Chong (Lead Author), National University of Singapore, Department of Biological Sciences.

Marcus Aik Hwee Chua, National University of Singapore, Department of Biological Sciences.

Victor Corral-Verdugo PhD is a Professor at Division de Ciencias Sociales University of Sonora, and lead author of *Psychological Approaches to Sustainability: Current Trends in Theory, Research and Applications* (2010, Nova Press).

Ding Ding MPH is with the Department of Public Administration at North Carolina State University. Her research fields include health policy analysis and non-profit organization management.

Prakash C. Dixit PhD was Professor and Chairman of the Department of Geology and Mining at Anton de Kom University of Suriname, Paramaribo, Suriname, South America.

Chigbo Joseph Ekwealo PhD is a Senior Lecturer in the Department of Philosophy, University of Lagos. His PhD is in Environmental Philosophy and he is the Editor of the *Journal of African Environmental Ethics and Values*.

Blanca Fraijo-Sing PhD is a Professor of Psychology with the University of Sonora, Mexico. Her academic interests focus on developing interventional programs of Environmental Education with children. She received the Interamerican Award on Environmental Psychology, as a graduate student, in 2005.

Kevin Halsey JD is a Professor of Environmental Law at Lewis and Clark College, Portland, Oregon, and co-lead for the Ecosystem Services Consulting team at Parametrix.

Hamim Hamim PhD is an Associate Professor at Bogor Agricultural University, Bogor, Indonesia.

Anne M. Hansen PhD works at PDRI in Arlington, Virginia, where she is a Senior Human Capital Consultant with research interests in selection and assessment methods, measurement issues, and organizational justice.

Paul G. Harris PhD is the Chair Professor of Global and Environmental Studies at the Hong Kong Institute of Education.

Mark E. Hillon, PhD in Management.

Cassandra Johnson-Gaither PhD is a Sociologist with the USDA Forest Service'sSouthern Research Station's Understanding Changing Social and Natural Systems Research Group.

Peter N. Jones PhD is the Director of the Bauu Institute where he works with indigenous peoples on ethno-medicine, cultural, and natural resource management, and social justice projects.

Justus Kithiia PhD is a Lecturer at the School for Field Studies, Centre for Rainforest Studies, Australia. His research concentrates on pro-poor climate change risk responses in East Africa.

Derk Loorbach PhD is an Associate Professor at the Dutch Research Institute for Transitions (DRIFT), Erasmus University, Rotterdam. He is co-author of *Transitions to Sustainable Development: New Directions in the Study of Long Term Transformative Change* (2010, Routledge).

Anna Lyth PhD is a Research Associate at the School of Geography and Environmental Studies at the University of Tasmania (Australia), and the Sustainability Research Centre, University of the Sunshine Coast, Australia. Her area of expertise is integrated planning for climate change mitigation and adaptation.

Michael Marder PhD is the Ikerbasque Research Professor of Philosophy at the University of the Basque Country, Vitoria-Gasteiz. He is the author of *Plant-Thinking: A Philosophy of Vegetal Life* (2012, Columbia University Press).

Jacob A. Massoud PhD is a Professor of Business and Leadership at Dominican University of California.

Sheila McNamee PhD is a Professor of Communication at the University of New Hampshire and Vice President of the Taos Institute. She is co-author of *Research and Social Change: A Relational Constructionist Approach* (2011, Routledge).

Nalini M. Nadkarni PhD is a Professor of Biology at the University of Utah. She co-founded the Sustainable Prisons Project in the state of Washington, and she is the author of *Between Earth and Sky: Our Intimate Connections to Trees* (2009, University of California Press).

Mei Lin Neo, National University of Singapore, Department of Biological Sciences.

Daniel Jia Jun Ng, National University of Singapore, Department of Biological Sciences.

Asep Nurhalim is an Islamic Studies Lecturer at Bogor Agricultural University, Bogor, Indonesia.

David Victor Ogunkan is a Town Planner who is currently a research student in urban and regional planning. His current area of interest is urban social issues, specifically street children in Nigeria.

Dan J. Pacholke is the Director of Prisons with the State of Washington Department of Corrections. He co-founded the Sustainable Prisons Project.

David Patterson PhD is a Professor of Judaic Studies at the University of Memphis. He holds the Bornblum Chair of Excellence in Judaic Studies and is the Director of the University's Bornblum Judaic Studies Program.

G. G. Patthey PhD is a Professor of Applied Linguistics at Los Angeles City College; her academic research is in the areas of sociolinguistics and sociobiology, and discourse analysis.

Luluk Setyaningsih is a Lecturer and Researcher at the University of Nusa Bangsa Bogor, Bogor, Indonesia.

Kathy Shearin is a Program Supervisor for the East Multnomah Soil and Water Conservation District (EMSWCD). She manages the Sustainable Urban Landscapes Program.

Vandana Shiva PhD is a Professor and founder of the Research Foundation for Science, Technology and Ecology, a participatory, public interest research organization to protect biodiversity, defend farmers' rights, and promote organic farming.

César Tapia-Fonllem PhD is an Environmental Educator at the University of Sonora, Mexico. His areas of research include the development of instruments to assess sustainable behavior and its determinants. He received the Interamerican Award on Environmental Psychology, as a graduate student, in 2007.

Aina Thompson Adeboyejo PhD is an Associate Professor and a Registered Town Planner in the Department of Urban and Regional Planning, Ladoke Akintola University of Technology, Ogbomoso, Nigeria.

Tai Chong Toh, National University of Singapore, Department of Biological Sciences.

Ambassador Amado S. Tolentino Jr is currently with the International Council of Environmental Law (Philippines) and is the Executive Governor (for developing countries), of the International Council of Environmental Law. Previously, he coordinated the Association of Southeast Asian Nations (ASEAN) Experts Group on the Environment; Vice-Chair (Asia), International Union for Conservation of Nature (IUCN) Commission on Environmental Law; Environmental Law Consultant to the United Nations Development Programme (UNEP). Presently, he is the Executive Governor (for developing countries) of the International Council of Environmental Law.

Tammi Vacha-Haase PhD is a Professor of Counseling Psychology at Colorado State University, and was the author of the 1998 seminal article, Reliability Generalization: "Exploring Variance in Measurement Error Affecting Score Reliability Across Studies" (*Educational and Psychological Measurement*, 58, pp. 6–20), and was lead author for Vacha-Haase, T., C. R. Tani, L. R. Kogan, R. A. Woodall, and B. Thompson (2001) "Reliability Generalization: Exploring Reliability Variations on MMPI/MMPI-2 Validity Scale Scores" (*Assessment*, 8, pp. 391–401).

Fred Van Dyke PhD is Director of the Au Sable Institute, and author of *Conservation Biology: Foundations, Concepts, Applications* (2010, Springer), and *Between Heaven and Earth: Christian Perspectives on Environmental Protection* (2010, Praeger).

Bettina Wittneben PhD is a Research Fellow at Oxford University's Smith School of Enterprise and the Environment. Her research concerns international climate governance and institutional change.

Alison Kim Shan Wee, National University of Singapore, Department of Biological Sciences.

Siti Maryam Yaakub, National University of Singapore, Department of Biological Sciences.

Ding Li Yong, National University of Singapore, Department of Biological Sciences.

Preface

The book would never have been written without Dr Francine Neago, who introduced me to Datuk Rajah Indran in Kota Kinabalu, Sabah Malaysia. Datuk Indran and I set out to create an infrastructure which would facilitate the preservation of wild areas in the state of Sabah. Datuk Indran and I began discussions with Datin Mariyati Mohamed PhD, who at the time was the Director of the Institute of Tropical Biology and Conservation at the University of Malaysia Sabah. She and Datuk Indran had collaborated on the Lower Kinabatangan Scientific Expedition in 2002 along with Beniot Goossens PhD, who is currently the director of the Danau Girang Field Centre located in the area's Wildlife Sanctuary. Over the next several years, the discussions focused on the details of the infrastructure, its legal framework, its institutional foundation, its overarching administration, goals, biology, etc. These discussions were accompanied with various trips to different areas of Sabah, encompassing protected and unprotected, private and public lands.

As the discussions ebbed and flowed, a variety of agencies and individuals became involved. Over time I realized a discussion of values was missing. It was taken for granted that everyone involved valued and cared about the same things, had the same agendas, the same concerns, and the same vision. Upon further reflection, I realized that most of those involved were scientists and conservationists who were very task oriented, and did not have a significant background in the social sciences and ethnographic methodology. In short, they had no means at their disposal to include the values of the participants, so they acted as if everyone involved was there for the same reasons, and the why was simply a shared understanding held by everyone.

Sabah, Malaysia is a very diverse society; it is fair to say that there is no dominant majority. It is also fair to say that its economy is tied to its geography. As such there are multiple constituents and many segments of society, each with its own set of values. However, having different values does not preclude participants from sharing aspirations. Individuals can have shared goals and diverse values and motivations. Understanding others' values can lead to the crafting of projects which appeal to a diverse set of values, and motivate diverse participants to work together toward a common goal. The point of this book is to give individuals in the field of sustainable development a starting point from which they can gain an understanding of participants' values, a sense of the diversity of those values, and a sense of what can be accomplished when one is motivated by one's values.

Acknowledgments

This book would not have been published without the editors and editorial assistants at Routledge: Virjee Khanam, Ashley Wright, Helena Hurd, and Helen Bell; and Production Manager, Alison Evans, and copy editor, Joanne Osborn. This book would not have been possible without the effort, work, and encouragement of many individuals, including Datuk Rajah Indran, and the instrumental, facilitative support provided by the University of Malaysia Sabah, Institute of Tropical Biology and Conservation. Specifically, Datin Mariyati Mohamed PhD (the Director of the University at the time the book was developed), and the successor, Abdul Hamid Ahmad. Other faculty members who provided encouragement and support include Henry Bernard PhD, Bakhtiar Effendi Yahya PhD, Monica Suleiman PhD, and Noramly Bin Muslim PhD. Without my friend Syed Fadzil Al'Shahab I would have accomplished very little in Sabah.

All of the contributing authors deserve recognition, as do individuals who facilitated individual chapters. Several individuals, however, deserve special mention as without their encouragement and support the book would not have been possible: Carolyn E. Adams-Price PhD (life-long friend and champion); David Boje PhD, whose encouragement, support, and caring extends well beyond this book, and who made the book feasible as his efforts resulted in the participation of several authors; David Garson PhD introduced Ding Ding (Chapter 6); Steve Hendricks (*The Unquiet Grave*, Da Capo Press, 2007) introduced Peter Jones PhD (Chapter 10); Datuk Rajah Indran is responsible for Prakash C. Dixit PhD (Chapter 11); Simeon Chavel PhD (University of Chicago) introduced David Patterson PhD (Chapter 12); Lynn Humphrey (Recreation Planner, United States Forest Service (USFS), Department of Agriculture (DOA)) introduced Cassandra Johnson-Gaither PhD and J. M. Bowker PhD (Chapter 15); Frank Fromherz PhD introduced Paul G. Harris PhD (Chapter 18); Ruta Stabina (University of Oregon, Sustainability Leadership Program) introduced two authors: Kathy Shearin (Chapter 22) and Kevin Halsey JD (Chapter 25). Several biologists had previously recommended Ms Shearin as the most knowledgeable individual for sustainable landscaping. David Boje's support resulted in the participation of the following individuals and authors: Jacob Massoud PhD (Chapter 7), Mark E. Hillon PhD (Chapter 26), and Slawomir Magala PhD (Erasmus University, Rotterdam) who introduced Derk Loorbach PhD and Bettina Wittneben PhD (Chapter 9).

Frank Fromherzs PhD's initial support was invaluable. Fred Van Dyke PhD (Chapter 13) provided encouragement without which the book would never have come to fruition; Chapter 8 (Jack Appleton and Wallace P. H. Chang) would not have been possible without Bill Lennertz (National Charrette Institute (NCI)). Victor Corral-Verdugo PhD, primary author of Chapter 16, provided Blanca Fraijo-Sing PhD and César Tapia-Fonllem PhD the opportunity to include Chapter 24. Vandana Shiva PhD's (Chapter 1) participation was the result of the effort of one research assistant (RA): Annie Tzoneva. The initial outline of the book was developed with C. Edward Snodgrass PhD who was introduced by Carolyn E. Adams-Price PhD. The draft was brilliantly edited by Fred and Rebecca Kameny. Library and research support at the University Malaysia Sabah (UMS) was provided by Rukiah Ag. Amit, and at the Sabah State Library by Antonia Peter Sani. Several RAs were involved in the development of the book: Amy Hass, Vasiliy V. Safin, Ryan Lau, and Alex Perusse who assisted with the editing of the final draft. Finally, I must mention the world's most wonderful filing assistants: Michelle-Sarah Appleton and Evy Killough.

Introduction

Jack Appleton

The purpose of this book is to provide researchers and facilitators of sustainable development a starting point from which to include others' values in their projects. It is not a comprehensive guide on values research. It is an introduction, intended to provide the reader with a foundation from which they can develop the skills to understand participants' values – especially participants whose cultural and socio-economic background, and values are significantly different. What follows is a sketch of a roadmap of how to build co-creative capacity among sustainable development project participants by developing and engaging participants' values. At first, this appears to be a simple task: just ask, "what do you care about, what do you value?" Actually, those two questions should be asked, but they are not sufficient. Not because participants lie or are unaware of their values, but because values are often ambivalent, contradictory, and may change in intensity as the understanding of the situation changes. Facilitators' and participants' values can be inferred by observing behavior, and captured ethnographically. Values are at the heart of any inquiry: "No problem can be adequately formulated unless the values involved … are stated" (C. W. Mills, 1959, *Sociological Imagination*, Oxford, p. 129). Certainly sustainable development, generative though it may be, is all about threatening changes. An objective understanding of values is not sufficient; ideally one must also develop a subjective understanding. To conceptualize as C. W. Mills suggests requires both the objective and the subjective, what Clifford Greertz called "thick description."

Part I of the book provides a beginning for both an objective understanding and subjective insight. A subjective understanding is the purpose of Part II of the book. The purpose of Part III is to inspire a vision of what is possible when one engages participants' values. Part II is not a series of normative statements; the chapters are personal reflections and descriptions of values of specific segments of humanity. One should not presume that every member of each group holds the same considerations. The chapters are insightful starting points, examples of what one may find as one explores the values held by others. Part III of the book is designed to provide the reader with a sense of the possible, from the immediate environment of our homes (Kathy Shearin) to Ambassador Amado S. Tolentino Jr's work to bring caring for the environment to every corner of the globe.

Part I, anchored by Vandana Shiva in Chapter 1, starts by reminding us why sustainable development is important. In Chapter 2, Jack Appleton discusses why values need to be included in sustainable development research and practice. The chapter continues with the definition of values, and an explanation of how values simultaneously compete for awareness. Sheila McNamee, in Chapter 3, describes the ways in which the dominant discourse of individualism permeates our thinking about sustainability from a relational constructionist orientation. In Chapter 4, G. G. Patthey shows how the world that Sheila McNamee introduces is created and how it can be revealed through the field of linguistics, communication, and discourse analysis. In Chapter 5, Tammi Vacha-Haase and her colleagues shift the discussion from language to the world of statistics with a cautionary tale which explores the limits of statistics, their appropriateness, and their validity and reliability in the area of psychometrics. The authors discuss how the tools and the limitations of psychometrics are used. In Chapter 6, Ding Ding returns the reader to the world of language with a discussion of focus groups: what focus groups are, why we should use them, and how to conduct effective focus groups. David M. Boje and Jacob A. Massoud, in Chapter 7, bring us to the less structured reality storytelling by reminding us that we live a story, and that stories, collected appropriately, give insight into our values and our lives. In Chapter 8, Jack Appleton and Wallace P. H. Chang scale up the focus from the details of participants' stories to the world of communities by explicating the charrette process. Charrettes can be a defining aspect of a sustainable development project and with some vigilance can be considered an expression of the community's values. Chang takes the charrette and proves that while it is an Anglo-French invention, it can be effective in other settings. The methodology part of the book ends with Derk Loorbach and Bettina Wittneben, who remind us in Chapter 9 that all understanding and action is to a degree solipsistic and subjective. They argue that a learning-by-doing and a doing-by-learning does not foil Mills's desire for a scientific understanding of social processes, but enhances it if the participants are embraced.

Part II of the book is organized first by religion in order of historical appearance, and second by geography starting in the USA, then moving south, and then east to Asia and finishing in Africa. This is so that no sense of importance or priority is attached to the ordering of the chapters. No one chapter is more important or follows from another chapter. Part II starts in Chapter 10 with Peter N. Jones's well-focused discussion describing indigenous knowledge and epistemology, how it relates to an understanding of the environment, and how such an understanding cannot be separated from research or actions pertaining to indigenous peoples' knowledge and their environment. In Chapter 11, Prakash C. Dixit then takes the reader to the other side of the world, and into the world of the great religions, as he unravels values as practiced by Hindus. Dixit's optimistic message embodies his subject as he explores the possibility of resolving the environmental crisis through the teachings and values of Hinduism. David Patterson provides a contrast in Chapter 12 as he discusses another of the great religions, the Jewish religious tradition as it relates to nature and stewardship. For Jews, stewardship is not simply an inextractible way of life; it is the essence of their existence: a sacrosanct covenant. In Chapter 13, Fred Van Dyke explores how our humanity may well be the key to our own future. Van Dyke discusses recent thinking with regard to stewardship, humankind, and the environment, and of how Christianity fits into the larger discussion of stewardship and sustainable development. In Chapter 14, Hamim Hamim and his co-authors complete the discussion of the great religions with an explanation of Islamic thought toward the environment and how life on earth relates to existence after life on earth.

With Cassandra Johnson-Gaither and J. M. Bowker's Chapter 15, Part II shifts from religions to geography. The authors paint a more intimate portrait of human beings and their relationship to the environment by exploring African American perceptions of and interactions with wildlands. The authors argue that collective memories of forest labor, plantation agriculture, sharecropping, and lynching impact black Americans' perceptions and use of wildlands. Part II continues in Chapter 16, with an almost impossible task – the ascertainment and description of environmental values in Latin America, elegantly taken on by Victor Corral-Verdugo and his colleagues, whose research on this topic is unparalleled. Corral-Verdugo and his colleagues provide insight into the dispositions among Latin Americans toward the environment. The chapter includes a discussion of distinctive worldviews, beliefs, and values contextualized within their physical and social environment, and shaped by their colonial history. From the Americas, the focus shifts to post-disaster Japan, in Chapter 17 by W. Puck Brecher, and an exploration of how the Phoenix is rising on the wings of the Transition Town movement. Brecher explores how values in Japan radically altered after the tsunami disasters of 2011. From Japan, Paul G. Harris moves the discussion to China in Chapter 18, where he provides a contrasting anchor with his discussion of the environment in this country. Leaving Asia, in Chapter 19 Chigbo Joseph Ekwealo explores the wisdom left to us by the elders in Africa through the proverbs they have handed down. Part II ends with a discussion by Aina Thompson Adeboyejo and David Victor Ogunkan, who in Chapter 20 explore how in Nigeria what we value also brings us hope for the environment and motivation for our actions to care for it.

Part III of the book takes the reader from the micro to the macro. It explores examples of what is possible when individuals are motivated by their values. In Chapter 21, Michael Marder provides a foundation for consideration of the environment. Kathy Shearin shows us how to care for ourselves, the environment, and how to bring a sense of nature into our world in Chapter 22. Shearin's chapter begins with a discussion of landscaping at the level of the family home. It defines sustainable landscaping, and explains why it is important, and how it relates to the preservation of the environment. In Chapter 23, Nalini M. Nadkarni and Dan J. Pacholke, with Marc Bekoff, demonstrate what is possible with a segment of society which most would consider impossible to bring into the discussion of sustainability: prisoners. They show us it is possible to engage in a larger positive transformational process with any population. In Chapter 24, Blanca Fraijo-Sing and her colleagues extract the essential elements of environmental educational programs, such as those run by Nadkarni and Pacholke, and Bekoff, and develop a generalizable model for environmental education. Combined, these initial chapters provide a roadmap for changing how we interact with and care for our environment. Shifting focus, in Chapter 25 Kevin Halsey explores how businesses, communities, and interested parties can come together to simultaneously lower their costs, preserve the environment, and gain necessary resources through ecosystems services. Mark E. Hillon takes us inside the segment of society that Halsey engages in the sustainable development process, but that is far removed from Pacholke's: the corporate boardroom. In Chapter 26, Hillon explains how a shift in strategic thinking can protect the bottom line which is the concern of business strategy. In Chapter 27, Justus Kithiia and Anna Lyth take the reader out of the world of business and back into the community and society where the foundation of deep traditions is connected to the building of resilience in Africa. Kwek Yan Chong and his colleagues let us know that such considerations are not arriving a moment too soon, as they take us on a journey in Chapter 28 to explore Singapore's biodiversity in its marine, coastal, and terrestrial habitats after two centuries of development. The book ends with Chapter 29 by Ambassador Amado S. Tolentino Jr, who provides insight into what the future of environmental law will look like and how it is being forged at the United Nations (UN) with the goal of bringing the natural world into the world of legal rights to ensure effective environmental law implementation to attain sustainability of resources.

Introduction to Part I
Methods for understanding individuals' values

Jack Appleton

Part I of the book explores how to include values in sustainable development. Vandana Shiva starts the journey in Chapter 1 by explaining why we should care, why it is an urgent task, and what caring means. She lays out the path forward, a world operating upon new assumptions as we care for what we care about. To include values requires both an understanding of what values are (Chapter 2), and an understanding of what participants' values are (Chapters 3 through 8). Derk Loorbach and Bettina Wittneben end this part in Chapter 9 by reminding us that in order to understand someone else one has to understand oneself. To accomplish this, one has to genuinely engage and learn from others, and include oneself in the learning process. Accordingly, the authors enlighten the path by pointing out that the task and process of understanding values is "an ongoing process of learning-by-doing and doing-by-learning in which all actors contribute to envisioning, agenda building, experimenting, and evaluation." There are many ways to conduct research and to evaluate a participant's values: in-depth interviews, ethnographic observation, surveys, thematic apperceptive test evaluation, content analysis of associated literature, analysis of participant self-reporting and recording, psychometric testing, word association analysis, group participatory techniques, and so on. Some ways require significant training; others involve significant logistics, techniques, and methods. The methods explained in Part I will introduce the reader to solid empirical research methods and provide insight into the social science process. The chapters and this part are not encyclopedic, they are not a how-to; they are an introduction to the research process and research techniques. Each chapter provides a solid foundation from which to begin to understand how to conduct such research activities.

The order of the chapters from Chapters 3 through 8 are not indicative of a specific research epistemology. However, there are clear linkages. Discourse analysis (Chapter 4) is the primary tool one uses to produce systematic evidenced-based conclusions from recordings of interactions (interviews, group discussions, stories, etc.). Our language is not spoken in a vacuum, it is a social act, and as such it is a product, a manifestation, and a creator of our social reality. Without at least some understanding of this process within which conversations take place, an analysis of discourse may not make sense. Sheila McNamee's Chapter 3 leads off the direct discussion of methodology. McNamee is followed by Patthey in Chapter 4, who provides an introduction to the nuts and bolts of discourse analysis. The discussion shifts gears as surveys are often used to ascertain values. In Chapter 5, Tammi Vacha-Haase and her colleagues explore the world of psychometrics and provide wisdom and caution to those who use surveys and interpret survey data. Their discussion is crucial; this is not so much because one is expected to create a survey from scratch, but because the use of surveys is so common. It is reasonable to expect one to use existing survey instruments and/or to incorporate existing survey-based reports into one's work. This is especially true when there are large pools of identifiable participants to be considered. Vacha-Haase and her colleagues do not discuss any specific evaluative questionnaire or survey, but their discussion of validity and reliability provides a strong cautionary tale. In fact, the NEP (New Environmental Paradigm) and other instruments which measure anthropocentrism (the tendency to view the world as centered on and created for humans) and environmental values are relatively easy to find and use, but not so easy to interpret correctly.

The next three chapters in Part I discuss three techniques which involve direct interaction with participants for data collection: focus groups, stories, and charrettes. These techniques ultimately rest on social construction theory and discourse analysis for interpretation of the data generated. Focus groups that are routinely used in research on environmental values and community planning, and are a staple in charrettes, are introduced and explored by Ding Ding in Chapter 6. In Chapter 7, David M. Boje and Jacob A. Massoud introduce storytelling as a means of gaining insight into the values of the storytellers and their communities. Stories can be collected as part of charrettes, or focus groups, or on their own. Stories can also be collected at the same time as survey data is collected. Here again, the interpretative aspects of story collection are important: what stories tell us about participants' values requires an understanding of discourse and social construction. charrettes make sense for large-scale projects: neighborhoods, regions, cities, and so on (Chapter 8).

One of the elegant aspects of these techniques is that, for the purpose at hand, they are relatively easy to grasp and utilize effectively. An individual may not be able to go from economist, biologist, civil engineer, or planner to social psychologist quickly, but they can go from following their sense or hunch about what others care about to exploring what others care about in a systematic evidence-based manner relatively easily.

Finally, another aspect of these techniques that allows them to be useful in the development of an understanding of participants' values is that they are relatively value-neutral. They can be used across a wide variety of setting and circumstance, and across cultures, or within a multi-cultural setting. Wallace P. H. Chang's case study in Chapter 8 clearly proves that charrettes are valuable tools in non-Western settings. Stories and narratives are a universal among human beings, and focus groups can easily be structured to create a sense of security within which participants discuss their lives and their values. After all, who has not sat around and talked about life with their friends and family?

1 Caring for what we care about

Vandana Shiva

Caring is one of the most important yet most devalued values in the current dominant system which has reduced human beings to greed and competition, and transformed everything into a commodity. Caring for the earth and having reverence for the earth has been considered an impediment to progress. Women's economies based on caring have been considered as unproductive, and hence are not counted. Caring for other species and other people has been pushed aside in the blind and careless race of grabbing more resources, consuming more stuff, and competing to have the biggest share. However, this culture of greed has created a deep crisis of non-sustainability both at the ecological and social level. The ecological crisis is symptomatized in the depletion and pollution of resources, the disappearance of species, and the disruption of climate systems. The social crisis is symptomatized by the deepening inequality, the increasing violence in society – especially the violence against women – and the denial of billions of people to their rightful share of the resources of the planet to meet their basic needs of food and water, clothing and shelter. Caring must move to center stage as a value to avoid ecological collapse, social disintegration, and conflict.

Neoliberal economics, false hope and the commoditized devaluation of women and nature

The neoliberal economic model, which focuses myopically on "monetary growth," discounts women as their contribution to the economy is not counted in monetary, Gross Domestic Product (GDP) terms. This basic devaluation is where the violence against women begins. The more governments talk *ad nauseum* about "inclusive growth" and "financial inclusion," the more it excludes the contributions of women to the economy and society. Accordingly, within such economic models, production for sustenance is "non-production." The transformation of value into disvalue, labour into non-labour, knowledge into non-knowledge, is achieved by the most powerful number that rules our lives, the patriarchal construct of GDP. Others who desire a more sustainable and democratic society refer to it as the Gross Domestic Problem.

The current economic model shaped by capitalist patriarchy is based on the commodification of everything, including women. When we stopped the World

Trade Organization (WTO) Ministerial in Seattle in 1999, our slogan was "Our world is not for sale." An economics of deregulation of commerce, of privatization and commodification of seeds and food, land and water, and of women and children unleashed by economic liberalization degrades social values, deepens patriarchy, and intensifies violence against women.

National accounting systems which are used to calculate growth as GDP are based on the assumption that if producers consume what they produce, they do not in fact produce at all, because they fall outside the production boundary. The production boundary is a political economic creation that, in its workings, excludes regenerative and renewable production cycles from the area of production. Hence, all women who produce for their families, children, community, and society are considered "non-productive" and "economically" inactive. When economies are confined to the market place, economic self-sufficiency is perceived as economic deficiency. The devaluation of women's work, and of work done in subsistence economies of the South, is the natural outcome of a production boundary constructed by capitalist patriarchy. By restricting itself to the values of the market economy, as defined by capitalist patriarchy, the production boundary ignores economic value in the two vital economies which are necessary to ecological and human survival. They are the areas of nature's economy and sustenance economy.

Neoliberal economic reforms lead to the subversion of democracy and privatization of government. Economic systems influence political systems; governments discuss economic reforms as if they have nothing to do with politics and power. They talk of keeping politics out of economics, even while they impose an economic model shaped by the politics of a particular gender and class. Neoliberal reforms work against democracy. We have seen this recently in the US government pushing through "reforms" to bring in Walmart through foreign direct investment (FDI) in retail. Corporate driven reforms create a convergence of economic and political power, a deepening of inequalities, and a growing separation of the political class from the will of the people they are supposed to represent. This is at the root of the disconnect between politicians and the public which has been experienced during the protests that have grown since the Delhi gang rape in 2012.

Worse, an alienated political class is afraid of its own citizens. This alienation explains the increasing use of police to crush nonviolent citizen protests recently in Delhi and elsewhere, the alleged torture of Soni Sori in Bastar, the October 18th, 2012, arrest of Dayamani Barlain in Jharkhand, and the thousands of cases against communities struggling against the nuclear power plant in Kudankulam. A privatized corporate state rapidly becomes a police state. This is why the politicians must surround themselves with ever increasing VIP security, diverting the police from their important duties – the protection of women and ordinary citizens.

Economic systems influence culture and social values. An economics of commodification creates a culture of commodification, where everything has a price, and nothing has value. The growing culture of rape is a social externality of economic reforms. We need to institutionalize social audits of the neoliberal policies which are a central instrument of patriarchy in our times. If there was a social audit of corporatizing our seed sector, 270,000 farmers would not have been pushed to suicide in India since the new economic policies were introduced. If there was a social audit of the corporatization of our food and agriculture, we would not have every fourth Indian hungry, every third woman malnourished, and every second child wasted and stunted due to severe malnutrition. India today would not be the Republic of Hunger that Utsa Patnaik (2008) has written about.

I have repeatedly stressed that the rape of the earth and the rape of women are intimately linked, both metaphorically in shaping worldviews and materially in shaping women's everyday lives. The deepening economic vulnerability of women makes them more vulnerable to all forms of violence, including sexual assault, as we found out during a series of public hearings on the impact of economic reforms on women organized by the National Commission on Women and the Research Foundation for Science, Technology and Ecology.

The victim of the Delhi gang rape has triggered a social revolution. We must sustain it, deepen it, expand it. We must demand and get speedy and effective justice for women. We must call for fasttrack courts to convict those responsible for crimes against women. We must make sure laws are changed so that justice is not elusive for victims of sexual violence. We must continue the demand for blacklisting of politicians with criminal records. We must see the continuum of different forms of violence against women, from female feticide, to economic exclusion, and sexual assault. We need to continue the movement for the social reforms necessary to guarantee safety, security, and equality for women, building on the foundations laid during our independence movement and continued by the feminist movement over the last half century. The agenda for social reforms, social justice, and equality has been derailed by the agenda of economic reforms set by capitalist patriarchy.

In addition to all this, we need to change the ruling paradigm that reduces the society to the economy, and the economy to the market. The imposition of reforms in the name of "growth," fuelling the intensity of crimes against women while deepening the social and economic inequality, must be reversed. Society and economy are not insulated from each other. The processes of social reforms and economic reforms can no longer be separated. We need economic reforms built from a foundation of social reforms that correct gender inequality in society, rather than reforms that facilitate all forms of injustice, inequality, and violence. Ending violence against women also needs to include moving beyond the violent economy shaped by capitalist patriarchy to a nonviolent, sustainable, peaceful economy which gives respect to women and the earth.

The old industrial paradigm, agriculture and the theft of the earth from our children

The old paradigm of food and agriculture is clearly broken. As the report of the International Assessment of Agricultural Knowledge, Science and Technology for Development (IAASTD) carried out by 400 scientists over 6 years for the United Nations (UN) has noted, "business as usual is no longer an option" (IAASTD, 2009, p. 3). The old paradigm of agriculture has its roots in war. An industry that had grown by making explosives and chemicals for the first two world wars remodeled itself as the agro-chemical industry after the Second World War. Explosive factories started to make synthetic fertilizers, and war chemicals started to be used as pesticides and herbicides. In 1984, a gas leak from a pesticide plant in Bhopal killed 3,000 people immediately and 30,000 since then, making the Bhopal tragedy a stark reminder that pesticides kill. Pesticides in agriculture continue to kill farm workers; the Navdanya report, *Poisons in our Food* (Shiva and Singh, 2012), shows there is a link between disease epidemics like cancer and the use of pesticides in agriculture. A daily "cancer train" leaves Punjab, the land of the Green Revolution in India, with cancer victims.

The chemical push (the Green Revolution) changed the paradigm of agriculture. Farmers who embraced it inadvertently introduced carelessness into our relationship with the earth and soil, seed and biodiversity. If chemicals and fossil fuels can replace humans, we don't need farmers and we don't need to be concerned with the agro-ecosystem. Instead of farming and working with awareness of and care for ecological processes, agri-business's mass scale embrace of farming technologies and the accompanying chemicals allowed the agricultural industry to reduce agriculture (the production of food) to an external input system adapted to chemicals without regard to consequences other than increased yields (system outputs). The well-being and health of the entire agro-ecosystem with its diverse species was no longer taken into account. Instead of recognizing that farmers have been breeders over millennia, giving us the rich agro-biodiversity that is the basis of food security, breeding was reduced to uniform industrial varieties responsive to chemicals. Instead of small farms producing diversity, agriculture became focused on large monoculture farms producing a handful of commodities. Correspondingly, the human diet shifted from about 8,500 plant species to about 8 globally traded commodities: corn, wheat, spinach, etc. Science transformed agriculture into compartmentalized, fragmented disciplines based on a reductionist, mechanistic paradigm; in place of the traditional holistic approach that was in place and to which we have to return.

Just as GDP fails to measure the real economy, the health of nature, and society, the category of "yield" fails to measure real costs and real output of farming systems. As the UN observed, the so called High Yielding Varieties (HYVs) of the Green Revolution should in fact be called High Response Varieties since they are bred for responding to chemicals, and are not high yielding in and of themselves. The narrow measure of "yield" propelled agriculture into deepening monocultures, displacing diversity and eroding natural and social capital.

The social and ecological impact of this broken model has pushed the planet and society into deep crisis. Industrial monoculture agriculture has pushed more than 75 percent of the agro-biodiversity to extinction. Because of toxic pesticides, 75 percent of the bees have been killed Seventy-five percent of the water on the planet is being depleted and polluted as it is consumed through intensive irrigation of chemically intensive industrial agriculture. The nitrates in water from industrial farms are creating "dead zones" in the oceans. Chemical industrial farming causes 75 percent of the land and soil degradation. Forty percent of all greenhouse gas emissions responsible for climate change come from a fossil fuel. The fossil fuels used to make fertilizers, run farm machinery, and move food thousands of miles contribute to carbon dioxide emissions. Nitrogen-based fertilizers emit nitrogen oxide which has a global warming potential approximately 300 times greater than carbon dioxide. Additionally, factory farming is a major source of methane. The chemically intensive industrial globalized system of agriculture is destroying the soil's capacity to grow foods, and with it our capacity to feed ourselves (Shiva, 2008).

While this ecological destruction of the natural capital is justified in terms of "feeding people," the problem of hunger has grown. One billion people are permanently hungry. Another 2 billion suffer from food-related diseases ranging from malnutrition and under-nourishment to obesity. When agriculture practices focus on the production of commodities for trade, instead of food for nourishment, hunger and malnutrition is the outcome. Only 10 percent of corn and soya grown is used as food. The rest goes for animal feed and biofuel. Commodities do not feed people, food does. A high cost external input system is artificially kept afloat with US$400 billion as subsidies. That is more than US$1 billion a day. The "cheap" commodities have a very high cost financially, ecologically, and socially. Industrial, chemical agriculture displaces productive rural families. It is debt creating, and debt and mortgages are the primary reason for the disappearance of the family farm. In extreme cases, as in the cotton belt of India, debt created by purchase of high cost seed and chemical inputs has pushed more than 127,000 farmers to suicide in a little over a decade. Getting out of this suicide economy has become urgent for the well-being of all life on earth.

It is falsely claimed that exploiting the earth creates economic value and economic growth, and that this improves human welfare. While human welfare is invoked to separate humans from the earth and justify her limitless exploitation, all of humanity does not benefit. In fact most lose. Pitting humans against nature is not merely anthropocentric, it is corporatocentric. The earth community has been reduced to humans, and humans have been further reduced to corporations as legal persons. Corporations then reshape part of humanity as consumers of their products and part of humanity as disposable. Consumers lose their identity as earth citizens, as co-creators and co-producers with nature. Those rendered disposable lose their very lives and livelihoods. Corporations as the dominant institution shaped by a capitalist patriarchy thrive on eco-apartheid. They thrive on the Cartesian legacy of dualism which puts nature against humans. It defines nature as female and passive subjugated. Corporatocentrism is thus also androcentric, a patriarchal construction.

The false universalism of human beings as conquerors and owners of the earth has led to the technological hubris of geo-engineering, genetic engineering and nuclear energy. It has led to the ethical outrage of owning life forms through patents, water through privatization, and the air through carbon trading. It is leading to appropriation of the biodiversity that serves the poor. Alienated, humans and corporations would like to "own" and trade in nature's services through the green economy.

The current crisis: why pricing nature is business as usual and won't work

Ignoring the earth's living and life-giving processes is at the heart of both non-sustainability and poverty. Non-sustainability is a result of disharmony with nature; it is a result of market laws having not just diverged dangerously from Gaia's laws and nature's laws, but actually becoming antagonistic to them. Nature has limits. The illusion of limitless growth based on limitless resource exploitation ignores ecological limits, and by ignoring limits creates scarcity.

The climate crisis is a result of putting pollutants into the atmosphere beyond the recycling capacity of the planet. To continue to add pollutants, while letting polluters make money through carbon trading, is a deepening of the war against the atmospheric commons.

Cyclones and hurricanes have always occurred. But as the Orissa Supercyclone, Cyclone Nargis, Cyclone Aila, Hurricane Katrina and Hurricane Sandy show, the intensity and frequency of cyclones has increased with climate change.

Using the earth as a trash dump is only one part of the current equation; the other is using the resources without consideration of their limits or the environment within which they are found and from which they are extracted. The crisis of species extinction is the direct result of destruction of their habitat and the direct attack on them through the arsenal of toxic chemicals. As Michael and Joyce Huesmann report in *Techno-Fix* "the present rate of species extinction is alarming according to various estimates, ranging from best to worst-case scenarios between 1,000 to 100,000 plant and animal species disappear each year, which translates into 2.7 to 270 irreversible extinctions everyday" (2011). According to the UN, species are disappearing at 1,000 times the natural rate of wildlife loss. More than one-fifth of the world's plant species are threatened with extinction. The UN Secretary General Ban Ki Moon cautioned that "we are bankrupting our natural economy. Maintaining and restoring our natural infrastructure can provide economic growth worth trillions of dollars each year. Allowing it to decline is like throwing money out of the window" (Ki-moon, 2010).

The United Nations Environment Programme's (UNEP's) report *Dead Planet, Living Planet: Biodiversity and Ecosystem Restoration for Sustainable Development* shows how nature is far more efficient than human-made systems (Nellemann and Corcoran, 2010). However, biodiversity is conserved when we love it, we care for it, we revere it, and we recognize its vital role in maintaining life. Protecting biodiversity is an imperative not just because it helps make money. It is important because it makes life.

For example, forested wastelands treat more waste water per unit of energy and have a 6 to 22 fold higher benefit cost ratio than traditional sand filtration in treatment plants. In New York, a filtration plant would have cost US$6 to US$8 billion plus US$300 to US$500 million per year as operating costs. Conserving the Catskills watershed at a cost of US$1 million to US$1.5 million was a far more effective way to provide clean water. If we destroy biodiversity and soil fertility with industrial monocultures in agriculture we have less food, not more. We might have more commodities, but not more food. Commodities are non-food, in fact anti-food.

The Chipko Movement saved Himalayan forests by putting the life of the forest above human life. Today the ecological services of the forests are a tradable commodity. As Pablo Salon (2011), the Bolivian Ambassador to the UN, stated at the General Assembly session on Harmony with Nature:

> The green economy considers it necessary, in the struggle to preserve biodiversity, to put a price on the free services that plants, animals and ecosystems offer humanity, the purification of water, the pollination of plants by bees, the protection of coral reefs and climate regulation.

According to the green economy, we have to identify the specific functions of ecosystem and biodiversity that can be made subject to a monetary value, evaluate their current state, define the limits of those services, and set out in economic terms the cost of their conservation to develop a market for environmental services; in other words, the transfusion of the rules of the market will save nature.

The illusion of such progress and growth measures the increased production and trade in commodities as growth, but fails to measure the death, destruction and decay of our rivers and aquifers, our land and soil, our atmosphere and climate maintaining process, our forests and biodiversity. However, it is the poor, the marginal, and the disenfranchised who bear the highest costs of ecological destruction and resource grab, but their deprivation does not count in the calculus of economic growth; poverty grows hand in hand with the ecological crisis.

Karl Polanyi (2012) has warned us against commodification and reduction of nature and society to the market. Commodification contributes to economic growth, but it undermines the rights of women and local communities, and the economies of both. It erodes local cultural milieus, and it destabilizes ecosystems by reducing their diversity and decoupling their integrity. As forests become valued only for carbon sequestration, or only for biomass production, rich diverse forest ecosystems are replaced with commercial monocultures. Accordingly, Polanyi (2012) explains the fundamental problem facing our modern economic world:

> A market economy must comprise all elements of industry, including labour, land and money. But labour and land are no other than the human being themselves of which every society consists and the natural surroundings in which all exist. To include them in the market mechanism means to subordinate the substance of society itself to the laws of the market (p. 75).

To this we would add "to include nature and nature's resources and processes in the market mechanism means to subordinate the substance of the earth's living processes to the laws of the market." Nature has been subjugated to the market as a mere supplier of industrial raw material and dumping ground for waste and pollution.

Ecological footprinting enumerates the need for a new way forward

Mathis Wackernagel *et al.* calculated the ecological footprint of human production and consumption (1997). The ecological footprint of an individual is a measure of the amount of land required to provide for all their resource requirements plus the amount of vegetated land to absorb all of that carbon dioxide emissions. In 1961, the human demand for resources was 70 percent of the earth's ability to regenerate. By the 1980s it was equal to the annual supply of resources, and since the 1990s, it has exceeded the earth's capacity by 20 percent: "It takes the biosphere, therefore, at least a year and three months to renew what humanity uses in a single year so that humanity is now eating its capital – the Earth's natural capital" (Wackernagel *et al.*, 2002).

The ecological footprint of all humans of course is not the same. In fact, not only is corporate driven consumerism eating into the earth's capital, it is eating into the poor's share of the earth's capital for sustenance and survival. This is at the root of resource conflicts across the developing world. An equitable ecological footprint is 1.7 ha/person. The average for the USA is 10.3 ha of land per person to provide for their consumption and absorb their waste. For the UK it is 5.2 ha, for Japan 4.3 ha, for Germany 5.3 ha, for China 1.2 h, and for India 0.8 ha (Wackernagel *et al.*, 1997).

When seeds, the source of life, are deliberately made non-renewable through technological interventions like hybridization or genetic engineering to create sterile seed, the abundance of life shrinks, growth is interrupted in evolution and farmers' fields, but growth of the profits of corporations like Monsanto increases. In India, farmers' suicides are linked to seed monopolies. This is why in Navdanya in India we defend seed sovereignty and farmers seed freedom.

If we dam rivers, and stop their life-giving flow, we do not have more water, we have less. More water goes to cities and commercial farms, but there is less water for rural communities for drinking and irrigation; there is less water in rivers for keeping the river alive. This is why we have been compelled to start the Save the Ganga Movement to stop large dams and diversions on the Ganges which are killing the river.

Caring for ourselves, our food and the earth: Gaia and the emerging paradigm of agriculture

Modest, neoliberal economic reforms and the economization of nature predicated on limitless growth in a panarchically limited world (a world where all systems are inter-related and related to nature, which is finite not infinite) can only be maintained for a limited amount of time by and for those powerful enough to grab the resources of the vulnerable. The resource grab that is essential for "growth" creates a culture of rape – the rape of the earth, the rape of local self-reliant economies, and ultimately the rape of women. The only way forward for the neoliberal model based on "growth" is through the subjection of ever larger numbers in its circle of violence. This way of reform will only lead to a violent end.

In nature's economy, an economy of sustenance, economic value is a measure of how the earth's life and human life are protected. Its currency is life-giving processes, not cash or the market price. A model of capitalist patriarchy that does not consider women's work and wealth creation to be of value deepens the violence by displacing women from their livelihoods and alienating them from the natural resources on which their livelihoods depend – the eco-agriculture system within which they live: the land, the forests, the water, the seeds, and biodiversity that envelop our lives.

A scientifically and ecologically robust paradigm of agriculture is emerging: ecological agriculture. The foundation of this is organic farming. It is not only an alternative to the broken paradigm of industrial agriculture, it is paramount to the survival of human beings and the eco-system which sustains us. At the ecological level, ecological agriculture and organic farming rejuvenate the natural capital on which sustainable food security depends – soil, biodiversity, and water. Chemical agriculture treats soil as inert and an empty container for chemical fertilizers. The new paradigm recognizes the soil as living, in which billions of soil organisms create soil fertility. The organisms' well-being is considered vital to human well-being. Chemical agriculture destroys biodiversity. Ecological agriculture conserves and rejuvenates biodiversity, enhances resilience, and increases the long-term sustainability of the planet. Chemical agriculture depletes and pollutes water. Organic farming conserves water by increasing the water holding capacity of soils through recycling organic matter. Biodiversity and soils rich in organic matter are the best strategy for climate resilience and climate adaptation.

While rejuvenating natural capital, ecological agriculture also rejuvenates social capital and increases human well-being and happiness. Organic agriculture increases output when measured across multifunctional benefits, instead of just the reductionist category of a single crop's "yield." In addition, it lowers the overall ecological footprint, and thereby increases agricultural capacity – not decreases it. As Navdanya's research (Shiva and Singh, 2011) on biodiverse organic systems has shown, ecological systems produce higher biodiverse outputs and higher incomes for rural families. When measured in terms of nutrition per acre, ecological systems produce more food. We can double food production ecologically. The false argument that genetically modified organisms (GMOs) are needed to increase food production is a desperate attempt to extend the life of a failing paradigm (Shiva and Singh, 2011).

Ecological systems of agriculture are based on care, compassion, and co-operation

The new paradigm of agriculture creates living economies and living cultures which increase the well-being of society and all life forms. That is why we, at

Navdanya in India, are very happy to work with the government of Bhutan on the transition to a 100 percent organic Bhutan. To further this transition and evolve the new paradigm of agriculture, the government of Bhutan, the International Federation of Organic Agriculture Movements (IFOAM), Biovision – headed by Hans Herren (the Chair of IAASTD), and Navdanya are planning a conference on Organic Agriculture in September 2013.

Care needs to be reintroduced into food and agriculture systems to make a transition to a new agriculture paradigm that protects the earth, our farmers, and our health. This transition includes a number of key shifts in thought and practice, from:

1   a reductionist, mechanistic paradigm of industrial agricultural research and its application to the holistic paradigm of ecological agriculture;
2   agricultural subsidies which support chemically-based, industrial monocrop produced foods to support for organic farming and the facilitation of access to both local and international markets;
3   a system of monocultures for commodity production based of subsidised external inputs to a system of eco-agriculture which is multifunctional and increases resilience by maintaining and enriching natural and social capital, protecting both biological and cultural diversity, the well-being of rural communities and livelihoods, and producing high quality, nutritious food;
4   the reductionist quantity measure of "yield" of commodities to the quality holistic measure of biodiverse outputs and multifunctional benefits;
5   treating farmers and peasants as disposable and dispensable to recognizing their central role in maintaining ecosystems, cultures, and local economies. For this, farmers must be guaranteed respect, dignity, fair returns, and democratic participation.

The natural laws that govern life on earth precede production, they precede exchange, and they precede the market. The market depends on Gaia. Gaia does not depend on the market. Both the earth and society come first. They are sovereign and autonomous. They cannot be commoditized, and reduced to the market.

Humanity stands at a crossroad. One road continues on the path of eco-apartheid and eco-imperialism, of commodification of the earth, her resources and processes. And this path must intensify violence against the earth and against people.

The second road is the path of making peace with the earth, beginning with the recognition of the rights of mother earth. This is the path of Earth Democracy. It is a path based on living within the earth's ecological limits and sharing her gifts equitably. It is a path based on deepening and widening democracy to include all life on earth and to include all humans who are being excluded by the so called "free market democracy" based on corporate rule and corporate greed. The path of Earth Democracy is the path of caring and sharing. It is the path to sustainable freedom.

References

Huesmann, M., and J. Huesmann. 2011. *Techno-Fix: Why Technology Won't Save Us or the Environment*. Gabriola Island, BC, Canada: New Society Publishers.

IAASTD (International Assessment of Agricultural Knowledge, Science and Technology for Development). 2009. *International Assessment of Agricultural Knowledge, Science and Technology for Development (IAASTD), Synthesis Report: A Synthesis of the Global and Sub-Global IAASTD Reports*. Washington, DC: Island Press.

Ki-Moon. 2010. Ecosystem Services Our Natural Capital; Allowing Their Decline Is "Like Throwing Money Out the Window", Secretary-General Tells High-level Biodiversity Event. *Secretary-General, SG/SM/13127, GA/10994, ENV/DEV/1160*. Retrieved on February 20th, 2012, from http://www.un.org/News/Press/docs/2010/sgsm13127.doc.htm

Nellemann, C., and E. Corcoran. 2010. *Dead Planet, Living Planet – Biodiversity and Ecosystem Restoration for Sustainable Development*. Arendakm, Norway: UNEP.

Patnaik, U. 2008. *The Republic of Hunger, and Other Essays*. Pontypool, UK: Merlin Press.

Polanyi, K. 2012. *The Great Transformation: The Political and Economic Origins of Our Times*. Mattituck, NY: Amereon Ltd.

Salon, P. 2011. Speech by Bolivia at UN Dialogue on Harmony with Nature. *pwccc.wordpress.com*. Retrieved on February 20th, 2012, from http://pwccc.wordpress.com/2011/04/20/speech-by-bolivia-at-un-dialogue-on-harmony-with-nature/.

Shiva, V. 2008. *Soil Not Oil: Environmental Justice in an Age of Climate Crisis*. Cambridge, Mass.: South End Press.

Shiva, V., and V. Singh. 2011. *Health Per Acre: Organic Solutions to Hunger and Malnutrition*. New Delhi: Navdanya.

Shiva, V., and V. Singh. 2012. *Poisons in Our Food – Links between Pesticides and Diseases*. New Delhi: Navdanya.

Wackernagel, M., L. Onisto, A. C. Linares, I. S. López Falfán, J. M. García, A. I. Suárez Guerrero, M. G. Suárez Guerrero. 1997. *Ecological Footprints of Nations: How Much Do They Use? – How Much Nature Do They Have?* Xalapa, Ver., Mexico: Centro de Estudios para la Sustentabilidad Universidad Anahuac, de Xalapa. Retrieved on February 20th, 2013, from http://www.ucl.ac.uk/dpuprojects/drivers_urb_change/urb_environment/pdf_Sustainability/CES_footprint_of_ nations.pdf.

Wackernagel, M., N. B. Schulz, D. Deumling, A. C. Linares, M. Jenkins, V. Kapos, C. Monfreda, J. Loh, N. Myers, R. Norgaard, and J. Randers. 2002. Tracking the Ecological Overshoot of the Human Economy. *Proceedings of the National Academy of Science* 99(14).

2 Including participants' values in the sustainable development process

Jack Appleton

A sustainable development project should start with a Participants' Values Analysis. Such an approach will increase the strength of the buy-in, in exchange for a slower start (systems principle: slower is faster when determining a leverage point). Overall leverage is increased due to the fact that participants' values are considered from the beginning. As a result, less resistance is encountered due to one of the parties protecting a hidden agenda, or introducing a new factor late in the negotiation process. After completing an initial project review, participants and constituents should be identified, and a Participants' Values Analysis should be conducted.

Sustainable development projects generally start with one party interested in developing a long-term solution to a specific natural resource related problem. Often the solution involves complex arrangements and multiple parties. While each party may enter the discussions in good faith, each does so for different reasons, with different values, with different concerns, and, most importantly, with different desired outcomes. These outcomes may or may not be congruent, and the values may or may not reflect a concern of the environment, or sustainability. More often than not, the facilitator, having been brought into the process by one or more of the interested parties, begins with a geo-resource analysis and a need analysis. The facilitator then develops a general framework from which the process proceeds. The immediately interested parties then proceed to the initial implementation stages with a variety of more specific studies, valuations, and process and project analysis, etc. As the participants' knowledge deepens, and as the development of the project progresses, often the social sphere of the project increases and newly interested parties emerge. As these parties engage in the process, and as the initial parties deepen their involvement, often heretofore unconsidered conflicts arise. Here is where a shift in the initial process would prove to be valuable and expeditious.

The initial process should be an ethnographic survey focused on the development of a values profile for each potentially interested party: not just the immediately interested parties. The goal being to identify what each party cares about and therefore to develop a prediction of what each party will come to view as a valuable outcome. The primary difference from what is normally done at the beginning of a project is that the assumption is the parties have heterogeneous not homogeneous values and agendas. This approach presumes that all parties involved can arrive at an agreement and that there is sufficient congruence within the project's scope to satisfy all concerned parties, or sufficient consensus to overcome entrenched opposition. The difference between this and traditional approaches lies in at which point in the process these issues emerge and are dealt with. By initially including participants' values, the accompanying concerns are genuinely engaged and do not fester and rise up late in the process, making them more difficult to deal with.

There is significant reason to assert that the earlier the heterogeneity is brought out, the greater the potential for the success. As facilitators engage each party in an ethnographic process focused on the development of a values profile, the potential for learning increases, the potential for trust among the parties increases, and the potential for resolving seemingly intractable considerations increases. Engaging at such an initial stage tends to increase the time horizon of the project in exchange for a stronger level of commitment by the involved parties, a deeper understanding of each party's aspirations and concerns, and a greater appreciation for the social complexities that often come to dominate and in the final analysis determine the later stages of the process. Patricia Wright's experience in Madagascar is instructive; although not a sustainable development project, it can be considered as such (Wright, 1994). Madagascar is a biologically diverse environment and an economically poor environment. It is also experiencing a rapid degradation of its natural environments and an exploitation of its natural resources. These conditions create the perfect conceptualization for a sustainable development scenario to be considered:

> The preservation of the remaining forests is a priority not only to conserve the rare flora and fauna, but also to maintain the watershed for the rivers. The forests contain the headwaters for many of the lowland areas. Streams that flow throughout the rain forest are pristine. They are a reliable source of healthy, clean drinking water. Without the drainage system afforded by the forests, erosion heavily silts the rivers. Rivers that are heavily silted make successful agriculture difficult. The water of the forests is also necessary for electricity. The biggest hydroelectric power dams are located near the forest because the headwaters are still protected. If the hills where the streams begin are deforested, the dams will no longer be of any use, either for rice production or for electricity. Crayfish are one of the forest's main products, found only in crystal clear streams. If the forest is cut, there will be no more crayfish. Deforestation also causes erosion, which leads to avalanches and mudslides that destroy homes and kill people during the rainy season.
>
> (Wright, 1994, p. 13)

These considerations also create the perfect conceptualization for a sustainable development approach utilizing an initial phase which starts with an ethnographically based Participants' Values Analysis.

For the purpose of discussion, one of the parties is interested, through self-consideration, in preserving the forest as a means of preserving their own self-interest: for example, crayfish producers, who then employ an ecosystems consultant who then approaches the logging interests and the hydro-electric interests (the immediate interested parties) to determine the feasibility of the development of a preservation agreement. At first glance, it appears the crayfish producers' values and interests align closely with the hydro-electric interests, but not so closely with the logging interests. Over time, as the process deepens, several other parties emerge as interested parties: farmers, environmental constituents, consumers of water and electricity (urban-based parties), etc. These alignments and "natural alignments" may or may not hold. With each party's inclusion a new set of considerations entangles the process. As the process moves forward, one could discover segments within each constituent group, for example, one could discover that a specific segment of the urban constituent group holds significant sway due to the fact that "[t]he spirits of the ancestors ... live in the forest" (Wright, 1994, p. 11). While such a consideration may well come forth initially and through a standard sustainable development evaluation process, it is less likely to do so, especially early in the process, as such a consideration is not within the realm of environmental scientific explication nor economic analysis, neither of which are concerned with spirits. In contrast, ethnographers and values are concerned with spirits.

Lacking such an understanding sets up a course of action whereby one of the interested parties obfuscates the process with a variety of objections and defensive routines while maintaining the "hidden agenda" of protecting the spirits due to the fact that the party has concluded that such an objection would be dismissed by the other parties involved who are proceeding on economic and scientific considerations. Such defensive routines prevent the process from moving forward, depress the possibility of productively engaging the parties, and mitigate the learning process which is critical to the development of the information necessary to structure a successful ecosystems services process and agreement (for an understanding of defensive routines see Argyris, 1985). The resulting increase in distrust among the parties, and the correct perception that at least one of the engaged parties has a hidden agenda, further erodes the potential for a successful conclusion: the development of a sustainable development agreement which provides for the needs of all of the interested parties: clean water, agriculture, aquaculture, electricity, and so on.

If, however, an initial phase starts with an ethnographically based Participants' Values Analysis, considerations such as values, beliefs, and cultural patterns would be an engaged aspect of the discussions from the outset, and the above "spirits"-based impediment would have a significantly diminished potential to impede the negotiative process. Ethnography is an intricate and time-consuming anthropographic methodology often taking years to successfully complete for just one segment of one population. Thus, what is being argued here is not that an ethnographic study of each concerned party is undertaken and the sustainable development process be held in abeyance until its completion. What is being promoted here is the undertaking of an ethnographically based Participants' Values Analysis, which, even in a complex and multi-partied situation, should take no more than a year, and can be accomplished in parallel to the required economic and environmental analysis which consumes the initial stages. Participants' Values Analysis should also include a development of a history of the area under consideration and the parties involved. In fact, the parallel development of such knowledge most likely will prove to be beneficial to the overall process.

The next concern that arises is the requisite knowledge and ability to undertake such an analysis. Most individuals involved in sustainable development do not have a strong background in the social sciences or clinical sciences; thus, they have a limited background to address such an analysis. Nonetheless, one does not need an extensive background to conduct such an analysis for the requisite purpose: the development of a sustainable development plan and agreement to which all parties will concur. The facilitator can conduct individual interviews, focus groups, have the interested parties tell stories, complete questionnaires, and so on. Through these processes and an analysis of the resulting data (transcripts of the conversations and stories, interviews, etc) the facilitator can produce a relatively clear, valid, and reliable description of the values, assumptions, and agendas that each party brings to the process.

Adam Kahane reminds us that "the complex and vital challenges we face cannot be addressed effectively by any one [participant], and so we need to build our capacity for co-creation" (2010, p. 127). In order to move forward together, "each actor's interests and needs and power need to be understood, recognized and taken into account" (Kahane, 2010, p. 135). The argument is simple: the co-creation of the capacity to understand, respect, and appreciate each other's interests and needs, and their source, that which we care about (our values), has to be the starting point, not a continuous residual issue that is dealt with when it's an impediment to the completion of a sustainable development project.

The first step is to develop a clear and useful definition of exactly what values are. To include values in sustainable development requires a careful definition of values: broad enough to cover a range of circumstances, but strict enough to be considered appropriate for practice. It has to be precise and clear enough that participants understand the concept of values and its boundaries (what is and is not a value), and simple enough that it can be quickly and easily utilized in a nonclinical and nonscientific setting.

According to Paul Bell, values "are a broader construct than attitudes and represent standards held by a person, culture, religion" (Bell, 2001, p. 26). Bell sees values as based on a collection of specific but related attitudes which rest upon some abstract principle. He points out an initial and pervasive difficulty: that attitudes and values are inferred from behavior and generally not directly expressed. Values represent behavioral tendencies and not absolutes (Bell, 2001, p. 26). Lewis Aiken defines attitudes as a "relatively stable, learned tendency to respond positively or negatively to a given person, situation, or object. Attitudes consist of cognitive, affective, and behavioral components. Examples of attitudes are political preferences, prejudices, scientific views, religious beliefs, and other complex response predispositions" (Aiken, 2002). Robert Gable and Marian Wolf (1993) turn to Gordon Allport for the following definition: "An attitude is a mental and neural state of readiness, organized through experience, exerting a directive or dynamic influence upon the individual's response to all objects and situations with which it is related" (Allport, 1954, p. 810). In accordance with Gable and Wolf, Stewart Allen *et al.* assert that "attitudes are tendencies to react favorably or unfavorably to a situation, individual, object, or concept" (2009, p. 33). This view leads to the notion of "consistency of responses to statements about ideas, people, and objects" (Gable and Wolf, 1993, p. 7).

Once the focus is on response, Bell's dilemma with regard to attitudes being ascertained indirectly is rendered moot, because responses are visible actions and statements, etc., all of which can be observed and studied. Attitudes perform, among other functions, the function of expressing values. Expressed attitudes reveal some basic value or values held by the entity articulating them (Triandis, 1971, p. 5). While there is some disagreement among scholars, for the purpose of this discussion and general definition, attitudes will be considered to be emergent from values, and therefore an expression of values (constructs that provide insight into underlying values). Thus, one has to return to define values more carefully.

Bell points out that attitudes develop within a normative, or value-based, context (2001, p. 26). Aiken echoes this sentiment, stating that a value is a sense of importance, utility, or worth attached to an object or construct (2002, p. 5). Gable and Wolf point out that values tend to be about ideas, such as what is desirable or undesirable, right or wrong, good or bad (1993, pp. 19–20). Allen *et al.* quote Milton Rokeach and Richard Hansis in defining values as "core conceptions of the desirable," and posits that values are "standards, or criteria" defining what is true, right, and beautiful (Allen *et al.*, 2009, p. 24). Values are sets of subjective preferences portrayed as objective conditions for life, but they are for the most part implicit in a world with a particular structure (Geertz, 1973, p. 131). Rokeach presents "values as standards that are to a large extent derived, learned, and internalized from institutions. These standards guide the development of a socially defined sense of self" (1979, p. 6). In simpler terms, one can have a positive attitude whereby positive is a value judgment regarding an attitude toward or about something. The attitude is an outward expression of an underlying value that is pertinent to a given situation, and this provides the context for the expression: a positive attitude.

Baruch Fischhoff differentiates between articulated and basic values. The former are characterized by a clear and expressed understanding of one's values across a diverse range of ideas and situations (Fischhoff, 2000, p. 628). The latter are characterized by the fact that "people cannot be expected to have articulated opinions on more than a small set of issues of immediate concern" (Fischhoff, 2000, p. 631). Fischhoff brings to the discussion the question of one's mindfulness or awareness of values and attitudes. Carl Rogers explains how values can be both articulated and basic constructs for the same person: "The value system is not necessarily something imposed from without, but is something experienced" (Rogers, 1951, p. 150). Thus, for Rogers, an individual or entity has both articulated and basic values at the same time.

What determines whether a given value is articulated or basic is experience. As one experiences diverse conditions and situations, one discovers or realizes one's values as they become known aspects of one's unconscious and implicit reality.

Kwame Anthony Appiah echoes Fischhoff (2000) and Rogers (1951) by following Bernard Williams's discussion of Isaiah Berlin's "Concepts and Categories: Philosophical Essays" (1979). Appiah argues that values reflect experience, culture, and the here and now: Fischhoff's issues of immediate concern. Appiah (2005, p. 147) states that according to Williams:

> if there are many and competing genuine values, then the greater the extent to which a society tends to be single-valued, the more genuine values it neglects or suppresses. ... The implication is that individuals require real choices, adequate options, ... To get the answer to this question right, we must make a distinction among kinds of value.

Appiah regards as genuine those values that are universal, that matter independently of our projects and identities (2005, p. 147). This is a view that has affinity with Fischhoff and Rogers. Appiah explains that for an individual the values distinction is not an abstract one between universal values, but a concrete distinction dependent on that which the individual brings into his identity and that which he values concretely. Appiah defines these as "project-dependent values" 2005, p. 227). One does not choose between vaguely held values that are concrete and abstract values. One chooses in favor of values that are tied to one's identity. This is the source of power in the values that one holds; they are not simply ideals, they are integrated into one's identity (Appiah, 2005, p. 243). The more strongly one identifies with an object, the greater the value placed upon that object. Conceptually and abstractly the object is the value itself – for example the value of honesty – and concern for such becomes part of the individual's identity, guiding behavior when embarking on an endeavor. The values expressed or of concern at any one moment are not the totality of values held by an individual in some sort of subconscious calculus which determines a ranking, but rather those values that relate to the project at hand through the individual's identity, and their identity's relationship to the project. Rokeach explains that values vary with a wide range of socioeconomic factors such as occupation, sex, age, reference group, and the social system within which one lives (1979). When one juxtaposes Rokeach's insights with those of Appiah, one sees that all the variables that Rokeach mentions are variables which influence our identity.

In short, values are concepts and objects for which individuals have a range of positive feelings. From our values our attitudes toward various objects emerge and are expressed. The characteristics of our attitudes are also shaped by the context, our behavior, our beliefs, and our level of understanding, and as these change our attitudes can change while our deeper values, some of which we are not even aware of, remain less malleable.

Expression of values in an organizational context

The values that an individual actor expresses or acts upon are often not those of the actor but of the actor acting as agent. One does not always act in accordance with one's own values and desires but in accordance with an entity that they represent. This observation is not a trivial concern when considering values in sustainable development. It is most probable that those involved in a sustainable development project are not involved by their own independent volition. Values, according to Geert Hofstede (2001), are not visible directly but can become evident through one's behavior (including language). Evidentiary behavior would include symbolic behaviors such as gestures, pictures, and objects, persons held in esteem (real or imagined), and rituals consisting of repeated collective activities (Hofstede, 2001). Hofstede expands values into dimensional scales which can be empirically verified as they are expressed in different cultural settings. These dimensions are power distance, uncertainty avoidance, individualism versus collectivism, masculinity versus femininity, and long-term versus short-term orientation (Hofstede, 2001, p. 29). Hofstede studied culture at the level of ethnic identity and nationality, not individual participant's values. Corporate cultural patterns most certainly can influence values, and vice versa. The same individual can definitely hold and express one set of attitudes and values within a given corporate setting, and then another set of attitudes and values in another setting (say at home with family). Corporate cultures, according to Allan Kennedy and Terrence Deal, "fall into four general categories" (1982, p. 107): the tough guy; work hard, play hard; bet your company; process. For Deal and Kennedy, values are the core of an organization, and everything emanates from the organization's values, formalized or not (1982, p. 21). The values held determine the choices made within an organization (1982, p. 22). The choices indicate what matters most to an organization and thus are the manifestations of its values (1982, p. 31). Charles Hampden-Turner views corporate culture in terms of its mediating influence on the behavior of the organization as it encounters and facilitates actions relative to encountered dilemmas (1990, p. 17). Hampden-Turner draws on Edgar Schein (2010), who defines values as a "sense of what ought to be." Over time, values are transformed and mitigated as they are tested: Did a decision or action based on a value work? Did it solve a problem? When testing values, one must consider espoused values and observed behavior; the two are often not congruent (Schein, 2010, p. 25). Values tend to lie between observable behavior and artifacts on the one hand and basic assumptions on the other (Hampden-Turner, 1990, p. 17). The distinction between espoused values and observed behavior is noted by Chris Argyris, who uses the term "theory-in-use" to refer to the factors and thinking patterns that a manager (or anyone) uses when making a decision (1985, p. 80).

Erving Goffman's (1959) theory of presentation explains the dilemma, noted by Argyris, facing the "organization man," who acts in accordance with the values of his organization, even if they are contrary to his own, or holds values that he does not express. It is true that Argyris and Goffman are discussing different phenomena, but there is a bridge between Argyris's and Goffman's notions: that over time individuals are not aware of their presentation of self. It becomes part of them and their identity. Their actions are in some sense a performance which matches the conditions at hand.

Thus, one can conclude that values are positive feelings toward objects which one cares about, or in other words, values are what one cares about. The expression of a value at any one time depends on a range of circumstances and variables, most of which are not within the control of the individual expressing or acting in accordance with a given value at a given time. For the purpose of including values in sustainable development, it does not matter if an individual is acting on their own behalf or as an agent for another person or entity. In both cases, the individual is a representative agent. What matters is that the values being expressed, that are "in-use," are contextual. The values that are relevant at any one moment are those which are tied to one's identity as it relates to the task at hand: in short, they are project-dependent.

This makes the inclusion of values in sustainable development both relevant and possible. The task is not to realign everyone's values to one framework, or to have everyone agree on which actions are required to bring about a sustainable future. Nor is the task to force agents to act in accordance with their "real" values as opposed to their presented values, espoused values, or working values. The task is to shape the question, the context, and the problem in such a way that each agent's project-dependent values align with and motivate his positive contribution to sustainable development. In other words, the object is not to change an agent's values which are antithetical to sustainable development so that they are compatible with sustainable development, but to structure problems so that the existing values of the participants contribute to sustainable development.

References

Aiken, L. R. 2002. *Attitudes and Related Psychosocial Constructs: Theories, Assessment, and Research*. Thousand Oaks, Calif.: Sage.

Allen, D. S., D. A. Wicker, F. P. Clark, R. Potts, and S. A. Snyder. 2009. *Values, Beliefs, and Attitudes: Technical Guide for Forest Service Land and Resource Management, Planning, and Decision Making*. Portland, OR: US Department of Agriculture, Forest Service, Pacific Northwest Research Station.

Allport, G. 1954. *The Nature of Prejudice*. New York: Addison-Wesley.

Appiah, K. A. 2005. *The Ethnics of Identity*. Princeton, NJ: Princeton University Press.

Argyris, C. 1985. *Strategy, Change, and Defensive Routines*. New York: Pitman.

Bell, P. 2001. *Environmental Psychology*. 5th edn. Mahwah, NJ: Lawrence Erlbaum Associates.

Fischhoff, B. 2000. Value Elicitation: Is There Anything There? In *Choices, Values, and Frames*. Eds. D. Kahneman, and A. Tversky. New York: Cambridge University Press, pp. 620–41.

Gable, R. K., and M. B. Wolf. 1993. *Instrument Development in the Affective Domain: Measuring Attitudes and Values in Corporate and School Settings*. Norwell, Mass.: Kluwer Academic.

Geertz, C. 1973. *The Interpretation of Cultures*. New York: Basic Books.

Goffman, E. 1959. *The Presentation of Self in Everyday Life*. Garden City, New York: Doubleday Anchor.

Hampden-Turner, C. 1990. *Creating Corporate Culture*. Reading, Mass.: Addison-Wesley.

Hofstede, G. 2001. *Culture's Consequences*. Thousand Oaks, Calif.: Sage.

Kahane, A. 2010. *Power and Love*. San Francisco: Berrett-Koehler Publishers.

Kennedy, A., and T. Deal 1982. *Corporate Cultures, the Rites and Rituals of Corporate Life*. New York: Addison Wesley.

Rogers, C. 1951. *Client-Centered Therapy*. Boston, Mass.: Houghton Mifflin.

Rokeach, M. 1979. *Understanding Human Values*. New York: Free Press.

Schein, E. 2010. *Organizational Culture and Leadership*. 4th edn. San Francisco: John Wiley and Sons.

Triandis, H. C. 1971. *Attitude and Attitude Change*. New York: John Wiley and Sons.

Williams, B. 1979. Introduction. In H. Hardy. Ed. I. Berlin. *Concepts and Categories: Philosophical Essays*. New York: Viking.

Wright, P. 1994. Ecological Disaster in Madagascar and the Prospects for Recovery. In *Ecological Prospects*. Ed. C. K. Chappel. Albany, New York: State University of New York Press.

3 Constructing values and beliefs

A relational approach to sustainable development

Sheila McNamee

Sustainable development is much more than good (or bad) science. While science can generate models and predictions of climate change, the results are of no consequence if communities do not translate conclusions into daily, planet-sustaining practices. Science is not independent of human interchange, and while the values inherent in sustainability/conservation projects focus on ensuring a livable future, scientific inquiry alone does not ensure that sustainable conservation practices will be realized.

Scientific research is useful when people generate new forms of living based on the research results and implications. We talk of pure science as science that reveals fundamental knowledge, and applied science as the practical application of scientific knowledge to the physical world. The field of sustainable development is clearly an applied science. The challenge for researchers in the field of sustainability is to work with communities in such a way that the practices which conserve our natural resources are embraced.

The application of sustainable practices may be limited by the ways that meaning has been constructed in the field of conservation. The terms "sustainability" and "conservation" have been equated with "giving up," "sacrificing," and "going without" the accustomed luxuries of daily life. Individuals in the field of sustainable development – engineers, biologists, economists, and others – see conservation and sustainable practices as enhancing our way of life, while the population at large understands the suggested shifts in practice as forms of sacrifice.

One way to explain this disparity between the general public and sustainability professionals is to understand the prominence of the modernist (individualist) worldview. Our taken-for-granted way of living in the world has "naturalized" the individual and his or her private, internal attitudes, beliefs, meanings, and traits. Our culture is interested in self-contained individuals (Sampson, 1993) and their private meaning-making capacities. Yet this way of viewing the world is not "the only accurate" one; it is a single option among many. In the remainder of this chapter I will articulate the dominant, individualist view, describe some of the limitations of this view, and offer a relational, constructionist orientation as an alternative. This alternative, I believe, offers sustainability professionals generative resources for working with the general public, to increase their level of awareness and reconstruct their attitudes and values concerning sustainable development.

Individualism and sustainability

Several scholars have argued that privileging individuals over community is dangerous. Christopher Lasch (1979), in *The Culture of Narcissism*, describes how our focus on the individual produces self-interest at the cost of communal betterment. Robert Bellah and his colleagues (1985) argue that the individualist tradition stands as a threat to any form of relational engagement when all efforts are focused on self-preservation. Each of us is centrally concerned with our own well-being, and yet we are dependent upon each other and our cultural institutions to "get ahead" or "be effective," and to "save the environment." Individualism as an ideology invites us to approach the world as if we alone can tame it. It is the individual who can solve problems, make decisions, think rationally, and act effectively.

It is therefore pertinent to sustainable development that the individualist proclivity presumes the ability of experts to transform a community's practices, values, and beliefs about conservation. When it is not possible for individual experts to successfully perform such transformations, we are left with the choice of scapegoating the individual, or blaming the broader cultural institutions for creating the unsolvable problem. It is far easier to blame our apparent inadequacies on "the system" or on another rather than on ourselves. In the face of failure or ineptitude, we begin to ask ourselves why we ever thought "the system" or another person could be counted on to help us achieve, succeed, thrive. Given such a phenomena, the domain of individualism has significant implications.

The limits of individualism

Individualism, as a mode of practice, is largely unquestioned within US culture. Most discussions of the development and implementation of new institutional activities and social policies focus on individuals' behaviors and attitudes rather than on communal relations. In our, American, culture we are hard-pressed to find an institutional context where attention is placed on anything but the individual. And for each individual citizen, others' actions are of concern only to the extent that they affect one's own well-being. This orientation has detrimental effects on sustainable development. If I am only looking out for myself, I am less concerned with how much my neighbors drive or what is their water consumption. As long as I can make my own lifestyle choices, I am content. Attention is placed on the transmission of information for the purpose of this discussion, on how experts on sustainable development can disseminate information concerning conservation in contrast to the building of communities and relationships within which people can collaboratively create new meaning and understanding about natural, economic, and social resources as they might ensure a generative future. The individualist orientation describes communication as the transmission or exchange of information, whereas the constructionist views communication as the creation of meaning.

With its focus on the transmission of information, the individualist tradition champions the self as an originator source of thought and action. Consequently, we educate individual minds, reward and punish individuals at work, and hold individuals responsible for all their actions, thoughts, beliefs, and more. In sum, the individual is the unquestioned, natural object of concern in our attempts to understand social life. To know anything about the complexity of social interchange, we assume that we must begin with the individual who is most obviously the basic unit of examination. Can we construct some alternative discourses for talking about how values and attitudes are constructed in the social world?

In fact, a number of social theorists and philosophers have challenged the idea of the self-contained individual. Rather than assume that intellect, knowledge, beliefs, values, and so forth are contained within people, the shift in orientation recognizes each as constructed within communities. Indeed, the very idea of private mental functioning, of a separate, "mindful" individual, is itself the byproduct of communal construction. Philip Cushman tells us that the fall of the feudal system coincided with the beginnings of individualism (1995, p. 364). Individualism as an ideology emerged in a particular historical moment. It was not naturally evident. And it emerged through collective coordination among citizens.

Richard Rorty (1979) argues that the idea of an interior mind reflecting an exterior nature is not a simple reflection of human existence but a historically situated convention. Historical studies document the shifting conceptions of mind. We no longer, for example, talk of "hysteria" or "soul" as manifestations of mind, and we continually add new mental realities to the ledger (Harre, 1979; Graumann and Gergen, 1996; Kutchins and Kirk, 1997). Anthropological work demonstrates different conceptions of the mind in different cultures (Heelas and Lock, 1981; Lutz and Abu-Lughod, 1990; Shweder, 1991). To the Buddhist, unity is significant; selfhood is not. Literary theorists call into question the long-accepted belief that the task of the reader is to locate the author behind the text – to ferret out the true meaning of a text. In contrast, deconstructionists such as Jacques Derrida (1976) illustrate how writing is a manifestation not of the author's mind but of systems of language that entail genres and traditions of writing. To them, writing is a culturally and historically contingent practice of effective language use. Thus, to read is to participate in culturally embedded practices of interpretation.

The implications of these critiques are significant: one does not constitute meaning alone, nor engage in a rational choice among competing goods, without having absorbed the intelligibilities of a community. Yet the individualist discourse is our dominant practice. It shapes cultural life by placing the self as the central origin of action. The result is that the self is prioritized. We value our own goals, needs, wants, and rights. Our chief concern is how we win or lose. And we only examine others' actions as they affect our own.

Individualist discourse generates a sense of fundamental independence or isolation. I'm never certain if I am being understood or not. Why should I pursue investments that might curtail my individual freedom? The byproduct of this stance is that relationships become artificial. Relationships "need to be worked on." And when working on a relationship becomes burdensome, we simply retreat to the self (what is best for *me*?). There are also deleterious effects on society. If everyone is self-absorbed, who cares about the environment? In this realm, gain for the individual is impoverishment for the community. Little attention is given in higher education to cooperative modes of learning. Business training emphasizes individual performance, and workshops abound in leadership and management training. Courts seek to allocate individual blame and remain blind to the broader social processes in which crime is embedded. And on both local and global levels, individualism promotes interminable conflict among incommensurate moral or ideological commitments. Is this a useful path for the future?

Individuals as a discursive option

To the constructionist, placing our focus on individuals is a "way of talking," or a discursive option. To consider individualism as a conversational resource rather than as an essential or fundamental reality is to shift the terrain of our discussion. Rather than simply reflect reality, our discursive tradition has created a particular kind of reality which includes features such as objectivity, individuality, uniform rationality, and progress. However, when individualism is seen as a discursive option (not a statement of how things "really" are), we recognize objectivity, individuality, uniform reasoning, and progress as byproducts of a particular approach to language rather than as descriptions of the essential nature of reality. This orientation provides us with some means for employing alternative resources. It allows us to see our words as byproducts of a discursive tradition.

Individualism is only one way of talking and thus only one way of being. Fully armed with the discourse of individualism, we are able to locate a broad array of qualities within individuals: intellect, leadership, sociability, agency, mental illness, insecurity, deviance, and perversion. It is individuals who reason, who lead, who relate, and who act intentionally. Thus, it is only reasonable to conclude that it is individuals who should become the focus of experts' attempts to change behavior and attitudes.

Such individualism has implications for sustainability. The future of the planet and the conservation of our natural, economic, and social resources require broad scale shifts in our cultural practice. To date, the most common approach taken in attempts to shift cultural practices has in fact emerged from contemporary, individualist sensibilities. The focus has been on (1) changing individual behavior, with the hope of changing attitudes, beliefs, and values, or (2) on changing individuals' attitudes, beliefs, and values, with the hope of changing their behavior. But what good are individuals' actions or beliefs, values, and attitudes if they stand alone? One of the most pressing challenges for sustainable development is creating conditions where the public at large engages with scientists and other sustainability professionals in co-constructing new ways of understanding our natural, economic, and social resources.

Instead of having "experts" inform the public about ways to sustain our planet and our livelihood, the "experts" must acknowledge their interdependence with the public. Without public participation, no sustainability practices will endure. There is a dire need to engage collaboratively. A constructionist orientation can facilitate the engagement process.

Toward potentials

Relational engagement emphasizes what people construct together. Constructionism (McNamee and Gergen, 1999; Gergen, 2009) proposes that meaning is always an emergent process. Meaning is not fixed. It is rather in constant flux, always open to new possibilities. Any sense of permanence arises from the skill we have in ritualizing our interaction. When we act, we invite others to co-construct the interaction. To the social constructionist, words and gestures (actions) are invitations into the creation of a particular scenario. My words and actions invite you to engage with me in cultural rituals. As Edward Sampson writes, "the most important thing about people is not what is contained within them, but what transpires between them" (1993, p. 20). The significance of placing meaning in the joint activities of participants, rather than in the heads of persons, is precisely the aspect of social construction that offers us alternatives to individualist attempts to alter the public's attitudes, beliefs, and values around issues of sustainability.

The process of constructing meaning

Meaning emerges as communities of people coordinate their activities with one another. The continual coordination required in any relationship or community eventually generates a sense of common practices. Patterns or rituals quickly give rise to standards and expectations (e.g. a community where perfect lawns are expected in each neighborhood). We come to expect the enactment of given patterns (everyone will take great care in producing a lawn that is thick and green). We implicitly construct a set of values associated with the performance (rich, lush lawns are a good thing). As these standards emerge and the coordinated activities become more and more entrenched within the relationship or community, a way of life is established – actually appearing as if "natural" and "normal" and transcendent of time or place or persons. This is a socially achieved reality, but we must be clear: it is as real as it gets (see Figure 3.1).

Meaning is always in motion; it is fluid and supple. Consistency is attributable to the coordinated achievement of participants. Stability can be credited to the participants' abilities to "play the language game" (Wittgenstein, 1953). To understand meaning, and thus reality, in these terms is to embrace the discourse of social construction where all meaning is dependent upon the coordination of people in relation to one another. Each configuration of people is likely to yield a

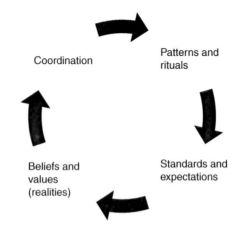

Figure 3.1 The relational construction of beliefs and values (meaning)

unique meaning, or one different from that of any other configuration. And thus, social construction is surely relativistic but surely not rampant. One is not free to simply construct the world at will. We are ultimately dependent on each other to make our worlds and therefore it is not the case that "anything goes."

Social construction focuses on dialogue as a practice that enhances the creation of new forms of understanding among different groups. It is a resource that moves us beyond largely failed attempts to change individuals' attitudes, values, and beliefs vis-à-vis issues of sustainability toward potentials for the development of sustainable action. The focal point is what people do together.

The difference of dialogue

Mikhail Bakhtin writes, "Truth is not … to be found inside the head of an individual person, it is born between people … in the process of their dialogic interaction" (1984, p. 110). He claims that dialogue is a responsive, multi-voiced activity, and as such is not limited to self-interest, psychological or relational improvement, or the crafting of cooperative, conflict-free ways of living. When we are responsive to others, our words and actions are not entirely our own; they carry traces of our histories of relationships and the beliefs and values that these relationships have crafted. Dialogue is a process of holding firmly to one's position while maintaining a curiosity and respect for another's very different position. This is what Bakhtin refers to as "responsivity."

The challenge is to find a way to approach important issues as understood and encountered in a plurality of ways. Doing so moves our focus away from an assessment of who is right and who is wrong or who is a good person and who is not. It places our focus on understanding very different beliefs and values on their own terms, temporarily suspending evaluation; it invites transformative dialogue where our focus is on making space for multiple rationalities as opposed to securing the rightness of our own morality through persuasive rhetoric. How might we begin the process of confronting the other dialogically?

Creating conditions for dialogue

We must create a context that invites a different form of conversation. Participants do not have to self-disclose in deeply personal and self-interested ways, or suppress differences of opinion, conflict, and discord. Nor must they ignore differential power positions or professional expertise. Rather, to be in dialogue is to holds one's own position while simultaneously remaining open to the often very oppositional, contradictory position of the other (Stewart and Zediker, 2002).

The act of holding one's own position while allowing others – often with diametrically opposing views – to do the same, and to be open and curious about the coherence of those very different positions, creates a unique relational context. It is a context, I believe, that is inherently democratic and concerned with broader issues of human and social well-being. It is a useful process for public deliberation and policy formation. It can create the space necessary for social equity and conflict resolution. Dialogue is a particular process that facilitates eventual decision and action in a humane and collaborative manner.

Resources for transformative dialogue

The values and beliefs that any person harbors are the byproduct of coordinated action within community. Our best resource for altering those values and beliefs is to create conditions that will allow for transformative dialogue. To participate in such a dialogue requires setting aside any notion of ultimate right or wrong, good or bad, and also temporarily suspending our proclivity to reach agreement. Instead, social construction as a philosophical stance invites us to coordinate diverse and complex views. This coordination can be achieved through a stance of uncertainty, genuine curiosity about differences, and generous listening.

Since we understand that values, beliefs, and realities are built from coordination within relationships, we can anticipate different and often incommensurate values and beliefs that will be housed within any one group or relationship. One might disagree with the ultimate belief that another is supporting, but still understand how it is that the other has come to support this belief. An individual's story is not wrong. By focusing on each other's stories, and not arguments of right and wrong and the underlying principles, others come to be seen as individuals who have a different story, a different rationale, a different history.

Rather than identify and disseminate lists of conservation practices (i.e. privileged abstractions), one might explore the very situated narratives of community members. It is more productive to initiate inquiry among citizens about their own personal understandings of sustainability in all forms – biological, economic, and social. Our collaborative conversation can begin by privileging what community members bring to the conversation. We do not create meaning, or understanding, alone. Meaning is jointly constructed and emerges within and from the joint activities of people.

Inquiry into issues of sustainability begins with investigations within the participating communities. How might we invite the stories of consumption within a community? Perhaps it would be useful to also invite community members to talk about what sustainability and conservation mean to them rather than assume that these abstract terms mean the same to everyone. If we are not responsive to others and if they are not responsive to us, we fail to construct what we intend (i.e. livable futures) and are left creating something entirely different. As we can see, what it means to act in ways that will sustain our environment and our well-being is easier to grasp in situated activity than through abstract discussion.

Additionally, it is useful for participants to engage in self-reflexive and relationally reflexive inquiry – to entertain doubt about their own certainties – by invoking skepticism about strongly held beliefs: is it certain that there is absolutely no other way to look at this situation? The inquiry can continue by invoking the doubtful voice of a friend, colleague, or mentor: how would my colleague or my friend think about this? This self-reflexive inquiry opens us to the possibility of alternative constructions, thereby transforming the nature of the interaction. Similarly, to pause and inquire about how "our" interaction is going recognizes that the meaning emerging in a particular interactive moment is a byproduct of "us," not of "you" or "me." Asking, "Is this the kind of conversation you were hoping we would have? Is there another way we could or should be doing this? Are there questions I should be asking you but I'm not?" acknowledges that we only have "power with" or "power to," and not "power over." How might sustainability experts' conversations with community members be different if they engaged in relational reflexivity?

The dialogue could continue by focusing on the coordination of multiplicities. In transformative dialogue the idea is to coordinate multiple discourses. The challenge is to become curious about all forms of practice and to explore the values and beliefs that give rise to them without searching for universal agreement. Can we create dialogic opportunities that invite generous listening, curious inquiry, and a willingness for co-presence?

Another dialogic resource is the use of familiar forms of action in unfamiliar contexts. Gregory Bateson talks about "the difference that makes a difference" (1972, p. 272) and Tom Andersen sees this difference as introducing "something unusual but not too un-usual" (1991, p. 33). Each of us carries many voices, many differing opinions, views, and attitudes – even on the same subject. These voices represent the accumulation of our relationships (actual, imagined, and virtual). In effect, we carry the residues of many others with us; we contain multitudes (McNamee and Gergen, 1999). Yet most of our actions, along with the positions we adopt in conversations, are one-dimensional. The challenge is to draw on these other voices, these conversational resources that are familiar in one set of relationships and situations but not in another. In so doing, we achieve something unusual.

Using familiar resources in contexts where we do not generally use them invites new forms of engagement. If our activities are invitations into different relational constructions, then we can focus on how utilizing particular resources invites certain responses in specific relationships, and different responses and constructions in others. All represent various attempts to achieve coordinated respect for the specificity of a given relationship and situation. If we can encourage ourselves and others to draw broadly on the conversational resources that are already familiar, perhaps we can act in ways that are just different enough to invite others into something beyond the same old entrenched beliefs and attitudes. To the extent that we can invite the use of the familiar in unfamiliar contexts, we are coordinating disparate discourses. What we are avoiding is co-opting one discourse as right and another as wrong. The novelty of enacting the old in a new context becomes fertile soil within which to craft generative transformation.

Finally, we might focus on the future, thereby creating room for imagining the future. The potential to reify a set of beliefs, making them static and immutable, is tremendous. Probably more important is the logic inherent in the focus on the past. By focusing on what has already happened, we unwittingly give credibility to causal models that are the hallmark of modern science. We privilege the logic by which what went before causes what follows. Such considerations inhibit imagining a new future. One cannot disconnect the past, present, and future. The past is embedded in a story, but there are many ways to tell a story. Not only do we harbor many voices, each with a different set of possible narrations, but others involved in the same "history" will very likely narrate it differently. Thus, the causality of past to present (and implied future) will take different turns, highlight different features, and celebrate different elements, depending on which story is privileged. Future-oriented discourse can enhance the coordination of diverse worldviews: the story of the future has not been written. By engaging in dialogue about the future, we underscore the relational construction of our worlds. We fabricate together the reality into which we might collaboratively enter.

The resources offered by a constructionist view of the creation of meaning shift our attention to what people do together. That is, we focus on collaborative, participatory processes from which the possibility for new understanding and new forms of action can emerge.

References

Andersen, T. 1991. *The Reflecting Team: Dialogue and Dialogue about the Dialogues*. New York: W. W. Norton.

Bakhtin, M. M. 1984. *Problems of Dostoevsky's Poetics*. Ed. and trans. C. Emerson. Minneapolis: University of Minnesota Press.

Bateson, G. 1972. *Steps to an Ecology of Mind*. New York: Bantam.

Bellah, R. N., R. Madsen, W. M. Sullivan, A. Swidler, and S. M. Tipton. 1985. *Habits of the Heart*. Berkeley, Calif.: University of California Press.

Cushman, P. 1995. *Constructing the Self, Constructing America*. Reading, Mass.: Addison Wesley.

Derrida, M. 1976. *Of Grammatology*. Baltimore: Johns Hopkins University Press.

Gergen, K. J. 2009. *An Invitation to Social Construction*. 2nd edn. London: Sage.

Graumann, C. F., and K. J. Gergen. 1996. *Historical Dimensions of Psychological Discourse*. New York: Cambridge University Press.

Harre, R. 1979. *Social Being*. Oxford: Blackwell.

Heelas, P., and A. Lock, eds. 1981. *Indigenous Psychologies*. New York: Academic.

Kutchins, H., and S. A. Kirk. 1997. *Making Us Crazy: DSM: The Psychiatric Bible and the Creation of Mental Disorders*. New York: Free Press.

Lasch, C. 1979. *The Culture of Narcissism*. New York: W. W. Norton.

Lutz, C., and L. Abu-Lughod, eds. 1990. *Language and the Politics of Emotion*. Cambridge: Cambridge University Press.

McNamee, S., and K. J. Gergen. 1999. *Relational Responsibility: Resources for Sustainable Dialogue*. Thousand Oaks, Calif.: Sage.

Rorty, R. 1979. *Philosophy and the Mirror of Nature*. Princeton, NJ: Princeton University Press.

Sampson, E. E. 1993. *Celebrating the Other*. Boulder, Col.: Westview.

Shweder, R. A. 1991. *Thinking through Cultures*. Cambridge, Mass.: Harvard University Press.

Stewart, J., and K. Zediker. 2002. Dialogue as Tensional, Ethical Practice. *Southern Communication Journal* 65(2–3), pp. 224–42.

Wittgenstein, L. 1953. *Philosophical Investigations*. Trans. G. Anscombe. New York: Macmillan.

4 Understanding values using critical discourse analysis

G. G. *Patthey*

Language is a medium of communication, but the words, sounds, and grammar of it do not simply put labels on experience for an easy transfer between interlocutors. Rather, such language features allow for systematic variations that help speakers to signal attitudes about the ideas they communicate. Listeners and readers attend to these embedded social signals as they negotiate how much of a given communication to understand and whether to block or filter some of it. In other words, human language contains multiple possibilities for interlocutors to shape their communications in accordance with their values. The constant negotiation of meaning between interlocutors complicates communication, and it complicates any description of language. Linguists often use the word "discourse" as a term to indicate language in use – as a tool that includes social and affective signals. Discourse analysis examines what people say or write in order to understand how people are using language to accomplish social and emotional goals along with communicating ideas.

A recent example of the way language choices slant communications can be found in a brief study of what is alternatively called "global warming" or "climate change." The very introduction of this topic allows for selecting between two different subject headings, each with quite different connotations. "Global warming" is associated with environmental problems, with Al Gore's *An Inconvenient Truth* (2006), and with the possibility that life as we know it is about to change radically, mostly for the worse; "climate change" is far more neutral, projects a more scientific aura, and is associated with the idea that the earth's climate simply cycles through various warming and cooling periods. Thus, a simple choice in subject headings can activate markedly different ideas about a given topic. These different ideas in turn reflect different worldviews and different priorities. Critical sociolinguists are alert to these activations of different associations. Turning their attention to everyday discourse, they define recurring speech events such as lectures or news reports about such topics as "global warming"/"climate change" and examine patterns of language choices to ascertain how speakers, listeners, writers, and readers are shaping each other's views of the world.

Critical discourse analysis starts with a version of the Sapir-Whorf hypothesis: human language mediates human experience, and thus influences human thinking. In other words, language does not simply reflect the values and preferences of individual speakers, it shapes them. According to Edward Sapir and Benjamin Whorf:

> Human beings do not live in the objective world alone, nor alone in the world of social activity as ordinarily understood, but are very much at the mercy of the particular language which has become the medium of expression for their society. It is quite an illusion to imagine that one adjusts to reality essentially without the use of language and that language is merely an incidental means of solving specific problems of communication or reflection. The fact of the matter is that the "real world" is to a large extent unconsciously built up on the language habits of the group. No two languages are ever sufficiently similar to be considered as representing the same social reality. The worlds in which different societies live are distinct worlds, not merely the same world with different labels attached.
>
> (Sapir, 1949, p. 69)

From a sociolinguistics perspective, language is a tool, but *never* a neutral tool. Every word is already imbued with meanings, allusions, and nuances that each new speaker has to negotiate anew. This is true for both oral and written language: writers often work hard at their task because they realize that their texts are open to various interpretations. Writing includes unique, additional challenges in human communication and reflection; however, the fundamental negotiation of meaning remains the same. Discourse analysts believe this indeterminacy of meaning to be a fundamental quality of human language.

The fundamental indeterminacy of meaning requires that people work out meanings for every interaction. Since it is typically possible to select between different sounds, words, and even grammatical possibilities to "say the same thing," different choices communicate not quite "the same thing" but rather what could be termed "the same thing with different attitudes," as demonstrated above by the choice of "global warming" versus "climate change." Norman Fairclough's example of reporting "redundancies in the car industries" as either "Thousands are out of work" or "Company directors have sacked thousands of workers" further illustrates this point. In the first communication, unemployment appears almost as a natural state of affairs, without identifying any particular cause or agency involved, whereas in the second, the subject–transitive verb–object sequence leaves no doubt as to who is to blame for the observed events (Mesthrie *et al.*, 2000, p. 327). The first communication includes an attitude of studied neutrality, appropriating the markings of objective science by using the passive voice; the second takes a much more accusatory stance, both in its sentential structure and in the decidedly biased significance of the verb "sacked." Variations or options like these make it possible to derive affective and social qualities from human communications.

Sociolinguists are interested in the realities and meanings that human beings construct with and through language. When linguists try to capture the creation and negotiation of meaning and try to come up with a scientific model of how it is done, the complexity of the process becomes readily apparent. Meaning appears stable across time, stable enough that philologists can create dictionaries, yet meaning is also created in the moment of use. Indeed, when linguists start to study language in use, they soon realize that speakers exploit that indeterminacy in their communications. Further, linguists realize that language is probably the original multi-tasking tool, as utterances, that is, sentences in use, always appear to address more than one communicative agenda. Utterances are multi-functional, and this quality depends on the indeterminacy of meaning. Speakers can choose a particular intonation, a particular stress-pattern, a particular choice among different alternatives – because the sum of their words will only become clear upon speaking. If we switch to the written medium, we find that each reader constructs the sum of the written words in a given text to reconstruct *a* meaning – not *the* meaning, as no such final, stable, inalterable meaning is possible.

Determining meaning requires interpretations, and something is always lost or at least altered in translation. That is, each interpretation of a given text requires something akin to a translation by the interpreter, and the interpreter produces only one possibility from a set of possibilities across speakers and across time. To make matters even more complicated, interpretations are rarely a matter between one interpreter and one text. The typical "text" is constructed on the spot by several speakers interacting, be that in conversation or mediated through writing. Each speaker contributes to this multi-authored "text," negotiating its joint creation simultaneously with the other interlocutors. This is enormously complex, yet human beings do it all the time without missing a beat.

Critical discourse studies examine written texts or mass media output rather than spoken discourse (Mesthrie *et al.*, 2000, pp. 326–30). In part, this is due to the relative ease of examining written rather than spoken discourse. Before critical sociolinguists can look for patterns of language choices, they have to define a regularly occurring form of discourse and gather a reasonable sample of language in use. Written forms tend to be already defined by the people who use them and readily available; in contrast, spoken forms of discourse like conversations are much more vaguely defined, have boundaries – beginnings and endings – that are sometimes hard to spot, and cannot be collected with quite the same ease. Studies of written texts or mass media output do, however, have some inherent limitations. They consistently reveal how information is "packaged" and manipulated to achieve certain desired effects, but rarely do they follow how the "package" is received by the intended audience, or even the more numerous unintended audiences that no doubt will follow.

Sociolinguists are aware of the challenges that come with inquiries into mass-mediated language processes involving large and distributed networks of interlocutors (Biber, 2006; Hull and Katz, 2006). Variables that have been found quite useful in a variety of critical studies of language use include speaking rights and responsibilities, topic control, and conversational pacing. Most of these variables have been applied to sets of data compiled from spoken discourse, some have been extended to print collections, and still others have been elaborated for written discourse. Marjorie Orellana (1996) and Deborah Poole (1994, 2008) examined negotiations of school values and procedures in elementary classrooms using both spoken language and written discourses. Consistently, teachers were found to have the right to speak pretty much whenever they want and for however long they want, whereas students were limited to providing correct responses and occasionally asking questions. Many other situations have defined roles that come with differentiated speaking rights. Powerful social roles come with the right to establish and maintain the topics of conversations and other speech events. People with less powerful social roles have to negotiate, and keep negotiating.

Speaking rights and topic control can often be ascertained more quantitatively by keeping track of how much different participants get to say, and how easily they can break in and put in their two cents. Thus, one of the first steps in most critical sociolinguistic inquiries is to establish the overall distribution of turns of talk and words produced, and to take note of who interrupts whom, how often, and at what points in a given set of interactions. All of these are related to power and control of the discourse.

Variables that have been found productive in critical discourse analysis include:

- Authorship or origin: People routinely make use of existing texts as they go about their business. A qualitative examination of the origin of their words, particularly in discourse generated within institutions (schools, hospitals, police stations, the US Congress, etc.) often turns into an archeological exercise into layers of allusions and quotations, and is quite revealing. The ideas of Mikhail Bakhtin (1981) about heteroglossia and multiple voices animating every utterance are particularly relevant in such inquiries.
- Use of jargon: Specialized vocabulary, or jargon, helps groups of speakers establish and maintain group boundaries. Jargon is a particularly salient feature of many professions and occupations, and monitoring its use is a helpful tool for studying registers, the type of "social dialect" associated with specific functions.
- Certainty or uncertainty: Every human language includes what could be called a "grammar of certainty," or multiple ways to incorporate various degrees of credibility or doubt into utterances and texts. This "grammar of certainty" is routinely exploited for purposes of politeness, but it can also be put to use to underscore or undermine the legitimacy of specific communications.
- Tentativeness: In line with projecting varying degrees of certainty, interlocutors take advantage of a number of recognizable linguistic cues such as hedges ("I think," "maybe," "you know") or tag questions ("It's not clear at all, is it?") to soften the force of their statements.
- Conversational support: compliment and criticisms: "Minimal responses" such as *mmh*, *wow*, or *yeah*, usually accompanied by matching body language, function as a verbal lubricant and support the ongoing production of particular stories or arguments in conversation. The occurrence of such discourse markers can be monitored and quantified. More overt forms of support come in the form of compliments and clear indications of approval addressed to speakers.
- Criticisms or clear indications of disapproval (the inverse) can also be monitored and quantified quite easily from a sufficiently rich transcript.

These variables can be quite challenging to operationalize for extended analyses of real language use, as they all involve a certain degree of interpretation. Rajend Mesthrie *et al.* (2000, pp. 237–39) provide a great example when they summarize sociolinguistic research on the use of tag questions in their chapter "Gender and Language Use." At first, tag questions were thought to be used more by women than by men to soften assertions, such as in "The way prices are rising is horrendous, isn't it?" (Lakoff, 1975, cited in Mesthrie *et al.*, 2000, p. 236). As more researchers examined tag questions, however, they found that the questions could express one of four distinct functions – epistemic, challenging, facilitative, or softening – depending on how they were used. Assigning a function to a given tag question required interpretive analysis on the part of the linguists, and a broader understanding of the speech event. Another researcher, Madeleine Youmans (2001), described the fluid and dynamic character of specific discourse markers, studying the use of different epistemic modals to express more or less politeness, and to assert or impugn the trustworthiness of others.

Just like tag questions, linguistic units like topic or signaling (un)certainty tend to be fluid and context dependent. They are negotiated in the speaking, and will shift as speakers respond to each other. Researchers studying these variables often use an ethnographic method called triangulation to evaluate their interpretations. Triangulation is a form of cross-referencing across data sets or across observations, and can also include having other qualified judges checking particular interpretations.

Critical discourse analysis usually requires several methods of analysis. Together with the required data collection, these multiple rounds of analysis can be quite time-consuming. Results are often tentative, as a particular analysis often leads to new questions that cannot be answered with the collected data. Despite all these difficulties, critical sociolinguists still find discourse analysis to be a task worth doing.

Critical discourse analysts are more interested in meaning than in variation per se. They are looking for patterns and the meaning of the discovered patterns. Since 2002, I have worked on mathematics instruction, using videotaped lessons from seven countries across the globe. The larger study is multidisciplinary and mostly descriptive at this point. That is, all the researchers working with these data are trying to understand mathematics instruction, and trying to understand whether differences between countries are due to cultural, institutional, or still other factors. The answer is actually all of the above, but a more interesting finding so far is that math lessons do not vary much across languages and countries. Furthermore, math teachers do not include many explanations of mathematical ideas. Instead, they keep drilling their students through mathematical problem solving, on an international scale. Learning math seems to mean doing math – in the sense of completing worksheet after worksheet of math problems – with relatively few comments about why problems are solved a particular way or even how the problem-solving steps might be relevant elsewhere (Patthey, 2009). This tendency presents quite a contrast with instruction in other subject areas where teachers do a lot of talking in most lessons.

This contrast in the frequency of explanations has piqued my interest and led me to wonder what could account for it. Language data alone, however, are not sufficient to answer this emerging research question. In fact, sociolinguistic analysis alone is probably insufficient, as the reasons for this unique yet internationally ubiquitous approach to mathematics instruction may lie in the history of mathematics as a discipline. To pursue this interest therefore requires historical research and perhaps also interviews with mathematics instructors about their teaching goals and methods. I do not yet know what it is about math-the-tradition, the discipline with a long and multicultural heritage, that will explain its emphasis on practicing rather than explaining mathematics. With a more in-depth understanding of the additional social and historical dimensions of the discipline, it should be possible to return to language data and discern how specific values unique to mathematics inform its everyday realization as a language-mediated subject in which explanations are skimped in favor of practice.

The contrast between "global warming" and "climate change" introduced above shall serve as a final illustration of both the promise and the limitations of critical discourse analysis. Early in 2011, I listened to a series of lectures about Antarctica and was struck by the use of the term "climate change" during these lectures. I did not recall hearing the term used much in earlier discussions of the Polar regions or of similar topics in human geography. I also suspected that the emergence of this term was related to the often acrimonious debates of "global warming" in the USA that followed the success of Gore's documentary film *An Inconvenient Truth* (2006). How could I turn this hunch into a testable hypothesis?

To examine whether my impressions reflected a measurable reality, I needed to follow the use of the two subject headings over time. The documentary *An Inconvenient Truth* had its première at the Sundance Film Festival in 2006 and won the Academy Award for best documentary in 2007. It also generated an almost immediate backlash from "global warming" skeptics, and brought to prominence an international debate about the reality and the science of "climate change". I decided to track the use of the two terms from mid-2006 to mid-2011 in two national newspapers, the *Los Angeles Times* and the *New York Times*, using each newspaper's website. Each newspaper appears to be using a different search algorithm, with the *New York Times* returning much higher counts than the *Los Angeles Times*, possibly by tracking all occurrences of a phrase rather than just those in titles or tags. Nevertheless, the criteria used by each newspaper were internally consistent, so the raw counts simply needed to be standardized to ascertain comparable trends over time. Table 4.1 presents the results of these two time series analyses using simple percentages for each newspaper for each year as a method of standardization.

The *Los Angeles Times* and the *New York Times* evidence strikingly similar distribution trends for the terms "global warming" and "climate change." From mid-2006 to mid-2007 both newspapers used the term "global warming" 60 percent and 59 percent of the time as opposed to "climate change" which they used 40 percent and 41 percent of the time. The next year the two terms were used with almost the same frequency, with the *New York Times* still favoring the term "global warming" (55 percent, compared to 51 percent for the *Los Angeles*

Table 4.1 Occurrence of the terms *global warming* and *climate change* in two newspapers, 2006–2011

	Los Angeles Times		New York Times	
	Global warming	Climate change	Global warming	Climate change
2006–7	71 (60%)	56 (40%)	1,291 (59%)	908 (41%)
2007–8	151 (51%)	145 (49%)	1,703 (55%)	1,388 (45%)
2008–9	146 (50%)	144 (50%)	1,456 (46%)	1,678 (54%)
2009–10	36 (33%)	73 (67%)	1,337 (38%)	2,156 (62%)
2010–11	72 (30%)	169 (70%)	947 (39%)	1,496 (61%)

Times). The year after that, the *Los Angeles Times* used both terms with almost the same frequency, while the *New York Times* reversed its earlier pattern, now using "global warming" only 46 percent of the time. The year 2009–10 brought a definitive shift toward "climate change," now used 67 percent of the time in the *Los Angeles Times* and 62 percent in the *New York Times*. This ratio increased to 70 percent in the *Los Angeles Times* during 2010–11 and remained at 61 percent in the *New York Times*. On the whole, the patterns found in the two newspapers confirmed my impression that the phrase "climate change" has come into much greater use since the success of Gore's documentary. Results also support the hypothesis that the distribution of the two terms reflects an attempt to shift and perhaps shape the discussions of "global warming" in the USA. However, they are insufficient by themselves.

Recall that I claimed that the two terms have different associations, with "global warming" perhaps having a more political sense and "climate change" a more scientific sense. To progress further in this analysis and support these interpretations of the two terms would require looking much more closely at where and how each term is used. First, the data base for the analysis would need to be expanded to include a range of texts in addition to the two newspapers. Second, the frequency of use for the two terms in political and scientific discourses would need to be examined to establish whether the proposed contrast in the sense of each term has any substance.

That's how sociolinguistics frequently progresses. We start with some interesting language use patterns, and a desire to understand these patterns. We define a representative data set and some key linguistic variables to see if our interpretive hunches have any substance. Our curiosity frequently takes us to other disciplines, as the discourse in question typically cannot be explained using linguistic variables alone. Eventually, armed with additional information about cultural, historical, and institutional backgrounds, we return to the discourse in question and try to ascertain whether these extra-linguistic processes can be glimpsed in the language use. Frequently, they can. We find that larger social processes are realized in and through the everyday practices of people, with language a most important tool. Sociolinguists will often apply many tools developed for a variety of sociolinguistic analyses, but they will then turn their attention to specific instances and discuss what they mean. Meaning is where it's at for a sociolinguist!

An enthusiasm for meaning does not eliminate the methodological problems inherent in examining it, so critical discourse analysts have attempted to develop a stronger theoretical foundation to complement their empirical studies. Critical sociolinguists view human language as the primary tool for socialization and enculturation in human societies (see Schieffelin and Ochs, 1995 [1986]). Human language is implicated in the construction and maintenance of any social system. Of particular interest to critical sociolinguists have been systems of privilege, such as those based on gender, ethnic origin, religious affiliation, or social class. Their focus on these systems has led to studies of the work done by and through language in exercising various forms of power, and hence the use of sociological writings theorizing about power in human affairs. Critical sociolinguists have also been interested in the more fundamental social processes at work in creating human families, human kinship systems, and many larger social groupings (as these seem to be derived from human kinship systems).

Sociolinguists have explored the writings of leading sociologists and social philosophers such as Pierre Bourdieu and Michel Foucault, as well as revisited ideas about language, the human mind, and human development as formulated by Mikhail Bakhtin and Valentin Voloshinov (discussed in Mesthrie *et al.*, 2000, pp. 321–22). The Bakhtin circle's theories about the heteroglossic nature of all human utterances could be likened to the indeterminacy of meaning discussed above. Lev Vygotsky's ideas, as developed in *Mind in Society*, also need to be mentioned (1978). Sociolinguists have drawn from all these sources, and they have developed a strong theoretical foundation, one that in turn has led to better grounded empirical work.

At issue is how human beings work out their identities, and their relationships and conflicts with each other. Any understanding of social systems must be based on an understanding of how people communicate, assert, and negotiate their values, and how they resolve conflicts. These conflicts occur when people interact, but they also occur when people negotiate inconsistencies between their preferences, their words, and their deeds. Such negotiations within and between people become apparent when one records interactions or interviews, and examines the resulting language data within an interpretive framework. Critical discourse analysis provides us with the theoretical and methodological tools to understand how people make sense of their worlds. It teaches us how to pay attention to the subtle and sometimes not-so-subtle ways that human beings inflect their communications with varying attitudes. It helps us see how a shift from "global warming" to "climate change" is about much more than semantics.

References

Bakhtin, M. M. 1981. *The Dialogic Imagination: Four Essays*. Austin, Tex.: University of Texas Press.

Biber, D. 2006. *University Language: A Corpus-Based Study of Spoken and Written Registers.* Amsterdam: John Benjamins.

Gore, A. 2006. *An Inconvenient Truth.* New York: Rodale.

Hull, G., and M.-L. Katz. 2006. Crafting an Agentive Self: Case Studies of Digital Story-Telling. *Research in the Teaching of English* 41(1), pp. 43–81.

Mesthrie, R., J. Swann, A. Deumert, and W. L. Leap. 2000. *Introducing Sociolinguistics.* Philadelphia: John Benjamins.

Orellana, M. F. 1996. Negotiating Power through Language in Classroom Meetings. *Linguistics and Education* 8(4), pp. 335–66.

Patthey, G. G. 2009. "Doing and (Not) Explaining Math: An Analysis of Mathematics Lesson Data from Seven International Settings." Invited Colloquium Presentation at the Annual Conference of the American Association for Applied Linguistics, Denver, CO, 21 March.

Poole, D. 1994. Routine Testing Practices and the Linguistic Construction of Knowledge. *Cognition and Instruction* 12(2), pp. 125–50.

Poole, D. 2008. The Messiness of Language Socialization in Reading Groups: Participation in and Resistance to the Values of Essayist Literacy. *Linguistics and Education* 19, pp. 378–403.

Sapir, E. 1949. *Culture, Language and Personality.* Berkeley: University of California Press.

Schieffelin, B. B., and E. Ochs, eds. 1995 [1986]. *Language Socialization across Cultures.* New York: Cambridge University Press.

Vygotsky, L. S. 1978. *Mind in Society: The Development of Higher Psychological Processes.* Cambridge, Mass.: Harvard University Press.

Youmans, M. 2001. Cross-Cultural Differences in Polite Epistemic Modal Use in American English. *Journal of Multilingual and Multicultural Development* 22(1), pp. 57–73.

5 Psychometrics

Measuring attitudes and values about the environment

Tammi Vacha-Haase, Anne M. Hansen, and Zinta S. Byrne

Conducting research on attitudes and values about the environment and sustainable development often requires the use of questionnaires or other types of assessment instruments. For example, when a researcher wishes to investigate attitudes toward sustainable development, a typical way to obtain this information is to develop a scale (a set of questions) designed to elicit individuals' views about the subject. Developing an instrument that measures what the researcher wants it to measure is not a simple process. How can the researcher be certain that the items in the questionnaire are really measuring attitudes toward sustainability? Can the researcher be sure that the same scale measures these attitudes consistently across people and time? The field of psychometrics helps to answer these questions.

Psychometrics is the field of study related to the theory behind and quality of psychological and educational measurement. Using psychometrics, researchers provide information about the consistency and accuracy of psychological assessment instruments. Assessment instruments, often referred to simply as tests, include, among others, questionnaires, observations, interviews, simulations (e.g. role-play), physical tests (e.g. vision, physical fitness), electronic tests (e.g. skin galvanic response meter), and combinations of all of the above. An accurate and consistent test is especially helpful for measuring difficult-to-observe characteristics or traits such as knowledge, values, attitudes, and personality. Attitudes and values cannot be seen, and determining whether they have been measured as precisely as possible cannot be accomplished through observation only. Thus, psychometrics allows researchers to judge the accuracy of their assessment of the attitudes and values that affect individuals' behavior.

Researchers and practitioners alike draw conclusions from the results of their measurement instruments; therefore, the quality of their decisions is based on the precision of their assessment. These decisions can influence both people and policies. For example, the US government's No Child Left Behind Act of 2001 requires testing in the schools to determine whether children in kindergarten through the twelfth grade are receiving an adequate education in Math and English; funding for schools and teachers is provided based on the results of these tests (Mayers, 2006). A local government may decide to continue allowing deforestation by a lumber company because a questionnaire on attitudes about paper indicated that people prefer reading printed books to electronic copies. Actions taken based on test results can have substantial impact and long-lasting effects; therefore, the accuracy of test results is critical.

This chapter explains how to use the tools of psychometrics to improve the measurement of attitudes and values, which in turn can lead to more informed decision-making. Two major aspects of psychometric information used in determining the accuracy and appropriateness of an assessment instrument, validity and reliability, will be discussed. Further, we provide an overview of psychometric theory in validity and reliability, describe sources of psychometric information, and present situations in which we explain why each type of information is useful, how it can be used, and the limitations of its use.

Validity

Researchers in sustainable development need to be able to draw reasonable conclusions about what they have measured. For example, researchers want to know if their test items adequately present the broad array of consequences associated with sustainable development, so that they can accurately determine to what extent people understand the impact of ignoring the consequences of development. They want to be able to predict from the results of their questionnaires which educational campaigns will have the greatest effect on people's willingness to recycle, invest in hybrid or electric cars, or support legislation to restrict toxic waste dumping in rivers. Evidence of measurement validity can provide support for predictions of this sort.

Validity refers to the extent to which an instrument measures the concepts that it is designed to measure. Establishing validity is a process of collecting evidence to support the conclusions that are drawn (Cronbach, 1951). It involves gathering information from various sources to compile evidence, typically referred to as the "process of validation". Validity can only be established to support specific conclusions for which we have evidence. That is, a test in and of itself can never be valid. A test can only be valid for a specific purpose. Therefore, one validates the *use* of the instrument and not the instrument itself. For example, if we develop a questionnaire to predict who is more likely to eat farmed salmon than wild salmon, we can validate the questionnaire for this purpose only. We cannot claim that we can also predict who will buy a hybrid car rather than a gasoline car. Hence, validity evidence confirms whether a test was designed to measure what it is supposed to measure (also referred to as "validity of measurement"), and whether the predictions that we claim to be able to make with the test can really be made (also known as "validity for decisions").

There are three major sources of validity evidence – criterion-related validity, content validity, and construct validity – each of which provides information to support the validity of a particular use of a scale. These types of validity are not mutually exclusive; each type contributes to the overall evaluation of validity evidence. Not all types of validity can be assessed for every test. For example, some questionnaires describe people's opinions, but without evidence to support

Table 5.1 Types of validity

Type of validity	Indicates …	Sources of information
Criterion-related validity	If a scale predicts a variable of interest	Correlation between the scale and criterion variable
Content validity	If the items represent the content area	Definition of construct; ratings from Subject Matter Experts (SMEs)
Construct validity	If the scale measures what it claims to measure	Discriminant validity; convergent validity; reliability; content validity; criterion-related validity

their predictive abilities, they should not be used to predict future behavior (see Table 5.1 for an overview).

Criterion-related validity

Criterion-related validity examines the extent to which a construct assessed by a scale is related to another independent variable of interest (a criterion). The criterion is selected based on the purpose of the test. Criterion-related validation studies examine the correlation between the construct of interest and what it should predict. The resulting correlation is known as the "validity coefficient." The higher the correlation, the more confidence we have that the scale is predicting the criterion. For example, if the purpose of a measure of environmental attitudes is to predict behaviors that protect the environment, establishing criterion-related validity (that the measure of attitudes is related to protective behavior) is essential. In this case, the predictor is attitudes and the criterion is a measure of actual behavior. If we wish to claim that the scale can be used to predict a specific set of behaviors, we must have evidence that supports this claim.

Within criterion-related validity there are two types of studies: predictive and concurrent. In predictive validity studies, researchers collect data on the predictor or the independent variable, wait a specified amount of time, and then collect criterion information (the dependent variable). These studies demonstrate the ability of the measure to predict one's future standing on a criterion. In contrast, researchers conducting concurrent validity studies collect both predictor and criterion information at the same time. Therefore, a concurrent study demonstrates the ability of a measure to predict one's current standing on a criterion.

A strength of predictive studies is that they assess the ability of a measure to predict future performance on the criterion. By waiting to collect the data, one is assured that it is truly the future score that is obtained – the score of interest. Because the predictor occurs before the criterion, one can be assured that the predictor is predicting the criterion and not vice versa. Thus, predictive studies are most appropriate for measures that claim to predict future standing or performance on the criterion. The disadvantage of predictive validity studies is that one has to wait the prescribed amount of time (up to a year or more) before being able to collect the criterion data. The result can be participant attrition, expense, loss of data, or other problems, especially when the wait time is long. Additionally, the results of the study are not known until after the prescribed amount of time.

An advantage of concurrent validity studies is that data on the criterion are collected at the same time as the predictor. This procedure is more cost-efficient, is less likely to result in participant attrition, and ensures that the results of the study are immediately available. Moreover, concurrent validity studies are beneficial when the purpose of a test is to explain performance on the criterion. A weakness of concurrent validity studies is that the collection of the predictor may interfere with or confound the collection of the criterion. For example, if a researcher wanted to investigate the influence of racial bias on behavior, participants might complete a questionnaire, and then take part in a group activity that involved people from different racial and ethnic backgrounds. If there was a correlation between the test score and participant behavior, the researcher could conclude that bias toward other ethnic groups predicts a certain behavior. However, it is possible that the *act* of answering questions about bias, rather than bias itself, affected participants' behavior. If a concurrent validity study is used as a proxy for a predictive study, the conclusions are weak; the criterion is not actually occurring at a time in the future. Hence, the resulting study cannot establish the directionality of the relationship between predictor and criterion.

Content validity

Content validity describes the extent to which the items in the scale are representative of the content area. Content validity is typically obtained when one is assessing a topic with concrete boundaries, such as the knowledge base of sustainable development. Content validity tells us to what extent our test items represent that knowledge base. In the field of environmental science, for example, this form of validity evidence answers the question "Does this scale measure attitudes about all the areas of sustainable development – economic, social, and environmental – that I wish to investigate?" (World Commission on Environment and Development, 1987; Vitalis, 2004).

To assess content validity, scale developers must first carefully define the content area. For example, how do we define attitudes toward the environment? Do they include attitudes toward humans, wildlife, plant life, or all three? After the content domain is defined, individuals knowledgeable about the content area, often referred to as Subject Matter Experts (SMEs), rate the extent to which the scale items are essential or otherwise representative of the content area. SMEs may be asked to rate how essential each item is to measuring attitudes toward the environment. One approach to quantitatively summarizing ratings is the Content Validity Ratio (Lawshe, 1975), which provides a measure of the agreement across raters that a particular item is essential or representative of a given construct. Thus, content validity tells us whether the test has been constructed adequately in terms of the item coverage. The wording of the items, language, and difficulty level are all considered (Messick, 1998) to prevent score results from being influenced by factors irrelevant to the construct. Factor analyses can also be used to assess whether items group together as expected (Sireci, 1998).

Construct validity

Construct validity also provides evidence that a scale is measuring what it purports to measure. It subsumes both content and criterion-related validity. Each new study contributes more information to the understanding of the construct and to the confidence that one is actually measuring and assessing that construct (Campbell and Fiske, 1959). One method for obtaining construct validity evidence is to examine the relationship of scores on a test with scores on other tests. One first determines which constructs should be related to the focal construct, and which should be unrelated. Construct validity evidence is obtained by showing that the focal construct correlates as expected with other similar constructs, and fails to correlate as expected with those to which it is hypothesized to be unrelated.

Two types of relationships are used to establish construct validity: convergent validity (correlates where it should) and discriminant validity (does not correlate where it should not) (Campbell and Fiske, 1959). Convergent validity demonstrates that the responses on a scale are related to responses from other scales that measure theoretically similar constructs. For example, if a researcher is developing a new measure of attitudes toward recycling, the scores on the new measure should be related to an existing measure of attitudes toward recycling. Discriminant validity provides evidence that the responses obtained on a given scale, let's say scale A, are unrelated to, or distinct from, scores obtained on other scales, let's say scale B, measuring other constructs that should not be unrelated because they are theoretically different. For example, a scale that measures attitudes toward marine animals should not be highly correlated with attitudes toward human use of national parks. Though there may be overlap between these attitudes, they should be distinct and not demonstrate a high correlation.

Beyond its relationships with other variables, a measure of a single construct should have homogenous items (questions that relate to the same construct). Thus, some researchers use factor analysis to demonstrate additional construct validity evidence. Factor analysis (Bryant and Yarnold, 1995) groups items according to their interrelationships. It reduces the items into similar factors, based on the assumption that responses for items measuring the same construct should be more closely related to each other than to items measuring different constructs. For example, if a theory suggests that an all-encompassing measure of sustainable development should assess social, economic, and environmental beliefs, then scores obtained on this measure should fall into those three categories.

Using validity information

It may be beneficial to use an established measure; however, widespread or previous use does not necessarily indicate that a test is psychometrically sound. How can a researcher determine if an existing scale has sufficient validity evidence? Evidence for content validity is usually set forth in the section of an article where the authors describe test development. Researchers should report the theory from which the scale was developed, the methods used to develop items, and the results of any quantitative analyses conducted to summarize judgments about items.

If a correlation table is reported in the results section, it can provide evidence of criterion-related validity (the correlation between the scale and the outcome variable of interest). Examining the pattern of correlations establishing that the measure of interest is like related scales but distinct from measures of other constructs can show indications of convergent and discriminant validity. Finally, factor analysis results, if provided, should show support for the homogeneity of items, thus supporting the theory of a single construct.

Evidence of validity is essential for establishing that a scale measures what it purports to measure. However, validity information is of little value if the scale does not accurately measure the attitude, value, or attribute of interest. To ensure accuracy of measurement, researchers assess reliability – another tool of psychometrics.

Reliability

Reliability provides an indication of the stability and consistency of score measurement. It provides information about how much of the observed scores on a test or scale are due to measurement error (something other than what is being measured), rather than true variation. It represents an estimate of how consistent scale scores are over time, across different versions of a test, or among scale items. Reliability estimates give information about the accuracy of a measure. Reliability does not indicate, however, whether what is being measured is what one purports to measure.

The reliability measures discussed herein are based on classical test theory (Cronbach, 1970), according to which each observed score on a scale has two components: the true score and the measurement error. Each individual has a true score that represents his or her actual standing or perspective on an attribute. However, because we cannot actually observe the true scores of attributes such as attitudes or values, only an observed score can be obtained.

Measurement error is defined as that which affects an observed score and is unrelated to an individual's actual standing on an attribute. Measurement error can come from a variety of sources, including which items are chosen and how they are written (e.g. difficult or poor wording), how the scale is administered (e.g. group setting, noisy or hot room, computerized responses), and characteristics of the individuals completing the scale (e.g. fear of tests, competitiveness, reading level). Reliability provides an estimate of how much of the variation

Table 5.2 Types of reliability

Type of reliability	Indicates …	Advantages	Disadvantages
Test-retest	Consistency of scores over time	Easy to use in most research settings	Requires two administrations; no estimate of reliability until after the second administration
Alternate forms	Consistency of scores across two forms of a test	Shorter waiting period between administrations than test-retest	Requires two administrations and at least two forms
Internal consistency: split-half	Consistency of scores across two halves of a test	Only one test and administration needed	Underestimates reliability (can be corrected with the Spearman-Brown formula); not good for very short scales
Internal consistency: alpha coefficient	Consistency of scores within a test	Only one test administration needed; stable estimate	Only useful for homogenous scales

in observed scores is due to error, rather than true variation on the attribute. The more error in measurement, the less the researcher is actually measuring the attribute. Therefore, it is important to establish reliability to confirm that the scores on the test are as accurate as possible.

There are several methods for obtaining a reliability estimate, known as the "reliability coefficient," for scores of a scale: test-retest, alternate forms, and internal consistency. Each of these methods produces a reliability coefficient and has different requirements, limitations, and strengths, and each provides different information about the consistency of a test. Researchers typically only report one type of reliability index – it is only in major test development projects (such as developing published tests) where multiple forms may be reported. For each type of reliability estimate described below, the following are included: a description of the estimate; the steps for collecting the reliability evidence; the advantages and disadvantages to each approach; and guidelines for choosing each type (see Table 5.2 for an overview).

Test-retest reliability

Test-retest reliability provides an estimate of the stability of scores on a test over time. This type of reliability is best used for attributes that are believed to be stable (e.g. IQ scores). If a scale measures something that is expected to change over time, such as lexical development, the results of this reliability coefficient will not be meaningful. To obtain a test-retest reliability coefficient, researchers should complete the following steps: give the measure to a group of respondents (Time 1); wait a specified period of time (depends on the attribute being measured); give the measure again to the same group of people (Time 2); and then calculate the correlation between the scores at Time 1 and at Time 2. The correlation coefficient is called the "reliability coefficient". The higher the coefficient (which functions just like a correlation coefficient and has the same properties), the more stable the scores on the measure and the less error in measurement.

Test-retest reliability has the advantage of using the same respondents and test items; therefore, it is unlikely that changes over time are due to item content or respondents, making it possible to rule these out as sources of error. However, there are difficulties in collecting this type of reliability information. First, it requires two test administrations that use the same respondents, which may be logistically difficult and may result in participant attrition. Second, using the same respondents may create carryover effects, where remembering test items from the first administration affects an individual's performance on the second administration.

Respondents also tend to repeat their guessing strategies and answering habits as well as their responses, which inflates the reliability estimate (Nunnally and Bernstein, 1994). Finally, it can be difficult to identify the optimal period between two test administrations; the time should be long enough to minimize carryover effects, but short enough to minimize attrition and stay within the time frame for attribute stability. Alternate forms reliability can overcome some of these disadvantages, as well as provide additional consistency information.

Alternate forms reliability

Alternate forms reliability examines the consistency of responses across two or more forms of a test. This type of reliability is best used when more than one form of a test will be given to different participants or when carryover effects are highly likely. To assess reliability, two different forms of the test are created, which should be nearly identical. Although the two forms should have different items, they should cover the same content area, reflect the same levels of the attribute, have the same number of items, and be presented in the same format. Both forms of the test are administered to the same group of people, and the relationship between the two forms is assessed. The resulting reliability coefficient indicates the consistency of scores over the two forms of the test. This approach controls for many of the carryover effects described with test-retest reliability and requires less time between test administrations; however, it presents its own drawbacks. Although the items on each form are different, information from the first form can still affect how respondents reply to items on the second form. To minimize this effect, researchers can randomly vary the sequence of forms among participants. Additionally, creating two forms of a test can be extremely challenging and time-consuming.

Internal consistency reliability

In contrast to the previously discussed reliability coefficients, measures of internal consistency require only one version of a test and one test administration. Internal consistency reliability provides an indication of the homogeneity of the scale items. It is a measure of how the items within a test are correlated. There are several ways to assess internal consistency. Two of the most often used are split-half reliability and alpha coefficient reliability.

Split-half reliability

Split-half reliability provides a way to assess internal consistency by dividing the items on a scale in half (e.g. take a twenty-item scale and create two ten-item scales) and calculating the correlation between the two halves. The test is first administered in its full form to a group of respondents. Then the scale is divided into identical halves, a process that essentially creates alternate forms from a single test (assuming that the test is indeed homogenous). The items can be divided randomly, or the test can be divided into even- and odd-numbered items. One should not split the test by moving the first half of the items into one scale and the second half into the other scale: the fatigue levels of respondents may increase from the first half to the second, causing careless answers or skipped questions and thus introducing error.

The primary disadvantage of split-half reliability is that reliability coefficients are affected by the number of test items in a scale: the fewer the items on the test, the lower the reliability estimate. Because split-half reliability divides the number of items in half, it underestimates the reliability of the *entire* test. This limitation can be statistically corrected by using the Spearman-Brown formula, which provides an estimate of what the reliability would be had the full set of scale items been used. Further information about the Spearman-Brown formula can be found in Jum Nunnally and Ira Bernstein (1994).

The alpha coefficient

The alpha coefficient (Cronbach, 1951) is another measure of internal consistency. It is calculated by creating all possible combinations of split-half reliabilities, correcting the reliability estimates for the number of items using the Spearman-Brown formula, and finally computing the average reliability coefficient. Alpha coefficients can be calculated in most statistical packages used in the social sciences, such as SAS and SPSS. By using all possible splits of the items, the alpha coefficient eliminates error due to the means used to divide items and provides a more stable estimate than only calculating one split-half reliability estimate. The alpha coefficient is affected by the number of items in the test and their average correlations. Thus, if a researcher obtains a low alpha coefficient (e.g. 0.50), either the test is too short or it does not have enough similar items (Nunnally and Bernstein, 1994).

Reliability differences and the generalization of reliability

Which type of reliability is appropriate to use depends on the details of the research. While types of reliability are not mutually exclusive, each provides different information, so a researcher may want to investigate more than one type of reliability for a single scale. To summarize, test-retest reliability is designed to measure stable attributes; alternate forms reliability is especially useful if the researcher needs to use two forms of the scale across people; and internal consistency reliability coefficients are designed for scales assessing attributes that are expected to be homogeneous. All these approaches to reliability provide estimates for a single set of test scores; they do not show that the scale itself is reliable. "A test is not reliable or unreliable. Rather reliability is a property of the scores on a test for a particular group of examinees" (Crocker and Algina, 1986, p. 144). To provide further evidence of reliability beyond a single set of scores, reliability generalization studies can be conducted.

Reliability generalization studies

Reliability generalization studies (Vacha-Haase, 1998) provide information about the average reliability of scores for a scale across existing studies. Reliability generalization studies also investigate the extent to which reliability estimates can vary across studies. Furthermore, they can identify the sources of variability in the reliability of scores, such as study or sample characteristics.

Once the reliability of the scale scores is estimated, the researcher must decide what conclusions can be made, and how the results can be used: questions of validity. The researcher must consider if there is sufficient reliability to be confident in the consistency of scale scores. Although there are no set standards, alpha coefficients of 0.7 and above are typically considered adequate for research, and 0.9 for decision-making (Nunnally and Bernstein, 1994). Another consideration is the effect of reliability on the relationship between variables. Reliability will affect how strongly the scale scores can be related to other variables (an issue of validity), such that low reliability will attenuate the correlation between the scale and variables of interest.

When using reliability of score results to describe the properties of a scale, one should consider several things. Reliability information can be reported to indicate both consistency of a test and homogeneity of items; however, these results should be reported with caution. The reliability information for a test is only a reliability estimate for the scores from a given study or sample (Pedhazur and Schmelkin, 1991). The reliability evidence gathered from a set of test scores is only for the scores, not the test; therefore, it can never be said that the scale itself is reliable. Additionally, the homogeneity of items can be one indication that a scale is unidimensional (that is, it only measures a single attribute). Nevertheless, internal consistency does not guarantee this; homogeneity is only one indication of unidimensionality, and further supporting evidence must be collected.

Establishing evidence of reliability is important for many reasons. Evidence of reliability of scores increases the likelihood that a scale can adequately measure the attitudes or values that one intends to measure. Further, reliability is a requirement for validity, establishing that a test measures what it is supposed to measure. If a scale can measure an attribute with relatively little error, researchers and policy makers can have more confidence in the conclusions that they draw from the scale.

Conclusion

In this chapter we have provided a basic introduction to psychometrics by describing two major principles of psychometrics: validity and reliability. The reader should be aware that the field of psychometrics also encompasses the theory and development behind test construction and measurement, which are beyond the scope and purpose of this chapter. By using information about the reliability and validity of measurement, researchers can increase the quality of conclusions and decision-making in their area of study. Furthermore, requiring researchers to provide reliability and validity information in published works allows others to determine the accuracy of their research, and gives them a sound basis on which to decide whether to use a pre-established scale.

References

Bryant, F., and P. Yarnold. 1995. Principal-Components Analysis and Exploratory and Confirmatory Factor Analysis. In *Reading and Understanding Multivariate Statistics*. Eds. L. G. Grimm and P. R. Yarnold, pp. 99–136. Washington, DC: American Psychological Association.

Campbell, D. T., and D. W. Fiske. 1959. Convergent and Discriminant Validity by the Multitrait-Multimethod Matrix. *Psychological Bulletin* 56, pp. 81–105.

Crocker, L., and J. Algina.1986. *Introduction to Classical and Modern Test Theory*. Belmont, Calif.: Wadsworth.

Cronbach, L. J. 1951. Coefficient Alpha and the Internal Structure of Tests. *Psychometrika* 16, pp. 297–334.

Cronbach, L. J. 1970. *Essentials of Psychological Testing*. 3rd edn. New York: Harper and Row.

Hambleton, R., H., Swaminathan, and H. Rogers. 1991. *Fundamentals of Item Response Theory*. Newbury Park, Calif.: Sage.

Lawshe, C. H. 1975. A Quantitative Approach to Content Validity. *Personnel Psychology*. 28, pp. 563–75.

Mayers, C. M. 2006. Public Law 107–110 No Child Left Behind Act of 2001: Support or Threat to Education as a Fundamental Right? *Education* 126(3), pp. 449–61.

Messick, S. J. 1998. Alternative Modes of Assessment, Uniform Standards of Validity. In *Beyond Multiple Choice: Evaluating Alternatives to Traditional Testing for Selection*. Ed. M. D. Hakel. Mahwah, NJ: Erlbaum. pp. 59–74.

Nunnally, J. C., and I. Bernstein. 1994. *Psychometric Theory*. 3rd edn. New York: McGraw-Hill.

Pedhazur, E., and L. Schmelkin. 1991. *Measurement, Design, and Analysis: An Integrated Approach.* Hillsdale, NJ: Lawrence Erlbaum.

Sireci, S. G. 1998. The Construct of Content Validity. *Social Indicators Research* 45, pp. 83–117.

Vacha-Haase, T. 1998. Reliability Generalization: Exploring Variance in Measurement Error Affecting Score Reliability across Studies. *Educational and Psychological Measurement* 58(1), pp. 6–20.

Vitalis, V. 2004. Science, Economics, and Sustainable Development: Making Measurement Meaningful. *Environmental Sciences* 1(2), pp. 201–30.

World Commission on Environment and Development. 1987. Our Common Future. Retrieved on July 15th, 2012, from http://daccessdds.un.org/doc/UNDOC/GEN/N87/184/67/IMG/N8718467.pdf?.

6 Determining environmental values using focus groups

Ding Ding

Introduction

Focus groups are a qualitative research technique to collect meaningful and profound information and have been widely used in social science. This chapter is intended to give readers a basic understanding of this widespread and promising research method. It concentrates on the application of focus groups and addresses focus groups from a social science practitioner's points of view. After exploring what focus groups are and why should we use them, it discusses techniques for conducting effective focus groups, the use of focus groups to determine environmental values, the new trend of virtual focus groups, and ethical issues associated with conducting focus groups.

Focus groups can be traced back to the 1920s, when group interviews were used for various purposes (Bogardus, 1926). Focus groups in something resembling their current form are generally accepted to have emerged in the 1940s with the groundbreaking work of Paul Lazarsfeld and Robert Merton, researchers in the Department of Social Research at Columbia University. They used focus groups to test people's reactions to propaganda materials and radio broadcasts during the Second World War (Cantril, 1944; Merton and Kendall, 1946; Lazarsfeld and Merton, 1948). Since the Second World War, focus groups have been used to uncover consumers' perceptions of products and marketing campaigns. The evident success of focus groups as a marketing tool greatly facilitated their application in other areas. Since the 1980s, focus groups have been widespread in mainstream academic research.

The typical focus group brings together eight to twelve qualified participants who discuss a predefined topic under the direction of a well-trained moderator. It usually lasts one and a half to two and a half hours and can be conducted at offices or online. Confusion may result from the improperly interchangeable use of some terms, including "group interview," "focus group interview" and "focus group discussion" (Frey and Fontana, 1991; Flick, 2007). Focus groups have been defined in a variety of ways, but fundamentally they are a way of getting information. For example, the engineers in a computer company are recruited by the Human Resources Department to share their opinions on how to improve Information Technology (IT) workers' creativity. David Morgan identified the key features of focus groups as follows: "they are a research method for collecting qualitative data, they are focused efforts at data gathering and they generate data through group discussion" (1998).

Benefits and limitations of focus groups

The main advantage of the focus group is that it provides a better opportunity to obtain rich and deep information than other qualitative methods. Focus groups take open-ended questions and elicit interaction between participants, and between participants and moderators. Participants are able to build on others' responses and come up with ideas they might not have thought of otherwise, or develop deeper insights than individual interviews or surveys would have engendered. Furthermore, the moderator and the observer can glean additional information about the topic being discussed through participants' body language and facial expressions. Other advantages include the ability to collect data from a group of people much more quickly and at lower cost, and to gather data from people with a lower literacy level, such as young children and non-native English speakers.

Focus groups have limitations as well. The first is that they are susceptible to response bias. The bias may come from moderators' perceptions to questions and their skills at facilitating discussions. It also may come from the participants' side. What participants say they think or do in focus groups may not be what they think or do in reality. Dynamics such as "Group Think" can enter the focus group, or simply because of the group dynamics the group can concentrate more on one aspect than it might have otherwise. Other drawbacks include misrepresentative information when discussion is dominated or sidetracked by a few individuals, and time-consuming data analyses after focus groups are conducted.

Also, focus groups may not be suitable for some sensitive personal topics, such as sexual behavior, stressful life events, weight control, and substance abuse. People tend to be reluctant to discuss subtle topics in front of strangers, regardless of the encouragement of the moderator.

Use of focus groups

Focus groups are commonly used at the early stage of research for exploration and discovery. They can also be used at late stages of research to facilitate deep understanding and interpretation of the results. These are some common uses of focus groups:

- gather information for a new or unknown topic of interest;
- obtain in-depth, meaningful information;
- develop a survey questionnaire;
- stimulate brainstorming and facilitate creative ideas;
- test people's perceptions, attitudes, responses, and beliefs about a product or service;
- diagnose potential problems of a product or service;

- interpret previously obtained research results;
- evaluate a program outcome;
- generate customized solutions for a specific audience.

How to conduct focus groups

Planning

Identifying the research question is the first step for research in any discipline. A focus group must begin with a clearly stated, appropriately defined problem that is worth investigating. The research question determines which research methods should be applied and what kind of information should be collected.

Careful and proper planning are essential for the focus group process to be successful. The planning of focus groups should answer several fundamental questions:

1. Why are the focus groups needed?
2. What kind information should be obtained through focus groups?
3. What actions should be conducted to complete the focus groups?
4. Where can one get resources to take actions?
5. What is the timeline for each step of the focus group?

Except for the general preparation, the planning should make detailed arrangements for each step of the focus groups. For example, planning related to recruiting participants should include a series of arrangements: identifying eligibility criteria and proper composition of participants; determining the resources and budget necessary to recruit participants; contacting and building relationships with potential participants; offering incentives to encourage people to participate; screening of and doing follow-up with the participants; and making participation more convenient, accessible, and comfortable.

Developing questions

The next step is to develop questions which elucidate the research problem. The first draft of questions can be written through brainstorming, expert panels, pre-focus surveys, and literature reviews. It is best to initially generate more questions than necessary, to allow for the later deletion of questions which do not capture information adequately, are culturally insensitive, or have other flaws. The draft questions will be sent to potential participants, researchers, and sponsors to test their readability, clarity, relevancy, and length, and then revised based on their responses.

There are three main types of questions in focus groups, which are used at different times. Engagement questions are used to get participants acquainted and create a comfortable discussion atmosphere. There are usually three to five questions of the second type, exploration questions, which are the core of the study. Finally, exit questions are used to allow participants to state their final opinion about crucial concerns and to check any missing information. All questions should be succinct and clear, explore different dimensions of the research questions, and be presented in an open-ended way, and participants should be allowed enough time to answer.

Moderating

A focus group is usually directed by a moderator who facilitates the discussion, and an assistant who takes notes or makes a recording. Having an unbiased and professional moderator is essential to achieve a focus group's goals. It is preferable to select a professional moderator who is good at communicating with participants and keeping the discussion on the right track. Qualified moderators should have adequate knowledge of the topic and a wide range of other skills, such as the ability to listen, think quickly, treat all participants equally and objectively, and manage time.

A moderator should clarify and rephrase questions when participants are confused. Effective moderators are able to probe participants for additional information. Unlike typical surveys, focus groups are not restricted by fixed choices but attempt to elicit as much information as possible. A participant may raise a topic or respond to others in a way that the moderator does not anticipate. The moderator should encourage this sort of spontaneity and get the facts behind the facts. Another characteristic of a good moderator is an ability to adjust questions or change their sequence. Otherwise, participants may spend too much time on information that is already known or bring up questions that change the research topic. The moderator should be able to assess quickly and accurately the contribution of each participant to the understanding of the group, and cut off irrelevant conversations or topics. In addition, silence sometimes gives clues, and a good moderator should be capable of dealing with silence and getting information from it.

Analyzing and reporting

As a qualitative research method, focus group analysis involves statistics to a limited extent, if at all. Instead, focus groups require the careful compiling and assessment of obtained information. In analyzing information, several principles must be kept in mind:

1. The analysis procedures should be predefined, consistent, and systematic.
2. The analysis should be verifiable by other persons.
3. The analysis should concentrate on key questions.
4. The analysis should be conducted as soon as possible after the focus groups.

The process of analyzing data usually begins by transcribing notes and recordings. Data are first grouped according to each question. For each question, answers are organized and classified into categories. Data are labeled and compared to synthesize the major themes and perspectives.

Collecting data of high quality and accurately reporting the data are the keys to getting valuable information from focus groups. Reporting is the process of conveying information to sponsors and decision makers. It is the intellectual and functional purpose of focus groups. The report should not focus on numbers or the frequency of answers, but rather identify patterns and perspectives. For example, a focus group could be applied to obtain local residents' opinions about building a new chemical plant. Focus groups provide depth such that simply reporting that, say, "20% of participants oppose building a chemical plant in their community; 50% of participants strongly oppose building a chemical plant" is not informative or meaningful given the type of data collected from a focus group. Instead, the report should identify the reasons behind the numbers: "the major reason for supporting the plant was the increased employment opportunity and other economic benefits to the community, while the main reason for opposing the plant was the potential damage to local environment and residents' health."

One pitfall of focus groups is that people tend to censor their ideas when other participants have backgrounds greatly different from their own, particularly with regard to education, income, and power. This tendency can reduce the quality and reliability of data. To avoid this pitfall and increase the value of information, researchers are often encouraged to conduct several focus groups and to aim for a high degree of diversity within each group. One must realize, though, that even in a project that involves vastly diverse groups, a small number of participants means that the focus groups have limited generalizability.

Case studies of focus groups

This part presents three cases studies to depict how to apply focus groups to determine environmental attitudes and values. Each case study discusses the purpose of focus groups, project size, description of participants, data collecting and analysis process, and the actionable results from focus groups.

Case 1: Corridor planning in Iowa

This focus group (Iowa State University Institute for Transportation, 2004) was part of a larger research project on transportation-related environmental projects in Iowa. The large project aimed to generate problem statements covering major environmental research and technology transfer issues, including air quality, energy, alternative fuel, corridor planning, and water quality. The specific purpose of the focus group was to identify initiatives to enhance statewide corridor planning.

The focus group consisted of eight participants, including researchers from Iowa State University, officials from the Iowa Department of Transportation and the Department of Natural Resources, materials inspection engineers, and roadside development specialists. The moderator first held brainstorming sessions and encouraged participants to list and rank ideas thought to be crucial to improve corridor planning. After identifying the ideas, the moderator probed participants to further specify and formulate important initiatives, including the specific procedures, resources, timelines, and benefits of each initiative.

The focus groups' results were analyzed and synthesized into four written initiatives for corridor planning: create a comprehensive database accessible to all levels of governments; develop a business case of environmentally friendly transportation; interchangeably utilize highway and expressway facilities; and conduct cost-benefit analysis of wetland mitigation (i.e. the protection, restoration, or creation of a wetland to compensate or make up for the destruction and/or disturbance of a wetland habitat). The initiatives further served as research problem statements in the larger project.

Case 2: Environmental issues and human behavior in low-income areas in the UK

A UK government agency conducted a project to explore the linkage of local environmental problems and global environmental issues with human behaviors in low-income areas (Power and Elster, 2005). The agency used focus groups, survey questionnaires, interviews with local managers, and a conference with policy makers to collect data.

The project consisted of 6 focus groups with approximately 12 participants in each group. Seventy-five residents in 6 low-income areas were recruited through local posters, social workers, and organizations. The participants ranged from 16 to 61 years of age, with 50 participants between 21 and 60 years of age. Among all participants, 60 percent were male, 56 percent were white, and 73 percent were involved with a community group.

The moderators began each focus group by asking the participants to name one thing that they liked about their local areas and three local environmental problems that most concerned them. Then the moderators asked the participants to rank the importance of a series of predefined wider environmental problems, such as global warming, rainforest destruction, and resource depletion. For both local and wider environmental problems, the moderators asked participants to explain why they thought these problems were important, what was the impact of the problems on their daily lives, who or what they thought was responsible for the problems, and whether they could think of any ways to help address the problems. After the focus groups, the participants were invited to complete a questionnaire covering questions about environmental concerns and actions.

The focus groups revealed that most participants were strongly aware of local environmental problems, such as litter and lack of green space, due to their direct impact on residents' day-to-day life. Participants were also familiar with wider environmental problems, such as global warming, species loss, and resource depletion. Participants blamed business and government for causing environmental problems. Participants felt a strong sense of personal responsibility for addressing environmental problems and were aware of the benefits of improving the environment.

Combining results from focus groups and other methods, this project proved that many residents in poor areas in the UK had a similar view of sustainable development to the rest of the country. They agreed that actions on environmental problems were timely and pertinent and that they were willing to act.

Case 3: Fuel economy label by environmental protection agency

The focus groups were used to redesign the fuel economy window sticker to reflect changes made by the Energy Independence and Security Act of 2007 and to help consumers purchase environmentally friendly vehicles (Environmental Protection Agency, 2010). The redesigned fuel label will be used in vehicles beginning with 2012 models.

The project was conducted by the US Environmental Protection Agency and the National Highway Traffic Safety Administration. The project used several methods (focus groups, online survey, and expert panel) to solicit public opinion on the label redesign. The pre-focus online survey and 32 focus groups were conducted in different locations at different times. Most focus groups consisted of 8 participants who had bought a new vehicle in the past 12 months and were the sole or primary purchase decision maker.

The first step was an online pre-focus survey to get the initial insights of potential participants. The survey collected information about the process of purchasing a vehicle, the role of fuel economy in this process, and how the fuel economy label affected the purchase decision. A total of 404 people finished the pre-focus online survey. After the online survey, 32 focus groups were conducted in Seattle, Chicago, Houston, and Charlotte in three phases between February and May in 2010. The first phase included 8 focus groups and collected information about existing fuel labels. The second phase involved another 8 focus groups to explore which fuel economy statistics consumers preferred to see on a window sticker and how well they understand those statistics. The third phase consisted of another 16 focus groups to evaluate label design in terms of content and look.

During the data collection process, the researchers identified some critical themes: keep the label simple; make it easier to compare vehicles; and accommodate the role of the label to the changing purchase process. The focus groups obtained meaningful information about people's comprehension of and reaction to fuel economy labels. An expert panel was conducted after the focus group to comment on and improve the draft fuel label created by focus groups. An online survey was then sent to new vehicle purchasers and intended buyers to test the understandability of the new fuel economy label and gauge how the label provided more information about efficient vehicles and shaped the purchase decision. The combined information of multiple methods yielded three versions of labels for public comment. The above case studies focused on diverse environmental issues and were conducted by various types of organizations in different countries. These case studies demonstrated how to apply focus groups with other data collecting methods to accumulate meaningful information and provide applicable results.

A new trend: virtual focus groups

With the rapid development and evolution of technology, conducting qualitative research through the internet is becoming increasingly popular and promising. One new trend is to conduct virtual focus groups, in which the group discussion is administered online.

In virtual focus groups, researchers use electronic or traditional means to promulgate information to targeted participants. Interested potential participants sign up for the online research project and complete profile forms. They are notified later about the scheduling of the focus groups. Virtual focus groups can be conducted in two ways: real-time focus groups process multiple information inputs simultaneously (through chat rooms, video teleconferencing, etc.); asynchronous focus groups collect and share information inputs across a span of time (through email, bulletin boards, etc.). In real-time focus groups, questions are written in advance to be completed by participants, typically in 90 minutes. In asynchronous focus groups, questions are brought up at the beginning of each day, and participants are given three to five days to offer their opinions.

Virtual focus groups have a high degree of anonymity, which can encourage participants to be more open and honest. Another advantage of virtual focus groups is that they expand access to hard-to-reach participants. Early virtual focus groups were used to collect data from participants who were geographically dispersed and physically immobile, including some types of patients, pregnant women, and people living in remote areas. Nowadays, virtual focus groups are often used to collect information from professionals such as doctors, lawyers, and executives. Finally, virtual focus groups reduce some of the costs associated with traditional face-to-face focus groups, such as the costs of facilities rental, travel, refreshments, recording equipment, and audio transcription.

The high degree of anonymity that accompanies the virtual focus group experience can also make participants more likely to disagree with or criticize other participants, with a consequent loss of insightful information gained from proper interaction among participants. The visual anonymity and psychological distance of the internet may undermine the impact of group interaction. Another major problem of virtual focus groups is that they have limited moderating. Moderators are required to have strong keyboard skills and familiarity with relevant software and technology. Even so, moderators of virtual focus groups lose visual cues from participants and find it more difficult to control the topics and pace of discussion. There is also the difficulty of maintaining security and confidentiality. It is difficult to prevent unauthorized people from gaining access to an online discussion through underhanded means. Last but not least, virtual focus groups are available to internet users only.

The virtual focus group will not necessarily replace the traditional in-person focus group. In some cases, virtual focus groups will be used in conjunction with face-to-face focus groups to better address research questions effectively and efficiently.

Ethical issues in focus groups

The focus group is an intensive human interaction process that involves several ethical issues. With all research methods encompassing human subjects, the fundamental rule of conducting research is to do no harm. Protecting participants is the first rule. Participants should be not be inconvenienced, and when recruited they should be informed of the goal of research and how the results will be used. At the beginning of a focus group session, the moderator should emphasize that participation is voluntary and that participants have the right to leave at any time if they feel uncomfortable.

Another major ethical issue of focus groups is the need to protect participants' privacy. Focus groups require participants to share their perception, understanding, and beliefs about specific topics. People often need to sacrifice their privacy to justify their standpoints. Researchers should devise procedures to keep participants' information confidential. For example, participants can be identified by number instead of by name, access to discussion transcripts and recordings can be limited, and some records can be destroyed after the research results are obtained. The researchers should also notify participants that there is always a risk that information will be inadvertently compromised, and that the participants should decide for themselves how much private information they wish to disclose. The researchers also need to require all participants not to share discussion information and to respect other participants' privacy. For sensitive topics, such as sexual behavior, drug use, and crime, the researchers can use small focus groups to reduce the risk that private information will be revealed.

A further ethical issue of focus groups is the risk of imposing stress on participants. In some cases, as when cancer patients or victims of domestic violence discuss their experiences, the participants may feel stress as they recount painful experiences. The discussion of controversial topics, such as the right to an abortion or the regulation of same-sex marriage, may cause fierce discussion among participants. In these situations, the researcher can ask an experienced expert to be present or on call to control the discussion. The researcher should also allow enough debrief time for participants who found the focus group stressful.

Focus groups usually include sponsors, researchers, and participants. All parties should be respected and protected. One common ethical tool to protect sponsors and researchers is a standard confidentiality agreement. It is an effective way to defend intellectual property and preclude disputes. Some sponsors may request that their identity be withheld from participants. Under these circumstances, the researcher should discuss the matter thoroughly with the sponsors to determine the proper scope of information accessible to the participants.

Sometimes the ethical issues are more troubling. For example, the researchers may learn of a legally reportable case of child abuse, or a participant who is carrying a contagious disease. In these instances, the researchers should report the incident to their supervisor and refer to the appropriate authorities and regulation to determine their obligation.

Conclusion

The focus group has developed into a powerful qualitative research method over the past 80 years. Since the 1980s, focus groups have been widely applied in social science and gained increasing coherence and scope. Focus groups can be used as a self-contained method or an adjunct method in a complex study. Different research tools have their unique strengths and drawbacks and are usually not interchangeable. Scholars and practitioners in the social sciences should grasp the principles of focus groups and apply diverse analytic approaches to better address research questions.

Acknowledgment

I'd like to thank David Garson PhD for his assistance. I'd like to thank Mr Jack Appleton for offering me this valuable opportunity and consistent support during the writing process.

References

Bogardus, E. 1926. The Group Interview. *Journal of Applied Sociology* 10(4), pp. 372–82.

Cantril, H. 1944. *Gauging Public Opinion*. Princeton, NJ: Princeton University Press.

Environmental Protection Agency. 2010. *Fuel Economy Label: Final Report National Service Center for Environmental Publications (NSCEP)*. Retrieved on July 15th, 2012, from http://www.epa.gov/nscep.

Flick, U. 2007. *Doing Focus Groups*. London: Sage.

Frey, J. H., and A. Fontana 1991. The Group Interview in Social Research. *Social Science Journal* 28, pp. 175–87.

Iowa State University Institute for Transportation. 2004. *Focus Group on Environmental Research and Technology Transfer Needs Related to Transportation*. Iowa: Iowa State University.

Lazarsfeld, P. F., and Merton, R. K. 1948. Mass Communication, Popular Taste, and Organized Social Action. In *The Communication of Ideas*. L. Bryson. Ed. New York: Harper and Row, pp. 95–118.

Merton, R. K., and P. L. Kendall. 1946. The Focused Interview. *American Journal of Sociology* 51, pp. 541–57.

Morgan, D. 1998. *The Focus Group Guidebook*. London: Sage.

Power, A., and J. Elster. 2005. *Environmental Issues and Human Behavior in Low-Income Areas in the UK.CASE report 31*. London: Centre for Analysis of Social Exclusion, London School of Economics and Political Science.

7 Determining environmental values
Storytelling at BP

David M. Boje and Jacob A. Massoud

This chapter offers a theoretical overview of storytelling research and consulting, and highlights several techniques for identifying values through storytelling. These tools may be applied by practitioners to promote change in a variety of organizational settings. Stories from British Petroleum (BP) will serve as our primary examples. The material represents an introduction to how to use storytelling to glean participants' values in the context of sustainable development and conservation. A complete blueprint is beyond the scope of the chapter. Storytelling offers an opportunity for researchers and practitioners of sustainable development.

Sustainable development involves broad societal issues ranging from environmental pollution to economic development; it represents a relevant challenge for social and natural scientists. The Brundtland Commission report, *Our Common Future* (UNWCED, 1987), defined sustainable development as development that meets the needs of the present without compromising the needs of the future. The report evaluated the four aspects of development and environmental protection: peace and security, economic development, social development, and proper governance (Friedman, 2006).

Sustainable development is defined by a complex set of criteria. As such, the values of participants in sustainable development projects remain an important yet often overlooked component of social science inquiry. There is a need for creative and cooperative approaches that include perspectives from multiple voices to enhance progress and motivate change. One means of fostering organizational change toward sustainability is through storytelling. This chapter situates storytelling within appropriate paradigms and illustrates the importance of story as living and reflexive. In addition, it will provide a bridge between simplistic uses of story and uses that are more important for environmental studies.

Common mythology treats stories and narratives as interchangeable

Practical guides to story and narrative fail to tell the narrative even when they tell the story. Narrative and story are not synonymous. Their differences present consequences for organizational behavior. David Boje argues that the behavioral study of people who actually tell narratives and stories, and their impact, is ignored

(Boje, 2006a, 2006b). Some advice books posit that leaders can transform an entire organization with a three-minute narrative with a coherent beginning, middle, and end. Tom Peters, in *Thriving on Chaos* (XXXX, pp. 482, 492–93), calls it a three-minute "stump speech." He encourages executives to tell the story several times a day. Stephen Denning (2000) repackaged the idea as the Springboard Story. In this approach, executives, managers, and sometimes all employees are put into story workshops to learn to tell their two-minute narratives, with the expectation that the organization will change its behavior. The empirical evidence shows that no such transformations result from such behavior. Such works focus on adapting story from mythology, fiction, or Native lore to inspire an organization to change its thinking and behavior (Parkin, 2004). Much like the stump speech and Springboard examples, the existent *in situ* narratives and stories go unexamined. People are assembled into workshops and read stories of Richard III, Coyote tales, Aesop fables, and so forth. Again, there is no empirical evidence that there is a carryover of changes in organizational behavior.

Another approach in story advice books is to elicit tacit knowledge from workers by having them tell stories in interviews and focus groups (Denning, 2005; Oliver and Snowden, 2005). During the process, the participant is storyteller and is encouraged to reveal some hidden knowledge through a story he tells. The assumption is that the tacit knowledge will accelerate knowledge sharing in learning organizations (or knowledge organizations). It is assumed that stories illustrate causal relationships that people do not recognize (Heath and Heath, 2007, p. 206). Further, it is assumed that the kinds of stories being elicited in the workshop are all similar to *in situ* stories back in the workplace. Again, the assumptions are without empirical proof of behavior. What is clear in the advice trade is that empirical study of actual story and narrative behavior is lacking.

Theories that treat narrative and story as different

Narrative is distinguishable from story. This is not a distinction without a difference; it is a necessary contrast with significant consequences for both researchers and practitioners. Mikhail Bakhtin explains that story is decidedly more dialogical than narrative (Bakhtin, 1993, p. 60). Polyphonic dialogism occurs when voices are engaged to debate one another, and multiple logics interact (Boje, 2008). Yiannis Gabriel (2000) argues that there is something more to story than a narrative. Jacques Derrida also distinguishes story from narrative:

> Each "story" (and each occurrence of the word "story," (of itself), each story in the story) is part of the other, makes the other part (of itself), is at once larger and smaller than itself, includes itself without including (or comprehending) itself, identifies itself with itself even as it remains utterly different from its homonym.
>
> (1979, pp. 99–100)

Derrida is more radical than Bakhtin, viewing narrative as an instrument of torture:

> The question-of-narrative covers with a certain modesty a demand for narrative, a violent putting-to-the-question, an instrument of torture working to wring the narrative out of one as if it were a terrible secret in ways that can go from the most archaic police methods to refinements for making (and even letting) one talk that are unsurpassed in neutrality and politeness, that are most respectfully medical, psychiatric, and even psychoanalytic.
>
> (1979, p. 94)

Italo Calvino imagines stories in relation to a space full of stories:

> I'm producing too many stories at once because what I want is for you to feel, around the story, a saturation of other stories that I could tell ... A space full of stories that perhaps is simply my lifetime where you can move in all directions, as in space, always finding stories that cannot be told until other stories are told first.
>
> (1979, p. 109)

For Calvino, story necessarily opposes itself in a web of stories. Taken together, each of these scholars implies that narrative is confining and controlling, whereas story can be emergent and stem from multiple perspectives.

What is important in making a distinction between narrative and story? We can look at the centering aspects of narrative in relation to more emergent and polyphonic aspects of story. This gives us a way to look at narrative and story as self-organization force and counterforce. Over time an emergent story can mummify into a narrative. And narrative can break up into fragments.

Empirical work on narrative and story

A 1991 study of storytelling in an office supply firm was based on eight months of recording *in situ* talk, conducting individual and focus group interviews, and doing participant observation (Boje, 1991). It was found that in general entire stories that include beginning, middle, and ending were rather uncommon. Instead, fragments were dispersed across many conversations, with many people co-creating them, content shifted with context, and there was terse-telling. In terse-telling, people assume that knowledgeable participants can fill in the blanks, and flesh out interpretations based upon what has not been uttered. This phenomenon of co-created story sensemaking is what Boje called the work of the "storytelling organization" (Boje, 1991). Leaders were shown to manipulate stories in conversation, using terse-telling and gloss, and inviting other tellers into the act to move along their agenda.

In 1995, a poststructuralist study of Disney as a *storytelling organization* indicated a struggle between official narratives and counterstories (Boje, 1995). The research revealed that Disney's official narratives deviated significantly from workers' and middle management's counterstories. After Walt Disney's death there was an imbalance, and narratives about Walt overpowered the stories that could have brought novelty and innovation into the Mouse Museum. The study analyzed how stories of leaders, long dead, are kept alive in annual reports. The practical implication is that in conversation, and written reports, there are particular story practices. People in their story work barely tell with the preferred narrative forms of beginning, middle, and end. Even the texts of annual reports show how stories are remade over time by shifting structure and emphasis. The story shifts from one year to the next (Boje and Rhodes, 2005, 2006; Boje and Rosile, 2008).

Viewing sustainability stories through a critical lens

As we have demonstrated thus far, narrative and story are interesting and powerful communication devices; storytelling research truly can provide practicality for practitioners. In storytelling research we look at relational aspects of narrative to story. How is a story changing over time? When does it stabilize into narrative?

The rebranding of BP cost approximately US$200 million (Werther and Chandler, 2005). Green initiatives changed BP's narrative identity over time to reflect environmental awareness. For example, in 2000 the name "British Petroleum" was replaced in many materials with the environmentally conscientious "Beyond Petroleum," the uppercase letters "BP" were changed to lowercase "bp," and the corporate logo became an organic sunburst symbol of yellow, white, and green known as the Greek Helios mark. Additionally, the company's gas stations were painted in the same colors to symbolize environmental responsibility and the sun (Beder, 2002). BP also adopted a new position on climate change, which is reflected by a series of print advertisements about global warming. A marketing firm, Ogilvy & Mather Worldwide, undertook this grand effort to reinvent BP and alter public opinion regarding BP's role in society.

This rebranding provides one with the opportunity to compare the official narrative to other sides of the story. It is not just *the* narrative but the interplay with multiple perspectives that becomes important to trace. Storytelling research allows us to analyze corporate narratives to see how they match up to enacted story actions. This is much in line with the work of Chris Argyris (1976) on espoused theory versus theory-in-use: "People hold two kinds of theories of action. First is the theory that they are aware of and report ... espoused theory. Second is the theory they hold and use and are not aware of which can be determined by observing their behavior; this we call their theory-in-use" (Argyris, 1976, p. 30). Thus, actual action and behavior do not always reflect what people espouse in their stories. This situation often creates a gap, which should be identified in order to align actions with attitudes and values. We will refer back to this gap and use several illustrations from BP that suggest that the company's green corporate stories are nothing more than greenwashing. Therefore, story context from BP will serve as our primary case study for story comparison.

Many mainstream storytelling consultants emphasize positive stories (Cooperrider *et al.*, 2000). Although their perspective holds value, it often falls short of effecting legitimate change in organizations. Critical perspectives are often necessary to achieve meaningful organizational change. Additionally, story consulting usually prescribes steps to change, but fails to analyze storytelling or the organization. Authors such as Denning (2000, 2005, 2007) and John Kotter (1996) recommend short narratives with a beginning, middle, and end. However, stories are not always short, and they certainly are not always so nicely structured. For example, the BP Prudhoe Bay disaster (discussed below) is not a two-minute story like a CEO's speech. It is complex, it is technical, and it contains a maze of twists and turns. Story analysis is required, because all the stakeholders in a situation will have their own stories.

Storytelling at BP

To make sense of the BP Prudhoe Bay disaster using story, we evaluated story fragments. The fragmented nature of the story, or stories, indicates a complex system of antenarratives. "Antenarrative is the fragmented, non-linear, incoherent, collective, unplotted and pre-narrative speculation, a bet" (Boje, 2001, p. 1). An antenarrative network displays complexity through antenarrative themes. Each possesses numerous interpretations; however, there is a commonality in the manner in which they form clusters and answer each other (see Figure 7.1).

Storytelling interaction among various authors denotes a network of story fragments that contains divergent realities. By intertextually evaluating an antenarrative one can demonstrate both sensemaking and attempts to control the narrative. The critical evaluation of antenarratives draws attention to poor organizational practices steeped in values. Through a process of identifying the negative stories and spin, organizations can move forward toward substantive organizational change and sustainability.

In theory, story shapes memory and counter-memory (Foucault, 1977). Corporate greenwashers employ a stylistic strategy story to regain and sustain a pristine image. Boje defines stylistic strategy story as an "orchestration of image, or more of a dialogism, among oral, print and video media, websites, gesture-theatrics, décor and architecture" (2008). Bakhtin (1981) describes five stylistic modes: artistic, *skaz* (everyday speech), everyday writing, scientific writing, and official narrative. These can be adapted to the stylistics strategy storying of corporate image (Boje *et al.*, 2006; Boje and Rhodes, 2006).

To be more precise, counter-memory is shaped by stylistic strategy story. Greenwashing is the creation of a counter-memory that subverts the writing of corporate history, corrupting its integrity. BP uses artistic image stylistics to tell a story counter to reality. This can be shown by the application of intertextuality analysis and image analysis to BP story data.

Intertextuality analysis: the BP example

Each text is theorized as a network of story fragments that refers to other texts. Thus, each text is an example of an antenarrative, with every story informed by other stories to which the storyteller and storylistener have been exposed, therefore *intertextuality* refers to antenarrative (Boje, 2001). The BP Prudhoe Bay

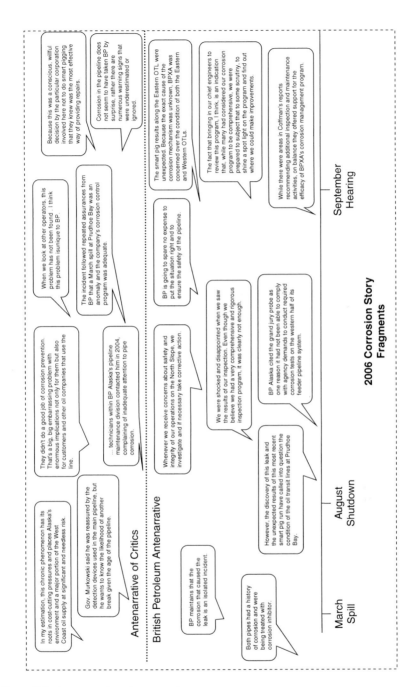

Figure 7.1 Antenarrative clusters and answers

disaster can be used to demonstrate the application of intertextuality analysis in sustainability research. BP depicts itself as environmentally responsible through its corporate website, numerous green advertisements, press releases, and several published documents (see www.bp.com). In the *BP Code of Conduct* (BP, 2005) the company summarizes its strong commitment to health, safety, security, and the environment (HSSE) It is clear from the *Code of Conduct* (BP, 2005)that BP is committed to an ethic of environmental protection, safety, and health, with a zero tolerance for accidents. Is it really? In this example, we demonstrate the use of storytelling to critically analyze BP's "true" commitment to sustainability.

BP often downplays, restories, and spins its side of the story to attain public legitimization. These efforts constitute BP's "official story", which surfaces in its publications and public communications. However, critics contend that the stories underlying BP's operations are symptomatic of greenwashing. However, these stories are fragmented and living. The events leading up to the Prudhoe Bay disaster of 2006 are recounted in many versions by numerous storytellers, with only bits and pieces of the whole. Antenarratives are a mechanism for various actors to influence and make sense of environmental accidents by constructing their own interpretive reality of the events. This system of antenarratives appears as intertextualities found in various media communications.

The storytelling that ensued regarding the largest oil spill in Alaska's North Slope constituted a scandal surrounding BP's method of pipeline inspection, and its delaying tactics. Each counterstory fragment illustrates part of a larger story of BP's consistent failure to protect the environment. Taken together, the fragments provide a relevant framework of narrative and counterstories, as antenarrative, surrounding the larger spill, smaller spills, and the subsequent reduction of North Slope crude oil production.

In the BP Prudhoe Bay study (Massoud and Boje, 2007), a variety of texts were intertextually analyzed, ascribing voice and affiliation to each antenarrative. Each story fragment was then re-evaluated within a network of stories and counterstories, as narratives by BP and its critics. This method provided a means to compare the trajectories of the many voices engaging in the antenarrative network of the Prudhoe Bay oil spills. The findings support Robert Gephart's work (1984), in which divergent realities emerged between the organizations that caused environmental damage and their critics. Antenarrative themes are clearly perceptible across various texts. Several of these themes directly raise the question of accountability at BP, and demonstrate BP's values in action, which differ from their espoused values.

Story fragments

Corrosion story fragments were a common theme with the Prudhoe Bay disaster. Questions concerning BP's corrosion prevention and inspection program became paramount throughout the disaster. The selected intertextualities analyzed illustrate both divergent realities concerning the corrosion problem and the antenarrative network. In the first story fragment, BP officials clearly espoused a belief that the corporation was unaware of any corrosion problems. Others point out, through counterstory, that BP's practices were well below the industry standards: "BP may have believed that using coupons and ultrasonic testing were sufficient to protect the infrastructure. But other industry leaders went well above and beyond regulatory requirements. They properly maintain their pipes. And they've avoided the problems that we've seen in recent months" (Congressional Record, 2006a). BP officials also denied their responsibilities. In practice, the company ignored signs that there were problems with their pipeline. For example, an engineering report predicted corrosion problems for BP's pipeline as early as 2001 (Congressional Record, 2006b). BP downplayed its prior knowledge of the corrosion problem, and it can be inferred that BP modified the report to de-emphasize the problem.

BP officials only "acted" surprised. The spill and shutdown clearly should have been prevented. Corporate elites opted to be reactive instead of attending to their environmental and economic responsibilities as true industry leaders would. Thus, BP denies accountability to the phenomenon in question through both the words of its officials and its failure to act in accordance with the *BP Code of Conduct* (2005) and other official statements. Such discourse reflects the "true" corporate values. Additionally, the company does so using the corporate "we" (Livesey, 2001). BP's use of the "we" dialectic materializes frequently, yet it falls short of moving to a discourse of accountability and sustainability, but statements like "We Have a Strong Commitment to Integrity" (Narrative Spin) are frequent. BP creates a dual reality marked by corporate image management. One has to look no further than the countless times that safety, responsibility, integrity, sustainability, and environment receive mention in official BP documents, advertisements, and press releases. The intertextual analysis manifested several poignant examples (Massoud and Boje, 2007). One such example implicates BP in a failure to be held answerable to its acknowledged commitment to the environment and safety. Consequently, the commitment is revealed as mere greenwashing. Lord Browne's letter in *Making Energy More: Sustainability Report* illustrates the divergent realities regarding BP's integrity and responsibility. In his letter, Browne states, "The actions we take are designed to enable our business to prosper and all our activities contribute to the delivery of our purpose as a business. Our focus is on safety and operational integrity, security of supply and the protection of people and the natural environment" (BP, 2006, p. 1). On the one hand, BP depicts itself as a socially responsible company; on the other hand, its actions reveal a different reality. Given the emergent story surrounding the Prudhoe Bay crisis, it becomes relatively easy to make the case that BP only espouses values of social responsibility. "The BP shutdown has brought to light what happens when a company turns its back on its responsibilities … The mess of a company's negligence must not be borne by the consumer, the environment or the community. Rather companies must stand up and take responsibility. And BP must be held accountable for its actions or inactions" (Congressional Record, 2006c).

In practice, these antenarrative fragments pin BP in storytelling fabrication and deceit. BP fails to answer its espoused integrity and responsibility.

Conclusion

We used story to identify environmental values. This chapter introduced storytelling as a means to foster change in organizations. It shows how organizations can support sustainable development by identifying their theories in action. In the examples drawn from BP, the company professed a commitment to safety, integrity, and environmental protection. However, the company's actions have not reflected its espoused values. Through a critical perspective and process the BP narrative was assessed from the perspectives of various stakeholder story fragments. Analyses, based on storytelling research, allowed this gap to be delineated. If taken into account by corporations such as BP, storytelling can lead to substantial changes toward sustainability in practice.

In conclusion, storytelling research is a legitimate tool for sustainable development research. Storytelling situated within an appropriate context highlights the differences between story and narrative. Combined with critical perspectives and antenarratives, instead of just simplistic positive stories that overlook environmental abuses such as those at BP, intertextuality analysis and image analysis become two of the many options available to practitioners and researchers for evaluating participants' values.

References

Argyris, C. 1976. Leadership, Learning, and Changing the Status Quo. *Organizational Dynamics* 4(3), pp. 29–43.

Bakhtin, M. M. 1981. *The Dialogic Imagination: Four Essays.* Ed. M. Holquist, trans. C. Emerson and M. Holquist. Austin, Tex.: University of Texas Press.

Bakhtin, M. M. 1993. *Toward a Philosophy of the Act.* Eds. M. Holquist and V. Liapunov. Austin, Tex.: University of Texas Press.

Beder, S. 2002. "bp: Beyond Petroleum?" in *Battling Big Business: Countering Greenwash, Infiltration and Other Forms of Corporate Bullying.* Ed. E. Lubber. Devon, UK: Green Books.

Boje, D. M. 1991. The Storytelling Organization: A Study of Storytelling Performance in an Office Supply Firm. *Administrative Science Quarterly* 36, pp. 106–26.

Boje, D. M. 1995. Stories of the Storytelling Organization: A Postmodern Analysis of Disney as "Tamara-land." *Academy of Management Journal* 38(4), pp. 997–1035.

Boje, D. M. 2001. *Narrative Methods for Organizational and Communication Research.* London: Sage.

Boje, D. M. 2006a. Pitfalls in Storytelling Advice and Praxis. *Academy of Management Review* 31(1), pp. 218–24.

Boje, D. M. 2006b. The Dark Side of Knowledge Reengineering Meets Narrative/Story. *Organization: The Critical Journal of Organization, Theory and Society* 13(5), pp. 739–45.

Boje, D. M. 2008. *The Storytelling Organization.* London: Sage.

Boje, D. M., E. Enríquez, M. T. González, and E. Macías. 2006. Architectonics of McDonald's Cohabitation with Wal-Mart: An Exploratory study of Ethnocentricity. *Critical Perspectives on International Business Journal* 1(4), pp. 241–62.

Boje, D. M., and C. Rhodes. 2005. The Virtual Leader Construct: The Mass Mediatization and Simulation of Transformational Leadership. *Leadership Journal* 4(1), pp. 407–28.

Boje, D. M., and C. Rhodes. 2006. The Leadership of Ronald McDonald: Double Narration and Stylistic Lines of Transformation. *Leadership Quarterly* 17(1), pp. 94–103.

Boje, D. M., and G. A. Rosile. 2008. Specters of Wal-Mart: A Critical Discourse Analysis of Stories of Sam Walton's Ghost. *Critical Discourse Studies Journal* 5(2), pp. 153–79.

BP. 2005. *BP Code of Conduct*. London: BP.

BP. 2006. *Making Energy More. Sustainability Report 2005*. London: BP.

Calvino, I. 1979. *If on a Winter's Night a Traveler*. New York: Harvest.

Congressional Record. 2006a. US Representative Deggette. September 7th.

Congressional Record. 2006b. US Representative Green. September 7th.

Congressional Record. 2006c. US Representative Tammy Baldwin. September 7th.

Cooperrider, D. L., P. F. Sorensen Jr, D. Whitney, and T. F. Yaeger. 2000. *Appreciative Inquiry: Rethinking Human Organization toward a Positive Theory of Change*. Champaign, Ill.: Stipes.

Denning, S. 2000. *The Springboard: How Storytelling Ignites Action in Knowledge-Era Organizations*. Boston, Mass.: Butterworth-Heinemann.

Denning, S. 2005. Stories that Tame the Grapevine. *Knowledge Management and Narratives: Organizational Effectiveness through Storytelling*. Eds. G. Schreyogg and J. Koch. Berlin: Erich Schmidt, pp. 73–100.

Denning, S. 2007. *The Secret Language of Leadership*. San Francisco: Jossey-Bass.

Derrida, J. 1979 Living On: Border Lines. In *Deconstruction and Criticism*. Eds. H. Bloom, P. de Man, J. Derrida, G.Hartman, J. H. Miller. New York: Seabury.

Foucault, M. (1977). *Language, Counter-Memory, Practice: Selected Essays and Interviews*. Ed. D. F. Bouchard. Ithaca, NY: Cornell University Press.

Friedman, F. B. 2006. *Practical Guide to Environmental Management*. Washington, DC: Environmental Law Institute.

Gabriel, Y. A. 2000. *Storytelling in Organizations: Facts, Fictions, and Fantasies*. London: Oxford University Press.

Gephart, R. P. 1984. Making Sense of Organizationally Based Environmental Disasters. *Journal of Management* 10(2), pp. 205–25.

Heath, C., and D. Heath. 2007. *Made to Stick: Why Some Ideas Survive and Others Die*. New York: Random House.

Kotter, J. B. 1996. *Leading Change*. Boston, Mass.: Harvard Business School Publishing.

Livesey, S. 2001. Eco-Identity as Discursive Struggle: Royal Dutch/Shell, Brent Spar and Nigeria. *Journal of Business Communication* 38(1), pp. 58–91.

Massoud, J. A., and D. M. Boje. 2007. Greenwashing through Stylistic Strategy Story: The Case of BP. *Standing Conference for Management and Organization Inquiry Proceedings*. March 29th–31st. Las Vegas, Nev.

Oliver, G. R., and D. J. Snowden. 2005. Patterns of Narrative in Organizational Knowledge Sharing: Refolding the Envelope of Art-Luddism and Techno-Fabulism. In *Knowledge Management and Narratives: Organizational Effectiveness through Storytelling*. Eds. G. Schreyogg and J. Koch. Berlin: Erich Schmidt, pp. 15–72.

Parkin, M. 2004. *Tales for Change: Using Storytelling to Develop People and Organizations*. London: Kogan.

Peters, T. 1987. *Thriving on Chaos*. New York: Knopf.

UNWCED: United Nations World Commission on Environment and Development. 1987. *Our Common Future (The Brundtland Report)*. Oxford: Oxford University Press.

Werther, W. B., and D. Chandler. 2005. *Strategic Corporate Social Responsibility: Stakeholders in a Global Environment*. Thousand Oaks, Calif.: Sage.

8 Charrettes in the sustainable development process

Jack Appleton

A charrette is a participant oriented, collaborative, community planning tool for projects that are for defined large geographic areas. The charrette process allows for the inclusion of the community, not just primary stakeholders, clients, and experts. It is an intense approach focused on developing a shared vision that can be implemented (National Charrette Institute, 2010, p. 34). The ideal charrette is a public activity that lasts approximately seven days, not including pre-charrette community outreach or community planning discussions, each of which can last one or two days. Including the preliminary charrette activities, preparation, meetings, research, discussions, and site visits, and post-charrette write up, the entire charrette process can take up to a year. Its success and value depend on systematic preparation.

The charrette is not a value-neutral facilitation process; it embodies a philosophy of project planning and design. Nor is it a panacea to be incorporated in all sustainable development projects and research. The process is a holistic, collaborative process characterized by a series of short feedback loops; it is inclusive and comprehensive (Lennertz and Lutzenhiser, 2006). A given project can be enhanced both in terms of the design and implementation by stating upfront sustainable principles as principles of the project.

The first step is an analysis of the project site area, which begins with interviews of key participants. A stakeholders' analysis is part of the pre-charrette phase, to ensure collaboration and inclusion. Stakeholders are individuals and entities that must be involved in the process to create meaningful collaboration (National Charrette Institute, 2010). Sustainable development practice and research often involve a significant number of people and entities. Providing a means of participation is likely to create an increase in cooperation among the interested parties. Generally, a site visit and meetings are part of the analysis by the core team and the key stakeholders (Lennertz *et al.*, 2010, pp. 25–26). Stakeholders should be grouped homogeneously to facilitate interaction and discussion by lowering risk, which should increase participation. The stakeholders' meetings are closed and confidential (Lennertz *et al.*, 2010, pp. 27). The engagement begins by developing an understanding of the project at hand: its geographic, political, economic, cultural, and social scope. If sustainability is one of the principles, environmental sciences have to be included as well. From the very beginning there is a collaborative effort: "a cross-disciplinary approach dictates that everyone who has a guiding influence on the project must be involved ... in an atmosphere of trust and respect" (Lennertz and Lutzenhiser, 2006, p. 26). Before the public charrette takes place a "cross-functional collaborative team process assures that no relevant piece of information is overlooked" (Lennertz and Lutzenhiser, 2006, pp. 30).

The core team begins its first meeting on site to develop a project assessment. The assessment results in a draft document called an OSM (Open Street Map – a general map of the geographic area which will be the focus of the Charrette) that sets forth objectives, strategies, and measures (Lennertz and Lutzenhiser, 2006, p. 34). The OSM "represents a shared agreement on a prioritized set of clear, specific, measurable, and achievable objectives among the primary stakeholders" (Lennertz and Lutzenhiser, 2006, p. 34). The final version of the OSM often requires negotiation and iteration among the principal individuals and the parties they represent. Early in the charrette planning process, the target community has to be engaged. This can be done with a public kickoff meeting that includes a clear explanation of the project, its purpose, its scope, and a solicitation for public involvement. Often a workshop is a component of the kickoff, to both elicit and model future public collaboration and involvement (Lennertz and Lutzenhiser, 2006, p. 49).

During the initial site visit, the primary stakeholders are interviewed. The interviews and focus groups must be planned, scheduled, confidential, and conducted with respect and professionalism (Lennertz and Lutzenhiser, 2006, p. 51). They should be "a series of friendly conversations into which the researcher slowly introduces new elements" (Spradley, 1979, p. 58) – beginning with concrete, objective questions, questions expressing the scope of the project and the interview, then moving toward more open-ended and expressive questions (Argyris, 1970, pp. 295–97). Each focus group should be conducted with a homogeneous grouping of participants in order to increase the level of participation, making the respondents less defensive and increasing their feelings of trust and safety (National Charrette Institute, 2010).

Early in the process the logistics of the multiday charrette have to be considered in detail – down to questions of scheduling, food, office space, and details of the tours. A charrette studio and a public meeting space have to be arranged. Wall space is a particularly precious commodity: it may have to be artificially set up (National Charrette Institute, 2010).

After preparation work of one to nine months, the public engagement phase of the charrette starts off with a public involvement and vision meeting. At this meeting the target area and the principles are presented. The participants then break up into groups to create goals, statements, and markups on the planning area, so that after the meeting the rendering team is able to produce a set of alternative renderings that encapsulate the various concepts expressed at the initial public meeting (National Charrette Institute, 2010).

There is an iterative process built into the charrette. Public collaboration is repeated twice, through an open house, a second public meeting, or both. Each time the feedback is incorporated into the final alternative plans. The stakeholders have private review meetings as well, to insure critical input from the key people and entities. In total there are four public meetings including a final meeting to present either the preferred plan or the alternatives that have been proposed as a result of the process. Charrettes are simultaneously web-based: the website must be kept current, and participants must understand that they have been recognized and included on it. Blogs relevant to the charrette should be engaged along with the local media (National Charrette Institute, 2010).

The on-site process begins with the setup of the studio, and the first public engagement begins with the site tours. Tours include core team members and stakeholders as necessary and are an indispensable part of the civic engagement process. The site visit is part of the planning for the public charrette, and thus the core team must complete it before conducting the public tours.

Day one of the public phase of the charrette begins with the first public meeting which is intended to gain legitimacy, explain the process, and encourage participation. The first public meeting's goal is vision development related to the site area. It can include breakout meetings and group discussions (instead of auditorium seating, people should be seated around large banquet tables). Groups should be small and self-organized to encourage participation. Groups should brainstorm big ideas, either after having the principles outlined to them or after being asked to generate the principles and goals themselves (National Charrette Institute, 2010). The principles can express values heretofore unspoken, or bring awareness to previously underlying values of which the participants were unaware. Guiding principles are followed by goals, objectives, and strategies which are directly tied to the achievement and measurement of the objectives – concrete, measurable results. These are followed by statements of tasks and activities.

Days two and three are when the core team takes all the presentation materials and works them into alternative proposals and plans. These alternatives become the focus of the iterative phase of the process – the second public meeting. Day two of the core charrette activity starts with the core team deciding on the alternative scenarios and the accompanying renderings, maps, charts, and other materials that will be created and presented at the second public meeting. Production teams are formed around alternative concepts (Lennertz *et al.*, 2010, pp. 29–34, 81–84). The core team and the materials production people spend the day developing the materials that will be utilized, presented, and needed for day three.

On day three, the designated team members meet with key stakeholders in a closed meeting where they preview the alternatives that will be presented and discussed at the public review meeting. The alternatives are adjusted as necessary to facilitate both the open public meeting and the continued support and involvement of the stakeholders. In the open public meeting, on the evening of the third day, the alternatives are presented and explained. An open house can be held as an alternative to a more structured public meeting. The idea is to have members of the public circulate, have discussions with people who present their views, and comment on the alternatives posted on the wall. The main purpose of the public meeting is iterative – to elicit interactive feedback. The subsidiary purpose of the meeting is ultimately to move the plan forward toward a synthesis, a plan that incorporates different points of views from the community into a single plan, or alternative plans (Lennertz *et al.*, 2010, pp. 33–34).

Days four through six of the charrette involve meetings with various individuals and groups that are more central to the project, and to the production of a single plan, or tightly presented alternatives from which a final plan will be selected afterward.

To support and facilitate these public and private activities, the on-site charrette studio should have both public and private space so that discussions and work are done simultaneously. As the plan is being synthesized, the studio has to accommodate both public and private space so that the core team can continue to work while stakeholders review the plan, and perhaps the public as well, through a gallery arrangement. The plan is presented for further feedback on the morning of day five, and another stakeholder meeting is held on the morning of day six. An optional open house can be held on the evening of day five. Days six and seven are taken up with closed stakeholder meetings, production meetings, and final preparation for the final public meeting (Lennertz *et al.*, 2010, pp. 36–37, 42–50). At the final public meeting, the basis of the report to be delivered to the client is then reviewed and revised, and the core team returns to the community roughly two and six weeks later for final review and revision meetings from which the final report is developed.

All aspects and specialties of the project are considered in a short feedback process. The initial public meeting has to be well planned and well run. Its success is material to the overall process. Start the meeting by introducing the core team; this should be done by someone in a position of authority. The charrette manager needs to introduce the scope of the project and its history, setting the principles and tone as well as the agenda for the public meeting and the charrette (Lennertz *et al.*, 2010, pp. 52–55, 74–78). The initial public meeting creates a context and framework for subsequent public involvement. It must address the work already done and the principles of the charrette. If these are not included, then the tenets of authenticity and genuine public participation are difficult to maintain. Immediately after being convened, the public meeting should address the principles of the project: principles differ from goals in that principles are immutable, often determined by law, developers' requirements, or funding. Principles are placed above goals and are absolutes that constrain the project.

A clear agenda must be part of the initial public meeting. Universal rules of conduct should be presented and posted, along with a schedule and a "buy-in" statement with some participation at the onset from the attending public participants. The facilitators, presenters, and so on are all introduced and their roles explained. The participants should be seated around tables so that participation is facilitated – not auditorium seating (Lennertz *et al.*, 2010, pp. 56–68). Public maps with tracing paper placed over them should be available at each table; the participants at each table can create statements of goals and themes that they place on the walls, using colored dots to indicate what they approve of or are concerned about. For example, a yellow dot might indicate an aspect of the plan that is a strong positive, while a blue dot might indicate that another aspect is problematic and needs to be changed. After being posted on the walls, weak and strong points are discussed by the spokesperson for each of the public groups formed at the tables. For a large project with multiple areas of consideration, tables can be arranged by topic or goal of the project. For example, one table might focus on transportation, another on the goal of walkable neighborhoods, and still another on open space.

Generally, there are two additional public meetings. Feedback from the first meeting is incorporated into revised plans by the core team. The revisions are then presented in private meetings with critical participants and experts. The second public meeting is essentially a repeat of the first public meeting, except that now the public is considering the revised materials. After the second meeting, the core team develops a preferred plan and presents it again to the critical stakeholders in private. The results of these meetings are then incorporated into the final plan, or into alternative final plans, which are then presented at the final public meeting.

Charrettes are incorporated into large planning projects for communities, cities, and regions. They begin with maps and drawings and generally end with maps and drawings. These maps and drawings (before or after) represent the graphically articulated hopes, aspirations, and dreams of a participatory community – not an entire community, but a community nonetheless. Obviously not every voice is heard, nor every suggestion incorporated. Maps, it should be noted, "not only serve to describe and prescribe but to facilitate reflection on what is described and experimentation with alternatives" (Argyris et al., 1985, p. 256). Their use as a tool to bring values into focus can be very effective and efficient, and while charrettes are not value-neutral, they can be useful across a variety of situations and cultures.

After Hurricane Katrina, students from Mississippi State University held a weeklong charrette sponsored by the Mississippi Renewal Forum (Walker and Seymour, 2008, p. 158). The idea was not new: charrettes had been used previously to teach and promote sustainability concepts in British Columbia and Seattle. The use of design charrettes to teach environmental and sustainability concepts had shown some promise in other venues: 32 percent of a group of schoolchildren from the fourth, fifth, and ninth to twelfth grades indicated in a survey that participation in a charrette had taught them ecological awareness (Walker and Seymour 2008, p. 159). Approximately 150 students and 20 faculty members and other professionals participated in the charrette sponsored by the Mississippi Renewal Forum. They divided into 24 teams, with each one responsible for developing a conceptual plan for a 6-square-mile (15.5-square-kilometer) area (Walker and Seymour, 2008, p. 151). The teams worked with each other and across disciplines, as each team had to consider the impact of its work on the adjacent team's assigned area. The participants utilized the principles of community, art, economy, and the environment, and were encouraged to think at both the micro scale and the macro scale. By integrating these themes holistically, the charrette process brought the tenets of sustainability into focus (Walker and Seymour, 2008, p. 162). While the specifics of sustainability or the pedagogical inclusion of sustainability was not directly assessed after the Mississippi Renewal Forum's charrette, a very high percentage of the participating students indicated that the charrette and interdisciplinary experience was very valuable in teaching them about sustainability (Walker and Seymour, 2008, p. 165). It is notable that the Mississippi Renewal Forum's charrette was large scale, involving 170 people for 5 days and covering an area of 144 square miles (373 square kilometers). It is also notable that it did not involve the participation of the general community within the area that the charrette targeted.

In Seattle in 2006, over 300 citizens participated in the "Green Future's Charrette" for two days, after much preparation. Professionals and students led 23 teams consisting of approximately 12 people each (Rottle and Maryman, 2006, p. 12). The result was "a spatial template for developing an integrated green infrastructure for all of Seattle" (Rottle and Maryman, 2006, p. 5).

> The centerpiece of the project was that it generated comprehensive vision plans including implementation strategies and priority recommendations for a city-wide open space network ... The open space plans were based upon a set of guiding principles; ... a regenerative green infrastructure ... to create a healthy, beautiful Seattle while maximizing our economic, social and ecological sustainability.
>
> (Rottle and Maryman, 2006, p. 10)

Each team worked on a specific geographic area, envisioning both a near time scale (20 years) and a far on time scale (100 years), in accordance with overall principles which where stated at the beginning of the public phase of the charrette. The preparation for the charrette, which took several months, was enhanced by the work of students from the University of Washington (Rottle and Maryman, 2006, p. 12). The result of the charrette was a planning document that is guiding the work of the Open Space Seattle 2100 Implementation Committee (Rottle and Maryman, 2006, p. 13).

In China, two charrettes of note were used to create design guidelines in the Pearl River delta region. Both charrettes were facilitated through international cooperation between academic and government entities. In 1999, one charrette in Zhongshan focused on environmentally sustainable urban design, property development, and architectural ideas. In June 2002, a charrette was conducted that expanded on that experience and focused on increasing concern for environmental sustainability when fostering urban conservation and redevelopment (Cody *et al.*, 2002, preface).

The planning for the 2002 charrette started in the fall of 2001. The charrette had approximately 100 local and international participants and focused on environmental sustainability, historic preservation, and transportation, among other topics. The participants were organized into six teams – each team blend-ing expertise, culture, nationality, experts, and students. After touring the study area (1 square mile/2.5 square kilometers), the teams worked intensely for 30 hours. On the third day, some of the teams focused on their planning, while others went back out in the field. By the evening of day four, the teams had produced a master plan and sketches (Cody., et al., 2002, pp. 2–3). Team 1, interestingly, expressed concern about "how to establish an effective process for community input … The team offered a solution that would knit the city together" (Cody., et al., 2002, p. 3). This remarkable example illustrates one of the reasons why charrettes are such powerful tools for sustainability. The team realized that without social sustainability, the human capacity to care for society and for the environment would break down. It is exactly these types of insights that the intense nature of the charrette process is designed to engender. The charrette was considered by the participants to be "an extraordinary experi-ence": it produced six concrete plans and a working relationship between the area's governing agencies, universities, and non-government agencies without which the charrette would not have been possible (Cody et al., 2002, p. 4). The participants did lament that there was not enough local citizen participation, which was an inhibiting factor. Without input from local residents the emergent plans relied heavily on the expertise of the participants – most of whom were not local to the area. One of the conclusions was that the "Charrette's sponsors and organizers agreed that future design events should include a series of work-shops with residents and merchants" (Cody et al., 2002, p. 4). This sentiment was reflected in some of the resulting recommendations: "for greater community consultation by engaging in a pro-active process of participation. … Bringing people from different professions, perspectives, cultures, etc. … A series of work-shops or 'mini-Charrettes' should be carried out in the residential and commer-cial areas" (Cody et al., p. 5).

The Zhongshan charrette focused on a demonstration site. Its purpose was to show that a charrette could be used to develop design guidelines for a munic-ipality in areas such as energy and resource conservation, building ecology, air quality, waste prevention and reclamation, landscaping using native species, and regional food security. The charrette was designed to consider issues of sus-tainability, urban planning, and development in an appropriate context relevant to the Zhongshan and Pearl River regions. The aim was to create a framework that could be generalized and exported to other municipalities. Participants were encouraged to develop solutions which allow for development and growth while protecting and enhancing the natural and cultural heritage. One of the tech-niques was to look at past sustainable traditions and how they could be fused with modern technology to develop a sustainable future compatible with the region's economic realities. The charrette adapted a definition of sustainability which emphasized the interaction of social and natural systems in a way that made explicit the relationships between the two and enhanced the long-term viability of both. This definition of sustainability fits very closely with resiliency concepts that are now emerging at the heart of sustainability thinking. It also aligns well with social sustainability frameworks, which encourage the application of sustainability principles to enhance the local community and economy.

In Zhongshan, economics was one of the principal concerns and areas of focus, because the economic success of a demonstration program would greatly improve its generalizability. Before the charrette, Zhongshan had already elevated itself in terms of concern for the environment by requiring open areas to make up at least 30 percent of every development. In addition to paying attention to the environment, Zhongshan has given consideration to its history, creating an urban pedestrian shopping street along which historic architecture has been restored. It has also enforced its environmental standards and in the process rejected some industries and closed others. The area considered for the demonstration charrette was relatively small, 0.15 square miles (0.4 square kilometers), but it was a diverse mix of environments and settlements and highly visible, being bounded by two waterways and transected by the region's major highway.

The charrette included 70 participants from the area, Beijing, Hong Kong, and the USA. It began with a site visit. After visiting the site the participants were divided into six groups of twelve members each. Pre-public event planning had taken three months. The public portion of the charrette lasted three days. The results have shaped the entire region, not just the target site. As the site of the first charrette of its kind, Zhongshan has become something of a reference for sustainable development throughout the region.

Case study: planning for sustainability in the Pearl River delta: the Zhongshan, China, demonstration charrette emphasizing sustainable development

Wallace P. H. Chang

Chinese University of Hong Kong's Department of Architecture and the New York Foundation for Architecture led a demonstration charrette which focused on environmentally sustainable urban design, property development, and preservation within an economically viable framework. The charrette took place on the 18th to the 20th of June 1999. The Hong Kong Institute of Architects and the Zhongshan Torch Hi-tech Industry Development Zone, among other organizations in southern China, sponsored the charrette in Zhongshan, China. The charrette teams each focused on a specific area such as energy and resource conservation, building ecology, air quality improvement, waste prevention and reclamation, native species landscaping, and regional food security. The exercise was designed to show that charrettes can be a valuable tool to foster sustainable development and an efficient means to create municipal-level development guidelines.

The Zhongshan charrette's challenge was to demonstrate the practical viability of sustainable planning and design through a charrette in light of the marketplace realities of Chinese development. In accordance with the Union Internationale des Architectes' (UIA's) China Sustainable Cities Project, its aim was to create an "applicable framework of sustainable planning concepts and processes that can be adapted to other cities in China and be a reference model for other developing regions" (Union Internationale des Architectes, 1999). Only when sustainability can be shown to offer real and lasting financial benefits to developers as well as city authorities will its principles be truly embraced and real change be effected. Through the Zhongshan demonstration charrette, and subsequent related actions and the dissemination of results, the aim was to show that sustainability makes sense not only in terms of the environment and social responsibility, but in the hard light of economics.

The location of the charrette was chosen because it is prominently situated near one of the fastest-growing regions of Zhongshan which is endowed with a wealth of cultural and natural features. It is a complex and challenging site, as well as a magnificent one which embodies the essence of the Pearl River delta's unique landscape. It was determined that the site holds great potential to become a model of environmentally responsible planning, design, and development for the region.

The Zhongshan charrette was purposely envisioned to be an interdisciplinary, collaborative design workshop intended to explore issues of sustainability and environmentally responsible architecture, urban planning, and development in the context of China's rapidly growing Pearl River delta region. Charrette participants were encouraged to scope out strategies, processes, and solutions that demonstrate how new development could proceed in a manner which protects and enhances China's rich natural and cultural heritage. In addition, the participants were encouraged to seek out the sustainable traditions of the past and integrate them with the technology of the present. The goal was the development of a socially, economically, and environmentally sustainable and resilient framework which could be naturally carried into the future and applied to other municipalities in the region.

Sustainability is a popular term in today's urban planning lexicon. For the Zhongshan demonstration charrette, the sustainability principle was stated as an ethic which seeks to minimize the impacts of human actions on the land, and to meet the needs of the present without compromising the ability of future generations to meet their own needs (United Nations Environment Programme, 1989). Sustainable planning, design, and development, then, refers to strategies of practice and intervention aimed at accommodating present human needs in a manner which considers the full spectrum of natural and cultural systems native to a site, and seeks a course of action minimally disruptive to those systems, ideally resulting in their enhancement and long-term viability. Sustainable development emphasizes relationships and processes rather than objects, and works with natural flows of matter, energy, and information rather than against them; conserves rather than wastes resources such as energy, water, and materials; encompasses the time dimension, showing sensitivity to historic character and to the unfolding of the future, including issues of management and maintenance; considers impacts at varying scales, from the local site to the larger region and beyond; and is socially and economically viable. It is a process of place making which invests spaces with meaning and identity, and enhances community. Sustainability reveals rather than disguises ecological processes and human relationships to them. It respects all users of a site, not just human beings (Brown *et al.*, 1995).

The linkage between economics and sustainability is critical at the local level as well. For sustainability to be embraced as a guiding principle in Chinese development, it must be shown to offer clear and compelling economic benefits. While Beijing may claim that sustainability is in the nation's best interest, unless developers themselves are impelled to choose it over degradation, little will be accomplished. This constraint poses a fundamental challenge to environmentally responsible planners and architects active in China, and was one of the central challenges of the Zhongshan charrette. Development must be proven economically viable. Only then will it have any real and lasting impact on China's expanding free-market system.

Deng Xiaoping and the architects of reform encouraged Gunagdong "to walk one step ahead" of the rest of China, and lead the nation on a path of change. Of the first four Special Economic Zones designated in 1980, three were in Guangdong. Leaders in Guangdong were given considerable freedom to distribute resources within the province, and the authority was able to manage affairs without answering directly to Beijing. Finally, the province was given new fiscal independence, and required to remit fewer taxes to the central government. These factors combined to place Guangdong at the forefront of Chinese development (Vogel, 1989, pp. 85–86). In Guangdong, the Pearl River delta would jump ahead as the foremost region in the province. The building boom of the post-Mao era transformed much of the Chinese landscape at a pace and scale unprecedented in history. The wholesale transformation occurred largely in the absence of comprehensive planning, and with little regard to short- or long-term environmental impact. China's physical environment has suffered immensely as a result. Though some cities have developed an environmental ethos – including Zhongshan, Dalian, and a handful of others – most have not; the net impact of the economic revolution on China's natural environment has been tragic.

Since the economic reform, Zhongshan has planned for parks, greenbelts, and open space, and has engaged in an extensive street tree planting campaign. The city has also constructed a number of major parks and open spaces. At the peak of the construction boom in the early 1990s, the city drafted standards for the real estate industry, requiring developers of each site to set aside an open space of not less than 30 percent of the total area. In 1994, the China Urban Planning Research Institute lauded Zhongshan for having achieved "Green City" status, and noted that it could easily achieve the even higher status of "Garden City" by 2010. Besides the "green" efforts, Zhongshan has also exerted much effort to promote cultural sustainability. For example, the Qijiang Riverside Park in the city center features a sculptural element based on the mythical journey of a Zhongshan native who travels overseas in search of work and eventually returns home to the place of his birth. It has also taken bold steps to preserve the fabric of the old urban center, creating a pedestrian shopping street where historic architecture has been restored. The city has made progress in combating water and air pollution. It has rejected more than 100 proposed projects that did not meet the city's environmental standards – several of which represented major investments. Existing plants are subjected to close monitoring, and once cited are required to cease polluting within a given time or be closed. More than 30 large factories have been closed in recent years as a result.

The charrette site

The site of the Zhongshan demonstration charrette occupies a long, narrow peninsula defined by the convergence of two tributaries of the Pearl River: the Xiaolan Channel to the north and the Shiqi River on the south which meet to form the Wenmen Channel). The lands to the north and west of the peninsula are rural and agricultural; across the water directly to the south is the Torch Hi-tech Industry Development Zone, while the urban center of Zhongshan is situated 1.9 miles (3 kilometers) to the southwest. The site is located partly within the administrative bounds of the Torch Development District.

The site is a low-lying area, approximately 4,519,200 square feet (420,000 square meters) in extent, with only minor topographic variation, the most prominent of which is a levee 7.3 feet (4 meters) in height. The site contains a rich array of natural environments and cultural resources, and holds great potential as a model development parcel. The site is also transected by the western Pearl River delta's principal north–south artery, the Guangzhou-Zhuhai Expressway. The road, built in 1995 and elevated on massive pylons, cuts across the site, providing vehicles above with a sweeping prospect of its extent.

The charrette goal

The goal of the charrette was to generate ideas for sustainable development in the Pearl River delta. Participants were encouraged to be imaginative in their proposals and not be bound by a rigid or prescriptive program. They were challenged to propose viable and realistic schemes for a sustainable community of 10,000 residents which would demonstrate principles of sustainability and serve as a model for development in the region. Toward this end, they were urged to consider the following nine questions in the design process:

1. Does the proposed design utilize renewable sources of energy, and use them efficiently?
2. Is it possible to develop on-site power generation, using biomass, wind, solar, or other forms of renewable energy?
3. Does the proposed design employ appropriate and locally available technologies?
4. Does the proposed design maximize engagement with the waterfront?
5. Does the proposed design consider the viability of urban agriculture and aquaculture, or retaining part of the site's agricultural uses as a source of sustenance?

6. Does the proposed design consider waste flows and address the issue of waste disposal and recycling?
7. Does the proposed design embrace and accommodate a diversity of socioeconomic groups?
8. Does the proposed design respond to the unique climatic conditions of the locality and the Pearl River region?
9. Is the proposed design economically sustainable – something that a developer concerned with the bottom line might actually choose to build?

After three months' preparation time, the Zhongshan charrette was formally launched between the 18th and 20th June 1999. Despite differences in language, background, and thinking patterns, more than 70 participants, including planners, architects, environmentalists, students, scholars, and government officials from Hong Kong, Zhongshan, Macau, Guangzhou, Beijing, and New York, were brought together to visit, discuss, and to design. By 18th June, through visits to the proposed site, the traditional water village, and other relevant projects, participants had gradually gained a further understanding about the workshop. Then they were divided into six groups of twelve members each and started discussing the issues and drafting proposals. By the end of the next day, 19th June, each group had to finalize its design proposal with drawings and working models. The results were reported accordingly in the afternoon of 20th June.

Although the charrette lasted for just three days, the collaborative efforts produced a multitude of concepts on sustainability which were available for future reference. Each of the six groups had a slightly different focus and mix of individual experience and backgrounds, and each group's recommendations were somewhat distinct:

Group 1: Create an ecological farm below the residential development and conserve the water landscape throughout the whole site, and include a water park as a prominent entrance feature to Zhongshan.

Group 2: Learn from the past while sustaining the present to nurture the future. Organize the site into three districts: high-density residential, a traditional water village, and an ecological garden.

Group 3: Develop a "living machine": public–private space, waste recycling infrastructure, community, water village, water and pedestrian transport, solar farm, and composting.

Group 4: Reinstate the historic fabric of the waterway. It used a fishing-boat metaphor: fish are kept alive in a water compartment, a tidal-responsive ecosystem that is self-purifying.

Group 5: Transform the energy cycle within the area to create a self-contained energy system though the application of modem technology.

Group 6: Create new and reuse existing village structures to provide denser mid-rise housing, an ecological teaching center; a monorail transport system and a water filtration system.

Zhongshan demonstration charrette's challenge and promise

The Pearl Delta has undergone enormous development. At the same time, the natural environment of the region has been degraded and threatened. The region is facing an unprecedented challenge. The Zhongshan demonstration charrette's challenge was to demonstrate the practical viability of sustainable planning and design in light of the marketplace realities of Chinese development. It showed promising results and proved that charrettes with environmental and sustainable principles could be of value to the region's planning process. To formulate proposals that are innovative yet professionally considered, environmentally advantageous, and cost-effective, a participatory workshop format can be organized to include those who have a direct impact on the environment and the region's development. Through charrettes, development proposals for the Wenmen Channel within the Torch Hi-tech Industry Development Zone can take into account the feasibility of sustainable concepts, and reflect a heightened awareness of building ecology, energy conservation, water and air quality improvement, waste reclamation, and ecological landscape design. The results of the charrette will be a future reference for sustainable developments in the region.

This Zhongshan charrette was the first environmental design charrette in China. It did not only inspire the idea of "sustainable development" per se, but it created a precious opportunity for similar minds to collaborate toward a common goal. Although the proposals made by the six groups would not be implemented, the understanding and viability of sustainable development in the Pearl River delta region was greatly enhanced. The Zhongshan demonstration charrette showed what can be done in an intense, short time by placing together experts and key individuals in a structured planning exercise. It has exemplified the future of planning in the region.

References

Argyris, C. 1970. *Intervention Theory and Method*. Reading, Mass.: Addison-Wesley.

Argyris, C., R. Putman, and D. M. Smith. 1985. *Action Science*. San Francisco: Jossey-Bass.

Cody, J. W., J. R. Richardson, and W. Chang. 2002. *Changdi Guangzhou, PRC: A Report on the Urban Environmental Design Charrette in the Pearl River Delta*. China: Department of Architecture, Chinese University of Hong Kong/Hong Kong America Center/School of Architecture of the South China University of Technology/People's Government of Yuexiu District, Guangzhou City (copy on file with author).

Lennertz, B. and A. Lutzenhiser. 2006. *The Charrette Handbook*. Washington, DC: American Planning Association.

Lennertz, B., D. Brain, and S. Coyle. 2010. *NCI Charrette System*. Portland, Oreg.: National Charrette Institute.

National Charrette Institute. 2010. NCI System Certificate Training Seminar, March 8th–10th.

Rottle, N., and B. Maryman. 2006. *Envisioning Seattle's Green Future*. Seattle, Wash.: Open Space Seattle 2100 Project, Department of Landscape Architecture, College of

Architecture and Urban Planning University of Washington. Retrieved on July 8th, 2011, from www.open2100.org (copy on file with author).

Spradley, J. P. 1979. *The Ethographic Interview*. Orlando, Fla:: Harcourt Brace Jovanovich.

Walker, J. B., and M. W. Seymour. 2008. Utilizing the Design Charrette for Teaching Sustainability. *International Journal of Sustainability in Higher Education* 9(2), pp. 157–69.

Case study references

Brown L., S. Kressel, and C. Royer. 1995. *Flowed Meadows Neighborhood: An Environmental Design Charrette*. Boston, Mass.: Boston Architectural Center.

Union Intemationale des Architectes. 1999. *The China Sustainable Cities Project*. Beijing: Working Group on Architecture and Energy.

United Nations Environment Programme. 1989. *15th Session of the Governing Council, Statement on Sustainable Development*. Nairobi: UNEP.

Vogel, E. 1989. *One Step Ahead in China: Guangdong under Reform*. Cambridge, Mass.: Harvard University Press.

9 Science and sustainability
A transition research perspective

Derk Loorbach and Bettina Wittneben

Introduction

Sustainable development has become a central guiding concept in scientific debates and policies characterized by complex and persistent problems (Scott and Gough, 2004). It aims to ensure economic welfare, social equality, and ecologic quality across society and generations. As society has changed into a network society, its fabric has frayed; modern problems have emerged that are so complex that top-down and expert approaches can no longer solve them. The embedded challenges defy solutions rendered from our current conceptions of knowledge, and the role of scientists in these processes is being challenged (Bolin *et al.*, 2000; Flyvbjerg, 2001; Gladwin *et al.*, 1995). A growing number of societal problems appear impossible to solve through existing institutions (Rotmans *et al.*, 2001). However, the network society, with its high degree of interconnectedness and availability of knowledge, simultaneously offers new ways of conceptualizing societal change, the role of knowledge, and influencing change. Society, comprised of individuals and organizations, is composed by complex, adaptive, self-organizing systems. The interplay between dynamic societal structures, individual actions, and technological innovations leads to changes in our societal systems, and periodically to profound transitions (Rotmans *et al.*, 2001).

Such a transition is needed to solve current complex problems and for sustainable development to occur. It is needed to address issues such as climate change, poverty, and equality, and at national and regional levels, and to inform policy related to sustainability. The ongoing processes of change need to be directed toward more sustainable systems; it is fundamentally uncertain what exactly is sustainable and thus how we should deal with the ongoing transitions. In this complex context, not only does the concept of sustainable development need to be adjusted, but the actors involved also need to re-evaluate their roles and practices (Loorbach, 2007).

Sustainable development is simultaneously a global and local challenge: global problems like resource depletion and climate change manifest themselves in different ways at the local or regional level. Various local problems and changes, in turn, add up to produce today's highly aggregated global challenges. The inherent complexities are context-specific and thus require sustainability problems to be approached with new problem-solving strategies: there are no grand solutions nor blueprint escapes. Rather than find solutions through disciplinary, expert-based approaches or technological solutions, the transition approach suggests we should identify the generic patterns of change involved in sustainability problems and figure out ways to work with such patterns and mechanisms to move more quickly toward sustainability. The transition perspective presented in this chapter offers a framework to identify, analyze and structure patterns of change in complex societal systems as a starting point for interventions. By necessity, such an approach requires the involvement of different sources of knowledge: disciplinary expertise as well as tacit and lay knowledge, and sharing a participatory process which results in the accurate framing of sustainability problems and effective solution strategies.

The transition approach does not offer a solution but an approach to our current problems. It perceives sustainable development as a structured and ongoing process of learning-by-doing and doing-by-learning, which moves us away from currently unsustainable practices. The subjectivity and incompleteness of the current scientific approach locks in an understanding of unsustainability that will fail the task at hand. A transition approach results in the co-creation of new knowledge. To be successful there must be a process of co-producing relevant knowledge and solutions in a learning-by-doing and doing-by-learning manner (Rotmans *et al.*, 2004). It is a new paradigm for sustainability research which can help to structure and scientifically ground the newly emerging research practices.

Transitions, transition management, and sustainable development

The combination of a reflexive, networked society coupled to a natural environmental system requires a form of reflexive modernization (Beck, 1994) which needs to be translated into fundamentally new practices, structures, and culture. The future development of our society is an area of continuing battle through debate: different actors perceive the contemporary problems of this world so differently that there is virtually no agreement on solutions. Whether the topic is climate change, development aid, or even the best strategy to combat pollution, fundamental differences in goals, interests, and strategy often prevent cooperation, consensus, or shared solutions. This type of problem is often called "wicked" (Rittel and Webber, 1973) or "unstructured" (Hisschemöller and Hoppe, 1996) in the literature, referring to the fact that the actors define these problems differently.

In addition to being defined and perceived differently, the problems of unsustainability originate from deeply rooted patterns of thinking and acting which are embedded in existing institutions and structures. Ultimately this means that they cannot be resolved by traditional means and approaches. Problems of unsustainability are by definition about different perspectives, unknown solutions, and an absence of consensus on the nature of the problem (Hisschemöller, 1993). For such persistent problems, a more fundamental reflection upon dominant values and perspectives is necessary to achieve the breakthroughs in thinking that enable transition processes.

Transitions are transformational processes in which existing structures, institutions, culture, and accompanied practices are broken down and new ones established. Societal transitions are defined as processes of change that alter the culture, structure, and practices of a societal system. These processes take a very long time to materialize – one to two generations – at the level of a societal system, although partial processes, for example, fundamental changes in thinking or radical innovation, can occur almost overnight. A societal transition is the result of interacting changes in all societal domains: for example, economy, ecology, institutions, technology, and welfare. Transitions as a phenomenon have been studied within several disciplines. Originally, the term was used to denote the "phase transitions" of substances as they changed from solid to liquid to gas, but since then the concept has been applied to a variety of shifts between qualitatively different states. These shifts are not linear but chaotic, and nonlinear; one model of change is punctuated equilibrium (Gould and Eldredge, 1977), and it has been applied in ecology, psychology, technology studies, economics, and demography (Gersick, 1991). The sociological concept of transition has its roots in population dynamics (Davis, 1945). Rotmans and colleagues (Rotmans *et al.*, 2001) have introduced the transition concept into the field of sustainable development, governance, and policy. In their view, a better understanding of structural societal change processes, i.e. transitions, will make it possible to formulate governance principles, methods, and tools to manage deep, structural change. Their work laid the foundation for the new field of transition studies (Rotmans *et al.*, 2004).

In this new research field, transition processes are studied from a variety of system perspectives: sociotechnical systems (Kemp *et al.*, 1998; Schot and Rip, 1997), innovation systems (Smits and Kuhlmann, 2004), and complex adaptive systems (De Haan, 2006; Van der Brugge and Rotmans, 2006). The different system perspectives on transitions have a number of basic commonalities:

1. The systems that are being studied are open and embedded in an outside environment with which the system co-evolves.
2. The external environment that influences the system is changing.
3. The system itself exhibits nonlinear behavior to adapt to its environment.

This process of adaptation takes place by means of changes in the system structure. Under certain circumstances, the environment and the system are so far out of tune that gradual adaptation is no longer sufficient and the systemic structure rapidly loses its effectiveness. Crises that undermine the dominant structure occur in the system until a turning point is reached and a new structure emerges. This view of systemic change hints at the emerging field of complexity and is a shared hypothesis underlying transition research.

A transition is a continuous process of societal change, whereby the structure of society or a subsystem of society changes fundamentally from one relatively stable system state to another through a co-evolution of its component structures. The complexity of a transition implies that it has a multitude of driving factors and impacts. A transition can be accelerated by one-time events, such as large accidents (e.g. Chernobyl) or a crisis (e.g. oil crisis) but is not caused by such events. Slow changes in the external environment determine the undercurrent for a fundamental change. Transitions thus are multi-causal, multi-level, multi-domain, multi-actor, multi-phase, and multi-speed processes.

In structuring this complexity and analyzing transitions, general patterns of complex system dynamics are taken as a starting point using common elements as a point of departure for analysis. The transition theory is therefore built on two main structural concepts: the transition is multi-phase and multi-level. These concepts are closely related and when combined help to analyze both the temporal dimension and the underlying dynamics of transitions. Embedded in a systems approach, these two concepts enable the rough analysis of any societal system in terms of the system state and the possibilities for agent-determined structural change. Transition management (Loorbach, 2007) is an intrinsic part of the theory as it conceptualizes the role of agency and can be used to analyze possibilities for influencing change.

A framework for transitions analysis

Although transitions are characterized by nonlinear, complex behavior, the process itself is a gradual one (Grin *et al.*, 2010). They can be described in terms of "degradation" and "breakdown" versus "buildup" and "innovation" (Gunderson and Holling, 2002) or in terms of "creative destruction" (Schumpeter, 1934). The central assumption is that societal structures go through long periods of relative stability and optimization, followed by relatively short periods of structural change. In this process existing structures (values, institutions, regulations, markets, etc.) fade away while new ones emerge. Multiple and interrelated innovations take place at varying speeds and levels. "Transition" is thus a collective term referring to a wide range of interconnected innovations at different levels in a "cascade of innovations" (Rotmans, 2005). The S-shaped curve therefore is a conceptual, descriptive model to reflect upon possible dynamics of a societal system and possible future trajectories. The central message of the S-curve is that structural change is not a gradual, linear process and that in the longer term structural change is to be expected.

From a complex systems perspective, the dynamics of a societal system are determined by their internal and external interaction with the internal and external environment: regimes, niches, co-evolution. An analytical model must be able to distinguish between system-specific, system-internal, and system-external developments. In a societal system, the dominant structure is called the "regime". Institutional structures give a societal system stability and guide decision making and the individual behavior of actors. At the regime level, a certain level of rigidity normally prevents innovations from altering the fundamental structure. At the micro level, innovations are created, tested, and diffused. External to the regime, the landscape dynamics define the characteristics and dynamics of the system as a whole, due to the fact that the system must adapt and co-adapt to its environment.

Neither the number of levels nor their boundaries are fixed: in between levels there could be other levels defined, for example, niche regimes as mini-systems between the micro and mesolevels. A patchwork of regimes (or subsystems), rather than one regime, is considered the dominant structure of this complex adaptive systems model. This structure enables the analysis of multiple regimes in which sub-transitions take place at different speeds and at different moments in time. Niches can finally be considered spaces within which innovations can mature and from there diffuse into the regime. In a complex systems view, niches can be part of the regime, exist outside the regime, or even exist in a semipermeable state providing the critical exchange between the system and its environment.

All models used to analyze societal systems are subjective constructions. The transition model is no exception. The fundamental question is which models are useful for what purpose. "A societal system" does not exist in reality, nor does a "regime." Any analysis of a system is arbitrary and only valid as long as it is supported or recognized by actors that operate within it, and it serves a useful purpose. Transition research presents itself as a new area for explorative research closely linked to innovative practice. The objective of transitions research is not to achieve objective analysis but to develop coherent, integrative, and long-term analytical tools that provide a basis for societal debate, policy, and reflection on future development (Loorbach, 2007). Transition research should stimulate and support the necessary problem-structuring processes, reflexive capacity, and social learning that create the conditions for sustainable change to occur.

Transition research and management in a sustainable development context

Sustainable development research and management seem almost impossible from a traditional mono-disciplinary perspective. Transitions are defined as all-encompassing transformational processes that can only be properly analyzed in hindsight. Transition management for sustainable development is in essence more an idea than an empirical fact or a hypothesis that can be empirically tested and validated. Although we can identify elements of transition management in historical transitions, and hypothesize upon what transition management could be and how we could actually operationalize it, it seems impossible to formulate straightforward hypotheses that can be tested through case studies or literature research alone. The nature of this research is to explore and underpin a new governance approach and to simultaneously develop an operational model. Almost by definition, this goal requires a new approach to interdisciplinary, participative, and applied research processes (Loorbach, 2010).

Transition theory challenges existing research paradigms. Influenced by complexity thinking, integrated approaches, and sustainability, a new research paradigm and field emerges in which the traditional gap between fundamental and applied research is bridged (Rotmans, 2005). The resulting field of theory and practice combines and integrates scientific disciplines. By its very nature the field is normatively driven transdisciplinary, integrating tacit and lay knowledge with scientific knowledge. The new research paradigm integrates practice, placing the researcher within the societal networks being studied (the very networks in which he or she has a specific role and influence). Transition theory is normative in its orientation toward sustainability while at the same time transition theory's research paradigm forms the gist of the research. In other words, the researcher is part of the community that is the subject of the research. Research is characterized by a focus on complexity, uncertainties, nonlinear development (also of knowledge), and sustainability.

Methodologically, the new research field of transitions requires research that is integrative, normative in its ambition, desires to contribute to societal change, and is participatory. Transition management is a unique example of such a research topic. The only way to achieve coherence between the theory and practice of transition management is through a learning-by-doing and doing-by-learning approach in which fundamental research, theory development, participatory research, and applied research are combined. The research methodology is unfolding during the research process: as new theoretical insights emerge, experimental and exploratory cases are used; conversely, when observations about operational processes inform or challenge theory, they need to be structured, integrated, and grounded. The process and the history of the research itself are integrated into the research – its reflexive quality has to be recorded, captured, and nurtured. The transition concept is an integrated assessment concept: a scientific "meta-discipline" that integrates knowledge about a problem domain and makes it available for societal learning and decision-making. It has a history of being applied first and foremost in the area of long-term environmental policy (Rotmans, 1998).

This consideration also relates to the concept of post-normal science (Funtowicz and Ravetz, 1994; Ravetz, 1999), which legitimates the involvement of diverse knowledge sources in science for policy by calling for extended peer communities and by emphasizing the inherent uncertainties and values in policy-related science. A key notion in integrated assessment and post-normal science is the acceptance of uncertainty and ambiguity. Sustainable development questions fit just such a paradigm. Its normative orientation provides a frame of reference to discuss and direct differences in perception, ambition, and understanding between actors. The rationale behind this assumption is that solutions for sustainable development can only be called sustainable when they are co-developed, implemented, and sustained by societal actors (Clark, 2003). Scientific knowledge related to sustainable development is not a goal in itself but rather a means to achieve progress. Scientists in the process of sustainable development are not providers of objective truths but part of the enquiry process. As such scientific knowledge, alongside political and social knowledge, becomes as subjective as the solutions and outcomes (Hisschemöller *et al.*, 2001).

Sustainability science practice increasingly involves cooperation with practitioners. It mainly refers to the field of global environmental and sustainability research and also emphasizes the importance of involving stakeholders in the knowledge-development process. While integrated assessment offers concrete tools and methods for complexity and sustainability research, sustainability science redefines the role of research and researchers at an abstract level. This is relevant for transition research since the ambitions behind transition research are similar to those behind sustainability science: scientific and societal impact based on the active and participatory role of researchers. This participatory role has become a new field of research in itself (Kasemir *et al.*, 2003; Van Asselt and Rijkens-Klomp, 2002). The central issue in this field is that participation in practice is often unstructured and ad hoc and that methods and tools for both participatory policy making and participatory (integrated) research need to be developed and tested (Van de Kerkhof, 2004). Although participatory methods (e.g. focus groups, consensus conferences, scenario exercises, simulation games) have a long history, they have been reinterpreted in their new context (Rotmans, 1998). So far, participation has been underdeveloped in scientific research as a means to generate knowledge with a higher relevance for society. Participatory science not only generates knowledge relevant for the situation for which it is developed but the participants internalize aspects of the knowledge generated, with the goal of enhancing its application. The participatory approach is thus an instrument for the transition researcher to transfer knowledge as well as to develop new theory.

The impact of transition management on policy making and its rapid development within the scientific community show a clear need for more of this type of participatory, normative, and integrative research next to more regular scientific research and knowledge. The research sketched above depends on the abilities of the researchers and practitioners involved to communicate clearly, to co-produce knowledge that is scientifically and socially relevant, and to develop pragmatic solutions. The pragmatic reflexive requirement requires finding adequate ways of dealing with a diversity of participants, differing normative interests and ambitions, and a variety of sources of knowledge. Development of competences and skills that enable the researcher to fulfill the required roles linked to research ambitions through training and experience should thus also form an explicit part of the transition research process, and the feedback looped training of the researcher.

Conclusion

Transition research is an overarching term that refers to a new type of research which requires a new type of researcher. Transition research is based on a systems approach to societal problems, and the participatory role of the researcher. Relevant knowledge and an understanding of complex, societal problems and phenomena are co-constructed in participatory processes between scientific experts and societal actors. Transition researchers simultaneously structure the processes that generate the required integrated knowledge. Transition researchers are scientists developing theory and reflecting upon practical experiences, who also act as participants, advocates, consultants, managers, facilitators, and negotiators. The broadening of the role of the researcher in governance and policy processes can be structured and more scientifically underpinned by the transition research perspective. In the context of sustainable development, there is a need for researchers to work in an interdisciplinary and transdisciplinary way and to act in different roles, depending on the process at hand. This does not exclude the role of experts and traditional desk research, but it does place their work in a broader and more integrated perspective.

Sustainable development in this perspective is not necessarily something that can be achieved, nor will a permanent agreement emerge as to what exactly constitutes sustainability. It is, however, exactly this ambiguity inherent in the concept of sustainable development that makes it an ideal starting point for structured debate about what in a specific context and moment in time is considered sustainable. When used in this way, sustainable development becomes a guiding notion in an ongoing process of learning-by-doing and doing-by-learning in which all actors contribute to envisioning, agenda building, experimenting, and evaluation. It is clear that in such a context, the criteria and conditions under which such a process takes place become highly important, as do the roles and abilities of all actors involved. We have argued that such general conditions and criteria can be formulated. Researchers in this process need to be reflexive and self-critical regarding their own findings and the value of the knowledge they produce, and realistic about how their knowledge can and will be used (Huault and Leca, 2007). As they engage societal arenas, researchers need to become more open to the values of others, their contributions and concerns in order to fulfill their multiple functions. In the short-term, perhaps traditional scientific authority will be undermined, but in the long-term its credibility and impact will prove it to be a valuable member of society, and not separate from it. In this multidisciplinary and self-critical context, it is necessary to be clear and conscious about the different roles that researchers play in participatory processes. Being explicit about this process of interrelatedness and reflexivity is the responsibility of researchers, while at the same time providing new opportunities for developing scientific methodology and research. If this can be achieved, research on sustainable development will be an integral part of sustainability.

References

Banerjee, S. B. 2003. Who Sustains Whose Development? Sustainable Development and the Reinvention of Nature. *Organization Studies* 24(2), pp. 143–80.

Beck, U. 1994. The Reinvention of Politics: Towards a Theory of Reflexive Modernization. In *Reflexive Modernization: Politics, Tradition and Aesthetics in the Modern Social Order.* Eds. U. Beck, A. Giddens, and S. Lash. Cambridge: Polity.

Bolin, B., W. Clark, R. Corell, N. Dickson, S. Faucheux, G. Gallopin, A. Gruebler, M. Hall, B. Huntley, J. Jaeger, C. Jaeger, N. Jodha, R. Kasperson, R. Kates, I. Lowe, A. Mabogunje, P. Matson, J. McCarthy, H. Mooney, B. Moore, T. O'Riordan, J. Schellnhuber, and U.

Svedin. 2000. *Core Questions of Science and Technology for Sustainability*. Retrieved on July 15th, 2012, from http://sustainabilityscience.org/content.html?contentid=776#en1.

Clark, W. C. 2003. Sustainability, Energy Use and Public Participation. In *Public Participation in Sustainability Science*. Eds. B. Kasemir, J. Jager, C. Jaeger, and M. Gardner. Cambridge: Cambridge University Press.

Davis, R. 1945. The World Demographic Transition. *Annals of the American Academy of Political and Social Science* 235, pp. 1–11.

De Haan, J. 2006. *How Emergence Arises*. Manuscript submitted for publication.

Flyvbjerg, B. 2001.*Making Social Science Matter. Why Social Inquiry Fails and How It Can Succeed Again*. Cambridge: Cambridge University Press.

Funtowicz, S. O., and J. R. Ravetz. 1994. The Worth of a Songbird: Ecological Economics as a Post-Normal Science. *Ecological Economics* 10(3), pp. 197–207.

Gersick, C. J. G. 1991. Revolutionary Change Theories: A Multi-level Exploration of the Punctuated Equilibrium Paradigm. *Academy of Management Review* 16(1), pp. 10–36.

Gladwin, T., J. Kennelly, and T. Krause. 1995. Shifting Paradigms for Sustainable Development: Implications for Management Theory and Research. *Academy of Management Review* 20(4), pp. 874–907.

Gould, S. J., and N. Eldredge. 1977. Punctuated Equilibria: The Tempo and Mode of Evolution Reconsidered. *Paleobiology* 3, pp. 115–51.

Grin, J., J. Rotmans, and J.Schot, in collaboration with F. Geels, and D. Loorbach. 2010. *Transitions to Sustainable Development: New Directions in the Study of Long Term Transformative Change*. New York: Routledge.

Gunderson, L. H., and C. S. Holling. 2002. *Understanding Transformations in Human and Natural Systems*. Washington, DC: Island.

Hisschemöller, M. 1993. *De Democratie van Problemen*. Unpublished manuscript. Amsterdam: Vrije Universiteit.

Hisschemöller, M., and R. Hoppe. 1996. Coping with Intractable Controversies: The Case of Problem Structuring in Policy Design and Analysis. *Knowledge and Policy: The International Journal of Knowledge Transfer*. Eds. M. Hisschemöller, R. Hoppe, W. Dunn, and J. R. Ravetz, pp. 40–60.

Hisschemöller, M., R. Hoppe, W. Dunn, and J. Ravetz. 2001. *Knowledge, Power, and Participation in Environmental Policy Analysis*. New Brunswick, NJ: Transaction.

Huault, I., and B. Leca. 2007. Toward a Critical Neo-institutionalism. Paper presented at the 5th Critical Management Studies Conference, Manchester.

Kasemir, B., J. Jager, C. Jaeger, and M. Gardner, eds. 2003. *Public Participation in Sustainability Science*. Cambridge: Cambridge University Press.

Kemp, R., J. Schot, and R. Hoogma. 1998. Regime Shifts to Sustainability through Processes of Niche Formation: The Approach of Strategic Niche Management. *Technology Analysis and Strategic Management* 10, pp. 175–96.

Loorbach, D. 2007. *Transition Management: New Mode of Governance for Sustainable Development*. Utrecht, Netherlands: International Books.

Loorbach, D. 2010. Transition Management for Sustainable Development: A Prescriptive, Complexity-Based Governance Framework. *Governance* 1, pp. 161–83.

Ravetz, J. R. 1999. What Is Post-normal Science? *Futures* 31(7), pp. 647–53.

Rittel, H., and M. Webber. 1973. Dilemmas in General Theory of Planning. *Policy Sciences* 4(2), pp. 155–59.

Rotmans, J. 1998. Methods for IA: The Challenges and Opportunities Ahead. *Environmental Modeling and Assessment* 3(3), pp. 155–79.

Rotmans, J. 2005. *Societal Innovation: Between Dream and Reality Lies Complexity.* Rotterdam, Netherlands: Erasmus Research Institute of Management.

Rotmans, J., J. Grin, J. Schot, and R. Smits. 2004. *Multi-, Inter- and Transdisciplinary Research Program into Transitions and System Innovations.* Unpublished manuscript, Maastricht, Netherlands.

Rotmans, J., R. Kemp, and M. Van Asselt. 2001. More Evolution than Revolution: Transition Management in Public Policy. *Foresight* 3(1), p. 17.

Schot, J. W., and A. Rip. 1997. The Past and the Future of Constructive Technology Assessment. *Technological Forecasting and Social Change* 54(2–3), pp. 251–68.

Schumpeter, J. A. 1934. *The Theory of Economic Development.* Cambridge, Mass.: Harvard University Press.

Scott, W., and S. Gough, eds. 2004. *Key Issues in Sustainable Development and Learning: A Critical Review.* London: Routledge.

Smits, R., and S. Kuhlmann. 2004. The Rise of Systemic Instruments in Innovation Policy. *International Journal of Foresight and Innovation Policy* 1(1–2), pp. 4–32.

Van Asselt, M., and N. Rijkens-Klomp. 2002. A Look in the Mirror: Reflection on Participation in Integrated Assessment from a Methodological Perspective. *Global Environmental Change: Human and Policy Dimensions* 12(3), pp. 167–84.

Van de Kerkhof, M. 2004. *Debating Climate Change.* Utrecht, Netherlands: Lemma.

Van der Brugge, R., and J. Rotmans. 2006. Towards Transition Management of European Water Resources. *Water Resource Management: Advances in Global Change Research,* special issue.

Introduction to Part II

Religious and ethnically based environmental values

Jack Appleton

Part II of this book is critical to the development of an understanding of participants' values. Participants are from all segments of the human population and thus encompass a significant heterogeneity in terms of their values, perceptions, and culture. Even among environmentalists there is a disparity of views and values, often creating a situation where there is agreement concerning what is to be done, but not agreement as to why (Norton, B. 1991. *Toward Unity Among Environmentalists*. Oxford: Oxford University Press). Values differ along a range of social and economic variables: race, ethnicity, nationality, sex, age, economic status, religion, religiosity, and so forth. The chapters in Part II are arranged into two thematic groups: religion and ethnicity. The first group focuses on religious traditions. Five of the world's great religious traditions are discussed, ordered in accordance with their historical appearance: indigenous peoples is first, followed by the modern religions of Hindu, Judaism, Christianity and Islam. The second group starts with an intimate portrait of African Americans, and then moves south with a discussion of Latin America. From the Americas, the discussion moves east to Asia with chapters on the recent developments in Japan and the environmental concerns of Chinese. Part II ends with chapters which illuminate the environmental values found in Sub-Saharan Africa. The ordering of the chapters thus implies that no one set of values described is inherently imbued with a different status or of greater importance.

It was consciously decided that the statements and descriptions in the chapters would not be normative statements of advocacy, but would be either personal statements, or descriptions of values held by a particular segment of humanity. A conscious attempt was made to include a diverse and significant range of statements of values that would provide insight into as much of humanity as possible. It was a conscious decision to not include a statement of values from a feminist perspective as a distinct statement. At least 15 of the authors are female (slightly less than half). That is a significant statement in and of itself. The inclusion of a Chinese perspective necessitated the inclusion of a Japanese perspective to deflect the tendency to divide humanity into oriental and occidental hemispheres. Despite the popularity of doing so, the statements are not being presented within a larger theoretical construct, and will not be discussed in such terms, for example, Geert Hofstede's work on the influence of culture and values on behavior is not discussed. Finally, these chapters provide insight, they are not definitive, and one should keep in mind that all values and all orientations can be found in all segments of humanity given that the segment is a significantly large population. In daily reality, all Chinese do not think this or do that, and the same can be said for Christians, and so on.

10 Indigenous peoples' environmental values

Peter N. Jones

Sustainable development is often characterized as a system of resource use that aims to meet current human needs while preserving the environment so that these needs can be met in the future. To ensure that the environment will continue to meet human needs, those working in the field of sustainable development have worked to develop policies and practices that guide development toward this goal. This has not been an easy or straightforward task, as different cultures hold different values toward the environment, including how to develop and sustain resource use. Within sustainable development discussions concerning the environment, much of the discussion has focused on two competing value systems: naturalism and universalism.

Naturalism centers on the view that everything is natural, and that everything there is belongs to the world of nature. Naturalism shows a deep connection to the world and others, and therefore prompts concern for the natural environment and its future. It is a common value system in discussions of sustainable development. However, because naturalism discounts the existence of any metaphysical possibilities in understanding influences on the environment, such as spirits or nonphysical forces, it increases the value placed on current life and the world as it is known to exist. Specifically, naturalism insists that the world of nature must form a single sphere that is free from incursions by metaphysical entities (Sagoff, 2004).

Universalism centers on the core belief in one common truth. In terms of the environment and sustainable development, universalism argues that despite multiple perspectives, there is one central value toward the environment that underlies all the diverse perspectives (Hubin, 1994).

Both naturalistic and universal approaches to the environment are homogeneous, in that they both argue for a central value – either naturalistic or universal – in the sustainable development discourse. This focus has resulted in the exclusion of other value systems that do not fall within these two general frameworks, including those of indigenous peoples, who hold a diversity of alternative perspectives and values toward the environment. These alternative perspectives cannot be properly encompassed within either naturalistic or universal environmental value systems, and as such provide an important alternative to the dominant discourse concerning sustainable development.

In much of the sustainable development discourse, economic and social development are considered important components of the field, along with protecting the environment and its resources. For example, the United Nations' (UN's) 2005 *World Summit Outcome* document (United Nations, 2005) refers to the "interdependent and mutually reinforcing pillars" of sustainable development as economic development, social development, and environmental protection. Indigenous peoples have argued that this framing is incomplete, and that sustainable development needs to also include a cultural component. For example, Article 1 of *The Universal Declaration on Cultural Diversity* (UNESCO, 2001) states that "cultural diversity is as necessary for humankind as biodiversity is for nature"; and that in any form of development it is necessary to consider "one of the roots of development, understood not simply in terms of economic growth, but also as a means to achieve a more satisfactory intellectual, emotional, moral and spiritual existence." Under this framing, indigenous cultures and cultural diversity are seen as an essential pillar in the sustainable development discourse.

Indigenous peoples

There are many definitions of "indigenous peoples," including those given by the people themselves. The most straightforward formulation of the term is James Clifford's: indigenous peoples are "native" to a particular place, original to their lands rather than having migrated from elsewhere. Indigenous peoples are therefore the "first peoples" or original inhabitants of a particular area (Clifford, 2007). As a result of their continuous and long-term connection with the land and environment, they have developed unique cultures, values, and specific knowledge concerning their environment.

Furthermore, many indigenous communities claim their histories and oral traditions have been literally created from the land, and thus their lands are filled with geographic and environmental features directly tied to these histories and oral traditions. For example, the Cherokee people of the southeastern USA view the Great Smokey Mountains as a sacred landscape. The significance of this region and its connection is illustrated in Cherokee oral tradition, which connects the people to the mountains, valleys, rivers, lakes, and forests of their homeland. Understanding the connection between the Cherokee and their environment is vital to understanding Cherokee history and identity, as well as Cherokee values toward the environment. According to Christopher Oakley (2009, p. 9):First, the Great Smokey Mountains provided the setting for many of the important legends and myths that explained Cherokee society and worldview. Likewise, the numerous waterways of the Smoky Mountains, vital to Cherokee existence in many practical ways, were also important settings for oral traditions. And finally, the native plants and animals of the mountains played important roles and characters in Cherokee mythology.

The Cherokee, along with other indigenous peoples, are tied in a very deep way to their lands, and part of their identity is directly taken from the land in which they live. This long-term, continuous, and deep symbiotic relationship with the land has allowed indigenous peoples to develop specific values and knowledge concerning the environment, including knowledge of how best to manage and sustain the environment to meet current and future needs. This knowledge, often termed "traditional ecological knowledge," or simply "traditional knowledge," is "a cumulative body of knowledge, practice, and belief, evolving by adaptive processes and handed down through generations by cultural transmission, about the relationship of living beings (including human) with one another and with their environment" (Berkes, 2008, p. 7).

Indigenous peoples argue that for sustainable development to be comprehensive and holistic, it is necessary to include indigenous traditional knowledge in the discourse (International Fund for Agricultural Development, 2003). This knowledge is commonly articulated in ways that nonindigenous peoples in sustainable development discussions find difficult to understand and to access, often because it exists in a social or even spiritual framework that falls outside the dominant value systems of naturalism or universalism.

Anthropologists and social scientists have attempted to articulate some of this traditional knowledge in terms of nonindigenous paradigms and frameworks. For example, Roy Rappaport (1967, 1984) used a systems approach to argue that the ritual pig feasts conducted by the Tsembaga people of Papua New Guinea helped to regulate the balance between human and pig populations, resulting in a sustainable resource and environment. In a more complex context, Stephen Lansing and James Kremer (Lansing, 1987, 1991; Lansing and Kremer, 1993), using agent-based models and computer simulations, have argued that the traditional Hindu water temples and priests on the Indonesian island of Bali help to regulate water usage, thus making the traditional agricultural system more sustainable than new green revolution technologies and innovations. More recently, several people have explicitly argued that indigenous traditional knowledge should be included in sustainable development discussions (see Harmon and Putney, 2003; Posey, 1999; Tiedje, 2007; Williams and Baines, 1993).

Traditional knowledge and indigenous values toward the environment

As each indigenous culture has developed its own unique traditional knowledge based on its history and relationship with the environment, the traditional knowledge of each indigenous culture has embodied the values of the particular group or community toward the environment. As noted above, however, traditional knowledge is often excluded from discussions of sustainable development because it is articulated in ways that do not fall under the dominant paradigms of naturalism and universalism. It does not fall under naturalistic paradigms because methods of acquiring and accumulating traditional knowledge, although often encompassing empirical research and experimentation, also includes dreams, revelatory experiences, oral traditions, and personal experience. These latter methods of obtaining knowledge are grounded in an ontology that includes metaphysical possibilities, whereas naturalism limits ontology to a world that is free from the influence of metaphysical possibilities.

Traditional knowledge is likewise incapable of being placed within a value system grounded in the paradigm of universalism. Because traditional knowledge is grounded in local environments and communities, and the knowledge that it embodies is in turn tied to the local environment, it is the opposite of a universal value toward the environment. This is true even when traditional knowledge from a community in one environment is compared to another community in an almost identical environment: the traditional knowledge of the two groups will hold similarities, but also striking differences.

This does not mean that traditional knowledge and the values that it promotes toward the environment should not be included in sustainable development discussions. On the contrary, it is because of the unique diversity of indigenous peoples and their traditional knowledge toward the environment that they should be included in the sustainable development discourse. As noted in Article 1 of *The Universal Declaration on Cultural Diversity* (UNESCO, 2001), "cultural diversity is as necessary for humankind as biodiversity is for nature." If we are to achieve the goals of sustainable development, it is essential that we include indigenous peoples and their traditional knowledge, precisely because they do not fit within the dominant frameworks of naturalism and universalism.

Indigenous peoples have argued for the importance of traditional knowledge and the need for it to be included in environmental management and sustainable discourse. In many cases their arguments can be found in charters, declarations, and other statements issued by the indigenous communities themselves. For example, in the Northern Territory of Australia, the Mary River Statement, issued and signed by over 80 indigenous experts from across the province, explicitly states: "Indigenous Peoples have rights, responsibilities and obligations in accordance with their customary laws, traditions, protocols and customs to protect, conserve and maintain the environment and ecosystems in their natural state so as to ensure the sustainability of the whole environment" (NAILSMA, 2009). As the Mary River Statement confirms, indigenous peoples have valuable knowledge concerning the environment and how to sustain it, and they must be included in sustainable development discussions because this knowledge cannot be separated from the people and the environment. The difficulty, therefore, is in understanding just how traditional knowledge is articulated and how to include it within the sustainable development discussion.

The Yanyuwa people from Wurdaliya country in the Northern Territory of Australia have what is known as *namu-Yuwa ki-Wundanyukawu*, which can roughly be translated as "Law for the Sea Turtle." This traditional knowledge involves a deep and complex understanding of the Yanyuwa people and their special relationships with *Wirndiwirndi* (flatback sea turtles [*Natator depressus*]), *malurrba* (green sea turtles [*Chelonia mydas*]), and all other *Wundunyuka* (sea turtles). As inhabitants of the Wurdaliya country for thousands of years, the Yanyuwa people have acquired traditional knowledge concerning sea turtles that is comprehensive and has been continually refined over hundreds of years. Furthermore, as Richard Baker (1989) discusses in depth, the Yanyuwa traditional knowledge has allowed them to maintain a sustainable lifeway that is in harmony with the local environment. Any discussion of sustainable development along the coast of the Northern Territory would benefit from including Yanyuwa traditional knowledge.

This traditional knowledge is often articulated, shared, and passed on from one generation to the next through songs, which explain *na-ngalki* (what makes people who they are), as well as the relationship of the Yanyuwa people to all the animals, plants, and things on and moving across Yanyuwa country (Johnston, 2009). These songs cannot be easily incorporated into the sustainable development discourse, not only because they fail to fit nicely within naturalistic or universal value systems but also because the knowledge and meaning found within the songs can only be understood while in Yanyuwa country. Therefore, if traditional knowledge is to be incorporated into sustainable development discussions, the indigenous peoples who hold that knowledge must be included.

Traditional knowledge is intricately tied to the local environment. Likewise, the values toward the environment that are found in traditional knowledge are uniquely tied to each indigenous group. These values are found in traditional songs and oral traditions, as in the Yanyuwa example, as well as being embodied and articulated in the very language of each indigenous group. This is often clearly demonstrated by examining the language and meanings of words that each indigenous group employs in discussing the environment. Plant and animal names among most indigenous groups are rarely truly arbitrary labels, even though the arbitrariness of words has been taken as a fundamental characteristic of human language since at least Ferdinand de Saussure (1996 [1907]). Most plant and animal names have descriptive force (Hunn, 1996), which, as Brent Berlin has noted (1992, pp. 255–59), facilitates the process of learning names and remembering the relevant properties and roles of the plants or animals named; in addition, this convention permits values toward the environment to be encompassed in the name itself.

In the traditional vocabulary of the Hupa, Yurok, and Karuk indigenous peoples of California, even the most common objects of experience are often named for the roles they play in the mythology, folklore, and cultural practices of the people and the environment (O'Neill, 2008). Far from representing frozen historical derivations devoid of living meaning, these descriptive nouns continue to act as repositories of traditional knowledge, directly expressing the values held by the indigenous peoples toward the thing named. For the Hupa, Yurok, and Karuk people, words used in discussing their traditional knowledge carry within them the values that these peoples hold toward the environment, along with the role that the named thing plays in the larger ecosystem. Again, the traditional knowledge of the Hupa, Yurok, and Karuk peoples fails to be properly encompassed under the naturalistic and universal value systems, simply because the knowledge and values are embodied in the specific words and language of the people, and not in the natural world itself or in some universal value. Likewise, if Hupa, Yurok, and Karuk traditional knowledge is to be included in sustainable development discussions, indigenous speakers of the language must be included, for the traditional knowledge is expressed and articulated in the language and the speaking of that language.

The values that indigenous peoples hold for the environment and that are embedded within their traditional knowledge are expressed and articulated not only through songs, oral traditions, and language, but also within other rituals and practices. Many of the rituals and cultural practices of indigenous peoples directly embody and reinforce the values that they hold for the environment, from the First Salmon Feasts held by many indigenous peoples of the Pacific Northwest of North America to ritual "burnings" found among many indigenous peoples around the world. For example, the Bhil tribal people of the Phulwari Sanctuary in southern Rajasthan, India, are known for their *agni snan*. These are ritual events performed to fulfill promises that communities have made to their local mountains if certain boons such as gifts of health, wealth, and prosperity are granted. Such ritual practices are described by Bhils as "fire baths" or "black skirts" for the way they can leave an entire slope darkened, as the ritual culminates in setting the top of a mountain on fire (Snodgrass *et al.*, 2008). Initially, the state government attempted to remove the Bhil tribals from the sanctuary and prevent them from performing this ritual. However, these ritual fire baths and the traditional knowledge that dictates their performance are now recognized as a central component of maintaining a healthy forest, as they promote diversity in habitats and stimulate growth. Likewise, another ritual called "spreading saffron" (*kesar bantna*) involves ritually closing off degraded sections of the forest from further use for five or more years (Snodgrass *et al.*, 2008).

The values of the Bhil tribals toward the environment are directly embodied in their ritual and cultural practices, and these rituals and cultural practices articulate their traditional knowledge concerning how to sustain the environment. As managers are slowly becoming aware, to sustainably manage the environment within the Phulwari Sanctuary it will be necessary to incorporate Bhil tribal rituals and cultural practices into the management of the sanctuary (Foundation for Ecological Security, 2010).

As the above examples demonstrate, indigenous peoples' traditional knowledge is completely tied to their environment, and they articulate this knowledge through songs, language, rituals, and cultural practices that have endured for generations. This continuous interaction with the environment has enabled indigenous peoples to view and value the environment in ways quite distinct from those that characterize the naturalistic and universal frameworks. Furthermore, the feedback loop between the people, their environment, and the development and propagation of their knowledge results in a recursive understanding of time and place. For many indigenous peoples, time and place intersect repeatedly, with ancient memories being kept alive in modern landscapes.

The "memoryscapes" are constantly created and recreated through the performance of songs, dances, rituals, and cultural activities, the retelling of stories, and the reallocation of place names (Nabokov, 2002, p. 145). The perpetuation of these memoryscapes allows indigenous peoples to transmit and refine their traditional knowledge from one generation to the next. For example, the Nimiipuu of present-day Idaho live within an environment replete with oral traditions and ancient memories revolving around different keystone species such as salmon *Oncorhynchus spp.* The environment and the oral traditions and ancient memories that it embodies for the Nimiipuu reinforce their traditional knowledge and the values they hold toward the environment. This value system is directly tied to sustaining the environment and its resources, as the very identity of the Nimiipuu is contingent on the yearly appearance of salmon and other resources (Jones, 2005).

Similarly, the Ta'utujil Maya of the Lake Atitlan area of Guatemala believe that they occupy *r'muxux kaj, r'muxux r'uwachulew*, which roughly translates as "the navel of the sky, the navel of the face of the earth" (Christenson, 2009, p. 98). The surrounding volcanoes and mountains are the abode of gods and powerful ancestors, while Lake Atitlan bears the primordial waters of creation, suffused with animative power capable of regenerating and sustaining life, as well as the capacity to destroy it. Like the environment of the Nimiipuu of present-day Idaho, that of the Ta'utujil Maya is a memoryscape in which important events periodically recur (Farriss, 1984). Because of the way the Ta'utujil Maya value the environment, they take into account not only past actions but also their possible recurrence. This worldview is a radical departure from naturalistic and universal values concerning the environment, and offers a unique contribution to sustainable development discourse.

Traditional knowledge, indigenous values, and sustainable development

Indigenous peoples around the world hold unique and essential values toward the environment, values that are embodied within their traditional knowledge. These values are essential to sustainability precisely because they do not fit within the dominant value frameworks of naturalism and universalism, and also because they embody values that are grounded in the local environment through time.

At the beginning of this chapter it was noted that sustainable development is often characterized as including economic and social development while protecting the environment. This characterization is lacking a cultural component, which may be found within the values that indigenous peoples hold toward the environment. However, because traditional knowledge and its values do not fit within the value frameworks of naturalism and universalism, it has proved difficult to include this fourth component into sustainable development activities. The component cannot be simply presented in a written document or easily incorporated into other value systems that are already at play within the sustainable development arena. Rather, it is necessary for indigenous peoples and their traditional knowledge to be included within the sustainable development arena in a holistic and meaningful way. That would mean incorporating indigenous peoples and their traditional knowledge while preserving their own value framework.

Accomplishing this goal would involve bringing indigenous peoples directly into the sustainable development discussion by incorporating their songs, oral traditions, language, cultural practices and rituals, and memoryscapes within sustainable development methods, theories, and policies. This is not an easy process, because these articulations of traditional knowledge and environmental values do not fit within naturalistic or universal value systems. As Australian Government Lands and Coasts (2004) recommends in its *Guidelines for Indigenous Participation in Natural Resources Management,* those working in the sustainable development arena need to ask local indigenous communities to help establish an appropriate process for gaining indigenous input into sustainable development planning. In the end, this will make sustainable development policies and practices more comprehensive and holistic, bettering their chance of meeting current human needs while preserving the environment so that these needs can continue to be met in the future.

References

Australian Government Land and Coasts. 2004. *Guidelines for Indigenous Participation in Natural Resources Management.* Retrieved on March 10th, 2011, from http://www.nrm.gov.au/publications/guidelines/indigenous-participation.html.

Baker, R. M. 1989. *Land Is Life: Continuity through Change for the Yanyuwa from the Northern Territory of Australia.* PhD thesis. Adelaide: Department of Geography, University of Adelaide.

Berlin, B. 1992. *Ethnobiological Classification: Principles of Categorization of Plants and Animals in Traditional Societies.* Princeton, NJ: Princeton University Press.

Berkes, F. 2008. *Sacred Ecology.* New York: Routledge.

Christenson, A. J. 2009. Ancestral Presence at the Navel of the World: Francisco Sojuel and Santiago Atitlan. In *Landscapes of Origin in the Americas: Creation Narratives Linking Ancient Places and Present Communities.* Ed. J. J. Christie. Tuscaloosa, Ala.: University of Alabama Press, pp. 98–119.

Clifford, J. 2007. Varieties of Indigenous Experience: Diasporas, Homelands, and Sovereignties. In *Indigenous Experience Today.* Eds. M. de la Cadena and O. Starn. Oxford: Berg, pp. 197–223.

Farriss, J. 1984. *Maya Society under Colonial Rule: The Collective Enterprise of Survival.* Princeton, NJ: Princeton University Press.

Foundation for Ecological Security (FES). 2010. *Assessment of Biodiversity in Phulwari-ki-Nal Wildlife Sanctuary: A Conservation Perspective.* Anand, Gujarat: Foundation for Ecological Security.

Harmon, D., and A. D. Putney, eds. 2003. *The Full Value of Parks: From Economics to the Intangible.* Lanham, Md.: Rowan and Littlefield.

Hubin, D. 1994. The Moral Justification of Benefit/Cost Analysis. *Economics and Philosophy* 10, pp. 169–94.

Hunn, E. S. 1996. Columbia Plateau Indian Place Names: What Can They Teach Us? *Journal of Linguistic Anthropology* 6(1), pp. 3–26.

International Fund for Agricultural Development (IFAD). 2003. *Indigenous Peoples and Sustainable Development: Roundtable Discussion Paper for the Twenty-fifth Anniversary Session of IFAD's Governing Council*. Retrieved on March 12th, 2011, from http://www. ifad.org/gbdocs/gc/26/e/ip.pdf.

Johnston, S. 2009. Narnu-Yuwa Ki-Wundanyukawu [Law for the Sea Turtle]. *Kantri Laif* 5, pp. 16–17.

Jones, P. 2005. Identity through Fishing: A Preliminary Analysis of the Impacts to the Nez Perce as a Result of the Damming of the Clearwater and Snake Rivers. *Cultural Dynamics* 17(2), pp. 155–92.

Lansing, S. 1987. Balinese "Water Temples" and the Management of Irrigation. *American Anthropologist* 89, pp. 326–41.

Lansing, S. 1991. *Priests and Programmers*. Princeton, NJ: Princeton University Press.

Lansing, S., and J. N. Kremer. 1993. Emergent Properties of Balinese Water Temple Networks: Co-adaptation on a Rugged Fitness Landscape. *American Anthropologist* 95, pp. 97–114.

Nabokov, P. 2002. *A Forest of Time: American Indian Ways of History*. Cambridge: Cambridge University Press.

NAILSMA (North Australian Indigenous Land and Sea Management Alliance). 2009. *Mary River Statement*. Northern Territory: Charles Darwin University.

Oakley, C. 2009. *The Center of the World: The Principle People and the Great Smoky Mountains. Landscapes of Origin in the Americas: Creation Narratives Linking Ancient Places and Present Communities*. Ed. J. Christie. Tuscaloosa, Ala.: University of Alabama Press, pp. 3–14.

O'Neill, S. 2008. *Cultural Contact and Linguistic Relativity among the Indians of Northwestern California*. Norman, Okla.: University of Oklahoma Press.

Posey, D. A., ed. 1999. *Cultural and Spiritual Values of Biodiversity*. London: Intermediate Technology Publications.

Rappaport, R. 1967. Ritual Regulation of Environmental Regulations among a New Guinea People. *Ethnology* 6(1), pp. 17–30.

Rappaport, R. 1984. *Pigs for the Ancestors: Ritual in the Ecology of a New Guinea People*. Prospect Heights, Ill.: Waveland.

Sagoff, M. 2004. *Price, Principle, and the Environment*. New York: Cambridge University Press.

Saussure, F. de. 1996 [1907]. *Saussure's First Course of Lectures on General Linguistics*. Ed. and trans. G. Wolf. Tarrytown, NY: Pergamon.

Snodgrass, J. G., S. K. Sharma, Y. Singh Jhala, M. G. Lacy, M. Advani, N. K. Bhargava, and C. Upadhyay. 2008. Lovely Leopards, Frightful Forests: The Environmental Ethics of Indigenous Rajasthani Shamans. *Journal for the Study of Religion, Nature, and Culture* 2(1), pp. 30–54.

Tiedje, K. 2007. The Promise of the Discourse of the Sacred for Conservation (and Its Limits. *Journal for the Study of Religion, Nature, and Culture* 1(3), pp. 326–39.

UNESCO (United Nations Educational, Scientific and Cultural Organization). 2001. *The Universal Declaration on Cultural Diversity, United Nations Educational, Scientific and Cultural Organization*. Retrieved on March 15th, 2011, from http://portal.unesco.

org/en/ev.phpURL_ID=13179&URL_DO=DO_TOPIC&URL_SECTION=201. html.

United Nations. 2005. *2005 World Summit Outcome, United Nations General Assembly, 60th Session*. Retrieved on April 4th, 2011, from http://www.who.int/hiv/universalaccess2010/ worldsummit.pdf.

Williams, N., and G. Baines, eds. 1993. *Traditional Ecological Knowledge: Wisdom for Sustainable Development*. Canberra: Canberra Center for Resource and Environmental Studies, Australian National University.

11 Hindu traditions and the environment

Prakash C. Dixit

Jane Goodall often says, "We are stealing the planet from our children." If we continue to develop with the same values which have allowed us to steal the planet from our children, the consequences will be tragic. However, value systems which could enable us to effect a midcourse correction do exist. Recognizing various dimensions of human life, the Indic traditions have built an enduring foundation for an environmental friendly value system and a balanced lifestyle (Singhvi, 1995). From the classical knowledge of Vedas, Upanishads, Bhagvat Gita, and Hindu epics to the contemporary ideals of a just world order, Hinduism and ecology are completely intertwined.

Values as practiced by Hindus can play a pivotal role in creating a world system where the sanctity of nature is revered by humans such that they might live and grow in harmony with all other entities and elements of our universe. This system is almost diametrically opposed to that which has prevailed for the last half-millennium. An effort is made here to explore the potential and possibility of resolving the environmental crisis by constructing an alternative worldview through the philosophies, teachings, and values of Hinduism.

Defining Hindu and Hinduism

The term "Hindu" does not occur in any of India's ancient religious texts. Even frequently used terms "Vedic Dharma" (the religion of Vedas) and "Sanatana Dharma" (timeless religion) are alien to this spiritual system. Sarasvati (1995, p. 28) of Kanchi Peetham (one of the five highest Hindu pontiffs) clearly states that our basic texts do not refer to our faith by any name. It is "the religion without a name" (Sarasvati, 1995). We call this primeval religion *Dharma*, which variously means "way of life," "righteous conduct," and "basic ethical and moral duties." He further claims that in the remotest times of human history there was only one *Dharma*, which was not very different in its moral, behavioral, and cultural values from the religion we now call Hinduism.

Dharma is a Sanskrit word for a system of values that upholds, sustains, or supports an entity. The word "religion" is a poor synonym of the word "*Dharma*." The entire edifice of *Dharma* is based on universal natural laws and enables its followers to be contented and happy. Maintaining and conserving the world at large is the aim of *Dharma*. "It operates in accordance with time, space, and conditions, and yet maintains a balance, lest society stray from eternal principles" (Seshagiri Rao, 2000, p. 24). Seshagiri Rao adds that the concept of *Dharma* gives us a model of cosmic and social equilibrium, representing unequivocally the principle of preservation. As a part of this process, worldly development and prosperity are considered the results of proper care and management of natural and human resources (Seshagiri Rao, 2000).

When the Persians conquered parts of northwest India, they called the people they encountered Hindu. Thus "Hindu" was originally a geographic and not religious term used initially by Persians and then Greeks (Frawley, 1992). Hinduism is basically a blend of traditions from ancient Dravidian, Aryan, and Indus civilizations, and tribal practices that evolved over millennia. It is proposed here to use the term "Hinduism" in place of *Dharma*, as it is universally understood and is the faith of almost a billion people. It is often held that Hinduism has no beginning and precedes recorded history. It was not founded by any human person. It is definitively claimed that its tenets were revealed to adherents while they were in their deep meditative state. Millennia passed before they were codified and the foundation scriptures written down. In that vast period of time its tenets were passed on from guru to disciple in an unbroken chain.

Thousands of spiritual traditions arose and evolved in India, in a multitude of forms. Many of these traditions traveled to other neighboring lands in Asia and took on their own local flavor. Examples abound from Nepal, Thailand, Indonesia, Cambodia, China, Korea, and Japan (Bharati, 2010). These traditions are interlinked, and as they evolved they borrowed and lent ideas, rituals, and beliefs among themselves. There are real and apparent contradictions in many of these traditions, including in Buddhism and Jainism, and yet there is no question of any acrimonious relationship between them. Swami Veda Bharati clearly states that it is not "religious tolerance but rather acceptance of all paths as valid, depending on each person's mind and understanding of the divine Name and Form or formlessness. It is the view of polymorphous Ultimate Reality" (2010, p. 212).

Basic tenets of Hinduism

Talking of its profundity, David Frawley states that "the Hindu mind represents humanity's oldest and most continuous stream of conscious intelligence on the planet." (2001, p. 12). It is most tolerant and democratic. It does not oppose science, scientific explorations, and technological innovations, as these are the methods of finding truth. Unlike adherents of other faiths, a Hindu can even question his own scriptures and gods, as seeking ultimate truth is the paramount goal of Hinduism. It "does not seek to impose itself upon people from the outside through force or persuasion" (Frawley, 2001, p. 13).

A Hindu individual follows a four fold value system in order to have a life of complete fulfillment. These values pertain to morals, *dharma*; values related to economic well-being, *artha*; values guiding desires for beautiful entities and enjoyment, *kama*; and spiritual values leading to liberation, *moksha*. A Hindu is expected to follow the strict path of truth, as the Hindu tradition follows the dictum, "*satyamevajayate*" (truth alone triumphs). Hindus are supposed to contest for righteousness by all positive means at their command. Their scriptures counsel: "If you protect righteousness, the righteousness shall protect you." Caring and sharing are the hallmarks of Hinduism and from these stem service to humankind and hospitality to unannounced guests, *atithi*. *Kshama* or forgiveness is Hinduism's cornerstone.

Hindu scriptures speak of certain virtues and qualities to which all followers should aspire, although the emphasis may differ with traditions and sects. They include *Ahimsa* (nonviolence), compassion, tolerance, contentment, hospitality, respect for living beings, austerity, protecting the helpless and less fortunate, truthfulness and honesty, cleanliness and purity, high moral character, and personal reflection (self-observation). For Hindus, however, nonviolence is supreme conduct, *ahimsa paramodharmah*, as all life is divine and sacred. Hindus following the path of nonviolence is reflected in the prevalence of vegetarianism among them. Hinduism today is the most widely practiced and most diverse religion on Earth, with innumerable traditions and sects. The Hindus have unspoken freedom to choose their own path for salvation according to their individual beliefs and temperaments. All their religious practices are accepted, respected, and revered. A Hindu sees the existence of God in all things, living and nonliving. There is some kind of commonality of values among all Hindus.

Hindus believe that Vedas and Agamas are impersonal, *apaurusheya*, and have the highest scriptural authority. There is only one God, an omnipresent, omnipotent, all-pervading Supreme Being, which is also ultimate reality, *Brahman*. Rig Veda (1.64.46), however, adds "*ekamsadvipraabahudhaavadanti*" (the wise may call it with many names). Every individual is governed by the law of cause and effect karma. Georg Feuerstein (2007, p. 21) calls it "law of retribution" or "moral causation," which in his opinion "is an expression of the deep interconnectedness and orderliness of the cosmos." Owing to the cycle of birth and death, all souls go through the process of rebirth unless their karmas are resolved.

Normal Hindu religious practices include simple devotion, austerity, yoga and meditation, selfless service, temple worship, chanting holy hymns, reading scriptures and following guru's guidance, observing festivals and going through various rituals to propitiate deities, and going on pilgrimage. Love, nonviolence, and strict following of good conduct (*dharma*) basically define the Hindu path.

Hindu values and the environment

Hindu teachings clearly realize the importance of preserving the ecological state of the Earth. The Vedas and other scriptures unambiguously enunciate that a Hindu requires reverence for all beings that are in bond to all others and are an expression of divinity itself. Hinduism and ecology are interwoven, as they both follow natural laws. Hinduism has always treated nature not as a source of sustenance but as a source of life. The concept of "*vasudhaivakutumbakam*" declares that all that is alive on this planet belongs to one single family. Unlike the modern concept of progress, which essentially pertains to economic development, the Hindu concept, which is called *mangalya* (collective welfare), is a state where no one has insurmountable problems and the natural, cultural, and social environment is conducive to overall welfare (Misra, 1997). Collective welfare in Hinduism includes all living and even nonliving entities such as mountains, rivers, lakes, and oceans, which are treated as sacred. Thus, reverence for nature is a part of Hindu thought and creates a strong ecologic base.

The law of *karma* is most profound in Hinduism and is supposed to be one of the laws of the mind. It follows simply the principle of cause and effect. If there is an action, its consequences are inevitable. Simply speaking, it is "as you sow, so shall you reap." No one can escape the consequences of an action. Hindus believe that in all situations they have to pay for their karmic dues. Speaking of the massive killing of the animals for human consumption, Georg Feuerstein and Brenda Feuerstein (2007, p. 58) go to the extent of stating, "Our (karmic) debt to the animal kingdom is massive." This tends to prevent Hindus from wrong actions and thus *karma* in effect becomes the law of opportunity where, by following their actions, individuals can grow to their full potential. This is also at the root of the respect that Hindus have for nature. Not an herb is taken from the Mother Earth by a traditional Ayurvedic doctor without asking for forgiveness in special prayers (Bharati, 2010).

The Vedas tell us that whatever happens in the cosmos happens because of Rita – the eternal or cosmic law. In human activity the Rita manifests itself as the moral law (Misra, 1997). The Hindu perspective on the environment laid the foundation of today's ecology on these basis millennia in advance. Rig Veda (6.48.17) commands: "Do not cut the trees because they remove pollution."

There are certain sects in Hindus who are defenders of environment (Dwivedi, 2000, p. 16), and prominent among them is Bishnoi sect whose villages are the greenest in the middle of the Thar Desert in Rajasthan, India. This is a 400-year-old tradition "whose followers adhere to 29 principles including total non-violence and non-violation of all nature" (Bharati, 2010, p. 90). It is perhaps the only community in the world which has given its blood to conserve the environment. T. S. Rukmani (2000, p. 103) places on record that "in 1753 three hundred and sixty three men, women, and children sacrificed their lives protecting their trees by hugging them."

The marvellous *Prithvi Sukta* Hymn to the Earth occurs in the twelfth chapter of the *Atharva Veda* (AV), consisting of 63 verses by Rishi Atharvan who taught about the relation of humans with the Earth (Sohoni, 1991). Values, attitudes, and ideals for the material, intellectual, and spiritual progress of human society are also defined in it (Sohoni, 1991). According to its translator, "The Prithvi Sukta may be regarded as an anthem of the human race ... conveying enlightened philosophy, spiritual thought, acute advice regarding the ideal human relations, deep perception of political dynamics and guidance concerning economic, physical and material processes – all set in a harmonious synthesis, surcharged with exalting purpose" (Sohoni, 1991). The twenty-seventh verse of *Prithvi Sukta* says, "We invoke the Earth upon which foliage and trees are firmly held, unthreatened, the Earth which is equipped with all good things in a stable environment of harmony" (Sohoni, 1991). It is clearly a description of the Earth endowed with all its wealth and harmony. Regarding the evil impact of pollution and the importance of life-giving water, the *Prithvi Sukta*'s thirtieth verse says, "O' Earth, may only pure water flow for our bodies. May all the water on Earth remain pure and unpolluted. May harmful substances be away from us. May only good actions occur at our instance" (Sohoni, 1991).

The importance of environmental ethics in the Hindu scriptures has been repeatedly emphasized. Manu, the Hindu law giver and author of the famed Manusmriti, vehemently defended the environment. Not only the common people but kings and princes accepted this as part of their *raja-dharma* (royal duty). A famous case in point is that of a prince in Rajasthan in the last century, who would tell his officers and people, "If you cut a branch you cut my finger" (Gold, 2000, p. 317). Among Hindus it is common to identify the human body with objects of nature. This kinship shows an inherent respect for all of existence.

Hindu values and sustainable development

Hindu values direct humanity to be judicious and frugal when using any natural resource. Hinduism emphasizes a modest living. Mahatma Gandhi epitomized "simple living and high thinking." Sarasvati stressed, "Neither too much ease nor too many comforts" (1995, p. 118). Ancient Hindu sages realized that the conservation of nature was essential. Had humanity obeyed this command, we would not be knocking today at the gates of hell. As stated earlier, the concept of *vasudhaivakutumbakam* (viewing all life on Earth as belonging to a single family) has been advocated by the Hindus as a way of promoting an ecologically responsible approach to global change (Dwivedi, 2000).

The very first verse of the *Prithvi Sukta* clearly states guidelines for a healthy Earth: "Truth, force of authority and duty, gravitational compulsion, dedication, creative energy, perfect knowledge, and sacrifice: these support and uphold the Earth; may these elements … magnify my field of activity" (Sohoni, 1991). In Hinduism, water is considered a powerful medium for purification. It is also thought to be a source of vigour and energy for our entire existence. There is no religious ritual for Hindus in which water is not used. All Hindu scriptures therefore command that water must be kept pure and its sanctity maintained. Rig Veda (10.9) is dedicated to the life-giving ability of water, not only physically but also spiritually. It is a prayer that a plentiful supply of pure water will always be available.

Sustainability is often presented as a remedy for today's tumultuous world, but Jeffrey Sachs (2004), among others, justifiably raises serious doubts about our ability to support a burgeoning population in the poor countries of the world, and the possibility that economic pressures will not only strain global ecology but also create acute conflicts between nations. Reconciling human needs and wants with the state of the Earth and having the courage to seek a remedy would undoubtedly be the positive choice as well as one compatible with Hindu values.

Let us see what the *Prithvi Sukta* has to say about this in its second verse: "May this Earth ... support all human beings, in all their diversity of endowment, in mutually supportive harmony and prosperity" (Sohoni, 1991). The *Prithvi Sukta* does not stop there. It returns to the topic in its fourteenth verse, AV(12.1.14): "May this Earth so charged with positive force, neutralise that element which impels ill-will, aggressive intention, subjugation of human beings and their elimination" (Sohoni, 1991). Will the powerful coterie of nations hear this message from the Vedas?

Sustainability in contemporary terms is generally understood as material progress without any environmental degradation. Here is a relevant passage from the thirty-fifth verse of the *Pirthvi Sukta*: "O' pure Earth, may that we utilize your soil well (for creative production) without causing you injury or harm and disturbing any vital element in you" (Sohoni, 1991). Again, in its fortieth verse, the *Prithvi Sukta* cautions about our actions: "May our Earth provide us with the wealth we desire, may our effort have proper direction, and may providence also assist us" (Sohoni, 1991). This same Hindu text speaks of the torch bearers who should carry the message of sustainable development. Contrary to the vision of those who derive only fear from the present state of the Earth, the forty-eighth verse of this text, AV(12.1.48), proclaims: "The Earth endures people of all temperaments, good and bad, but the blessings of the Earth are derived by the ones with nobility of mind, following the path of right conduct" (Sohoni, 1991). And finally, in the fifty-sixth verse, the *Prithvi Sukta* clearly lays down what is right for humanity: "O' Earth, in the villages, forests, assemblies, committees and other places on Earth, may what we express always be in accord with you" (Sohoni, 1991). Could there be any better, more sensible way of expressing what we must do for this planet?

The majority of Hindus live in South Asia, but there are also sizable populations throughout the world (Rukmani, 2001). Most Hindus carry with them their values, their culture of tolerance, and try to live in harmony with the majority of their adopted lands. Many immigrant Hindus have created their own sacred rivers, mountains, lakes, and seas and follow their rituals and other spiritual practices in the local settings of their adopted lands. One commonly hears stories of their having done so in Mauritius, Suriname, Guyana, Trinidad, and Fiji. Wherever possible they still use herbs, plants, and, of course, spices in the same way as in India. There is no doubt that the culture and values of the international Hindu community can encourage local communities to appreciate nature as a sacred source of life which we should preserve as best as we can.

Globalization, Hindu values, and the state of the environment

With the invocation of a new global economic order, Hindu values are under great strain. Cracks are appearing in extended families, a hallmark of Hindu values, as their members find greener pastures in faraway places in India and abroad under new economic pressures. The waves of new technologies are bringing their own culture along and are affecting Hindu society even more acutely as the new social norms are at complete variance with the Hindu attitudes. In India, where the Hindus are concentrated in colossal numbers, industrial and infrastructure development have wrought horrors, and large chunks of urban areas and natural systems have sunk into environmental chaos. Economic considerations have taken the upper hand and the environment is obviously the worst casualty, owing largely to poor literacy and scant awareness. Today, the most sacred rivers like the Ganga, Yamuna, and several others, which Hindus were never tired of worshipping, have become gutters. Burgeoning population pressures have made a once self-sufficient food state into nearly an import-based one. The Green Revolution and agriculture based on chemical fertilizers and pesticides have contaminated the soils and dangerously polluted dwindling groundwater reservoirs. India and its proud Hindus face the worst ecological crisis in their history.

Kelly Alley (2000) questions why political and religious leaders cannot come together on such vital issues as the pollution of the Ganga, the holiest river of India. Anil Agarwal (2000, p. 172) also wonders, "Is Hinduism culpable?"; being Hindu is an individualistic religion *dharma* and actions are confined to their own well-being, and therefore the social good (civil community) is lost. This could be happening because of the social, economic or even cultural compulsions in modern times, but the genuine values of Hinduism which teach only universal good, cannot be faulted. One must acknowledge that current serious political and social structures complicate preserving natural systems in accordance with Hindu traditions. Well-meaning actions are often manipulated by opportunistic political parties, and parochial religious groups. Even the most unsuspecting Hindu personalities involved in saving the environment have been dragged into controversies (Sharma, 2002). Political parties and groups are often disingenuous when they take up issues invoking Hindu values; they mostly end up opening an ugly debate on secularism and communalism. In the process, the vital spiritual and religious energy that could have been gainfully utilized to save those natural systems that Hindus always thought sacred is regretfully lost. The other important point is that many of these earnest and genuine religious leaders who talk of preserving the sanctity of rivers and mountains may lack basic scientific knowledge and an awareness of the environment.

Hindu leaders, especially in India, find it impossible to believe that the government and bureaucracy would do much to keep the sacred spaces clean and pure; they are inclined to further their goals on their own initiative, by invoking the grace of God and adopting non-cooperative agitation and passive resistance as taught by Gandhi. Passion and emotional energy, however temporary, could help in a good cause. Alley (2000), however, doubts if any coordinated effort is possible between Hindu leaders, politicians, and environmental activists to preserve sacred spaces, because each group has a limited agenda, a narrow perspective on the problem, and a very different approach to solutions. This problem may arise in other situations around the world when religious tenets and practices are to be used as the instruments of sustainable development. New economic forces, technological culture, political pressures, and the breakup of the social fabric are today adversely affecting Hindu values and attitudes. A serious consequence is that these values cannot play their full role in a new kind of revolution that would preserve the environment.

Hope, possibilities, and opportunities

Before we invoke Hindu values and attitudes as possible instruments in redirecting our efforts for sustainable development policies, should we not ask ourselves whether charity should begin at home? Why is the environmental crisis so serious in the heartland of South Asia, and especially India, where the Hindu population is concentrated? The Indian subcontinent has passed through colossal periods of aggression, colonialism, and exploitation by foreign powers. The last 60 years witnessed the worst kind of communal holocaust, disabling military conflicts and arms races, cross-border incursions, and so-called armed class struggles and terrorism. To these could be added large periods of ineffective political leadership, disastrous economic planning, and an absence of infrastructure, education, and health for the citizens. Corruption and misappropriation of national and social funds almost complete this shabby picture. Obviously ecology became the worst casualty. The only thing that survived was a functional democracy which has proved to be a beacon in this vast area of darkness.

At the global level, there is hope that we can achieve a sustainable way of life in the next half-century if all people, businesses, and governments worldwide commit themselves to the right course of action without delay. But is it possible to achieve the necessary changes in political decision-making, public conscious-ness, and education? The developing countries hold the key. In these countries economic and environmental conditions are desperate, and in spite of campaigns for globalization and economic liberalization, the gap between rich and poor has been widening.

In any model of sustainability, equity and justice must remain paramount. Development must provide not only material comfort but also an enriched human life. The global community must devise new, innovative strategies to attack the vicious cycle of poverty and environmental degradation. Doing so will require that rich countries decrease their consumption. As for the developing world, it must recognize that rising human populations together with the commensurate rise in consumption will cause additional stresses to the finite resources of our planet. For the survival and sustainability of the planet, all nations, societies, and religious communities will need to make sacrifices and forget their differences. Interfaith dialogue is a necessary precursor. Meetings of the world's religious and spiritual leaders at the highest levels have had outcomes that augur a new hope and understanding. Mary Evelyn Tucker and John Grim (2007, p. 6) state that "we are discovering that the human heart is not changed by facts alone but by engaging visions and empowering values." Lynn White Jr concludes that "more science and more technology are not going to get us out of the present ecologic crisis until we find a new religion, or rethink our old one" (1967, p. 155).

It is only apt that we assess the use of Hindu values when creating policies for sustainable development. In the Vedas and other Hindu texts there are detailed accounts of nature and instructions on how to protect it. Educated and competent cadres of Hindu leaders will have to explain to their community and the world at large the relevance of the original spirit of Hindu reverence for nature to save the environment. O. P. Dwivedi (2000) explains how Hindu concepts of eco-care and what he calls *dharmic* ecology could be pragmatically and effectively utilized to create a harmonious environment across the religious and spiritual traditions. In Dwivedi's scheme of things there is no place for religious bigots and parochial elements. He advocates a completely open and absolutely secular approach. Following Dwivedi and other Hindu thinkers, it is possible to suggest some steps for using Hindu ecological philosophy and values to reduce the damage done to our environment.

Hindu leaders should take the initiative in saving the green Earth in a transparent and sincere manner. Secular institutions should be assisted in their efforts to pursue the goals of sustainable development without the impression of a hidden agenda. While political and social discussions could create an amicable world, the emphasis should only be on the universal values (Hindu or otherwise), so that efforts to save the Earth will be inclusionary. Most sincere and influential Hindu leaders, in tandem with like-minded leaders from other faiths, could take up the initiative to create a global family in the true spirit of *vasudhaivakutumbakam*, and to serve all beings equally and without any reservation (*sarva-bhuta-hiteratah*).

If Hindu dharmic values are propagated and practiced as taught by the scriptures, the causes of environmental degradation – greed, exploitation, inequality, poverty – will gradually disappear. A case in point is the work of Dr A. P. J. Abdul Kalam, the former president of India, an observant Muslim and an avid reader of Hindu scriptures, who cites cultural values to inspire the young generation of his country to participate in projects which will clean the environment. If similar projects happen everywhere through value-based voluntary work, small clean and green areas will eventually become larger, giving a new dimension to the environmental movement and sustainable development. M. S. Swaminathan (2002), the father of India's Green Revolution, counsels that India should draw on the wisdom of the past in order to solve the problems of today. In his view, the ancient Indian messages of "*antyodaya*" (starting the development process with the poorest person) and "*sarvodaya*" (social inclusiveness for all on an equitable basis) offer the only hope for future.

Hindus could be part of an active worldwide movement, strictly following Gandhian lines in preserving and protecting sacred spaces as well as places of ecological, historical, cultural, and spiritual importance. This is now possible as many Hindu leaders are respected and listened to around the world. The Hindu diaspora may play a significant role in this process. Sunderlal Bahuguna, a Gandhian activist and famed progenitor of the Chipko Movement in the Himalayas, is well known for his objection to the selling of natural resources, which were once revered as sacred. Do we have the courage to go against this onslaught and opt for alternative ways to keep the Earth going and green? Or do we wait for the day when the culture of technology and markets will learn a new and different lesson in a distant future when it is already too late?

The Indic environmental ethos views life as a gift of togetherness, mutual accommodation, and interdependence (Singhvi, 1995). If these values are to play a meaningful role in implementing sustainable development, then spirituality, morality, and universality will be its guiding lights.

Acknowledgments

I am deeply indebted to Dr Swami Veda Bharati, Spiritual Head of Swami Rama Sadhaka Grama, Rishikesh, and Chancellor of the HIHT (Himalayan Institute Hospital Trust) University, Dehradun, India, and Ir. Manish Dixit of Contexcity BV, Delft, the Netherlands, for critically reviewing the manuscript, and to Dr Swami Veda Bharati for the use of his personal research library. My grateful thanks go to Datuk Rajah Indran, Advisor for Biology Conservation of the University Malaysia Sabah, Malaysia, for his helpful suggestions.

References

Agarwal, A. 2000. Can Hindu Beliefs and Values Help India Meet Its Ecological Crisis? In *Hinduism and Ecology*. Eds. C. K. Chappel, and M. E. Tucker. Cambridge, Mass.: Harvard University Press, pp. 165–79.

Alley, K. D. 2000. Separate Domains: Hinduism, Politics, and Environmental Pollution. In C. K. Chappel, and M. E. Tucker. Eds. *Hinduism and Ecology*. Cambridge, Mass.: Harvard University Press, pp. 355–387.

Bharati, Swami Veda. 2010. *What is Right with the World: Human Urge for Peace*. Rishikesh, India: Ahymsin Publishers.

Dwivedi, O. P. 2000. Dharmic Ecology. In *Hinduism and Ecology*. Eds. C. K. Chappel, and M. E. Tucker. Cambridge, Mass.: Harvard University Press, pp. 3–22.

Feuerstein, G. 2007. *Yoga Morality*. Prescott, Ariz.: Hohm Press.

Feuerstein, G., and B. Feuerstein. 2007. *Green Yoga*. Saskatchewan, Can.: Traditional Yoga Studies.

Frawley, D. 1992. *From the River of Heaven: Hindu and Vedic Knowledge for the Modern Age*. Delhi: Motilal Banarasidass.

Frawley, D. 2001. *Hinduism and the Clash of Civilization*. New Delhi: Voice of India.

Gold, A. G. 2000. If You Cut a Branch You Cut My Finger: Court, Forest, and Environmental Ethics in Rajasthan. In *Hinduism and Ecology*. Eds. C. K. Chappel, and M. E. Tucker. Cambridge, Mass.: Harvard University Press, pp. 317–36.

Misra, R. P. 1997. The Indian World-view and Environmental Crisis. In *Integration of Endogenous Cultural Dimension into Development*. Ed. B. Saraswati. New Delhi: Indira Gandhi National Centre for the Arts. Retrieved on January 22nd, 2008, from http://ignca.nic.in/cd_05016.htm.

Rukmani, T. S. 2000. Literary Foundations for an Ecological Aesthetic: Dharma, Ayurveda, the Arts and Abhijnansakuntalam. In *Hinduism and Ecology*. Eds. C. K. Chappel, and M. E. Tucker. Cambridge, Mass.: Harvard University Press, pp. 101–25.

Rukmani, T. S., ed. 2001. *Hindu Diaspora: Global Perspective*. New Delhi: Munshiram Manoharlal.

Sachs, J. D. 2004. Sustainable Development. *Science* 304 (5671) p. 649.

Sarasvati, C. S. 1995. *Hindu Dharma: The Universal Way of Life*. Bombay: BharatiyaVidyaBhawan.

Seshagiri Rao, K. L. 2000. The Five Great Elements (Panchamahabhuta): An Ecological Perspective. In *Hinduism and Ecology*. Eds. C. K. Chappel, and M. E. Tucker. Cambridge, Mass.: Harvard University Press, pp. 23–38.

Sharma, M. 2002 *Saffronising Green*, Seminar. 516. Retrieved on November 29th, 2007, from http://www.india-seminar.com/2002/516/516%20mukul%20sharma.htm.

Singhvi, L. M. 1995. *Environmental Wisdom in Ancient India*. The Summit on Religions and Conservation, Atami, Japan, 7 April. Retrieved on March 22nd, 2007, from http://www.ecomall.com/greenshopping/eastgreen2.htm.

Sohoni, S. S. 1991. *Hymn to the Earth: The Prithvi Sukta*. New Delhi: Sterling Publishers.

Swaminathan, M. S. 2002. July–Sept. How Green Will Our Earth Be? *Life Positive Plus* 1(1), p. 72.

Tucker, M.E., and J. Grim. 2007. Daring to Dream: Religion to the Future of the Earth. In R. R. Ruether. Ed. *Reflections: A Journal of Yale Divinity School* Spring. 4(9). Retrieved on June 13th, 2012, from http://www.yale.edu/reflections/leadstory.pdf .

White Jr, L. 1967. The Historical Roots of Our Ecological Crisis. *Science* 155(3767), pp. 1203–7.

12 The Jewish tradition of stewardship

David Patterson

In the Hebrew Scriptures that form the foundation of the Jewish tradition, it is written, "The earth is the Lord's, and all that is in it; the world, and all who dwell in it" (Psalms 24:1). In the same Scriptures, however, we read, "The heavens belong to the Lord; the earth He gave to humanity" (Psalms 115:16). A contradiction? Not at all, at least not from the standpoint of Jewish tradition. The assertion that the earth belongs to the Holy One derives from the teaching that the earth and everything in it, all of its fruits, come into being through the never-ending utterance of the Creator. Therefore, despite our labor to reap the harvest from the land, when we place a piece of bread in our mouths, we say a blessing acknowledging God as *hamotzi lechem min ha-aretz*, that is, as the One "who brings forth bread from the earth." The Israelites may have gathered the manna from the earth, but it came from heaven, that is, from the dimension of height that belongs to the One God, as it is written: "This is the bread that the Lord has given you to eat" (Exodus 16:15). Still, it is we who must till the soil, reap the harvest, and attend to the land.

Hence, there is no contradiction between the two verses from the Psalms: the height of the heavens belongs to God, while the stewardship of the earth belongs to humanity. This height of the Holy One is a metaphysical height; it is what makes our stewardship of the earth matter, before any decision or action on our part. From a Jewish perspective, this stewardship is rooted in a covenant between the Creator and the human being who, through that covenant, is a partner in the act of creation. Indeed, the very movement of creation implies such a covenant: as the thirteenth-century sage Nachmanides has noted, the Hebrew words for "covenant" and "created," *brit* and *bara*, are cognates (Nachmanides, 1971, p. 112). The covenant of creation, moreover, is made of commandments (*mitzvot*), including the commandments regarding the care of this world. While some may suppose that the issue of stewardship is a modern one, in the Jewish tradition it is as old as creation itself.

In the Torah, the most fundamental commandment on stewardship comes with the creation of the first human being, suggesting that stewardship lies at the core of the reason for our existence: "God created man in His own image, in the image of God He created him, male and female He created them. And God blessed them and said to them, be fruitful and multiply; fill the earth and subdue it, and rule over the fish of the sea, the birds of the heavens, and every living thing that moves upon the earth" (Genesis, 1:27–28). Because the commandment to rule the earth is from the Holy One, it is a commandment not merely to rule but to sanctify and elevate the earth. For the fulfillment of a commandment establishes a connection between God and His creation; indeed, the root of the Hebrew word for "commandment," *mitzvah*, is *tzavta*, which means "connection." Only the human being created in the image of the Holy One can connect the Creator with His creation through the fulfillment of the commandments. Much more than a matter of caring for the environment, stewardship is a means of connecting with the Creator.

Fulfilling the commandment of stewardship, the human being rules over the earth in such a way as to affirm the sanctity of the earth and all its creatures. Thus, in establishing dominion over the earth, the human being attains a vertical dimension and, with it, human dignity. Rabbi Joseph Soloveitchik explains "there is no dignity without responsibility ... Only when man rises to the heights of freedom of action and creativity of mind does he begin to implement the mandate of dignified responsibility entrusted to him by his Maker" (Soloveitchik, 1965, p. 16). The word for "responsibility" in Hebrew is *achariyut*; its root is the word *acher*, which means "other." The responsibility that defines dignity therefore entails an orientation toward something higher than oneself, toward another, both human and Divine, for the sake of whom we take on the stewardship of the earth. The commandment to rule over the earth, then, implies a prohibition against profiteering, exploitation, and other enterprises that treat the earth as if it were nothing more than the raw material we tap to suit our personal desires, rather than a Divine creation subject to Divine commandment. Dominion does not mean domination. From a Jewish standpoint, there is far more at stake in our environmental stewardship; redemption itself hangs in the balance.

Redemption is nearest when God is most manifest; the key to the manifestation of God, according to Jewish tradition, is adherence to His commandments. In modern and postmodern times, having grown deaf to the Divine commandment, we have shoved God farther than ever into obscurity. If there is no commanding Voice behind our treatment of humanity and the earth we share, there is no reason to act in any manner except the one that suits us. The poisoning of our planet is the result of much more than mere greed; it is the outcome of a philosophical stance that situates the self at the center of all reality. We have leveled all of creation into a sameness, so that a human being has no more inherent value than an animal. The result is a confusion of tongues in the discourse surrounding environmental stewardship.

The postmodern problem of stewardship

Much of postmodern thinking is beyond parody, and there is nothing humorous about the threat of postmodernism to environmental stewardship. The notion of a Divinely commanded stewardship so central to the Jewish tradition and to the responsible care of the earth is alien to postmodern thought. Many postmodern thinkers are known for their environmental advocacy. Peter Singer asserts "The only thing that distinguishes the infant from the animal in the eyes of those who claim it has a 'right to life,' is that it is, biologically, a member of the species *Homo sapiens*, whereas chimpanzees, dogs, and pigs are not" (Singer, 2001, p. 20). Singer determines that "speciesism" is ethically wrong, since all living things should be considered equal. Singer blames Judaism for the unfounded "privileging" of the human being. The "emphasis on the sanctity of every human life," he correctly points out, comes from "the Hebrew view of creation" (Singer, 1996, p. 165). In contrast to the Hebrew belief, he proposes a view based on "reason": "Only those who prefer religious faith to beliefs based on reasoning and evidence can still maintain that the human species is the darling of the entire universe" (Singer, 2001, pp. 206–7). Reason-based beliefs cannot determine anything sacred or holy about animals or the environment. Thus, Singer frees himself (and human beings) from the absolute commandment of stewardship; Singer frees himself to act in any manner that suits him.

The Jewish tradition, by contrast, avows the sanctity of all human life over animal life, so that one may destroy the amoeba to save a human being while at the same time prohibiting the extermination of another people. Only with this hierarchy, and not with the postmodern leveling of all things into the same thing, can we understand both care for the environment and care for humanity in terms of an absolute injunction. Only by appealing to the Divine commandment can we respond to the questions of "Why?" and "In the name of what?" with regard to our care of the environment. From a traditional Jewish viewpoint, the oft-touted "harmony with nature" is the opposite of the steward-ship of nature. Why? Because in nature only the fit survive, in a never-ending power struggle. Once the human being is considered part of nature, and not the steward of nature, he or she is justified by power alone. Which means that nei-ther the oppressor nor the polluter can be in the wrong. According to Martin Heidegger, "The expression 'will to power' designates the basic character of beings; any being which is, insofar as it is, is will to power" (Heidegger, 1979, p. 18). From a Jewish standpoint, and contrary to postmodernism, true steward-ship lies in a dominion over nature expressive of our servitude to the Creator and to His children. In other words, stewardship is possible only where the stronger party comes to the aid of the weaker. Reducing humanity to a species and the human being to a specimen, postmodern thinking plays into the hands of a totalitarianism grounded in the rule of might over nature as well as over humanity.

From a postmodern standpoint, the value of a human being is relative to a value determined by cultural contexts and natural accidents, such as race, class, and gender. It may lie in power or wealth, in anything that makes one person "feel good" about another or, more importantly, about himself. But because all these traits are rooted in contingencies, the postmodern human being, as well as nature itself, can have only a contingent value. Therefore, in postmodern consciousness there are no absolute demands: we treat both human beings and animals in any way we please. As we have seen, in matters of "rights," postmodernists such as

Singer place animals in the same category as human beings; and then are shocked when human beings are treated like animals.

Postmodernists no longer hear the commanding Voice that rises up from the earth and all that is in it to command us to watch over and care for God's creation. Instead we listen to the sounds of wolves and whales and ocean waves, as we curl up in the illusion that we are "communing with nature." In order to hear the commandment to attend to nature, as well as to the outcry of our neighbor, we must attend to the Voice that speaks from beyond nature, and not to the "sounds of nature." Worship of nature is the idolatry that must, from a Jewish perspective, be opposed. Once made into an idol, nature is rendered mute. And we are rendered deaf. One thing needed in the project of environmental stewardship is a capacity for hearing the commanding Voice of the God of nature.

The God of nature in Jewish tradition

According to Maimonides's *Moreh Nevuchim* 1:51, Jewish tradition divides ontological reality into four components: mineral (*domeh*, literally "silent"), vegetable (*tzomeach*, "that which grows"), animal (*chai*, meaning "alive"), and human being (*medaber*, that is, a "speaking being"). This sequence from silent being to speaking being characterizes the Jewish understanding of creation: all that is derives its being from Divine utterance. Inanimate matter is called *domeh* not because God is silent but because at that level of creation, the Divine utterance is most muted. Since the human being is created in the image and the likeness of the Holy One Himself, God speaks loudest through the summons and the plea of the humanity around us. And because the human being is a speaking being, a human being is capable of response – is "response-able" or responsible – for the beings that do not attain the level of speech. Deuteronomy 8:3 tells us: "Man lives not by bread alone, but by every utterance from the mouth of God does man live." According to Rabbi Steinsaltz, it means that "man does not live only from the calories provided by bread, but from Divine energy. Superficially I am only eating matter, however, in fact I am ingesting language, because the raw material of bread is the Divine word" (Steinsaltz and Eisenberg, 2000, p. 147). What is said of bread may be said of every atom of nature. Instilled with something that exceeds its ontological reality, the physical is also metaphysical; the material is also spiritual. Every "item" is also a "vessel" of the supernal Voice, by which all things exist and through which we are commanded to the stewardship of all things. The God of nature speaks in the imperative: the Voice that creates nature also commands the human being to care for nature. For both nature and the human being are vehicles of the Divine presence.

What, then, does Jewish tradition teach about the God of nature? The Torah begins with: "*Bereshit bara Elokim ...*" ("In the beginning *Elokim* created ..."). Hence, Jewish tradition associates God as *Elokim* according to gematria (a method of interpretation based on numerical values of Hebrew letters), *Elokim* has the same numerical value as *hateva*, which is "[the] nature" or physical reality (Horowitz, 1993). Therefore in the aspect of *Elokim*, who is the Creator of heaven and earth, God and nature are of a piece. Jewish teaching is that nature teems, as it were, with the Divine sparks of the Creator's ongoing utterance (see, for example, Zohar I, 19b). Furthermore, the word *teva* refers to something deeply imprinted into an object; a coin imprinted with an image, for example, is a *matbea* (a cognate of *teva*). Just so, nature is imprinted with *Elokim*, as the body is imprinted with the soul. Says the Midrash, "just as the Holy One, blessed be He, bears His world, so the soul bears all the body" (Pirke de Rabbi Eliezer 34). Just as the body is saturated with the soul, so is nature saturated with God.

Although nature overflows with the Divine Presence, it is, as we have seen, a silent presence. The *neshamah* that makes the human being a speaking being – the breath upon which the word vibrates – is what enables humanity to reign over a silent nature as a means of serving the God of nature. Only a speaking being can have dominion over the earth. Because only one who has a capacity for utterance can affect the creation made of Divine utterance. And only one who can affect creation faces the task of becoming more than he is, better than he is, through his stewardship of nature.

According to Jewish tradition, environmental stewardship thus matters not merely because it is commanded; rather, it is commanded because our care for the environment and the creatures of nature affects all of creation (Chaim, 1992, p. 24). According to Jewish tradition, animals have no rights to any sort of treatment; rather, human beings, as speaking and therefore responsible beings, are commanded to treat animals with a certain consideration and sensitivity. Hence, the Jewish prohibitions against cruelty to animals. So when Abraham asked Shem why God preserved their lives, Shem explained that it was because they stayed up all night every night feeding the animals (Midrash Shochar Tov 37:1; Weissman, 1980, p. 157). From the perspective of Jewish tradition, it is because God commands us concerning a stewardship of animals, and not because animals have "natural rights," (Deuteronomy 22:10, 25:4). Indeed, without the commandment to extend Sabbath observance to resting one's animals, animals may suffer any cruelty. For the Sabbath is precisely the insertion of the Eternal One into His temporal creation to sanctify creation by commanding His children with regard to the treatment of His creation.

Thus, in the Jewish tradition there is a bond between the God whose Name is Sabbath (see Zohar II, 88b) and the God of nature. As the Maharal of Prague has taught, the six days of Creation correspond to the six directions of physical space: what was created in the first six days was the physical, ontological reality of the natural world. The seventh day, however, transcends the other six to give them meaning: it is the dimension of the holy (Peli, 1988, pp. 11–12). From the Jewish perspective, Sabbath observance is the key to kindness to animals, clean air, and pure water. The Sabbath is to time what the human being is to nature. Just as time derives its meaning from the Sabbath, so nature derives its meaning from the human being who adheres to the Divine commandment to watch over all of creation.

Our stewardship includes more than the treatment of animals. The Torah, for example, commands us to allow the land to rest and lie fallow every seventh year (Leviticus 25:4) and prohibits the destruction of fruit-bearing plants (e.g. Deuteronomy 20:19). It contains laws concerning what may be planted in a given tract of land (Leviticus 19:19), as well as laws that determine when we may gather fruit from a tree (Leviticus 19:23–25). Significantly, the chapter from Leviticus where we find the latter two commandments also includes commandments regarding the treatment of other human beings, particularly our elders (Leviticus 19:32) and the stranger who dwells among us (Leviticus 19:33–34). This is no coincidence: once again we find that our responsibility for how we treat the earth is tied to our responsibility for how we treat our fellow human being. Further, the laws of Torah that pertain to the land pertain specifically to the Holy Land. It turns out that the Jewish tradition surrounding the Holy Land is central to its tradition of stewardship.

Where Jewish tradition is concerned, the holiness of any land begins with the holiness of the Holy Land. If the Land of Israel (*Eretz Yisrael*) is not the Holy Land, then all the religious traditions that rest upon the biblical testimony rest upon an illusion. Which means: if there is no Holy Land, then no land is holy. Because the Land of Israel is holy, Jewish tradition has a whole range of commandments concerning the treatment of the Holy Land, commandments that imply a certain holiness about all of the earth. Just as the Jewish people are chosen to attest to the chosenness of every human being, so is *Eretz Yisrael* deemed holy to attest to the holiness of all of nature. In keeping with the gravity and the depth of stewardship that belongs to such a testimony, the first of the six orders of the Talmud is *Zearim*, which concerns our treatment of the earth in the process of planting and harvesting the fruits of the earth. As the first order in the Talmud, it is the one most fundamental to our existence in this world. The holiness of the Holy Land derives neither from its history nor from its shrines but from the divine commandments concerning the stewardship of the land, from the *mitzvot*, which as we have seen are not just "commandments" but also "connections" between God and the land.

Stewardship lies precisely in this accountability before the Creator who entrusts His creation to our care – before the Creator called *Elokim*. One must think in Jewish terms to determine these connections that join together God, nature, and the human being. As Creator, God brings the earth into being through the word, and God's word is Torah. Therefore, to hear the Voice that sustains nature – the Voice that speaks both from within and from beyond nature – is to hear Torah, which includes both the stewardship of nature and service to humanity. Judaism teaches that the human soul, like nature, is made of God's utterance: the soul is made of Torah (Steinsaltz, 1989, p. 32). The connection between the soul and nature as utterances of God can be seen in the linkage between *adam* and *adamah*, between the "human being" and the "earth." Thus, we realize more profoundly the definitive interweaving of our relation to the earth, the *adamah*, and our relation to other human beings, the *adam*. Our stewardship over the earth is meaningless without a care for the other human being. Since both are made of Torah, the poisoning of the earth is more than a pollution that may pose a health hazard – it is an act of desecration that threatens the soul.

From the Jewish point of view, nature is a means of sanctification. Earth, air, and water harbor a holy fire that can be released when put to proper use, as prescribed in the Torah. The idea is not to be at one with nature – it is to be at one with Torah. We can use wood, for example, to make a Holy Ark for the Torah scrolls, or we can use it to make a weapon. We can use ink to write a Torah scroll, or we can use it to sign a deportation order. We can transform the food we eat into acts of loving kindness or into acts of violence. Whichever action we choose, we either release the divine sparks hidden in the natural world or we veil them. Either way we create angels, according to the Talmud, for good or for evil (see Avot 4:11; Chagigah 41a). We have no ethical relation to nature. But we do have a sacred obligation, that is, a commanded relation. Our treatment of nature is a matter of manifesting holiness in the world. What connects each to the other is the Torah that constitutes both.

The Torah is made of commandments and the soul is made of Torah, the soul is made of commandments. Therefore, when we violate a commandment of Torah, we damage the soul. And since, like the soul, nature is made of Torah, our violation of nature also damages the soul. Thus, according to Jewish tradition, our every action either elevates or desecrates all of creation on all levels, both physical and spiritual. We refrain from polluting nature not only because of the potential harm to human life but also because pollution of the earth obstructs the view of the heavens. Which is to say: it blocks the channeling of holiness into the world. Thus, Jewish "environmentalism" is not simply about putting an end to logging or saving the white owl; it is about elevating the material and natural environment to release God's hidden holiness into the world. And how is the world, including nature itself, elevated? Through the Divine commandments of Torah.

The stake in stewardship

The talmudic sages teach that since the destruction of the Temple, which is the symbol of God's dwelling in the world, the table where guests sit in our home has taken the place of the altar (Menachot 97a; Chagigah 27a). For the host is always a host to someone who, in a sense, is a stranger, no matter how well we know the one whom we invite to our table. And God too is a stranger in this world. Like the Holy One, the guest is always from elsewhere; therefore we must make him feel at home, just as we must make the Holy One feel "at home" if we are to fulfill the purpose of creation. In fact, our hospitality toward a fellow human being is precisely how we make the Holy One feel at home, as it is written in the Mekilta: "When one welcomes his fellow man, it is considered as if he had welcomed the Divine Presence" (Mekilta, Amalek). That is why we must refine ores, fell trees, build roads, develop fuels, weave cloth, plant crops, build fires, and do everything else required to lay a table for our fellow human beings. We elevate all these things from the earth by dwelling upon the earth, and dwelling upon the earth requires the triumph over nature. To be turned over to a stark, pristine nature is to be rendered hungry and homeless, left to the mercy of the wilderness.

Our choice

Whichever action we choose, to be at one with nature or to be at one with Torah, we make a choice between life rooted in goodness and death rooted in evil. Like the Torah itself (see Deuteronomy 30:15), the Voice that speaks from within and from beyond nature summons us to choose life. The environmentalist movements reminiscent of Heidegger's and Singer's thinking would eliminate the dimension of height and hierarchy and thus level the human being to the status of all natural beings. So leveled, chickens cooped up for slaughter are easily compared to Jews crammed into gas chambers. So leveled, the human being has no obligation to nature or to anything else. For only a higher being can be obligated in relation to a lower being. And only a being who is higher than nature can be a steward of nature. At stake is far more than a clean environment: at stake is the life of the soul.

References

Chaim, C. 1992. *Let There Be Light*. Trans. R. Blumberg. Jerusalem: Feldheim.

Heidegger, M. 1979. *Will to Power as Art, Nietzsche, vol. 1*. Trans D. Krell. San Francisco: Harper and Row.

Horowitz, I. 1993. *Shnei Luchot HaBrit*. Jerusalem: Kolel Avrekhim HaTotzaat Sefarim.

Nachmanides. 1971. *Commentary on the Torah. vol. 1*. Trans. C. B. Chavel. New York: Shilo.

Peli, P. H. 1988. *The Jewish Sabbath: A Renewed Encounter*. New York: Schocken.

Singer, P. 1996. *Rethinking Life and Death: The Collapse of Our Traditional Ethics*. New York: St. Martin's.

Singer, P. 2001. *Animal Liberation*. New York: Harper Perennial.

Soloveitchik, J. 1965. *The Lonely Man of Faith*. Northvale, NJ: Jason Aronson.

Steinsaltz, A. 1989. *The Sustaining Utterance: Discourses on Chasidic Thought*. Trans. Y. Hanegbi. Northvale, NJ: Jason Aronson.

Steinsaltz, A. and Eisenberg, J. 2000. *The Seven Lights: On the Major Jewish Festivals*. Northvale, NJ: Jason Aronson.

Weissman, M., ed. 1980. *The Midrash Says, vol. 1*. Brooklyn, NY: Bnay Yakov.

13 Christian stewardship

Fred Van Dyke

The definition of sustainable development, first offered in *Our Common Future*, is "meeting the needs of the present generation without compromising the ability of future generations to meet their own needs" (World Commission on Environment and Development, 1987). Christianity founded on fundamental tenets to "love your neighbor as yourself" (Leviticus 19:18) and to "treat people the same way you want them to treat you" (Matthew 7:12) would seem to be an obvious resource in establishing moral and ethical warrant for considering future generations as our "neighbors," and giving attention and concern to their rights and welfare. Sustainable development is founded on the principle of identifying and meeting real human needs, while simultaneously prescribing and submitting to self-imposed limits on resource consumption and the use of technologies that harm the environment. In these goals, Christianity shares a view of human beings as a species uniquely created and valued by God, made "in His image" as his personal representative to creation (Genesis 1:26), at the same time prescribing an attitude to material possessions and resource consumption marked by restraint, frugality, and contentment with what one has (I Timothy 6:6–11), supported by the hope of a transgenerational future community living under the rule of God (I Thessalonians 4:13–18; Revelation 21:1–7). The major tenets of Christian belief speak to fundamental questions of sustainable development and conservation. Christian belief and behavior arise from four normative sources: the Bible, theology, historical Christian tradition, and the church. These compartments are not absolute, and their boundaries are semipermeable. To examine the relationship between Christian belief and environmental stewardship one has to consider all four.

Lynn White Jr identified the Judeo-Christian tradition, and especially western Christianity, as the underlying cause of the emerging environmental crisis (White Jr, 1967). White asserted that the Judeo-Christian tradition taught that nature had no reason to exist except to serve human beings. Christianity, in White's view, established a dualism of humanity and nature and taught that "it is God's will that man exploit nature for his proper ends" (White Jr, 1967, p. 1205). White Jr's essay became one of the most influential works of its generation. *Historical Roots* by White Jr, republished widely in the 1970s, became a staple in discussions of ecological ethics (Krebs, 1972). The Judeo-Christian tradition was vilified from landscape architecture (McHarg, 1969) to pollution and species extinctions (Ehrlich and Harriman, 1971).

Much has changed in the interpretation of the Judeo-Christian tradition. By the 1990s, Baird Callicott was explaining "the Judeo-Christian Stewardship Environmental Ethic is especially elegant and powerful. It also exquisitely matches the requirements of conservation biology" (Callicott, 1994, p. 36). The foundation of this perceptual transformation has been a re-examination and reapplication of the historic teachings of the Scripture and the church.

God, humans, and nature

The two oldest statements of Christian faith, the Apostles' and Nicene Creeds, begin: "I believe in God, the Father Almighty, Maker of heaven and Earth." Genesis 1 opens the biblical story with an account of creation that is singular in its essential points compared to other creation narratives of its time. First, God exists independent of nature and is the creator of it, not vice versa. God molds a chaotic nature into an orderly cosmos characterized by establishing natural functions. Unlike in the creation stories, there is no conflict between God and nature in Genesis 1. The creation is derived from God and separate from him. Nature is not divine, and its entities and processes are not objects of worship. Although nature is not divine, every part of it is repeatedly declared to be "good" by God, giving matter a derived intrinsic goodness. For the Jews, God revealed himself to them and could not be manipulated because God alone was divine. The Jews regarded the natural world with greater respect and care, receiving it as a trust to them from God. Living creatures, imbued with intrinsic goodness pursued their own ends and purposes. According to Michael Northcott, Thomas Aquinas taught: "each and every creature tends toward this – that it may participate in the Creator and be assimilated to the Creator insofar as it is able." And in this context, "God deliberately brings about multitude and distinction in order that the divine goodness may be brought forth and shared in many measures. There is beauty in the very diversity." Northcott continues "God not only causes the universe to come into being but he is the origin of the purpose which every kind of being pursues in the course of its life, which is why each purpose which is pursued according to nature can be described as inherently good and right" (Northcutt, 1996, pp. 227–29).

Genesis 1 establishes the "goodness" of all created things, humans are a special "kind" of creature, different from all others as God says, "Let us make man in our image, after our likeness, and let them rule over the fish of the sea and over the birds of the sky and over the cattle and over all the earth, and over every creeping thing that creeps on the earth" (Genesis 1:26). Christian teaching affirms that nature is good, but it also affirms that humans rule over nature as a representative of God to nature; that is what it means to be made in the "image" of God. This doctrine is part of the foundation of Christian belief that nature is good, and that humans are uniquely responsible for its care. If, however, these doctrines are misunderstood, they can justify the abuse of nature. Human beings rule over nature because nature is not "sacred nature." This allows for a sharp distinction between God and nature (Passmore, 1974, p. 9).

White Jr focused on Genesis's mandate for humans to "rule and subdue" the Earth (Genesis 1:28). Much of modern environmental ethics, such as Aldo Leopold's the land ethic, are designed to correct this misunderstanding of that mandate. Leopold wrote, "A land ethic changes the role of Homo sapiens from conqueror of the land community to plain member and citizen of it. It implies respect for his fellow-members and also respect for the community as such" (1966, p. 240). The idea that humans are to be the "conqueror" of nature is not a logical consequence of Christian teaching

However, as western Christian belief and practice developed, two interpretations of the Genesis mandate emerged. The conservative understanding placed emphasis not on humans transforming nature but on humans transforming themselves to the realities of God and the world he had created. In this view, attempts to transform nature were acts of impiety and violations of the rights of God. As late as the sixteenth century, a Spanish commission under the reign of Philip II rejected proposals for making two rivers navigable because "if God had so willed that these rivers should be navigable, then he would have made them so with a single word … It would be a bold infringement of the rights of Providence if human hands were to venture to try to improve what God for unfathomable reasons has left unfinished" (quoted in Schillebeeckx, 1968, p. 55). In this conservative strain, nature was not to be treated as sacred, but it was to be respected by being left alone.

The "radical" view exemplified by Sir Francis Bacon saying that "knowledge is power." This view rested on the logic that everything was for human use; humans could modify nature as they chose. The "knowledge" to which Bacon referred was the knowledge of science and the art of technological application. The "power" he aspired to was power over nature. Bacon hoped science and technology would be used in the name of God to restore to humanity the dominion they had held over nature before the Fall (Genesis 3). "It is a restitution and reinvesting (in great part)," wrote Bacon, "of man to the sovereignty and power (for whatsoever he shall be able to call the creatures by their true names [i.e. understand them scientifically] he shall again command them) which he had in his first state of creation" (cited in Passmore 1974, p. 19). Science and technology thus held the promise that it could restore humans to the position they had held before the Fall. Bacon was espousing a Christian heresy, and Bacon's error was to allow science and technology, rather than direct human effort, to restore humanity to an unfallen condition. Although his views were not Christian, Bacon expressed his ideas in theological terms. And this identification has supported the accusation that Christian beliefs about nature were responsible for environmental destruction.

Ruling and subduing: taking human responsibility seriously

The conservative view of the human relationship to nature is deeply rooted in biblical construct to "rule" in the kingdom of God. The biblical meaning of "to rule" is far different from its worldly connotation. God instructed Moses regarding the conduct of their king to the Israelites: "he shall not multiply horses for himself, … nor shall he greatly increase silver and gold for himself." The instructions continue with the admonition that the king's first duty is to write out a copy of the Law in the presence of the priests, and then to read and meditate on it daily "that he may learn to fear the Lord his God, by carefully observing all the words of the Law and these statutes." Jesus was even more explicit: "whoever wishes to become great among you must be your servant, and whoever wishes to be first among you shall be your slave" (Matthew 20:25–27). This perspective is consistent with the instructions given to Adam: "The Lord God planted a garden toward the east, in Eden, and there he placed the man whom he had formed … Then the Lord God took the man and put him into the Garden of Eden to cultivate it and to keep it" (Genesis 2:8, 15).

The verbs rendered here as "cultivate" and "keep" are elsewhere usually translated as "serve" and "protect." They are sacred expressions of service to God, not merely agricultural tasks for the purpose of sustenance. The words of Genesis 2:15 express the fact that in Eden, God created a "sacred space" and installed man as its priest (Walton, 2001, p. 196). Thus, the correct understanding of the text is not that the world was created for humans but that humans were created for the world. Made in the image of God, Christians have, historically, believed that human beings are both uniquely authorized and empowered for the duties of stewardship, and therefore must take such responsibilities seriously. These ideas are expressed repeatedly in the historical teachings of the church. For example, the Swiss reformer John Calvin seems to implicitly understand this definition of how to "rule" over nature and also, in a surprisingly modern way, seems to grasp the concept of "sustainability" and exalt it to the level of Christian virtue and duty: "Let him who possesses a field, so partake of its yearly fruits, that he may not suffer the ground to be injured by his negligence; but let him endeavor to hand it down to posterity as he received it" (cited in Young, 1994, p. 40). Such instruction should have led Christians to develop a theologically well-grounded environmental ethic. Unfortunately, this has not been the case, as most Christian traditions forgot to display the characteristics of Christ's service when in positions of authority.

Nonhuman creatures as moral subjects: the diversity of life and the Trinity

Christians believe that individually created "things" are to be perceived as good, and that their collective diversity is a condition to be esteemed and valued. After the flood, God institutes a covenant of protection. Nonhuman species are explicitly named as the objects of God's concern and the beneficiaries of his protection: "I will remember my covenant between me and you and all living creatures of every kind. Never again will the waters become a flood to destroy all life" (Genesis 9:15). In Exodus and Leviticus, God institutes a pattern of rest for the land (Leviticus 25:2, 25:23). God's ownership of the land was enforced through the practice of "Jubilee." Every 50 years property acquired by individuals had to be returned to the former owners. Thus, land could not be accumulated indefinitely as a possession of the wealthy.

Although the Bible makes it clear that nature is not divine, it states just as clearly that nature is an active and explicit witness to God's power and attributes:

> The heavens are telling the glory of God; and their expanse is declaring the work of His hands. Day to day pours forth speech, and night to night reveals knowledge. There is no speech nor are there words; their voice is not heard. Their line has gone out through all the Earth, and their utterances to the end of the world.
>
> (Psalm 19:1–4)

> Paul is even more forceful: "Since the creation of the world his invisible attributes, his eternal power and divine nature, have been clearly seen, being understood through what has been made, so that [unbelievers] are without excuse" (Romans 1:20). Jesus himself constantly uses natural objects and processes to explain what "the kingdom of God is like." In doing this he demonstrates his underlying belief that creation displays the glory of God in addition to revealing God's providential care.
>
> (Matthew 6:25–34)

Such beliefs have had profound implications in the development of the conservation movement. It was the conviction that nature was an object of God's care that inspired the US conservationist John Muir to advocate its preservation. Speaking of the Grand Canyon in Arizona in an essay entitled "God's First Temples," Muir wrote:

> Instead of being filled with air, the vast space between the walls is crowded with Nature's grandest buildings – a sublime city of them, painted in every color, and adorned with richly fretted cornice and battlement spire and tower in endless variety of style and architecture. Every architectural invention of man has been anticipated, and far more, in this grandest of God's terrestrial cities.
>
> (1997, pp. 742–43)

Muir understood that if nature and its creatures were the objects of God's concern, the battle for their preservation must be framed in moral absolutes; speaking of his beloved Sierras in California, Muir wrote:

> The battle we have fought, and are still fighting, for the forests is part of the eternal conflict between right and wrong, and we cannot expect to see the end of it … The smallest forest reserve, and the first I ever heard of, was in the Garden of Eden; and … yet even so moderate reserve as this was attacked. … So we must count on watching and striving for these trees, and should always be glad to find anything so surely good and noble to strive for.
>
> (1896, p. 276)

The linkage of humanity and nature in sin, judgment, and redemption

Christians believe that sin is a destructive force unleashed by choices that affect the entire created order. Therefore, the Fall is not an event whose consequences are confined to human beings as both humans and nonhuman nature are affected by the effects of sin; both stand in need of redemption from it. The basis for this belief is exemplified in the prophetic writings as well as in Genesis:

> Listen to the word of the Lord, O sons of Israel, for the Lord has a case against the inhabitants of the land, because there is no faithfulness or kindness or knowledge of God in the land. There is swearing, deception, murder, stealing and adultery. They employ violence, so that bloodshed follows bloodshed. Therefore the land mourns, and everyone who lives in it languishes along with the beasts of the field and the birds of the sky, and also the fish of the sea disappear.
>
> (Hosea 4:1–3)

Thus, the prophet makes the radical claim that human sin has ecological consequences. The corrupting power of sin disrupts the entire created order.

Sin is therefore the fundamental problem not only of the human condition but of the environmental condition, and so it is not only humans that stand in need of redemption but all of creation. Christians understand the prophecy of Isaiah as foretelling this redemption and reconciliation: "And the wolf will dwell with the lamb, and the leopard will lie down with the young goat, and the calf and the young lion and the fatling together" (Isaiah 11:6). Isaiah's words express the prophetic vision that nature and its nonhuman creatures have an eschatological future because for these events to occur, these creatures must be present in the coming kingdom of God. Jewish theology echoes this sentiment. The Messianic hope of the Old Testament is that one day a descendent of David would arise who would rule the Earth perfectly because "the Spirit of the Lord will rest on Him, the spirit of wisdom and understanding, the spirit of council and strength, the spirit of knowledge and the fear of the Lord" (Isaiah 11:2).

Christians have shown a recurring historical tendency to separate the doctrines of creation and redemption into separate spheres of theology, describing the effects of the atonement in personal terms that achieve reconciliation between God and human beings. Paul links them by making Jesus Christ the agent of both. He describes the atonement's effects in cosmic terms that achieve reconciliation between God and the created order. The atonement, the death of Christ, is the means through which Christ redeems the cosmos he created. The expectation of cosmic reconciliation in Christ was widely assumed and unashamedly proclaimed:

> It is well, then, in treating this subject, to speak first of the creation of the universe, and of God its Artificer, in order that one may duly perceive that its

recreation has been wrought by the Word who originally made it. For it will not appear at all inconsistent for the Father to have wrought its salvation in Him through whom He made it.

(Athanasius, 1903, pp. 42–43)

Platonic intrusions into Christian theology followed the Patristic period (100–451CE), intrusions which emphasized Plato's view of the material as an imperfection of the true "essence" or "spirit" of a divine form. As these ideas gained prominence in Christian theology, the concept of a redeemed creation all but disappeared. However, it did not vanish; it was kept in the writings of such notable reformers as John Wesley. One of Wesley's most famous sermons, "The General Deliverance," argues that animals will share in the redemptive work of God in the new creation. Wesley argues that the "dominion" given to humans in Genesis 1:28 was not exploitation but rather the authority to convey divine blessing, as God's image and representative, to other creatures, just as the text of Genesis 2:15 indicates. "So that man was God's viceregent upon earth, ... the prince and governor of this lower world; and all the blessings of God flowed through him to the inferior creatures" (Wesley, 1872, p. 244). Wesley argues that these creatures will be restored, not to their original state in Eden, but to a better and higher state: "As recompense for what they once suffered, while under the 'bondage of corruption' ... they shall enjoy happiness suited to their state, without alloy, without interruption, and without end" (1872, pp. 249–50).

Contemporary expressions of stewardship

Contemporary Christian expression and behavior, especially among American evangelical Christians, could be used to support White Jr's argument (1967). In the 1990s, surveys of US religious attitudes toward the environment appear to show that low levels of environmental concern are correlated with biblical literalism. However, the Bible is not the cause of lower support for environmental spending; it is rather the pretext of those whose rigid 'style' inclines them both to resist environmental concern and insist on religious certainty. As early as 1970, the American Baptist Church adopted its "Resolution on Environmental Concerns" (American Baptist Church, 1970), and similar statements by numerous other denominations began to appear, especially in the 1980s and 1990s. On January 1st, 1990, on the World Day of Peace, Pope John Paul II added his voice in his official message, which he entitled "The Ecological Crisis: A Common Responsibility" (National Catholic Rural Life Conference, 2008). The World Council of Churches issued similar and repeated statements on environmental responsibility (World Council of Churches, 2008). In 1992, the Joint Appeal by Religion and Science for the Environment involved the participation of 115 signatories, the vast majority of them Christian. Christian statements and activism in fact became so common during this period that by 1998, Carl Pope, then president of the Sierra Club, issued a published apology to Bartholomew I, patriarch of the Orthodox Church: "We acted as if we could save life on Earth without the same institutions through which we save ourselves" (Pope, 1998, p. 14).

Today, all of the world's religions support conservation; faith-based organizations (FBOs) are functioning and growing all over the world in every faith tradition. They include groups like the Islamic Foundation for Ecology and Environmental Sciences (IFEES), the Coalition on the Environment and Jewish Life, the Buddhist conservation organization Tzu Chi, and the one with my favorite acronym, the African Muslim Environment Network (AMEN). Because of their growing role in conservation, FBOs have become a subject of intense interest among older, established national and international conservation organizations. Today, organizations like the National Wildlife Federation, Conservation International, and the World Bank have full-time positions, or in some cases entire programs and divisions, devoted to working with FBOs. The theologically based stewardship model of conservation that has developed in Christian conservation FBOs leads to many practices congruent with those of the conservation community. Differences in ethical premises, based on the Christian beliefs outlined to this point, have latent but significant implications that affect the overall purpose of conservation and sustainable development and the fundamental problem that conservation and development practices are intended to solve. One Christian FBO, A Rocha International, can serve as an example.

A Rocha, Portuguese for "the rock," began as an obscure effort on the coast of Portugal by two British missionaries, Peter and Miranda Harris, who established and combined an ornithological field station with a church that met in the same location (Harris, 1993). Today, A Rocha has grown to an international organization with established or developing chapters in 19 countries. It defines itself as an organization that seeks to be intentionally and identifiably Christian in understanding conservation as a biblical expression of environmental stewardship, oriented to the needs of local communities, cross-cultural in its willingness to work with people of divergent backgrounds, committed to cooperative efforts with multiple interests and organizations, and dedicated to serious conservation research, management, and education (A Rocha International, 2008). Its contributions have been increasingly recognized by the conservation community at large, leading to A Rocha's inclusion as a member among the organizations and nation-states of the International Union for Conservation of Nature (IUCN), the only FBO of any faith tradition that has been so far included. A Rocha's emphases on human community and cultural transformation are integral features of its efforts. In pursuing these ends, A Rocha and other Christian FBOs often employ methods different from those of traditional conservation organizations, methods that reflect their different goals and priorities. For example, A Rocha's Kenya chapter has worked effectively with local residents and government officials in the Arabuko-Sokoke Forest, the largest remnant of dry coastal forest in East Africa. A Rocha has developed the Arabuko-Sokoke Schools and Eco-Tourism

Scheme (ASSETS) to establish community involvement in local conservation. In this effort, A Rocha, Kenya, has developed facilities and services for tourists who come to see the forest's noteworthy plant and animal life, and it then diverts funds generated from these activities to provide scholarships for local school children ("eco-bursaries") and to nature conservation. In similar ways, Christian conservation FBOs like the Au Sable Institute (Au Sable Institute, 2008), the John Ray Initiative (John Ray Initiative, 2008), and Restoring Eden (Restoring Eden, 2008) and others have emerged as originators of substantive initiatives in education, development, research, and policy in environmental conservation and sustainable development since the 1980s.

A Rocha and other Christian conservation FBOs try to bridge the traditional "communications gap" that has historically existed between Christian and other organizations and their programs (World Commission on Environment and Development, 1987). They recognize the immensity of modern conservation problems, problems that have often led the secular conservation community to pessimism and despair. The Christian perspective in conservation and sustainable development is a hopeful one, however, based on the expectation of redemption accomplished in the resurrection of Jesus Christ, and through that resurrection an eventual reconciliation and redemption of all things, including all things on Earth, to God's eternal and redemptive purposes.

This hope is present in A Rocha and other Christian FBOs, and pervasive in the many individuals active in conservation who identify themselves as Christians. In 2005, Simon Stuart, leader of the IUCN's Biodiversity Assessment Team, published a letter with 30 other Christian conservationists from around the world in the journal *Conservation Biology* that attempted to explain the basis of this Christian hope in the context of their own work:

> Christians are committed by their biblical beliefs not only to the conviction that God himself cares for his universe in a daily and ongoing way but also that he helps and guides people in their conservation efforts. We are, therefore, not on our own against the relentless forces of unsustainable development and rapacious materialism. Every time we celebrate a conservation success story such as the recovery of the white rhinoceros in southern Africa, we are strengthened in this present hope that God is working with us to redeem his creation.
>
> (2005, pp. 1690–91)

Secular advocates of conservation and sustainable development cannot, no matter how much they would like to or how correct they are, tell policy makers what to do. Christians, on the other hand, can develop and implement conservation and sustainable development practices and policies as virtues and seriously engage policy makers with the hope of promoting a tradition that can ascribe transcendent goals and values to sustainable development. Christians can direct such efforts toward stewardship; not merely as immediate superficial tactical strategies and technical solutions, but as genuine lasting change not only in the details, but in people's current relationship with nature.

References

A Rocha International. 2008. *What We Do*. Retrieved on September 4th, 2012, from http://www.arocha.org/int-en/work.html.

American Baptist Church. 1970. *Resolution on Environmental Concerns*. Retrieved on June 30th, 2012, from http://www.abcusa.org/LinkClick.aspx?fileticket=65jubmGQN9o%3d&tabid=199.

Athanasius. 1903. *On the Incarnation of the Word of God*. Trans. T. H. Bindley. London: Religious Tract Society.

Au Sable Institute. 2008. Retrieved on September 12th, 2012, from www.ausable.org.

Callicott, J. B. 1994. Conservation Values and Ethics. In *Principles of Conservation Biology*. Eds. G. K. Meffe and C. R. Carroll. Sunderland, Mass.: Sinauer, pp. 24–49.

Ehrlich, P., and R. L. Harriman. 1971. *How to Be a Survivor*. New York: Ballantine.

Harris, P. 1993. *Under the Bright Wings*. Vancouver, BC: Regent College Publishing.

John Ray Initiative. 2008. Retrieved on September 12th, 2012, from www.jri.org.uk.

Krebs, C. J. 1972. *Ecology: The Experimental Analysis of Distribution and Abundance*. New York: Harper and Row.

Leopold, A. 1966. *A Sand County Almanac with Essays on Conservation from Round River*. New York: Sierra Club/Ballantine.

McHarg, I. 1969. *Design with Nature*. Garden City, NY: Natural History Press.

Muir, J. 1896. Address on the Sierra Forest Reservation. *Sierra Club Bulletin* 1(7), pp. 275–77.

Muir, J. 1997. *Nature Writings*. New York: Library of America.

National Catholic Rural Life Conference. 2008. *The Ecological Crisis: A Common Responsibility*. Message of His Holiness Pope John Paul II for the Celebration of the World Day of Peace, 1 January 1990. Retrieved on September 12th, 2012, from http://conservation.catholic.org/ecologicalcrisis.htm.

Northcott, M. S. 1996. *The Environment and Christian Ethics*. Cambridge: Cambridge University Press.

Passmore, J. 1974. *Man's Responsibility for Nature: Ecological Problems and Western Traditions*. New York: Charles Scribner's Sons.

Pope, C. 1998. Reaching beyond Ourselves: It's Time to Recognize our Allies in the Faith Community. *Sierra Magazine* November–December, pp. 14–15.

Restoring Eden. 2008. Retrieved on September 12th, 2012, from www.restoringeden.org.

Schillebeeckx, E. 1968. *God the Future of Man*. New York: Sheed and Ward.

Stuart, S. N., G. W. Archibald, J. Ball, R. J. Berry, S. D. Emmerich, D. M. Evans, J. R. Flenley, K. J. Gaston, D. R. Given, A. G. Gosler, P. Harris, J. Houghton, E. D. Lindquist, D. C. Mahan, M. D. Morecroft, D. C. Moyer, D. Murdiyarso, C. Nicolson, A. Oteng-Yeboah, A. J. Plumptre, G. Prance, V. Ramachandra, J. B. Sale, J. K. Sheldon, S. Simiyu, R. Storey, L. G. Underhill, J. Vickery, and T. Whitten. 2005. Conservation Theology for Conservation Biologists: A Reply to David Orr. *Conservation Biology* 19(6), pp. 1689–92.

Walton, J. H. 2001. *Genesis: The NIV Application Commentary*. Grand Rapids, Mich.: Zondervan.

Wesley, J. 1872. The General Deliverance. In *The Works of John Wesley Vol. 6*. Grand Rapids, Mich.: Zondervan.

White, L., Jr. 1967. The Historical Roots of Our Ecologic Crisis. *Science* 155, pp. 1203–7.

World Commission on Environment and Development. 1987. *Report of the World Commission on Environment and Development: Our Common Future*. New York: Oxford University Press.

World Council of Churches. 2008. *Justice, Peace, and Creation*. Retrieved on July 15th, 2012, from http://www.wcc-coe.org/wcc/what/jpc/index-e.html.

Young, R. A. 1994. *Healing the Earth: A Theocentric Perspective on Environmental Problems and Their Solutions*. Nashville, Tenn.: Boardman and Holman.

14 Islam and stewardship

Hamim Hamim, Luluk Setyaningsih, and Asep Nurhalim

Islam teaches its followers to have concern for their natural surroundings. The roots of Islamic teachings on environmental practices can be found in the Islamic Holy Books, the Quran and the Hadith. Professors Yusuf Qardhawi (2001) and Ali Yafie (2006) have worked on the writing of an Islamic basic rule, a *Fiqh*, specifically regarding the environment. A *Fiqh* is a part of Islamic law that explains many activities and practices required to be understood and implemented by Muslims. In his book, Qardhawi (2001) explains that maintaining and protecting the environment have close correlations with many basic Islamic teachings such as the Islamic foundation (*Tauhid*), Islamic morals and behavior (*Akhlaq*), the Islamic basic rule (*Fiqh*), Islamic purposes (*maqashid syar'iyyah*), and the knowledge of Quran and Hadith. Islam teaches its followers to do good deeds with the only expectation being a reward from God in the Hereafter. Muslims believe that God created the universe for the good of humankind, with all of nature following His will.

> And the heaven He has raised high, and He has set up the Balance. One may not transgress the balance. One must observe the weight with equity so as to not make the balance deficient. And the earth He has put for the creatures. Therein are fruits, date-palms producing sheathed fruit-stalks [enclosing dates]. And also corn, with leaves and stalk for fodder, and sweet-scented plants. Then which of the Blessings of your Lord will you both deny?
>
> (Al-Rahman 55:7–13)

Homo sapien, according to Islam, is a special creature different from other creatures such as plants and animals – therefore human beings receive the mandate to manage nature in accordance with the will of the Almighty Creator. Allah says: "And [mention, O Muhammad], when your Lord said to the angels, 'Indeed, I will make upon the earth a successive authority'" (Quran 2:30). Humans can understand what is good and should be done, and what is bad and should be avoided and abandoned. Therefore, human beings can receive lessons from God about commands and prohibitions as well as about the worship of his Lord: "And indeed We have honored the Children of Adam, and We have carried them on land and sea, and have provided them with *At-Taiyibat* [lawful good things], and have preferred them above many of those whom We have created with a marked preference" (Quran 17:70).

As special creatures, human beings have a mandate to manage our earth with consideration for other life. This command is expressed in several verses of the Quran as well as in the Hadiths of the Prophet Muhammad. For example, Allah says: "And do not do mischief on the earth, after it has been set in order, and invoke Him with fear and hope; Surely, Allah's Mercy is (ever) near unto the gooddoers" (Quran 7:56). Allah also says: " if anyone killed a person not in retaliation of murder, or (and) to spread mischief in the land – it would be as if he killed all mankind, and if anyone saved a life, it would be as if he saved the life of all mankind" (Quran 5:32). As some scholars have observed, more than 95 verses in the Quran are devoted to the environment and several *hadiths* (sayings) also explain what Muslims should do for nature and the environment, both individually and as a community.

Stewardship and the Islamic Hereafter

Islam always relates the action in this life with life Hereafter. One of the most important teachings of Islam is that there is a durable relationship between recent life in the world and the Hereafter. In performing all deeds, a Muslim is required to consider both the recent world and implications for the Hereafter. "Muslims believe that scales of deeds will be set up on the Day of Judgment, and that no soul shall be wronged: 'Whoever has done an atom's weight of good shall see it'(Quran 99:7–8)" (Katheer, 1999). Allah also says: "He it is, Who has made the earth subservient to you (i.e. easy for you to walk, to live and to do agriculture on it, etc.), so walk in the path thereof and eat of His provision, and to Him will be the Resurrection" (Quran 67:15). Therefore, a Muslim is required to have knowledge of life in the universe (science and technology) and of Islamic religion (theology). This paradigm is implemented in almost all countries that are predominately Muslim. With an understanding of the close relationship between the life of the world now and life in the Hereafter, people will realize that Great God's creation was not in vain. Humans are commanded to study, observe, and pay attention to the universe. By studying the universe they will have knowledge and lessons from God, recognize the causes of harm to nature, and know how to avoid or repair the natural environment. Islam teaches its followers to avoid activities that pollute, because they will damage the environment and humankind itself, and Allah does not like them. Allah says: "But seek, with that (wealth) which Allah has bestowed on you, the home of the Hereafter, and forget not your portion of legal enjoyment in this world, and do good as Allah has been good to you, and seek not mischief in the land. Verily, Allah likes not the mischief-makers" (Quran 28:77).

The Quran teaches us that the greatest damage to nature is induced by human hands, driven by humans' desires and wishes, and their disregard of God's commandments. Consequently, God may inflict punishment: "Evil has appeared on land and sea because of what the hands of men have earned, that Allah may make them taste a part of that which they have done, in order that they may return" (Quran 30:41). Allah makes people realize that they have done something wrong with the hope that they will refrain from repeating their bad deeds and return to the teachings of Allah.

The close relationship between recent activities in the world and the Hereafter should encourage Muslims to act with sincerity. *Ikhlas* is doing everything only for God. Through the concept of *ikhlas*, we will be willing to do things on behalf of animals, plants, and the universe, knowing that God will repay us with merit and goodness: "they were commanded not, but that they should worship Allah, … and perform As-Salat (Iqamat-as-Salat) [daily prayers] and give Zakat [alms]: and that is the right religion" (Quran 98:5). The Prophet Muhammad also said: "Muslims will always earn the reward of charity for planting a tree or sowing a crop which birds, humans, or animals then eat from" (Al-Bukhari, 2004). This verse and the *hadith* assert that everyone who believes in Allah will worship him through prayer and by providing charity, and assistance to the underprivileged as well as to other creatures to maintain the balance that Allah has created and that provides for humankind.

Muslim behavior and the environment

Ikhlas is a very important concept in Islam, because without it the deeds of a Muslim are not worthy. Keeping this concept in mind, Muslims do good deeds for the benefit of others and the environment, including animals, plants, and the universe. Many *hadiths* of the Prophet Muhammad encourage people to do good deeds, including for the environment. Yusuf Al Qardhawi (2001) said that there are many *hadiths* as complement to the verses of Quran that emphasized the importance of growing the crops and trees. In Islam each human being is a servant of God, appointed as *khalifah* (vicegerent) in this earth and assigned by God to manage this natural world in a good manner. Humans are appointed as the managers of the earth because God has given to humankind sufficient intelligence to grasp knowledge through guidance from His Messengers (Prophets) and by learning what happens in nature and the universe. Therefore, all events in the universe become a natural laboratory for human learning. Allah says: "Verily! In the creation of the heavens and the earth, and in the alternation of night and day, there are indeed signs for men of understanding" (Quran 3:190).

Islam also considers noble works that could save living things such as plants and animals, and the environment. Only human beings can do these good deeds. Animals are sometimes displaced by human needs, such as the needs for housing, agricultural fields, and industrial sites, and as a result they may lose their habitats and sources of food and drink. It is only humans who have the ability to prevent these animals from dying of hunger or thirst. In Hadits, the Prophet Muhammad said: "Whenever Muslims plant a tree, they will earn the reward of charity because of the food that comes from it; and likewise what is stolen from it, what the wild beasts eat out of it, what the birds eat out of it, and what people take from it is charity for them" (Bin-Al-Hajjaj, 2004). The Prophet is also reported to have said: "Muslims will always earn the reward of charity for planting a tree or sowing a crop which birds, humans, or animals then eat from" (Nawawi, 2010).

The Prophet related to his companions the story of a man who found a dog panting from thirst. He narrated: "The man went down into a well, filled his shoes with water and offered it to the dog to quench its thirst. The Prophet said, 'Then Allah was grateful to him and forgave him his sins.' The companions asked, 'O Messenger of Allah! Is there a reward for us with relation to animals?' He replied, 'There is a reward with every living creature'" (Al-Bukhari, 2004). Such *hadiths* show that Islam provides respect and reward for anyone who cares about the fate of God's creatures.

If we consider what happens in nature, God has created the universe in harmony. The plants as producers become food for small creatures such as grasshoppers, ants, and butterflies, or large animals like monkeys, and also help to protect water. The small animals will become food for the larger ones, such as wolves, snakes, lions, and tigers. All living things will decompose after death, thus producing the chemical compounds required by plants. This ecosystem works in balance and has been sustained for a long time (Naeem *et al.*, 1999). Yet if people cut down too many trees, the source of water and food for animals will be lost, and some animals will starve. Therefore, the forests must be managed wisely to avoid harming God's most defenseless creatures (Hasan, 2009). God is wrathful toward those who disregard this duty. Allah says in Quran (2:205): "And when he turns away (from you 'O Muhammad SAW'), his effort in the land is to make mischief therein and to destroy the crops and the cattle, and Allah likes not mischief." This is in line with the Islamic prohibition against eating the meat of various fanged beasts and strong hoof animals such as wolves, tigers, and snakes. "The Prophet Muhammad (peace be upon Him) prohibits eating all the wild animals with fangs and every bird with strong claws" (narrated by Muslim (Bin-Al-Hajjaj, 2004)). We can assume, moreover, that if it is forbidden to obtain the meat of these animals for food, the prohibition is even stronger if the animals are killed only to clothe and decorate the human body. Early Islamic scholars did not discuss this matter in detail, but the assumption has held for a long time. Now, with greater knowledge of natural science, we are aware of the important role of these wild animals in our natural ecosystems.

Islam's dietary restrictions (*Halal*) extend to animals such as deer and rabbits that do not have fangs and sharp nails. Although the ban is considered temporary, it is understood that the hunting of these wild animals should be controlled and avoided. God forbid that anyone who is undertaking a ritual pilgrimage (*haj*) in Mecca should hunt and eat meat from these animals, as suggested in the Quran:

> O you who believe! Kill not game while you are in a state of Ihram for Hajj or 'Umrah [pilgrimage], and whosoever of you kills it intentionally, the penalty is an offering, brought to the Ka'bah, of an eatable animal [i.e. sheep, goat, cow, etc.] equivalent to the one he killed, as adjudged by two just men among you; or, for expiation, he should feed Masakin [poor persons], or its equivalent in Saum [fasting], that he may taste the heaviness [punishment] of his deed. Allah has forgiven what is past, but whosoever commits it again, Allah will take retribution from him. And Allah is AllMighty, All-Able of Retribution.
>
> (5:95)

Moreover, Islam even completely forbids its followers to eat many kinds of wild animals that have strong claws, sharp fangs, like tigers, snakes, lions, and eagles. "Forbidden for my ummah (to eat) all the claws of birds and all the fangs of the beast" (narrated by Abu Dawud). There is no particular logical explanation for the Prophet's prohibition so far, but the biologists understood that those animals normally occupy the top of the biology tropic that is very limited in number and therefore vulnerable to extinction, and these species are part of the endanger species based on Red List Criteria (Vié *et al.*, 2009).

Islam and the environmental crisis

If goodness toward nature's plants and animals is commanded by Allah, then the command to be good to other human beings undoubtedly is even stronger. Muslims are commanded to work for the goodness of humankind today and for the future, and not for the badness of them. This commend is either for man or women, as Allah says: "Whoever does an evil deed will not be recompensed except by the like thereof; but whoever does righteousness, whether male or female, while he is a believer – those will enter Paradise, being given provision therein without account" (Quran 40:40). God commands Muslims to learn from nature and from history what has happened in previous generations, so that we can avoid disasters in the future. Allah says in the Quran: "Many similar ways (and mishaps of life) were faced by nations (believers and disbelievers) that have passed away before you, so travel through the earth, and see what was the end of those who disbelieved (in the Oneness of Allah, and disobeyed Him and His Messengers)" (3:137).

Today all humans are faced with the frightening threat of climate change due to global warming. Drought has hit many countries in Africa, Asia, and Australia, resulting in higher food prices. According to data from the World Food Program and the United Nations Food and Agriculture Organization (UNFAO) in 2011, thousands of people in the Horn of Africa have died of starvation due to prolonged drought (UNFAO, 2011). In other countries, heavy floods and tornados have damaged buildings, settlements, and agricultural lands. Research has shown that climate change has been driven by human activities that increase greenhouse gases and, because of deforestation, decrease the absorption of carbon dioxide. This situation should make us aware that climate change is God's warning about the destructive effects of human activities, in particular the increase in carbon dioxide emissions since the beginning of the eighteenth century (IPCC, 2001). We need to be aware that God has created the universe including our earth in balance (Yahya, 2001). Human beings, plants, animals, and the ecosystem are dependent on each other, and human activities may cause balance disorder (Naeem *et al.*, 1999). It is our responsibility to face the challenge of climate change with serenity and to work hard to mitigate its effects. God has created the universe in balance (Quran 55:7–13), but human activities might cause them to unbalance.

Islamic teaching suggests that humans can take four steps to restore the imbalance they have caused:

1. Be patient and return all things to Allah (Quran 2:155–156).
2. Evaluate the weaknesses and our mistakes as we do (Quran 3:135).
3. Make improvements for the future (Quran 28:54).
4. Work together and help each other (Quran 5:2).

By following these steps, humans can restore the balance now and into the future. These steps toward restoration follow the teachings of the Prophet Muhammad (peace be upon Him), who said: "The believers are amazing, everything will be good for him, [because] if the disaster struck he be patient, and be patient is good for him" (narrated by Muslim (Bin-Al-Hajjaj, 2004)). In addition to being patient, a Muslim is asked to evaluate him or herself for any actions taken, whether those actions be connected to worshiping God, associating with humans, or associating with nature. Humans often act in haste and without thought to the consequences of their acts. Therefore, the evaluation process is critically important. Evaluation, known in Islam as *muhasabah*, is something that should be done continuously. In a *hadith*, Umar bin Khattab, the companion of the Prophet Muhammad, said: "Evaluate yourself before you are evaluated [by God in the Hereafter]" (narrated by At-Tirmidzi) (Al-'Uthaimin, n.d.). Humans who evaluate themselves, then when they do wrong they will realize it and ask forgiveness from the Lord. Without such forgiveness, in the Hereafter God will respond to bad and destructive acts with punishments:

> And those who, when they have committed *Fahishah* [a multitude of sins] or wronged themselves with evil, remember Allah and ask forgiveness for their sins; – and none can forgive sins but Allah – And do not persist in what [wrong] they have done, while they know. For such, the reward is Forgiveness from their Lord, and Gardens with rivers flowing underneath [Paradise], wherein they shall abide forever. How excellent is this reward for the doers (who do righteous deeds according to Allah's Orders).
>
> (Quran 3:135–36)

By understanding their present conditions and past actions, human beings are able to repair damage while maintaining the development required for living their life in a sustainable manner. This great task must be initiated from the individual, then by families and communities, and then at the national and international levels. Individual changes are the key to success; otherwise, changes will never happen. Allah says: "Indeed, Allah will not change the condition of a people until they change what is in themselves" (Quran 13:11).

Islam teaches us that every individual should be responsible for all activities performed by themselves or by their family, a principle that reflects the interconnectedness of individual, family, and community. Because the individual is under the control of the family, the family will become a representation of the community. The following excerpt exemplifies Islamic teachings on this subject (Quran 66:6):

> And the Prophet Muhammad said: "Each of you is a leader and he will be asked about the lead. A man/husband is the leader for his family and he will

be asked about the lead. Woman/wife is the leader of the family of her husband and child and he will be asked about them.

(Al-Bukhari, 2004)

The role of individuals and families in performing the great task can start with small things such as taking out the trash properly, using water efficiently, not consuming foods and beverages to excess, not wasting electricity, and in general not being extravagant. In Islamic teachings, extravagance and waste are strongly prohibited: "O Children of Adam! Take your adornment, while praying and going round the Ka'bah, and eat and drink but waste not by extravagance" (Quran 7:31); "And give to the kindred his due and to the Miskin and to the wayfarer. But spend not wastefully in the manner of a spendthrift. Verily, spendthrifts are brothers of the Shayatin, and the Shaitan is ever ungrateful to his Lord" (Quran 17:26–27). Islam also encourages rightful acts to be performed by the government to support the sustainable use of nature. In Islamic teachings, as emphasized by many Islamic scholars, the government has the task of maintaining natural resources for the benefit of its inhabitants. Islamic scholars have noted that when the Prophet Muhammad was alive, He made the effort to build a common conservation area known as a Hima that could not be disturbed, an effort that was continued by several caliphs after Him, such as Abu Bakar and Umar ibn Khattab (Muhammad et al., 2006). Islam also emphasizes that actions must be taken in anticipation of our future life in this world and on the day of judgment. People who are obedient to Allah always foresee how their actions will outline the future: "O you who believe! Fear Allah and keep your duty to Him. And let every person look to what he has sent forth for the morrow, and fear Allah. Verily, Allah is All-Aware of what you do" (Quran 59:18). Muhammad also said: "If there are still seeds in your hand, and even though you know that tomorrow will be doomsday, [please] plant them!" (narrated by Ahmad) (Muhammad et al., 2006; Cisse, 2008).

These verse and *hadith* confirm the importance of doing something for the days to come, because what we do today will have implications for the future. If today we act respectfully toward nature, then we will get goodness in the future. But if we are unmindful of the future, or act in a way that worsens our natural environment, we will reap disasters in the future. God's reply will depend on our actions, not the results we have achieved, because sometimes positive actions will have an impact only much later. Therefore, Islamic teachings are very much concerned with long-range efforts to improve our environment.

Islam is concerned with and supports efforts to mobilize cooperation for the common good, and at the same time forbids efforts to mobilize that are evil and sinful. Allah says in the Quran (5:2): "Help you one another in AlBirr and AtTaqwa [virtue, righteousness and piety]; but do not help one another in sin and transgression. And fear Allah." Verily, Allah is severe in punishment. Working together is the key to the success of everything. The natural world is too big to be repaired by a single person or by a few people. That is why it is important to identify the Islamic values underlying the campaign to improve the environment.

References

Al-Bukhari, M. B. I. 2004. *Shahih Al-Bukhari*. Beirut: Daar Al-Thouqi Al-Najah.

Al-'Uthaimin, M. S. n.d. *The Muslim's Belief*. Trans: M. Al-Johani. Retrieved on July 15th, 2012, from http://www.islamworld.net/docs/aqeedah.html.

Bin-Al-Hajjaj, M. 2004. *Al-Musnadu Al-Sahihu bi Naklil Adli (Shahih Al-Muslim)*. Cairo: Daar Al-Syuruq.

Cisse, T. Cheikh Amadou Tijaan. 2008. *Islam, the Environment and the use of Vetiver Grass*. Retrieved on August 24th, 2011, from http://groups.msn.com/PepiniereNaajBaal/_whatsnew.msnw.

Hasan, S. 2009. Measuring Illegal Logging: An Islamic Environmental Jurisprudence. *Indonesian Islamic Law Journal* 1(1) pp. 60–65.

Intergovernmental Panel on Climate Change (IPCC). 2001. *Summary for Policymakers. Climate Change: The Scientific Basic*. Cambridge: Cambridge University Press.

Katheer, I. 1999. *The Tafseer of The Quran*. Retrieved on July 15th, 2012, from www.qurancomplex.com.

Muhammad, A. S., H. Muhammad, R. Mabrur, A. S. Abbas, A. Firman, F. M. Mangunjaya, K. I. B. Pasha, and M. Andriana. 2006. *Fiqih Lingkungan [Islamic Environmental Jurisprudence]*. Jakarta: Conservation International Indonesia.

Naeem, S., C. F. S. ChapinIII, R. Costanza, P. R. Ehrlich, F. B. Golley, D. U. Hooper, J. H. Lawton, R. V. O'Neill, H. A. Mooney,O. E. Sala, A. J. Symstad, and D. Tilman. 1999. Biodiversity and Ecosystem Functioning: Maintaining Natural Life Support Processes. *Issues in Ecology* 4, pp. 1–12.

Nawawi, I. 2010. *Riyadhus Shalihin*. Subarjono Digital Library. Retrieved on January 3rd, 2012, from http://www.niknasri.com/wp-content/uploads/2010/01/Riyadhus-Shalihin-1.pdf.

Qardhawi, Y. 2001. *Ri'ayah al-Bi'ah fiy Syari'ah al-Islam [Protecting the Environment in Islamic Law]*. Cairo: Daar Al-Syuruq.

United Nations Food and Agriculture Organization (UNFAO). 2011. *The Crisis in the Horn of Africa*. Retrieved on February 12th, 2012, from http://www.fao.org/crisis/horn-africa/home/en.

Vié. J-C. C. Hilton-Taylor, and S. N. Stuart. 2009. *Wild Life in a Changing World*. Switzerland: International Union for Conservation of Nature (IUCN).

Yafie, A. 2006. *Merintis Fiqh Lingkungan Hidup [Environmental management and protection according to Islamic law in Indonesia]*. Jakarta: Ufuk.

Yahya, H. 2001. *The Glory in the Heaven*. London: Ta-Ha Publishers Ltd.

15 The social construction of African-American environmental values

Cassandra Johnson-Gaither and J. M. Bowker

Introduction

Memories are not all of pastoral picnics (Schama, 1995, p. 18). Maurice Halbwachs argues that memory is socially constructed, that is, it is only retained in groups or communities of people (1980). For events to withstand the test of time there must be a mutual sharing of information about such events, otherwise memories die. Memories do not exist apart from the social milieu of their mnemonic community. Being social creatures, humans experience the past collectively (Zerubavel, 1996). Few studies have explored the historical relationship of African Americans to wildlands, and how the collective experience and memories influence a contemporary African-American wildland ethic (Taylor, 2000). We focus on African-American impressions of wildlands because these landscapes form a significant part of Americans' core identity. Empirical studies indicate a significant difference in the way African Americans and whites interact with America's wildlands (Gramann, 1966). An understanding of African-American collective memory may well provide insight into why these differences exist.

Collective memory involves the relaying or handing down of cultural history from generation to generation. Successive generations can be influenced by events even though subsequent generations have no direct memory of such events. Today, African Americans have no personal memories of slavery, and the population of blacks alive today who labored in southern turpentine and lumber camps during the first half of the twentieth century is negligible. Still, American blacks recollect stories about hardships that occurred while working in turpentine camps, and of wildland lynchings that took place in backcountry woods. These "memories" contribute to the formation of African Americans' ethnic identity.

Daniel Stokols refers to the historical symbolism of landscapes as social imageability or the perceived social field of a milieu (1980). This is the "capacity of a place or type of place to evoke vivid and collectively held social meanings among its occupants or potential occupants" (Stokols, 1980). Social imageability can arise through environmental symbolism, which is a gradual process of assigning meaning to a place or landscape based on past experiences. According to Stokols, this symbolism can come about even for people who have no direct contact with an area (Stokols, 1990, pp. 641–46). The history of a place can be passed down to successive generations such that the place can come to symbolize a certain atmosphere or mood even though no direct personal contact has been established.

Simon Schama's description of Yosemite valley shows how the white, middle-American view of wildlands and wilderness constructs these areas as benign places – spiritual, sanctified refuges distinct from the profanity of human modification (1995, pp. 7–9). Middle America imagines wildlands as mystical places having the power to transform one's essence because wild nature is perceived as sacred. One enters a wilderness but emerges somehow changed. One of American wilderness' earliest advocates, John Muir, located the divine in nature. He describes wild nature as a "window opening into heaven, a mirror reflecting the Creator" (cited in Nash, 1967, p. 125). The idea of wildlands as benevolent entities also abounds in the secular realm. Frederick Jackson Turner proposed that wilderness, the actual physical aspects of primeval forests and unchartered territory, helped to establish American democracy (1953). Early white Americans had the unique experience of vast, open lands, and the freedom to explore these places and appropriate them; this unrestricted freedom resulted in American "individualism, independence, and confidence," ideal characteristics which distinguish Americans from others (Nash, 1975). Similarly, John Hammond argues that wilderness is good because it contributes to a uniquely American character and is symbolic of American national heritage (1985).

Thomas Greider and Lorraine Garkovich also argue that perception of the natural environment is a social construction (1994). As such it is largely the result of the observer's imagination. The constructed image is influenced, in part, by a community's past relationships with particular environments. Wild places for African Americans may be what cultural geographers refer to as "sick places" which evoke horrible memories of toil, torture, and death (Bixler and Floyd, 1997).

The African-American community, when compared to white Americans, exhibits a less positive relationship with America's wildlands. Evidence suggests that the community's collective memories of negative experiences such as slavery/plantation work in forests, sharecropping, and lynching have contributed to blacks having a negative apperception regarding wildlands. The institutions of slavery, forest work camps, and sharecropping exploited black labor, and lynchings were essentially acts of terror perpetuated against blacks in wildland areas. There are also indications that there are some positive connections between blacks and wildlands. African Americans have always fished and hunted in wildland settings and are returning to the rural South to establish homesteads adjacent to wildlands. To better understand these apparent discrepancies and to set the discussion of black land memories in context, the following section reviews the literature on black interaction with wildlands, including African-inspired ontology, black concern for the environment, and the progression of American environmentalism. The working relationship of blacks with both wildlands and other natural areas are discussed and placed in the context of mainstream environmentalism evolution.

African Americans and American environmentalism

National parks and forests are held in high regard. This is, in large part, because the early environmentalists who founded the American environmental movement were influenced by European intellectuals from the Enlightenment who romanticized nature. One result of such an origination is that American environmental recreation is essentially an avocation of white, college educated, middle to upper income males (Lucas, 1989). Research on wildland recreation shows a relative lack of black participation in outdoor activities that occur in such areas. Jack Goldsmith reports that national park visitors are mostly white, despite the Park Service's intent to attract a more ethnically and racially diverse visitor base (Goldsmith, 1994); regional level household surveys show blacks are significantly less likely than whites to interact with wildlands (Johnson *et al.*, 1997). James Gramann also found African Americans were less likely than whites to engage in wildland recreation, with fishing and hunting being the exception (1996). Even for a wildland-based activity like hunting, Stuart Marks' multi-ethnic investigation of rural, male hunters in North Carolina showed that blacks, compared to whites and Native Americans, were much less likely to report that they enjoyed the aesthetics of nature when hunting (1991).

Recent empirical work, however, shows few significant differences between blacks and whites in terms of their concern for wilderness (Cordell *et al.*, 2000). Moreover, Paul Mohai's work calls into question the assumption of black apathy for the environment (Mohai, 1990). African-American interest may be demonstrated in non-conventional environmental forms such as concern for community integrity (i.e. clean, crime-free neighborhoods and workplace conditions) rather than concern for wildlands and wildlife habitats. To understand this one must understand the history of the African-American community.

Dorceta Taylor chronicles the rise of the American environmental movement and the parallel, particularistic histories of non-whites. She identifies four periods of environmental thought (1997). This comparison of mainstream white interests and periphery groups shows how issues of basic civil liberties were the chief concerns of marginalized groups during the time when whites were concerned with environmental protection. The first environmental period, 1820 to 1913, can be considered the pre-(environmental) movement era. The related environmental paradigm or environmental philosophy (exploitive capitalist paradigm, ECP) was based on exploitation and intense extraction of natural resources. The next phase, 1914 to 1959, is the early environmental movement. Romantic views of the environment framed the natural world in idealistic terms. As discussed earlier, romanticism endows wild areas with a mysticism which exceeds the actual physics of the resource. The third phase of the environmental movement began in the early 1960s with Rachel Carson's 1962 book, *Silent Spring*, during which the mainstream of the environmental movement focused on pollution such as air and water contamination. The previously romanticized view of nature was replaced by the new environmental paradigm. The latest environmental phase is the Post-Three Mile Island/Love Canal era from about 1980 to the present.

Pre-movement era: slavery, sharecropping, lynching

According to the 1820 US Census, there were approximately 1.5 million slaves in the USA. There have been numerous accounts written about the "nightmare of drudgery" under which most blacks lived. The majority of slaves worked on plantations where their primary task was toiling on the land. An ex-slave is quoted in Lerone Bennett Jr: "it seems the fields stretched 'from one end of the earth to the other'" (Bennet Jr, 1968, p. 87).

Though slaves lived close to nature like other racial/ethnic groups of the period and extracted sustenance from the land (when permitted), they could not explore the wider environment. The very condition of being a slave dictated a life of extreme restrictions. The slave stood as antonym to the American myth of unrestricted wilderness exploration. Taylor remarks that while free white men had the privilege of discovering wildlands, slaves were severely circumscribed in their movement by a white, male dominated society that enacted slave codes in each slaveholding state (2000). Even free blacks were subject to the circumscriptions contained in these laws (Genovese, 1972).

The ambiguity that contemporary blacks appear to experience with wildland environments may well have begun with the slave experience. Elizabeth Blum writes that slaves assigned a multitude of meanings to wilderness (2002). Though black movement was severely restricted, slaves still managed to covertly access wildlands which provided a place of escape, either temporarily or permanently, from the oppression of plantation life. Blum's interpretation of early black American wildland interaction is consistent with the growing preservationist sentiments described by Taylor during this era. At the same time, however, Blum also stresses that slaves perceived both fear and danger in wilderness. Slaves especially dreaded wild animals and, to a lesser extent, other humans, and supernatural forces believed to inhabit wildlands. The wilderness was a place to be avoided for many, and some slave parents were concerned that their children needed to understand the potential danger wilderness contained. Blum's description of slave wildland interaction suggests, again, that blacks did not view these terrains as romanticized landscapes removed from human influence but rather in more practical terms. Wilderness was both perceived and used as a haven but was also kept at bay (Blum, 2002).

In addition, plantation agriculture and related tasks in forested wildlands served to create a negative imagery of such places among blacks. While descriptions of black labor on cotton, tobacco, and plantations are plentiful, relatively few accounts exist of slave work specifically in wildland environments, such as naval stores operations, especially turpentining (Averit, 1921). Gaynelle Wright's ethnohistorical account of turpentining in southern pine forests notes that black labor in the naval stores industry has been overlooked by historians because of confusion in the nineteenth century as to whether naval stores products should have been classified as industrial or agricultural products (1979).

Turpentining took place in remote pine forests. Workers used hatchets or hacks to make incisions into trees. Carved receptacles or "boxes" (later, attached cups) collected the crude gum or oleoresin that flowed from the opened spots in the trees. Periodically, workers would empty collected crude gum into a larger storage bin for later distillation. The turpentine extraction period ran from about March or April until November. Until the 1930s, turpentining was a purely extractive operation. The longleaf pine forests were viewed much like minerals to be extracted rather than as renewable resources (Croker, Jr, 1979).

The exploitation and subjugation associated with plantation agriculture during slavery impacted black perceptions of wild areas. This point is crucial as black land memories have been informed by negative social constructions and emerge not only from direct work in wildlands but also from work associated with land in general. William Cronon suggests that race is not the only factor; there is evidence of class-based differences in wildland appreciation (1996). The nineteenth century agrarian working class did not romanticize or idealize wildlands because their livelihood was more directly dependent upon land resources (Cronon, 1996, p. 15). This was true not only for African Americans involved in plantation agriculture but also for poorer whites and others living close to the land. Nonetheless, the historical black wildland relationship can be distinguished from that of white America due to the overlap of class oppression with racism, specifically the fear that arose from the dreadful things that happened to African Americans in the wildlands of the South. African Americans, due to their subjugated position, have not belonged to an elite which appropriated wild spaces as a cultural ideal. The subordinate position prevented such a positive and romantic association. Middle-class white Americans saw themselves civilized in contrast to African Americans whom they believed were more primitive by nature. Furthermore, European racism placed blacks on a par with the wild and uncivilized; both images have left a deep impression upon the collective black wildland memory (Turner, 1953).

After the Civil War, blacks continued to be kept in a virtual system of "involuntary servitude" by Jim Crow laws which were enforced by legal and extra-legal means, including vigilante groups such as the Ku Klux Klan; and black mobility was restricted by white southern landowners who used debt incurred by blacks through sharecropping and tenancy arrangements to enforce segregation and to restrict the activities of African Americans. In effect, blacks were rendered immobile and compulsively tied to the land through planter-backed ordinances such as "enticement laws, emigrant agent restrictions, contract laws, vagrancy statutes, the criminal-surety system, and convict labor laws" (Daniel, 1985, p. 6). Agrarianism remained the dominant economic system in the USA until the last decade of the nineteenth century.

When slavery ended, blacks felt they had a right to the land that they had helped cultivate during slavery. They reasoned that their work had contributed substantially to both the southern and northern economies. Blacks realized that land ownership would be crucial in uncoupling them from the exploitative plantation economy. Vincent Harding writes of the newly freed slaves: "Of course the search for land, the need to hold on to land, was still central to the black hope for a new life in America" (1981, p. 315). Vernon Wharton, cited in Jay Mandle, also states: "their [ex-slaves'] very lives were entwined with the land and its cultivation; they lived in a society where respectability was based on ownership of the soil; and to them to be free was to farm their own ground" (Mandle, 1978, p. 106). The denial of land to blacks left the overwhelming majority of blacks landless and effectively perpetuated the pre-emancipation plantation economy (Mandle, 1978).

In 1896, the Supreme Court's *Plessy v. Fergusson* decision ruled that blacks had no rights which whites were bound to respect. Thus, the twentieth century started with blacks solidified in a subordinate position. Significantly, wider black participation in American democracy became possible because of Booker T. Washington's 1895 "Atlanta Compromise," which was an official black acquiescence of Jim Crow and social inequality (Harlan, 1974, pp. 583–87).

Early environmental movement: black migration, turpentining, lumber camps, sharecropping, lynching

The 1890s marked the end of rural agrarianism as the dominant economic system in the USA. By the early part of the twentieth century, industrialization had replaced agrarianism as the primary economy. Yet in 1914, blacks were still, according to Mandle, mostly "southern, rural, and poor" although the "Great Black Northern Migration" had already commenced and its net effect would continue over the next four decades. Blacks remaining in the rural South were still mostly employed in agriculture and domestic or service positions because opportunities for other viable employment in the region remained limited (Mandle, 1978). After the Civil War, naval stores operations moved from plantations to camps established by "producers" who secured financing for the operations. Blacks continued to make up the overwhelming proportion of workers in the industry. The descriptor "Turpentine Negro" was a common term applied to blacks employed in this industry. They lived either in turpentine camps or backwood shanties. The dangerous working conditions were complemented with daily living conditions in the camps that were also dangerous and exploitative. Charlotte Todes describes typical conditions in the work camps:

> Negroes predominate in the turpentine camps of Georgia and Florida where exploitation of the workers is notorious. Mexican and Negro workers only are employed in the insect ridden cypress swamps. To cut cypress, the workers must wade in humid swamps, often up to their hips in water, and must live with their families in house boats built over the swamps. Living quarters for Negro workers are "match-box" shacks or box cars, segregated from white workers.
>
> (Todes, 1931, pp. 83–84)

Like plantations before them, turpentine camps continued to operate as microsocieties with a distinct set of morals, social norms, and economic guidelines (Wright, 1979). By the 1960s, traditional turpentining had ceased to be a significant industry in the South, due mainly to the lack of an available workforce.

Black respondents in Tze. I. Chiang *et al.*'s (1971) investigation cite exacting working conditions as reasons for seeking employment outside the forests.

Blacks also labored in the southern lumber industry, accounting for one-half of all southern forest laborers from 1910 to 1940 (US Census). Conditions reported in lumber camps are similar to those described in turpentine camps, with the same closed system of indebtedness and company dictated mores. Blacks usually performed the most dangerous work in timber processing. Typically, they loaded cut logs onto railroad cars that transported the timber to the sawmill or they comprised the "rail gang" which laid tracks for the makeshift rail line into the timber stands (Mayor, 1988). Todes also writes about working conditions for blacks in lumbering:

> To work at the heaviest jobs is the lot of the Negroes. In the woods, they fell and buck the trees, handle the hooks or tongs, form the labor gang in the skidder crew, work on railroad construction and do the heavy work in the loading process. In the mills, they ride the carriage or haul and stack lumber while the white workers handle the machines. In the Great Southern Lumber Company's camps where the white sawyers have an 8-hour shift, Negro workers riding the carriage or "rig" must work 10 hours a day. Whites workers get paid for two holidays a year but the Negroes get no vacations at all.
>
> (1931, p. 83)

The collective memory of turpentining and lumbering has been relayed to successive generations by word of mouth. For instance, Chiang *et al.*'s (1971) study reports that older blacks who had been turpentiners strongly discouraged younger family members from becoming involved in the work. Older blacks recounted the hardships involved in turpentining, and it was viewed as a low-class occupation. Official knowledge of turpentining and lumbering has been kept alive in official memory sites such as the anthropological databases contained in the Florida Folk Life Collection. Songs and folk tales recorded by southern turpentine workers in the 1930s are included in the 1930s Work Project Administration's database.

Lynchings served to further alienate blacks from wildlands as some of these acts occurred in isolated woodland areas (Raper, 1933, p. 6). For instance, eight of eleven black lynchings that took place in Florida in the 1930s happened in "open country" or wooded areas. The greatest number of lynchings occurred in the 1890s and then lessened towards the middle of the twentieth century, but the threat of such violence remained (Zangrando, 1980). The fact that some of the lynchings occurred in wooded areas sufficed to influence black perceptions of wildlands. Being that wildlands are unfamiliar landscapes, the frightening imprint of the wildlands becomes intertwined with the terror of lynching.

Modern environmental movement: environmental justice and black return to the land

In 1982, the African-American environmental justice movement began in Warren County, North Carolina, when African Americans protested the proposed citing of a hazardous waste landfill in their county (Szasa and Meuser,

1997). It focused attention on the inequitable distribution of hazardous and toxic waste sites in lower-income and minority communities (Bullard, 1990). Chief concerns of environmental justice advocates are issues relating to pollutants and environmental toxins which threaten the integrity of local neighborhoods and workplaces, both in urban and rural areas. These concerns of primarily female and lower-income groups have been contrasted with the goals of mainstream (majority white) environmental groups which seek to preserve federally designated wilderness areas and wildlife and fish habitats.

The environmental justice movement coincided with the return of blacks to the South, including the rural South. From 1970 to 1980, more than 1 million African Americans migrated to the South from the Northeast, Midwest, and West. This compares with an out-migration from the South of 0.95 million blacks during the same time period (McHugh, 1987). Blacks, like other race/ethnic groups, returned to the South because of better job prospects in the urban areas of the region, such as metropolitan Atlanta and Charlotte and Raleigh-Durham, NC.

In *A Call to Home: African Americans Reclaim the Rural South*, Carol Stack notes that blacks are also returning to rural regions of the South, despite the lack of viable economic opportunities or improved racial relations (1996). According to Stack, social conditions in some rural areas have not improved appreciatively since blacks left en masse a half century ago. Some blacks are moving back to the rural South because of the need to reconnect with family and to reclaim the land (1996). The recent black return to rural landscapes highlights the paradoxical relation of blacks with wildland environments. Blacks are returning to rural areas despite the hardships encountered in these places by earlier generations. Current trends suggest there is a desire in the African-American community to engage rather than avoid wildlands. Certainly, rural residence would provide more opportunities for blacks to interact with wildland places, less inhibited now by the constraints which accompanied their foreparents. This return migration indicates that there may be factors which mitigate black land memories, for instance increased urbanization and affluence among African Americans.

The contemporary, mostly urban, black population is farther removed from the land than its rural predecessors; present generations of African Americans may also be farther removed from negative images of wildlands. There is also a larger black middle class than 50 years ago, with greater access to information about wildland recreation resources and official data concerning environmental degradation. Blacks may now hold wildland attitudes similar to middle-class whites, even though blacks interact with wildland resources less than whites do. As more African Americans move into the middle class, and become more suburban, there may well be a shift in the collective construction of their perception of wildlands.

References

Averit, J. B. 1921. Turpentining with Slaves in the 30's and 40's. In *Naval Stores: History, Production, Distribution and Consumption*. Ed. T. Gamble. Savannah, Ga.: Review Publishing & Printing Company, pp. 25–27.

Bennett, L., Jr. 1968. *Before the Mayflower*. New York: Double Day.

Bixler, R. D. and M. F Floyd. 1997. Nature Is Scary, Disgusting, and Uncomfortable. *Environment and Behavior* 29, pp. 443–67.

Blum, E. D. 2002. Power, Danger, and Control: Slave Women's Perceptions of Wilderness in the Nineteenth Century. *Women's Studies* 31, pp. 247–67.

Bullard, R. D. 1990. *Dumping in Dixie: Race, Class and Environmental Quality*. Boulder, Co.: Westview.

Carson, R. 1962. *Silent Spring*. New York: Houghton Mifflin Company.

Chiang, T. I., W. H. Burrows, W. C. Howard, and G. D. Woodard Jr. 1971. *A Study of the Problems and Potentials of the Gum Naval Stores Industry*. Atlanta, Ga.: Industrial Development Division, Engineering Experiment Station, Georgia Institute of Technology.

Cordell, H. K., J. M. Bowker, C. Betz, and C. Johnson. 2000. July. *Wilderness Awareness and Participation: A Comparison Across Race and Ethnicity – Preliminary results: NSRE 2000*. Washington, DC: USFS.

Croker, Jr, T. C. 1979. The Longleaf Pine Story. *Southern Lumberman* 239, pp. 69–74.

Cronon, W. 1996. The Trouble with Wilderness or, Getting Back to the Wrong Nature. *Environmental History* 1, pp. 7–28.

Daniel, P. 1985. *Breaking the Land: The Transformation of Cotton, Tobacco, and Rice Cultures Since 1880*. Urbana, Ill.: University of Illinois Press.

Genovese, E. D. 1972. *Roll, Jordan, Roll: The World the Slaves Made*. New York: Pantheon.

Goldsmith, J. 1994. Designing for Diversity. *National Parks* 68, pp. 20–21.

Gramann, J. H. 1996. *Ethnicity, Race, and Outdoor Recreation: A Review of Trends, Policy, and Research. Miscellaneous Paper R-96-1*. Washington, DC: U.S. Army Corps of Engineers.

Greider, T., and Garkovich, L. 1994. Landscapes: The Social Construction of Nature and the Environment. *Rural Sociology* 59, pp. 1–24.

Halbwachs, M. 1980. *The Collective Memory*. New York: Harper and Row.

Hammond, J. L. 1985. Wilderness and Heritage Values. *Environmental Ethics* 7, pp. 165–70.

Harding, Vincent. 1981. *There Is a River: The Black Struggle for Freedom in America*. New York: Harcourt Brace Jovanovich.

Harlan, L. R. 1974. *The Booker T. Washington Papers, Vol. 3*. Urbana, Ill.: University of Illinois Press.

Johnson, C. Y., P. M. Horan, and W. Pepper. 1997. Race, Rural Residence, and Wildland Visitation: Examining the Influence of Sociocultural Meaning. *Rural Sociology* 62, pp. 89–110.

Lucas, R. C. 1989. A Look at Wilderness Use and Users in Transition. *Natural Resources Journal* 29, pp. 41–55.

Mandle, J. R. 1978. *The Roots of Black Poverty: The Southern Plantation Economy After the Civil War*. Durham, NC: Duke University Press.

Marks, S. 1991. *Southern Hunting in Black and White*. Princeton, NJ: Princeton University Press.

Mayor, A. H. 1988. *Southern Timberman*. Athens, Ga.: University of Georgia Press.

McHugh, K. E. 1987. Black Migration Reversal in the United States. *The Geographical Review* 77, pp. 171–82.

Mohai, P. 1990. Black Environmentalism. *Social Science Quarterly* 71, pp. 744–65.

Nash, R. 1967. *Wilderness and the American Mind*. New Haven, Ct.: Yale University Press.

Nash, R. 1975. Qualitative Landscape Values: The Historical Perspective. In *Landscape Assessment: Value, Perceptions, and Resources*. Eds. E. H. Zube, R. O. Brush and J. G. Fabos. Stroudsburg, Pa.: Dowden, Hutchinson, & Ross, Inc., pp. 10–17.

Raper, A. F. 1933. *The Tragedy of Lynching*. Chapel Hill, NC: The University of North Carolina Press.

Schama, S. 1995. *Landscape and Memory*. New York: Alfred A. Knopf.

Stack, C. 1996. *Call to Home: African Americans Reclaim the Rural South*. New York: Basic Books.

Stokols, D. 1980. Group x Place Transactions: Some Neglected Issues in Psychological Research on Settings. In *Toward a Psychology of Situations: An Interactional Perspective*. Ed. D. Magnusson. Hillsdale, NJ: Lawrence Erlbaum Associates. pp. 393–415.

Stokols, D. 1990. Instrumental and Spiritual Views of People-Environment Relations. *American Psychologist* 45, pp. 641–646.

Szasz, A., and M. Meuser. 1997. Environmental Inequalities: Literature Review and Proposals for New Directions in Research and Theory. *Current Sociology* 45, pp. 99–120.

Taylor, D. E. 1997. American Environmentalism: The Roles of Race, Class and Gender in Shaping Activism, 1820–1995. *Race, Gender, and Class* 5, pp. 16–62.

Taylor, D. E. 2000. The Rise of the Environmental Justice Paradigm: Injustice Framing and the Social Construction of Environmental Discourses. *American Behavioral Scientist* 43, pp. 508–80.

Todes, C. 1931. *Labor and Lumber*. New York: International Publishers.

Turner, F. J. 1953. *The Frontier in American History*. New York: Henry Holt and Company.

Wright. G. G. 1979. *Turpentining: An Ethnohistorical Study of a Southern Industry and Way of Life*. Master's thesis. Athens, Ga.: University of Georgia.

Zangrando, R. L. 1980. *The NAACP Crusade Against Lynching, 1909–1950*. Philadelphia: Temple University Press.

Zerubavel, E. 1996. Social Memories: Steps to a Sociology of the Past. *Qualitative Sociology* 19, pp. 283–99.

16 Latin Americans and the environment

Attitudes, beliefs, and values

Victor Corral-Verdugo, Blanca Fraijo-Sing, and César Tapia-Fonllem

The Latin American subcontinent hosts societies that exhibit particular idiosyncrasies in their interactions with the natural world. These idiosyncrasies are at least partially a result of people's exposure to their physical environment, while shared beliefs are a result of centuries of colonization, especially from Europe. Asian, African, and of course Native American influences are also manifested in people's attitudes toward the environment.

The sum of external cultural influences (western worldviews), local traditions (*autochthonous* systems of beliefs), and people's exposure to the particularities of the physical environment has resulted in certain Latin American attitudes toward the environment. These influences can support either pro- or anti-environmental behaviors. Although the link between attitude and behavior is not salient enough to consider attitudes as major determinants of ecological action, there is no doubt that these predispositions are significant predictors of such action (Scott and Willits, 1994; Corral-Verdugo and Armendáriz, 2000), and can be considered, at least, a platform upon which behavioral tendencies develop. Therefore, studying environmental attitudes, beliefs, and worldviews in this and other regions of the world is necessary to understanding what makes people behave in sustainable or anti-ecological ways.

Our description will be based upon research conducted mainly in Latin America, although research conducted in Europe, North America, and other regions is also discussed. We begin with a general description of the Latin American biophysical and cultural environment. Since a main feature of this environment is its diversity, a main point in this chapter is the consideration of social and biophysical variety in Latin America in promoting environmental attitudes, beliefs, values, and worldviews.

The socio-cultural geography of the Latin American environment

Latin America encompasses countries that are highly diverse both physically and socially. Socio-economic inequities, notorious throughout the region, make possible the existence of extremely rich families but also of social groups living under extreme poverty in the same country, region, or city. A significant number of Latin Americans face a daily struggle for subsistence, and against impunity, authoritarianism, and social injustice (Arriaga, 2000). Yet others live in relatively stable, prosperous, and democratic countries and regions. While many Latin Americans live in conditions similar to those experienced by citizens of wealthier nations (Brea, 2003), many others have no access to adequate education, employment, social security, health support, or commodities such as computers, the internet, and cars.

A considerable number of ethnic groups are present among Latin Americans: Europeans, Africans, Asians, Middle Easterners, and Native Americans (Brea, 2003). A significant proportion of Latin American societies consider themselves as members of western civilization, holding its cultural values. However, particular forms of collectivistic, modernistic, nondualistic, and holistic views of the world predominate in Latin American. This divergence from the individualistic, post-modernist, dualistic, and analytic worldview of European and Anglo-American societies (Schmuck and Schultz, 2002) makes necessary a special approach for studying interactions between environment and behavior in this region of the world. Since environmental researchers look for answers to the environmental dilemma in the prevailing worldview, the study of environmental attitudes in every country and culture is required to understand how societies cope with environmental opportunities and risk.

The dualistic (ecocentric versus anthropocentric) system of beliefs is used by western researchers as a universal paradigm for explaining environmental attitudes. The individualistic approach that emphasizes factors such as personal responsibility, competence, and motivation is supposed to lead people toward sustainability, in accordance with such a paradigm. Moreover, the rational, analytical component of the decision-making process is thought to be the one defining pro-environmental orientation. However, since most cultures of the world do not hold these Euro-American orientations, the study of holistic (combined eco-anthropocentric) worldviews, collective orientations, and affective-emotional determinants of sustainable behavior is one of the alternative approaches for studying environment-behavior interactions that should be considered in trying to characterize environmental attitudes in Latin America and elsewhere. In accordance with the particularities of the Latin American region, a significant number of studies characterizing environmental attitudes and behaviors among people of this region are investigated in this chapter using these alternative worldviews.

The biodiversity of the tropical, subtropical, and temperate habitats of Latin America is necessary for the well-being of the Earth. The neo-tropical ecological zone contains 68 percent of the world's tropical rainforests (UNEP, 1999). The Latin American region contains 40 percent of the plant and animal species on the planet, and is considered to have the highest floristic diversity in the world. The Amazonian valleys, the Andean mountains, the Brazilian Atlantic forest, and the forests of Meso-America are home to some of the world's richest ecosystems. Arid and semiarid vegetation occurs in the mountainous areas running from southern Ecuador to Chile, in northern Mexico, in northern Colombia, and in Venezuela, Argentina, and northeastern Brazil. Brazil, Paraguay, and Bolivia share some of the world's most important continental wetlands renowned for their diversity. Studying conditions and personal characteristics, including environmental attitudes and worldviews, that encourage people to conserve these rich scenarios is vital for the whole world.

Environmental attitudes and awareness

Exposure to environmental risks (Stern *et al.*, 1995), poverty (Dunlap and Mertig, 1996), contact with the natural world (Kals *et al.*, 1999), and a tradition of inclusiveness with nature (Allwood and Berry, 2007) are considered factors that influence pro-environmental attitudes. Since these conditions are prevalent in Latin Americans, their environmental awareness should be high when compared with other populations. Riley Dunlap *et al.* (1993) asked how concerned diverse national samples were about environmental problems, finding that a much larger proportion of Mexican adults (29 percent) rated the environment as the "most important problem," contrasting with the 11 percent of American respondents and 9 percent of German respondents. This study also showed that in Chile, Mexico, and Brazil, inadequate sewage systems, air and water pollution, and contaminated soil are seen as serious environmental problems. The loss of natural resources in Brazil and inadequate sewage systems in Uruguay were seen as especially serious environmental problems.

Stuart Oskamp and Wesley Schultz (2005) and Schultz (2001) examined underlying values related to environmental attitudes across 16 countries. They assessed biospheric values, reflecting concern about the well-being of all living things, and egocentric values indicative of self-oriented goals. Mexico had higher biospheric values then the USA and Germany. This finding seems to reveal a higher pro-environmental attitude of these Latin Americans.

Robert Bechtel *et al.* (1999) also showed that Mexicans and Brazilians scored higher than North Americans in a measure of ecocentric beliefs: the New Environmental Paradigm scale (NEP, Dunlap and Van Liere, 1978). These results were replicated comparing US, Japanese, Peruvian, and Mexican samples, with the Mexican sample producing the highest levels of agreement with the NEP (Bechtel *et al.*, 2006).

As for the relationship between attitudes toward nature and people's contact with the natural world, M. X. Bizerril (2004) evaluated Brazilian students' environmental perceptions of savanna-like vegetation. The author administered to students tests of knowledge and perception of the place biome's wildlife. Students who had more contact with the region's natural landscapes showed greater affection for it. Also, H. Tirado *et al.* (2007) found that with Mexican respondents, the greater the contact with the natural environment that was reported, the greater the feeling of inclusiveness with nature.

Daily environmental problems and hazards faced by Latin Americans make them especially aware of their environment, and perhaps more aware than their counterparts in North America and Europe. A history of contact with nature increases an individual's tendency to develop pro-ecological attitudes. This does not necessarily transform Latin Americans into more environmentally oriented citizens in terms of actual behavior. Pro-environmental attitudes are necessary, but not sufficient, to lead individuals and groups toward the goal of sustainable action.

Worldviews

Worldviews are systems of beliefs which reflect how people conceive human–nature relations (Bechtel, 1996). Several authors in the area of environmental beliefs consider that a dichotomy exists between two supposedly contradictory belief systems: the so-called Human Exception Paradigm (HEP) – an anthropocentric belief system – and the NEP of ecocentric nature (Dunlap and Van Liere, 1978; Dunlap *et al.*, 2000). However, others have not found a contradiction between these two environmental worldviews (Bechtel *et al.*, 1999; Castro and Lima, 2001). This discrepancy seems to be explained in terms of cultural differences. According to Victor Corral-Verdugo and Luz Irene Armendáriz (2000), North Americans and some Europeans tend to hold dualistic systems of belief. This is reflected in the apparent dichotomy between anthropocentrism and ecocentrism that they exhibit, meaning that in those cultures a person is either ecocentric or anthropocentric. Alternatively, Latin Americans seem more likely to hold holistic worldviews, in which anthropocentric and ecocentric beliefs are not seen as contradictory. Bechtel and colleagues (1999; 2006) found that in their samples from the USA, the NEP and the HEP covariate significantly and negatively: when one is high, the other is low. However, in their Brazilian and Mexican respondents such covariance was positive, indicating that Latin Americans could hold both systems of belief simultaneously. This implies that they could consider themselves members of an exceptional species (anthropocentrism) even while exhibiting a sense of responsibility for caring for the natural world (ecocentrism). Upper-class Peruvians were the only Latin American sample exhibiting the dualistic orientation. Bechtel *et al.* (2006) concluded that this result was due to the tendency among Latin American higher classes for the Euro-American worldview to predominate.

Bernardo Hernández *et al.* (2001) compared the environmental-belief factor structure of undergraduate students from Mexico with those of students from Spain. They assessed "progress," "naturalism," and "anthropocentrism" factors. Although naturalism and anthropocentrism negatively covaried in both samples, the correlation between "progress" and "naturalism" was negative in the Spanish sample and nonsignificant in the Mexican one, indicating again a nondualistic view of human–environment relations among these Latin Americans, while the Europeans tended to be more dichotomic in expressing their beliefs. Corral-Verdugo *et al.* (2008) suggest the emergence of a non-dichotomic, holistic New Human Interdependence Paradigm (NHIP) in diverse populations of the world. The NHIP envisages interdependence between human progress and nature conservation and conceives it as a dynamic process of integration and incorporation of human needs into natural processes. Based upon the results of Bechtel and colleagues (1999; 2006), Corral-Verdugo *et al.* (2008) designed and administered to Mexicans, Italians, French, and Indians an instrument assessing the NHIP scale. The factor structure of the instrument was found to be universal and proved to predict a measure of conservation behavior more saliently than the NEP-HEP instrument did. Additionally, the result indicated that this holistic worldview is present among Europeans of Latin culture (Corral-Verdugo *et al.*, 2008).

Environment, community, and self

Since Latin American societies are considered to be more collectivistic than individualistic (Hofstede, 1980), there is interest in studying how this inclination affects people's pro-environmental dispositions. Esther Wiesenfeld (1996) argues that a significant number of Latin Americans reflect the notion of community as a "we," understood as a compact and somehow homogeneous group; people belonging to the group feel, think, and behave in similar and predictable ways. The "we" implies a set of processes such as membership, inclusion, identity, feeling of belonging, and an emotional bond or sense of community which does not appear to vary across time and within members of the community. However, for Wiesenfeld the "we" is rather dialectic and dynamic: shared needs and group processes built across time allow for intragroup diversity, disagreements, and fluctuations in dimensions such as participation in environmental protection initiatives and other collective actions. Wiesenfeld stresses the importance of community context in facilitating the comprehension of people-environment transactions and individuals' actions for bettering the environment. She offers as evidence the research results of a number of Latin American authors (Wiesenfeld, 1997; Giuliani and Wiesenfeld, 2002; Jiménez-Domínguez and López-Aguilar, 2002). These authors demonstrate that collective efforts empower participants, increasing their autonomy and self-reliance and reinforcing their sense of community and identity. As attachment to place and to other people increases, they work together to solve problems of adaptation, including environmental challenges.

Effect of interventional programs on environmental attitudes

An important subject of research in the area of environmental attitudes is the effect of interventional programs aimed at promoting pro-ecological values. Following a recommendation by the United Nations Educational, Scientific and Cultural Organization (UNESCO, 1980) regarding the importance of developing behaviors oriented toward environmental protection, a number of interventions have been designed in Latin America aimed at promoting attitudes favorable to ecological preservation.

Teresa Gutiérrez-de-White and Susan Jacobson (1994), in Colombia, tested the effect of a teacher workshop about wildlife conservation on students' attitudes toward conservation, and found that the intervention was successful. J. Colvin (1993) described a series of environmental education workshops, which were attended by elementary-school teachers from the USA and Ecuador. He concluded that preserving biodiversity and the sustainable use of natural resources depended on the understanding, cooperation, and community participation of those who live in places where those teachers work.

A. Biaggio *et al.* (1999), in Brazil, intended to promote favorable attitudes toward the environment through debates among elementary-school children concerning environmental dilemmas. Although the authors did not find their results entirely satisfactory, their approach is potentially useful in trying to induce pro-ecological attitudes.

In Mexico, Blanca Fraijo (2003) developed a program intended to promote pro-environmental attitudes, values, knowledge, skills, and participation in elementary-school children. She based her intervention on the goals of environmental education proposed by UNESCO (1980), which conceives this process as an integration of behavioral tendencies and capacities with pro-environmental behavior. She also considered the framework suggested by Corral-Verdugo (2002), in which environmental education is used to promote pro-environmental competence (i.e. the possession of skills in response to social requirements intended to preserve the environment). Among those requirements, Fraijo (2003) demonstrated attitudes as personal characteristics significantly linked to pro-ecological behavior. Her program was found capable of producing congruence between skills and social and personal pro-ecological requirements, as recommended by UNESCO. L. Hernández-Martín del Campo and Corral-Verdugo (2005) tested the effect of a literature course on the development of pro-environmental values in Mexican teenagers. The course emphasized universal values contained in the works of recognized authors of the universal literature. After two months the students significantly increased their adherence to values of nature preservation, along with other universal values. More importantly, this program resulted in congruence between values and pro-social and pro-environmental behavior.

Latin America has been an important laboratory where the effect of intervention programs promoting pro-environmental attitudes has been successfully tested. Since these attitudes seem in turn to affect pro-ecological behavior this effort is a valuable and necessary part of the process of generating a citizenship committed to environmental protection.

Final comments

As demonstrated in this brief review of studies, idiosyncratic as well as universal psychological dispositions emerge from people-environment interactions in this region of the world. Some Latin American worldviews, values, and beliefs are particular, while others are shared with cultures outside the region. Since Latin America is one of the critically bio-diverse regions of the world, understanding how societies and individuals in this region react and became predisposed toward the environment is crucial for developing interventional strategies. According to a number of studies, exposure to environmental hazards, experience with resource scarcity, a tradition of inclusiveness, and contact with the natural environment make Latin Americans more aware of environmental problems than most citizens in the western world (Dunlap *et al.*, 1993; Bizerril, 2004; Oskamp and Schultz, 2005; Tirado *et al.*, 2007). This does not necessarily lead them toward overt pro-ecological behavior, yet it does configure a psychological basis on which people's pro-environmental dispositions could develop and eventually may manifest as sustainable actions (Corral-Verdugo and Armendáriz, 2000).

Studies have also shown that Latin Americans can hold either individual-istic or collectivistic cultural traditions. Thus, depending on the group, strat-egies intended to promote pro-environmental attitudes and behaviors can use individually-based or community participation approaches to solve environmen-tal problems. This explains why a number of Latin American authors are inter-ested in studying individual predictors of environmental commitment such as personal responsibility, competence, egoistic motives, self-esteem, etc. (Corral-Verdugo, 2002), while others are more inclined to look at community-oriented strategies to solve environmental problems (Wiesenfeld, 1997; Giuliani and Wiesenfeld, 2002; Jiménez-Domínguez and López-Aguilar, 2002; Hernández and Reimel de Carrasquel, 2004). Although many Latin Americans have either a dualistic or collectivistic worldview, many others exhibit a synthetic worldview of people-environment interactions (Corral-Verdugo and Pinheiro, 2009). In this latter case, individuals easily accept both ecocentric and anthropocentric visions of their role in nature (Bechtel *et al.*, 1999; 2006). This holistic approach, recog-nized as a "New Human Interdependence Paradigm," seems to be in accordance with one of the pillars of sustainable development – social sustainability – and slightly but significantly predicts pro-environmental behavior (Corral-Verdugo *et al.*, 2008). This approach, first described by Latin American researchers, seems to be emerging in (at least) European and Asian countries as well.

Finally, while recognizing the value that correlational and observational studies have for understanding how environmental attitudes manifest, a growing number of Latin American authors use evidence-based approaches for promoting pro-ecological attitudes, beliefs, and values. Especially in studies with children as a target population, researchers have developed successful interventions and strat-egies which have promise for increasing pro-environmental behaviors (Colvin, 1993; Gutiérrez-de-White and Jacobson, 1994; Biaggio *et al.*, 1999; Fraijo, 2003; Hernández-Martín del Campo and Corral-Verdugo, 2005). These interventions and the prospective studies on the psychological correlates of sustainable acting in Latin America will be markedly valued in the close future.

References

Allwood, C. M., and J. W. Berry. 2006. Origins and Development of Indigenous Psychologies: An International Analysis. *International Journal of Psychology* 41, pp. 243–68.

Arriaga, C. 2000. *Poverty in Latin America: New Scenarios and Political Challenges for Urban Habitat*. Santiago de Chile: Economic Commission for Latin America and the Caribbean.

Bechtel, R. 1996. *Environment and Behavior*. Thousand Oaks, Calif.: Sage.

Bechtel, R., V. Corral-Verdugo, M. Asai, and A. González-Riesle. 2006. A Crosscultural Study of Environmental Belief Structures: USA, Japan, Mexico and Peru. *International Journal of Psychology* 41, pp. 145–51.

Bechtel, R., V. Corral-Verdugo, and J. Pinheiro. 1999. Environmental Beliefs U.S., Brazil and Mexico. *Journal of Crosscultural Psychology* 30, pp. 122–28.

Biaggio, A., G. Vargas, J. Monteiro, K.Souza, and S. Tesche. 1999. Promoção de atitudes ambientais favoráveis atráves de debates de dilemas ecológicos [Promoting Favorable Attitudes Toward the Environment through Debates of Dilemmas with Ecological Content]. *Estudos de Psicologia* 4, pp. 221–38.

Bizerril, M. X. 2004. Children's Perceptions of Brazilian Cerrado Landscapes and Biodiversity. *Journal on Environmental Education* 35, pp. 47–58.

Brea, J. 2003. Population Dynamics in Latin America. *Population Bulletin* 58, pp. 3–36.

Castro, P., and L. Lima. 2001. Old and New Ideas about the Environment and Science: An Exploratory Study. *Environment and Behavior* 33, pp. 400–23.

Colvin, J. 1993. Workshops in the Forest: A Model International Environmental Exchange Program in Ecuador. *Journal of Environmental Education* 24, pp.23–25.

Corral-Verdugo, V. 2002. A Structural Model of Pro-environmental Competency. *Environment and Behavior* 34, pp. 531–49.

Corral-Verdugo, V., and L. I. Armendáriz. 2000. The 'New Environmental Paradigm' in a Mexican Community. *Journal of Environmental Education* 31, pp. 25–31.

Corral-Verdugo, V., G. Carrus, M. Bonnes, G. Moser, and J. Sinha. 2008. Environmental Beliefs and Endorsement of Sustainable Development Principles in Water Conservation: Towards a New Human Interdependence Paradigm Scale. *Environment and Behavior* 40, pp. 703–25.

Corral-Verdugo, V. and J. Pinheiro. 2009. Environmental Psychology with a Latin American Taste. *Journal of Environmental Psychology* 29, pp. 366–74.

Dunlap, R., G. Gallup, and A. Gallup. 1993. *Health of the Planet*. Princeton, NJ: Gallup International Institute.

Dunlap, R. E., and A. G. Mertig. 1996. Weltweites Umwelbewußsein: Eine Herausforderung für die sozialwissenschaftliche Theorie. In *Umweltsoziologie: Sonderheft Nr. 36 der Kölner Zeitschrift fur Soziologie un Sozialpsychologie*. Eds. A. Diekman and C. C. Jager.

Dunlap, R. E., K. D. Van Liere, A. G. Mertig, and R. E. Jones. 2000. Measuring Endorsement of the New Environmental Paradigm: A Revised NEP Scale. *Journal of Social Issues* 3, pp. 425–42.

Dunlap, R. G. and K. D. Van Liere. 1978. A Proposed Measuring Instrument and Preliminary Results: The "New Environmental Paradigm". *Journal of Environmental Education* 9, pp. 10–19.

Fraijo, B. 2003. *Competencias proecológicas del cuidado del agua en niños de primer grado de primaria [Water-conservation Proecological Competencies in First Graders at Elementary Schools]*. Doctoral thesis. Culiacán, Mexico: Autonomous University of Sinaloa.

Giuliani, F., and E. Wiesenfeld. 2002. Sustainable Development and Identity in Two Venezuelan Communities. *Environment and Behavior* 34, pp. 81–96.

Gutierrez-de-White, T., and S. K. Jacobson. 1994. Evaluating Conservation Education Programs at a South American Zoo. *Journal of Environmental Education* 25, pp. 18–22.

Hernández, B., V. Corral, S. Hess, and E. Suárez. 2001. Sistemas de creencias ambientales: Un análisis multi-muestra de estructuras factoriales [Environmental Belief Systems: A Multisample Covariance Analysis of Factor Structures]. *Estudos de Psicología [Spain]* 22, pp. 53–64.

Hernández, L. and S. Reimel de Carrasquel. 2004. Calidad de vida y participación comunitaria: Evaluación psicosocial de proyectos urbanísticos en barrios pobres [Quality of Life and Community Participation: Psycho-social Evaluation of Urbanistic Projects in Poor Neighborhoods]. *Interamerican Journal of Psychology* 38, pp. 73–86.

Hernández-Martín del Campo, L. M., and V. Corral-Verdugo. 2005. Enseñanza de valores a través de la literatura: Un estudio con adolescentes mexicanos [Teaching Values through Literature: A Study of Mexican Teenagers]. In *Niñez, Adolescencia y problemas Sociales*. Eds. M. Frías and V. Corral. Mexico City: CONACYT-UniSon.

Hofstede, G. 1980. *Culture's Consequences.* Beverly Hills, Calif.: Sage.

Jiménez-Domínguez, B., and R. López Aguilar. 2002. Identity and Sustainability in Two Neighborhoods of Guadalajara, Mexico. *Environment and Behavior* 34, pp. 97–110.

Kals, E., D. Schumacher, and L. Montada. 1999. Emotional Affinity toward Nature as a Motivational Basis to Protect Nature. *Environment and Behavior* 31, pp. 178–202.

Oskamp, S., and P. Schultz. 2005. *Attitudes and Opinions.* 3rd edn. Mahwah, NJ: Erlbaum.

Schmuck, P., and P. Schultz. 2002. Sustainable Development as a Challenge for Psychology. In *Psychology of Sustainable Development.* Eds. P. Schmuck, and W. Schultz. Norwell, Mass.: Kluwer/New York: Springer.

Schultz, P. W. 2001. The Structure of Environmental Concern: Concern for Self, Other People, and the Biosphere. *Journal of Environmental Psychology* 21, pp. 327–39.

Scott, D., and F. K. Willits. 1994. Environmental Attitudes and Behavior: A Pennsylvania Survey. *Environment and Behavior* 26, pp. 239–60.

Stern, P. C., T. Dietz, L. Kalof, and G. A. Guagnano. 1995. Values, Beliefs, and Pro-environmental Action: Attitude Formation toward Emergent Attitude Objects. *Journal of Applied Social Psychology* 25, pp. 1611–36.

Tirado, H., V. Corral, M. Maceda, E. García, A. Robles, V. Blanco, A. Rodríguez, J. C. Llanes, and S. Castillo. 2007. Factores afectivo-emocionales relacionados con el medio ambiente y su efecto en el comportamiento pro-ecológico [Affective-emotional Factors Related to the Environment and their Effect on Pro-ecological Behavior]. *Revista Mexicana de Psicología*, special issue, *Proceedings of the XV Mexican Congress of Psychology*, pp. 103–5. Mexico City: Sociedad Mexicana de Psicología.

UNEP (United Nations Environment Programme). 1999. *Global Environmental Outlook.* Nairobi: UNEP.

UNESCO (United Nations Educational, Scientific and Cultural Organization). 1980. *Environmental Education in the Light of the Tblisi Conference.* Paris: UNESCO.

Wiesenfeld, E. 1996. The Concept of 'We': A Community Social Psychology Myth? *Journal of Community Psychology* 24, pp. 337–46.

Wiesenfeld, E. 1997. From Individual Need to Community Consciousness: The Dialectics between Land Appropriation and Eviction Threat (A Case Study of a Venezuelan "Barrio"). *Environment and Behavior* 29, pp. 198–212.

17 Post-disaster Japan's environmental transition

W. Puck Brecher

Introduction

Several dramatic developments have overturned Japan's environmental discourse: the March 11, 2011, "triple disaster" (the 9.0 magnitude earthquake, tsunami, and nuclear meltdown at Fukushima, hereafter noted as 3.11); the ensuing and ongoing anti-nuclear movement; and growing antipathy toward the central government. An urgent call for greater local empowerment has crystallized amid this confluence of phenomena, empowerment to be informed by greater self-sufficiency at the grassroots level. Previously, Japanese self-empowerment initiatives had emerged to combat isolated environmental threats, variously winning short-term traction within local populations. These movements have recently declined, replaced by a more comprehensive, integrated discourse that locates environmental concerns within the contexts of energy policy, reconstruction, and human safety. Eclipsed by the horrors unleashed by 3.11, therefore, issue-based environmental activism all but vanished in post-disaster Japan. Taking its place, a new generation of environmental counter measures has coalesced around ideals like community, self-sufficiency, and resilience.

Japan's new grassroots environmental discourse is closely tied to the country's post-disaster anti-nuclear movement, and is distinctive in several important respects. Most significantly, it has become a majority position. Data from public opinion surveys on nuclear power varies widely, but nearly all studies conducted during the 18 months following 3.11 found most Japanese distrustful of the nation's nuclear program and in favor of reducing or eliminating it altogether. The most reliable estimates for the first half of 2012 place the percentage of Japanese espousing such positions at between 55 percent and 70 percent (Oguma, 2012, p. 18). Such attitudes have also exerted considerable influence during the public debate over the future role of nuclear power. Japan's pre-disaster energy plan called for increasing nuclear energy's share of national output from 27 percent to 40 percent. Post-disaster, not only did a sizeable majority support dismantling a major sector of the national energy infrastructure, it assumed this position with the knowledge that doing so may result in higher electricity prices, power shortages, rising unemployment, greater reliance on imported oil, increased carbon dioxice (CO2) emissions, local economic decline, and stricter energy-saving mandates. In a country whose citizenry has always defended its personal comforts and economic interests, the anti-nuclear movement is noteworthy for its presumed acceptance of economic risk and personal sacrifice.

Post-3.11 environmental discourse is also distinctive for its shift from issue-specific to general conservation. Community-based environmental activism has historically mobilized around a single problem, such as localized industrial pollution. As such, it has generally limited its objective to mitigating short-term problems rather than reforming unsustainable policies and infrastructures. For this reason, even the most successful green movements have typically dispersed after achieving short-term results. Wildlife habitat within the Fujimae Tidelands in Nagoya, for example, was successfully protected by a highly effective citizens' movement but then allowed to degrade after the campaign's conclusion (Yoshimura and Kato, 2005). Recontextualized by a national energy crisis, environmental advocacy is now finding resonance with mainstream values by transitioning toward community building (*machizukuri*).

One representative vestige of environmental activism camouflaged within the national energy debate is Japan's Transition Town (TT) movement, an emergent social force that is helping to fuel a renaissance in community-based conservation. After discussing the principles and practical challenges facing the TT movement, this chapter examines the TT phenomenon within the context of post-disaster Japan. It concludes that environmental activism in Japan is undergoing a major strategic shift toward community strengthening and away from explicitly green initiatives.

Transitioning: benefits, needs, and obstacles

According to Noriyuki Tanaka, the TT project, which BBC radio called "one of the most dynamic and important social movements of the 21st century" (Tanaka, 2011, p. 235), was formulated in 2004 by permaculture advocate Dr Rob Hopkins, who then launched the first TT in Totnes, England, two years later. Subsequent TTs adhere to a "franchise system," each fundamentally independent yet united by adherence to a dual premise. The first part is peak oil, the controversial assumption that the availability of affordable oil has peaked and that oil energy's increasing scarcity will precipitate a crisis that current social, economic, and industrial infrastructures are ill-equipped to handle. The second is global climate change, also a consequence of current dependence on fossil fuels.

TTs respond to these imminent threats by augmenting local resilience by maximizing their self-sufficiency and ability to endure infrastructural crisis. This objective calls for a series of strategic community-based measures to ensure renewable supplies of local resources. Hopkins' *The Transition Handbook: From Oil Dependency to Local Resilience* (2008) organizes these measures into a systematic process. Prescribed TT guidelines afford individual TTs considerable autonomy but also attempt to secure program fidelity by requiring organizers of TT startups to receive formal training. The program also requires core members to draft a constitution that clarifies TT objectives and outlines its conflict resolution protocols (Tanaka, 2011, p. 235).

TTs need not be independent settlements or residential collectives. They are intra-urban interest groups engaged in transforming their immediate living spaces. Transitioning energies are designed to crystallize and spread quickly by minimizing the personal burdens generally associated with more environmentally sustainable living. Realizing that drastic lifestyle changes are unrealistic for most, the TT concept takes the self-empowering, environmentalist ideals of ecovillages and transfers them to existing residential communities. That is, it attempts a practical conversion of neighborhoods into ecovillages (Barrett, 2011).

Diffusion of the TT idea is also facilitated by the implicit legitimacy it garners as a homegrown local empowerment movement led by neighborhood residents. It does not have to contend with stereotypes faced by liberal environmental organizations, extremist religious groups, or marginal political factions. Indeed, an emerging TT takes deliberate steps to avoid becoming a source of public suspicion. Contrary to environmental non-governmental organizations (NGOs) that attempt to generate support with anger, fear, or guilt, the TT program is designed to offer residents an enjoyable, positive experience. The transition process in Totnes, for example, achieved long-term traction by proceeding at a natural pace that allowed for gradual adjustment. Its initiatives were also implemented without significant visible changes to the community (Katô, 2011, p. 90). TTs position themselves as defenders of economic resilience by supporting sustainable local businesses and industries. The greater implication of this focus on micro-level transformation is the presumption that the collective impact of disparate localized movements will catalyze macro-level societal change. Its approach echoes the paradox that, as Malcolm Gladwell writes in his study of societal transformation, "in order to create one contagious movement, you often have to create many small movements first" (2002, p. 192).

The potential benefits of the transition philosophy make it a largely unassailable proposition in Japan. Regardless of its specific initiatives, its community-building agenda combats depopulation and aging trends afflicting many of Japan's rural areas. Local leadership of community or neighborhood-scale conservation projects lighten administrative burdens on the top while generating solidarity below. It promotes synergistic partnerships while fostering greater local pride, self-esteem, and commitment to self-reliance. It may also provide residents with incentives to acquire new knowledge and skills. In many cases, local environmental conservation programs are able to act more expediently, more flexibly, and more economically than initiatives generated from above. They are less apt to become gridlocked or diluted by concessions to opposing interests. Transition groups able to establish close, interdependent relationships with political authorities are also more likely to represent local interests and thereby garner greater local acceptance.

Broad skepticism toward the ability of central, prefectural, and even local governments to actualize timely, effective conservation measures also indicates a need for greater community-based involvement in Japan. The absence or inadequacy of local representation within administrative bodies underscores the same need, particularly for grassroots initiatives that address issues of immediate local concern. Top down conservation tends to be late, slow, underfunded, and remedial rather than preventative, and it is disinclined to utilize local knowledge.

Benefits and needs notwithstanding, TT initiatives face a number of potential obstacles. They may confront the same conflicting views, objectives, and interests that typically hamstring governments. A conservation group must not only arbitrate internal conflict, it will be unlikely to win over the larger community if its projects significantly threaten local economic interests. In such cases, projects may stall or be forced to accept concessions that compromise their effectiveness. Moreover, most conservationist ventures will be carried out under the aegis of local administrations. Navigating difficult bureaucratic channels to obtain permissions and compliances may slow progress, and a proposed nature conservation program may even encounter legal obstructions. Communities may also be crippled by financial constraints. Dependence on local sponsors and donors can delay or stall projects. In addition to procuring financial resources, a TT must also acquire the knowledge, skills, and voluntary labor to sustain itself indefinitely (Trotman, 2008, pp. 3, 6, 11–12). The Transition model accepts that citizen initiatives cannot overcome such obstacles independently. Transitioning must proceed through the momentum of a community-wide movement.

Japan's TT movement

Peak oil proponents point out that post-3.11 Japan has indeed suffered an unforeseen energy shock, though from nuclear power rather than oil. And its resilience has been tested. Following the meltdown at Fukushima, Japan's 50 nuclear reactors, which had supplied about 27 percent of the nation's electricity, were systematically decommissioned. From May to July, 2012, Japan was nuclear free. Even as the country suffered rolling blackouts and energy price hikes, many Japanese bitterly opposed the government's decision to restart two reactors in Ôi, Fukui Prefecture. Meanwhile, the central government itself remained ineffectual and unpopular, with public sentiment toward national politics swinging between apathy and anger. In July, 2012, a Japan Broadcasting Corporation (NHK) poll found that 52 percent of Japanese supported none of the seven current political parties, the highest percentage since NHK started administering the polls in 2004 (NHK News Web, 2012). Communities understood that they could not rely on assistance from the state and so would have to respond independently.

Japan's TT movement flourished in this context. While ongoing prior to 3.11, its popularity was catalyzed by a spectrum of post-3.11 anxieties. In the summer of 2011, the country claimed a respectable 14 TTs. One year later, that number had exploded to 31, with many additional communities following suit independent of formal TT affiliation. The disasters and subsequent energy debacle made TT principles self-evident. Japanese no longer questioned the need to prepare for infrastructural crisis, they were experiencing it firsthand. To this extent, the anti-nuclear demonstrations ongoing through 2011–12 were not exclusively anti-nuclear, but rather expressions of affirmation for the sort of grassroots renaissance being advanced through the TT program. Local self-sufficiency had become a matter of common sense.

Enhancing self-sufficiency is a process of securing sustainable supplies of local resources. It calls for developing renewable (e.g. solar, hydro, biomass, and wind) energy infrastructures, expanding local agriculture, and minimizing waste, the most effective means of doing so to be determined independently by local TTs.

TTs also call for greater economic independence. Even communities that secure local supplies of energy and food cannot attain maximal resilience while remaining dependent on a vulnerable external economy. Economic independence rests on the collective efforts of producers, distributors, and consumers, and will gather little momentum without collaboration from local businesses.

One way that transitioning addresses this need is by instituting local currencies. In addition to keeping money within the community, local currencies support businesses by encouraging local production and trade, helping to protect the local economy from external economic shocks, and reducing the need for middlemen. Among TTs in Japan's Greater Tokyo area – Fujino, Sagamiko, Hayama, Kamakura, Yokohama, Kamogawa, Takao, Koganei, Hachiôji, Setagaya, and Shibuya, as well as TTs in nearby Chiba, Kanagawa, and Saitama Prefectures – nearly all are experimenting with currencies and voucher systems. Those whose limited memberships preclude deployment of an actual currency host role-playing games and mock transaction exercises to show prospective members how capital circulates and impacts local economic independence.

TT Fujino was the first to experiment with a local currency. About 90 minutes west of central Tokyo and known for its woodlands and artists, Fujino is the hub of Japan's TT movement and the country's first official TT. Though its currency, called the Yorozu, was originally introduced in a role-playing capacity to attract more community business owners, when the TT Fujino's membership reached about 100 households, the currency was launched as both actual and symbolic capital for members to purchase goods and services. Because transactions occur face to face in a "marketplace," they enhance communication, collaboration, and cooperation. Rather than patronizing chain stores that pump capital out of the local economy, Yorozu users help reduce dependence on external goods that require middlemen and energy for transport.

Momentum accompanying the launch of the Yorozu elicited several other local initiatives. One is Fujino Electric Power Company (*Fujino denryoku*) which holds outreach sessions to promote installation of renewable energy generation facilities in private homes, as well as workshops on converting used cooking oil to biodiesel auto fuel. Its annual Festival of Lights (*Hikari matsuri*), a three-day solar-powered celebration of local art and music, also functions as a TT promotion and recruitment event. (As a long-term investment, private generation of solar power became even more attractive in the summer of 2012 when the government passed a feed-in-tariff system requiring power companies to buy surplus electricity from private citizens.) Leading by example, Fujino Electric has fitted its headquarters with donated 20-year-old solar panels, allowing it to drop off

Figure 17.1 Satoyama Nagaya in Fujino

the public power grid. Surplus power will be used to supply an electric vehicle charging station.

TT Fujino's signature monument is Satoyama Nagaya, a co-housing structure accommodating four families, eleven people (see Figure 17.1). The building was designed by architect Yamada Takahiro, one of its residents, in the architectural style of nineteenth-century tenements, or row houses (*nagaya*). Completed in February 2011, much of the structure was built using local wood, bamboo, and earth. The insulating properties of the traditional mud walls obviate the need for air conditioning, its windows and skylights also helping to regulate indoor temperatures. The sod roof (on the left in Figure 17.1) provides additional insulation. Each family occupies its own private living quarters but shares a common dining area, kitchen, guest room, baths, and laundry facilities. Members also share a fruit and vegetable garden. A hand pump transfers collected rainwater to an outside sink and then to a garden irrigation system. Collected rainwater also supplies the toilets. Solar panels help charge electric appliances, including an electric bicycle. Residents, who completed much of the construction themselves, unanimously extol the efficiency of their co-housing arrangement and report satisfaction with their progress toward maximizing energy independence and minimizing their environmental footprint.

Fujino's greatest contribution to Japan's TT movement is the Permaculture Center of Japan (PCCJ), a collaborative organ of TT Fujino. Not only does PCCJ offer permaculture training for TT members and local farmers, but also the training in TT leadership required of aspiring TT organizers. While some Japanese obtain training in the UK, most receive it at Fujino before launching TTs in their own communities. TT Fujino members have translated *The Transition Handbook* (Hopkins, 2008[BIBXXX]) into Japanese for this purpose.

Fujino is an exceptional case, for while Japan's TT startups are proliferating rapidly, most cannot yet claim substantial memberships. The fact that many TT leaders trained at Fujino's PCCJ and are inveterate networkers has resulted in a tangible uniformity among Greater Tokyo TTs. All rely on websites, blogs, and social networking for self-promotion. Many have also established TT bars or cafés, attractive public spaces that serve as outreach centers to interface with their communities. Common activities include film screenings, festivals, and information exchange sessions. They also hold workshops or talks promoting solar and other renewable energy systems, permaculture, recycling, composting, and experimentation with local currencies. All events carry a dual objective: promoting sustainable urban development through voluntary citizen action, and providing enjoyable experiences that enhance community solidarity.

Integrating community building and enjoyment is integral to the movement's own sustainability. Methods vary. TT Kamakura, for example, sponsors group "treasure hunt" hikes (*aru mono sagashi*) designed to restore neighborhood pride while educating residents about their local history, environment, and culture. Interspersed with recreational events like tofu-making workshops and barbeques, TT Kamakura hosts study groups that educate members about responsible energy use and assist in solar panel kit assembly. Its Transition Salon serves as an outreach forum where interested residents join potluck meals and discuss issues of concern, such as the town's declining youth population, marriage rate, and birth rate, and how to reverse these trends by attracting new resident families.

TT Yokohama is the primary organizational force, and thus the primary presence, at the summer Tanabata festival held in the neighborhood of Ôkurayama. Here members advertise future activities and workshops, and promote an "Ampere Down" campaign encouraging locals to convert their homes' standard 50 amperage service to 30 amps. The conversion not only saves energy and money, it promotes awareness by requiring households to modify domestic energy use. Conscious of representing itself as a town-building and revitalization initiative rather than an environmental intervention, TT Yokohama functions seamlessly alongside local craftspeople, small business owners, organic vegetable vendors, and charity groups soliciting donations for victims of 3.11. As a homegrown initiative, it operates as a communal insider and its environmental agenda is understood as interdependent with community interests.

Newly established TTs like that in Yokohama are not yet piloting forceful local transitions. They do represent, however, a multiplicity of community-building groups and trends emerging in post-disaster Japan. TTs' networking efforts bring them into contact with an extraordinarily diverse and energized body of NPOs (non-profit organizations) working on everything from beach cleanups to charity soccer camps. Community Crossing Japan, for example, an NPO seeking to unite local communities, expects to reach 200 member communities by 2015.

The grassroots momentum building since 3.11 helps such upstart groups expand their base and play more participatory roles within this emergent public sphere.

Many communities are implementing transition-like measures independently of the TT movement. Resident groups in Ueda City, Nagano Prefecture, have visited and networked closely with Tokyo area TTs and adopted TT energy-saving and community-building strategies. Their outreach events endorse a comprehensive overhaul of the city's energy infrastructure that includes extensive use of solar, hydro, wind, biodiesel, and biomass power generation. The NPO Ueda Citizen Energy (*Ueda shimin enerugii*) has initiated a transition toward this vision through a roof-sharing program allowing residents without roofs to invest in solar power. Investors buy and install solar panels on the roofs of "lender" homeowners with the two parties sharing the profits. Ueda has also instituted a system of using silk cocoons (*mayu*) as local currency, called Maayu. A number of local establishments participate in this program. One private academy, for example, allows payment of up to 20 percent in Maayu, while a kimono shop accepts payment of up to 10 percent in Maayu for kimono and 20 percent for shoes, sandals, and clogs. Ueda residents can also conduct transactions at a monthly Maayu market or via an online bulletin board. The system's aim is not to establish a capitalistic barter economy, but to foster goodwill and an amicable business culture.

The unifying and restorative effects of strong local bonds are regularly illuminated by great human tragedy. Daniel Aldrich has found, for example, that social capital (social relations) played a larger role in the recovery of Tokyo neighborhoods following the great 1923 earthquake than physical infrastructure or economic capital. Recovery, measured in terms of population growth rates, was accelerated more effectively by strong social networks, community currency programs, and community activities than by infusions of material aid or infrastructure renovation (Aldrich, 2012). The healing process following the Great Hanshin (Kobe) earthquake in 1995 followed the same pattern (Shaw and Goda, 2004). Post-3.11 surveys conducted throughout Japan also show that safety, conservation, peace of mind, relationships, and "a sense of togetherness with others" stood out as people's top priorities (Edahiro, 2011). It is no surprise, then, that emotional fallout from these tragedies has prompted more Japanese to take stock of the sociopolitical potentials of community solidarity and to discover community strengthening as a more viable veneer for grassroots environmentalism than overtly green initiatives. Will this turn be impulsive and temporary, or will it help to alter Japan's approach to sustainable development permanently?

A series of pre-disaster civil and legal developments indicate that broad sectors of Japanese society had been moving in the direction of the sort of environmentally-oriented community building sought by Japan's current TT movement, and that 3.11 only accelerated this process. As Jeff Kingston (2004, pp. 15–17) and others have observed, this trend can be traced to the mid-1990s, when ineffectual governmental responses to a similar confluence of human and natural disasters energized Japanese civil society. During the intervening years, prolonged economic stagnation further eroded public faith in the top-down administrative model that had piloted Japan's postwar recovery. In addition, more permissive NPO laws ignited an explosion of new grassroots interest groups. During this same period, stricter emissions standards and lower projected earnings fueled greater corporate commitment to green business. Further still, the country's increased role in international environmental issues instilled a greater sense of national responsibility for combating global environmental problems. Such developments suggest that Japan had been inching toward a new order characterized by a comparatively decentralized distribution of power and a stronger, more engaged civil society (Brecher, forthcoming).

Japan's TT movement should not be understood as a fleeting reaction to tragedy, but rather as representative of a larger evolutionary process. In contrast to issue-based green movements and environmental NGOs seeking to incite public alarm, Japanese TTs are attuned to the practical and psychological needs of a post-disaster society. Their platforms and outreach efforts are intentionally localized. Rather than promoting abstract concepts like "nature conservation" with uncertain local relevance, TTs endorse neighborhood unity, pride, and collaboration; rather than petitioning, boycotting, or demonstrating, all of which are confrontational and stress intra-community relations, TTs sponsor enjoyable experiences such as local currency role-playing games and educational hikes; and rather than leveling attacks on industry, TTs selectively endorse local industry and promote economic resilience. Such strategies protect TTs from public censure and allow members to take collective control over their own transition.

As a practical, community-centered approach to grassroots empowerment, transitioning is a compelling proposition for growing numbers of Japanese. Moreover, as a model of sustainable development it shares common philosophical ground with an emergent civil society disposed to actualizing greater local self-determination. By responding to widely resonant values and concerns, Japanese TTs and likeminded grassroots groups are positing themselves not as marginal to but as ambassadors for the mainstream.

Acknowledgments

Interviews with Nagaya residents were conducted by Emi Takahashi. The photograph in Figure 17.1 was taken by the author.

References

Aldrich, D. P. 2012. Social, Not Physical, Infrastructure: The Critical Role of Civil Society after the 1923 Tokyo Earthquake. *Disasters* 363, pp. 398–419.
Barrett, B. 2011. *Transition Fujino – Prospects for a Better Future.* OurWorld 2.0. Retrieved on 10th August, 2011, from http://ourworld.unu.edu/en/transition-fujino-%E2%80%93-prospects-for-a-better-future/.
Brecher, W. P. Forthcoming. Precarity, Kawaii (Cuteness), and their Impact on Environmental Discourse in Japan. In *Imagining the Lost Generation: Representations of Japan's "Unequal Society" (kakusa shakai) in Popular Culture.* Eds. R. Rosenbaum, and W. K.Iwata. Oxford: Routledge.

Edahiro, J. 2011. How Japanese Lifestyles and Awareness Changed after the March 11 Great East Japan Earthquake. *Japan For Sustainability Newsletter* 111, November.

Gladwell, M. 2002. *The Tipping Point: How Little Things Can Make a Big Difference.* New York, NY: Back Bay Books.

Hopkins, R. 2008. *The Transition Handbook: From Oil Dependency to Local Resilience.* White River Jct., Vt: Chelsea Green.

Kingston, J. 2004. *Japan's Quiet Transformation: Social Change and Civil Society in the Twenty-First Century.* London and New York: Routledge Curzon.

Katô H. 2011, Winter. Toranjishon taun no bôken: 'dasseichô' shakai he no 'ikô' wa sude ni hajimatteiru. *Kotoba* 2, pp. 88–93.

NHK News Web. 2012. *Noda naikaku fushiji 56% hossoku irai saikô.* 12 July. Retrieved on August 10th, 2012, from http://www3.nhk.or.jp/news/html/20120709/k10013457951000.html.

Oguma E. 2012. *Japan's Nuclear Power and Anti-Nuclear Movement from a Socio-Historical Perspective.* Paper presented at "Towards Long-term Sustainability: in Response to the 3/11 Earthquake and the Fukushima Nuclear Disaster," Conference at the Institute of East Asian Studies, April 20–21. Berkeley, Calif.: University of California.

Shaw, R., and K. Goda. 2004. From Disaster to Sustainable Civil Society: The Kobe Experience. *Disasters* 281, pp. 16–40.

Tanaka, N. 2011. Transition Initiatives: A Grassroots Movement to Prepare Local Communities for Life after Peak Oil. In O. Mitsuru. Ed. *Designing our Future: Local Perspectives on Bioproduction, Ecosystems and Humanity.* Tokyo: United Nations University Press, pp. 234–43.

Trotman, R. 2008. *The Benefits of Community Conservation: A Literature Review.* Auckland, NZ: Auckland Regional Council.

Yoshimura, T., and R. Kato. 2005. Waste Management Activities in Nagoya City, Japan: Local Government and Community Partnerships. In *Innovative Communities: People-Centered Approaches to Environmental Management in the Asia-Pacific Region.* Eds. J. Velasquez, M. Yashiro, S. Yoshimura, and I. Ono. Tokyo: United Nations University Press.

18 Environmental values in China

Paul G. Harris

Introduction

The natural environment is declining at an alarming pace. It is an understatement to say that China is one of the developing countries experiencing rapid industrialization and modernization. Its economic activity and associated demand for energy are increasing much faster than in most countries. Alongside its economic expansion, China is experiencing its own environmental problems. Environmental pollution and degradation cost the country roughly 10 percent of its gross domestic product, even leading to *negative* economic growth in some provinces and contributing to social unrest (Huang, 2007; Economy, 2010). Alarmingly, China has surpassed the USA to become the largest national source of carbon dioxide, the most important greenhouse gas causing global warming and resulting climate change (Netherlands Environmental Assessment Agency, 2007). Environmentally sustainable development is therefore extremely important both for China (and the Chinese people) and the world.

Attitudes toward the environment in China are ambiguous (Harris, 2004, p. 145). These attitudes are indicators of how the Chinese view the natural environment. They are important precursors of individual Chinese behaviors, and the policies and actions of the Chinese government, to combat environmental problems. They are indicators of whether China's people and government will practice environmentally sustainable development and preservation of nature sometime in the future. To be sure, China already has what we can call a policy *toward* the environment – many environmental regulations and a national strategy for sustainable development – but arguably it does not yet have a policy *for* the environment. Such a policy requires placing the environment at the center of concern, if only for the instrumental purpose of protecting the people in China who rely on it for their health, livelihood, and survival. Such a policy likely requires changed values among China's people and a change of thinking on the part of its government.

This chapter is based on Chinese survey data, secondary sources (e.g. Chinese print media and scholarly reports) and analyses in tertiary literature including early work on the subject. Data on environmental values in China can be sketchy and ambiguous. As Yok-shiu Lee has pointed out, compared to well-developed social science research in the West, "the research base for China's environmentalism is still in its infancy. Only recently have researchers in [China] begun to unveil the complex contours of China's environmental consciousness" (Lee, 2005, p. 35). In short, getting a precise understanding of Chinese environmental attitudes and priorities is probably impossible. Nevertheless, one can develop a general sense of people's values toward the environment. With this in mind, the remainder of the chapter reviews environmental awareness and values in China before briefly looking at environmental action there.

Environmental knowledge

What are the perceptions and values of people in China toward environmental issues? Which environmental issues do they care about the most? Before answering these questions, it is first important to consider knowledge of ecological issues. Environmental knowledge can be defined as a general knowledge of facts, concepts, and relationships concerning the natural environment and its major ecosystems (Fryxell and Lo, 2003, p. 47). It involves perception of environmental protection efforts, "scientific knowledge of environmental protection" and "perceptions of general environmental conditions and specific environmental problems" (Xi et al., 1998, p. 6).

Generally speaking, people in China are convinced to varying degrees of the seriousness of environmental pollution. However, survey findings and tertiary literature suggest quite limited environmental knowledge, most of which is garnered from the media (Xi et al., 1998). Despite their close relationship with the environment, Chinese farmers' knowledge of it is weak. About 80 percent of the farmers surveyed do not understand the causes of environmental degradation in their villages, and in one study 84 percent of them did not understand that agricultural fertilizers contribute to environmental pollution (Zhu, 2001). Villagers appear to know little about ecology (Qi, 2000). This level of environmental knowledge in villages is not surprising given the limited environmental education there.

Environmental knowledge among younger city dwellers seems to be higher. A poll conducted in Yunnan Province found that nearly half of those questioned (45.8 percent) linked environmental protection only to sanitation, with only 11.4 percent of respondents making the connection between environmental protection and nature (Wang, 2002, p. 41). In Lian Yun Gang City, 68 percent of survey respondents understood that the goal of environmental protection was to create a harmonious relationship between people and the natural world (Yi et al., 2002, p. 31). But in Panyu City of Guangdong Province, the average score of respondents for environmental knowledge was 4.02 out of a possible 13. Similarly, the overall score of Guangdong's city residents was 4.94 and that of villagers was 3.78 (Ma, 2003, p. 40). Residents of Panyu were found to lack the most basic knowledge required to protect the environment, with most respondents to a survey (88 percent) not knowing, for example, that disposable utensils would create environmental pollution (Ma, 2003, p. 40). In Henan Province, environmental knowledge among both city residents and villagers was found to be low (Li, 2002).

Awareness and concern

Koon-Kwai Wong argues that deteriorating environmental conditions have led increasing numbers of Chinese to become aware of the need for environmental protection (Wong, 2003). For example, a 1996 pan-China survey determined that almost one-third of the people studied thought that environmental pollution was extremely serious (Ma and Jian, 2000, pp. 204–205), and a 1998 survey found that nearly 57 percent of respondents in 31 provinces believed that China's environmental situation was very serious (Li, 2001). A survey performed in 2000 concluded that environmental protection and environmental degradation were a top concern of people living in urban areas (United States Embassy (Beijing), 2000). A 2002 survey found that 62.5 percent of people in China were of the opinion that environmental protection was extremely important (Cui, 2002, p. 86). Though we cannot make perfect comparisons across these and similar surveys due to varying survey methods, there is a trend toward more Chinese placing emphasis on the issue of environmental protection.

Surveys from different locations reflect some consensus in Chinese thinking about the environment. One survey conducted in Beijing suggested that a majority of respondents had a clear understanding of the "preciousness" of the natural environment, the limitations of natural resources, the limited capacity of the earth to absorb waste, and the effects of population and lifestyle on the environment (Tang, 2000). Beijing respondents had a "clear and strong" sense of environmental responsibility, and they often had a sense of urgency to protect the environment (Tang, 2000). University students in Beijing are environmentally conscious and recognize that environmental degradation in China is a serious problem (Wong, 2003, p. 519). Most residents of Shanghai believe that the environment is the greatest challenge facing the world in the twenty-first century (Luo, 1998). Similarly, most people in Hongzhou think that environmental pollution and environmental protection are issues requiring urgent attention (Qi, 2000, p. 94). In Hubei Province, most respondents placed environmental protection among the top three most important issues faced by the people there, with 17.6 percent of respondents placing it first (Zhu and Hui, 2003). In Panyu, 45 percent of residents surveyed were very worried that environmental pollution would harm their health (Ma, 2003, p. 40).

Nevertheless, depending on location, livelihood issues and other concerns are often greater than worries about the environment, and one survey of Chinese officials found that they generally mirrored public attitudes: the environment was not among their greatest concerns (*China Youth Daily*, 2003). In recent years, environmental concern has grown as industrial, water and air pollution has grown. Arguably, the 2008 Olympics raised awareness of environmental issues – not least because drastic efforts to reduce air pollution in Beijing during the games were generally successful, only to be reversed shortly thereafter. In general, however, it seems evident that in the midst of China's ongoing transition to a largely unregulated capitalist economy, there are many other issues on people's minds in addition to environmental changes, and those issues are frequently viewed as being of greater importance or urgency. Naturally, concern about the environment can be very high in locations where pollution is severe, quite often leading to demonstrations and social unrest. Unfortunately for millions of Chinese people, the number of such places is itself very high indeed.

Environmental proximity

Based on a variety of surveys, it is clear that the most important environmental problems for people in China are those that are spatially closest to them or that most directly affect them. Those that are least important are distant issues, such as ecosystem-wide problems (e.g. climate change). For example, a government survey found that in the late 1990s the greatest environmental concerns were air and water pollution; 26.6 percent of city residents and 30.3 percent of villagers were concerned about water pollution, with the ratio for air pollution being 29.4 percent and 23.9 respectively (SEPA, 1999, pp. 22–23). A 2002 survey seeking people's views on what they considered the most important environmental problems found that large numbers (71 percent) were most concerned about water pollution, with air pollution and domestic waste pollution considered the next most important environmental issues (Wang, 2002, p. 42). Xiaolin Xi *et al.* (1998, pp. 1–29) argue that people ranked water pollution, air pollution, noise, and solid waste as the top four most important environmental problems. Insufficient green space in urban areas and "public area pollution" (e.g. garbage, spitting, and smoking) were also viewed as very serious problems in many people's minds. According to Xi *et al.*, these are "problems people encounter in their everyday lives. Other, more remote problems, such as worsened biodiversity, shrinking cultivated land, deforestation, desertification, and sea pollution, are excluded from the priority list for environmental protection" (Xi *et al.*, 1998, p. 12).

Surveys of public attitudes in different parts of China reinforce these findings. Among their environmental concerns, according to Jun Tang, Beijing residents care most about air and water pollution (Tang, 2000, p. 25). According to another survey, most Beijing residents are concerned about the problems of sewage treatment and pollution (Jin and Ming, 2001). A survey of residents of Hangzhou in Zhejiang Province suggests that the people there are most concerned about noise and water pollution (Qi, 2000, p. 94). Most of these people hold the opinion that lack of fresh air and quiet surroundings are the major environmental concerns. They also believe that air pollution, unnecessary water use, and domestic waste are important environmental problems (Qi, 2000, p. 95). In Hubei Province, the environmental issues of greatest concern are air and water pollution and rubbish (Zhu and Hui, 2003). Shanghai people care most about air pollution, city green space, water quality, and noise (Luo, 1998, p. 40). Residents of the city of Panyu care about environmental issues related to daily life, but few are concerned about global issues like climate change (Ma, 2003). Garbage is viewed as a serious problem by nearly 60 percent of residents in both Beijing and Shanghai (Xi *et al.*, 1998, p. 11).

Large majorities of people in Beijing and Shanghai believe that biodiversity, pollution from pesticides, and deforestation are serious problems. However, in Beijing and Shanghai, fewer people believe that dust storms (42 percent) – which are common in Beijing and some other parts of China – desertification (38 percent), and ocean pollution (38 percent) are serious problems. In contrast to Panyu, 62 percent of respondents in these cities think that climate change is a serious problem (Xi *et al.*, 1998, pp. 11–12). University students in Beijing also regard water pollution, soil erosion, and air pollution as the most urgent environmental problems in China (Wong, 2003, pp. 519–36). That some urban residents place such high emphasis on somewhat broader ecological issues suggests that more education has enabled them to distinguish between questions of sanitation and the built environment, on the one hand, and the wider natural environment on the other.

With these and other findings in mind, broadly speaking we might say that the Chinese public's environmental concerns are primarily focused on water and air pollution, particularly insofar as they relate to daily life. With the exception of some survey data of urban university students, people in China are indifferent toward the broader ecological environment, as reflected in limited concern about issues such as stratospheric ozone depletion and climate change (Cui, 2002, p. 87). The upshot is that people in China primarily express great concern about environmental problems and pollution affecting their daily lives. Global environmental issues are generally not considered urgent.

Environment vs development

While the concept and practice of sustainable development has gained prominence across China, in many parts of the country it remains a low priority relative to economic growth and wealth creation. This may explain why almost half of Chinese believe that economic development "unavoidably" causes harm to the natural environment (Li, 2001). A survey by the State Environmental Protection Administration (SEPA) suggested that people view local economic development and creation of economic infrastructure as more important than environmental protection (Cui, 2002, p. 87). In Shanghai, only a quarter of people surveyed were of the opinion that "environmental protection was more important than economic development" (Luo, 1998, p. 41).

In contrast, one survey in Zhengzhou of Henan Province found that when there is a conflict between protecting the environment and economic development, the majority of people would give "first consideration" to the environment (K. T. Li, 2002). In Fujian Province, 70 percent of residents surveyed supported sacrificing convenience to protect the environment (L. Li, 2002). However, signalling where future elites place economic development, more than half of Beijing University students (53.7 percent) ranked "promote economic development" and "maintain economic stability" as the most important developmental objectives in China. Only 11 percent of those students chose "protect the environment" as their first priority (Wong, 2003, p. 31).

Variables underlying values

What explains people's attitudes toward the environment in China? The more environmental knowledge people have, the stronger their environmental consciousness (Huang, 2002). Higher education levels and more frequent newspaper reading were two major variables that increase people's understanding of environmental problems (Zhou, 2002). People who have received a university education have much higher environmental awareness (Hong, 1998). Age is also a factor: teenagers' environmental knowledge is higher than that of older people (SEPA, 1999, p. 23). These findings are confirmed by surveys of people in the cities of Chongqing and Beijing. The Chongqing survey showed a direct correlation between environmental awareness and educational level, and confirmed that in areas with higher standards of living people had higher expectations of environmental quality (Zhou, 2002). According to a 2000 survey of Beijing residents, the higher the educational level of respondents, the lower their satisfaction with environmental conditions in the city (Jin and Ming, 2001). More broadly, people's attitudes are generational: those who experienced poverty – whether directly or indirectly through family narratives – are focused on escaping and avoiding poverty above all else, even at the cost of environmental harm, and young people are much more individualistic and consumption oriented.

Environmental action

As suggested above, many people in China say that they are aware of environmental issues and that they are willing to pay for environmental protection. However, they often do not "practice what they preach," instead commonly demonstrating indifference toward environmental protection. Shu Yi Cui argues that only about 8 percent of Mainland Chinese have a high "environmental participation ratio." People call for environmental protection, but their interest wanes when it comes to their behaviors (Cui, 2002, p. 87). Indeed, some surveys show that in "local areas" people seldom act to prevent pollution. For example, "Say much but do less" is how Tian Fang Ma describes the environmental value of residents in Panyu, where a vast majority of residents surveyed (80 percent) said that they wanted to participate in environmental protection activities – but their behaviors did not reflect this (Ma, 2003). In Hangzhou, Zhejiang Province, three-quarters of people surveyed said that they viewed sanitary protection the same as environmental protection, claiming that they would not litter roads, parks, and other public spaces. However, Weifeng Qi argues that littering reached serious proportions in Hangzhou, suggesting that people were not describing their behaviors accurately or honestly (Qi, 2000, p.95). Kun Tao Li has shown that the majority of both city and village residents in Zhengzhou, Henan Province, were indifferent to joining in environmental protection activities (K. T. Li, 2002).

According to a survey by SEPA, only about 25 percent of the public would consider environmental factors when shopping (Cui, 2002, p. 87), although (paradoxically) 63.5 percent of people would choose "green" products and 35 percent of them said that they would pay higher prices when shopping if it would promote environmental protection (Cui, 2002, p. 87; Li, 2001, p. 123). In one "green consumption" survey, almost 79 percent of the people surveyed said that they would consider environmental factors when shopping (Chen, 1999). In Hubei Province, 47.6 percent of survey respondents said that they were willing to accept higher prices for products or services for the sake of protecting the environment, while only 16.8 percent of people were not willing to do so (Zhu and Hui, 2003). In sharp contrast, however, in Zhengche 62 percent of people said that they were not willing to pay for environmental protection (Wang, 2002, p. 41), and in Fujian Province, 28.6 percent of residents had no "green-consumption consciousness" whatsoever (Li et al., 2002, p. 34). Views of industry managers seem to be similarly ambivalent: Gerald Fryxell and Carlos Lo (2003, p. 47) found that "Chinese managers profess relatively strong environmental values. Chinese managers reported high levels of adherence to various environmental ethics." Nevertheless, industries continue to pollute at an alarming and increasing pace.

These findings suggest that many people in China are at least expressing a substantial willingness to consider environmental issues when making consumption and other life decisions. But actions rarely fully reflect these expressed sentiments: most Chinese opt to buy products that are the least expensive simply because they are too poor to consider alternatives, regardless of those products' environmental impacts.

Conclusion

This chapter has reviewed some findings on Chinese environmental attitudes and priorities, based largely on reports of Chinese surveys up to about the year 2000. Much of the survey data is sketchy and even contradictory, but an overall picture does emerge, especially in four areas of concern: knowledge, attitudes, values, and behavior.

Knowledge of ecology and environmental issues is limited outside major urban areas and areas with good education, although it has been increasing in recent decades due to education campaigns and media coverage. For most Chinese, the environment is mainly an issue of sanitation and health. There is limited understanding of how human behavior affects the environment and especially about global environmental issues. The exceptions are among more educated people. Basic ecological and environmental knowledge is a prerequisite for attitudes and behaviors that are less harmful to the environment. The most obvious implication of this is that basic education, encompassing ecological issues, should be a greater priority.

Attitudes toward the environment in China are segmented along a variety of lines: geography, age, education, wealth, and status. Individuals in each segment

tend to have different attitudes toward the environment. More educated, affluent, and urbanized people have more pro-environmental attitudes. Attitudes are
directed toward different problems: first to domestic issues (sanitation, drinking
water, indoor pollution), then to local issues (water and air pollution), on to
national issues (acid rain, desertification, deforestation), and – most rarely – to
global issues (ozone depletion and climate change). The vast majority of Chinese
are concerned about their home environment and perhaps their neighborhood,
but not the surrounding area, often not beyond their most immediate surroundings. In short, people in China say they care about environmental problems that
affect them very directly and most immediately.

With regards to values, the Chinese have an instrumental view of nature:
the environment exists for the benefit of people. Considering apparently pro-
environment philosophical traditions in China, aesthetic and ethical valuations
of the environment and nature are surprisingly low (Harris, 2004). The environment is seldom people's first priority. Both people and the government consider
poverty alleviation, economic development, and individual wealth creation to
be most important. Other valuable goals, such as social stability, are also often
more important to people than the environment. When asked about the relative
importance of economic development versus environmental protection, the split
is roughly half in favour of one over the other. However, the overall sense of environmental responsibility is low; people are generally not concerned enough to
accept personal responsibility for environmental protection. Instead, they expect
the government to take care of environmental protection.

The findings for behavior somewhat mirrors that of values: environmental
behavior in China is often ambivalent. While people may express concern about
environmental conditions and even say that they are willing to act to protect the
environment, this does not often coincide with behavior. Benefits to oneself are
essential for most people to act willingly on environmental issues. People will
generally choose immediate comfort and convenience over environmental protection, especially if there is any significant economic cost associated with pro-
environmental behavior (e.g. buying green products). Even the simplest actions
are resisted; less than half the people in most areas will choose not to litter. More
educated and affluent people, despite having more knowledge of ecology and
expressing concern about the environment and a willingness to protect it, are not
much more willing to *act* in pro-environmental ways than less educated people
and the poor. Self-interest is a common theme. This helps to explain the rising
number of environmental protests: as pollution affects people directly, for example by contaminating drinking water or severely fouling local air, it moves up
people's list of priorities, sometimes rising to the top until the government agrees
to do something about it.

China is still in the relatively early stages of what may be a long period of
major economic growth. This is quite frightening from an environmental perspective given the severe pollution that the country has experienced in recent
decades. The findings described here suggest that much more has to be done

to increase environmental knowledge and raise environmental values among the people of China. The implications go well beyond China itself. Given its enormous contribution to global environmental problems, not least of all climate change, the extent to which environmental values take hold in China will greatly determine whether humanity continues to live beyond the carrying capacity of the earth or instead changes course toward genuinely sustainable development.

References

Chen, T. 1999. Green Consumption and Environmental Problems Survey [Lu Se Xiao Fei Yu Huan Bao Wen Ti De Tiao Cha]. *Market and Demographic Analysis [Shi Chang Yu Ren Kou Fen Xi]* 5(1), pp. 42–43.

China Youth Daily. 2003. Issues of the Most Concern for Chinese Officials in 2002 (*Zhong Guo Ling Dao Gan Bu Zai Er Ling Ling Er Nian Zui Guan Xin De Shi Qing*). December 18th, p. 1.

Cui, S. Y. 2002. Public Environmental Consciousness: Existing Situation, Problems, and Strategy [Gong Zhong Huan Jing Yi Shi Xiang Zhuang, Wen Ti Yu Dui Ce]. *Theory Journal [Li Lun Xue Kan]* 4(110), pp. 86–87.

Economy, E. C. 2010. *The River Runs Black: The Environmental Challenge to China's Future.* Ithaca, NY: Cornell University Press.

Fryxell, G., and C. Lo. 2003. The Influence of Environmental Knowledge and Values on Managerial Behaviours on Behalf of the Environment: An Empirical Examination of Managers in China. *Journal of Business Ethics* 46, p. 47.

Harris, P. G., ed. 2004. "Getting Rich is Glorious": Environmental Values in the People's Republic of China. *Environmental Values* 13(2), pp. 145–65.

Hong, D. 1998. A Comprehensive Judgement and Sampling Analysis of Citizens' Environmental Awareness [Gong Min Huan Jing Yi Shi De Ke Xue Ping Pan He Chou Yang Fen Xi]. *Science and Technology Review [Ke Ji Dao Bao]*, pp. 15–16.

Huang, C. 2007. Environmental Expenses Erode Heated Economy. *South China Morning Post.* 4 August, p. A5.

Huang, X. S. 2002. The Public's Awareness of Environmental Protection and Environmental Protection in the Three Gorges Reservoir Area [Gong Zhong Huan Bao Yi Shi Yu San Xia Ku Qu De Huan Jing Bao Hu]. *Journal of Chongqing Three Gorges University [Chong Qing San Xia Xue Yuan Xue Bao]* 18(3), p. 103.

Jin, Y. J., and J. Ming,. 2001. Environmental Protection: How Much Do You Know about Beijing People's Concern Level [Huan Jin Bao Ku, Jing Cheng Bai Xing Guan Zhu Cheng Du Zhui Duo Xiao]. *Journal of Beijing Statistics [Beijing Tong Ji]*, pp. 16–17.

Lee, Y. F. 2005. Public Environmental Consciousness in China. In *China's Environment and the Challenge of Sustainable Development.* Ed. K. A. Day. London: M. E. Sharpe.

Li, K. T. 2002. On the Public's Environmental Consciousness [Zhenzhou Gong Zhong De Huan Jing Yi Shi]. *Journal of Henan Textile College [Henan Fang Zhi Gao Deng Zhuan Ke Xue Xiao Xue Bao]* 14(2), p. 32.

Li, L. 2002. Investigation and Analysis of Public Environmental Attitudes in Fuzhou City [Fuzhou Shi Gong Zhong Huan Jing Yi Zhi Tiao Cha Fen Xi]. *Fujian Environment [Fujian Huan Jing]* 19(5), p. 33.

Li, L., J. Huang, W. H. Lu, S. N. Wang, and X. Hu. 2002. The Investigation and Analysis of Public Environmental Attitude in Fuzhou City [Fuzhou Shi Gong Zhong Huan Jing Yi Zhi Tiao Cha Fen Xi]. *Fujian Environment [Fujian Huan Jing]* 19(5), pp. 32–34.

Li, N. N. 2001. Environmental Consciousness and Environmental Behaviour [Huan Bao Yi Shi Yu Huan Bao Xing Wei]. *Learning Sea [Xue Hai]* 1, pp. 122–23.

Luo, X. 1998. Shanghainese Environmental Consciousness Micro-Investigation [Shang Hai Ren De Huan Jing Yi Shi]. *Journal of Society [She Hui Xue]* 5: 40–41.

Ma, R., and R. G. Jian. 2000. China Residents' Differences in Environmental Consciousness and Attitudes between Cities and Villages [Zhong Guo Ju Min Zai Huan Jing Yi Shi Yu Huan Bao Tai Du Fang Mian De Cheng Xiang Cha Yi]. *Social Science Scientific Research [She Kua Ke Xue Zhan Xian]* 1, pp. 204–7.

Ma, T. F. 2003. On the Present Condition and the Countermeasures of the Environmental Awareness of Panyu Residents [Panyu Ju Min Huan Jing Yi Shi Xiang Zhuang Fen Xi Ji Qi Due Ce]. *Journal of Panyu Polytechnic [Panyu Zhi Ye Ji Shu Yuan Xue Bao]* 2(2), p. 40.

Netherlands Environmental Assessment Agency. 2007. *China Now No. 1 in CO$_2$ Emissions; USA in Second Position.* Press Release. Retrieved on June 19th, 2007, from http://www.pbl.nl/en/dossiers/Climatechange/moreinfo/Chinanowno1inCO2emissions USAinsecondposition.

Qi, W. 2000. Survey and Review on Environment Consciousness of Citizen: Taking the Example of Hangzhou in Zhejiang [Cheng Shi Shi Min Huan Jing Yi Shi Diao Cha Yu Ping Jia]. *Journal of Planners [Gui Hua Shi]* 16(3), pp. 94–95.

SEPA (State Environmental Protection Administration). 1999. The Whole China's Public Environmental Consciousness Investigation Report [Quan Guo Gong Zhong Huan Jing Yi Shi Diao Cha Bao Gao]. *Peoples' Forum [Ren Min Lun Tan]* 7, pp. 21–23.

Tang, J. 2000. The Social Analysis of Beijing Residents' Environmental Attitudes and Environmental Behaviour [Beijing Ju Min Huan Bao Tai Du He Huan Bao Xing Wei De She Kuai Xue Fen Xi]. *City's Problem [Cheng Shi Wen Ti]* 5 (97), pp. 24–25.

United States Embassy (Beijing). 2000. Environment Tops Urban Worries. *Beijing Environment, Science, and Technology Update.* 3 November.

Wang, Y. B. 2002. Zhenche People's Individual Attitudes and Behaviour in Environmental Protection [Yun Nan Kun Min Zhe Che Min Zhong Huan Jing Bao Hu Tai Du He Xing Wei]. *Social Sciences in Yunnan [Yun Nan She Hui Ke Xue]*. 1, pp. 41–42.

Wong, K. K. 2003. Environmental Awareness of University Students in Beijing. *Journal of Contemporary China* 12(36), pp. 519–36.

Xi, X., F. Lihong, and D. Xueming. 1998. *Public Environment Awareness in China: An Analysis of the Results of Public Surveys.* Report prepared for the Centre for the Integrated Study of the Human Dimensions of Global Change, Carnegie Mellon University. December. Beijing: National Research Centre for Science and Technology for Development, Ministry of Science and Technology.

Yi, S. T., T. Song, Y. R. Lu, and Y. Z. Xiong. 2002. Questionnaire Investigation Survey and Analytical Research on Lian Yun Gang Citizens' Environmental Awareness [Lian Yun Gang Shi Min Huan Jing Yi Shi Wen Juan Tiao Cha Ji Fen Xi Yan Jiu]. *Huanjiang Daobao* May, pp. 30–31.

Zhou, Y. 2002. Chongqing Cities and Surrounding Suburbs Citizens' Environmental Awareness/Attitude Situation Analysis [Chong Qing Zhu Cheng Qu. Ji Jin Jiao Ju Min Huan Jing Yi Shi Diao Cha]. *Chongqing Environmental Science [Chong Qing Huan Jing Ke Xue]* 1(24), p. 15.

Zhu, C. R., and L. Hui. 2003. Public Environmental Consciousness of Hubei Province [Hu Bei Gong Zhong Huan Jing Yi Shi Kao Cha]. *Journal of Economic Tribune [Sheng Qing Yan Jiu]* 15, pp. 55–56.

Zhu, Q. 2001. The Investigation and Reflection on Chinese Farmers' Environment Consciousness [Guan Yu Nong Min Huan JIng Yi Shi De Diao Cha Yu Si Kao]. *The World of Investigation [Diao Yan Shi Jie]* 1, p. 29.

19 African environmental values expressed through proverbs

Chigbo Joseph Ekwealo

Africa today is occupied by people of various ethnic groups: Blacks, Portuguese, Asians, and Arabs. Naturally, these people all have their distinctive consciousness, informed by their own worldviews and ideology. In the postcolonial era, Africans owe their epistemological allegiance to different westernized, colonial powers. Some therefore wonder if there can be distinctly African philosophical and environmental views which will hold for everyone, sufficient to warrant the locution "African thought." Although they are correct to raise the question, there are general orientations in African thought such that the label can be justified (Momoh, 2000), just as we use the locutions "German philosophy," "Continental philosophy," and "Greek philosophy" despite contrasting ideologies and views within each school of thought. As Kwame Nkrumah, Frantz Fanon, Ali Al'amin Maxrui, and other critical thinkers have said, the present African is a three-headed person, one who carries a triple heritage of traditional African, Asian-Islamic, and Judeo-Christian philosophical ideas. Here we present environmental principles springing from the precolonial African traditional heritage, which represents the foundational consciousness of the people.

African environmental values are substantive principles, beliefs, and doctrines embodying their worldviews, which are underlain by a consciousness of the relationship between humans and so-called inanimate entities such as minerals, plants and vegetables, and animals (Ekwealo, 2008, pp. 214–16). These values are a binding force and a basis for mental and behavioral responses to life and reality. With them the individual African knows the basis of their actions, the logic of their convictions, and the context of their reasoning. Some of these values are pansophism, godlessness, complementary dualism, existential gratitude, live and let live, sacred feminine, and *Nwanne, Ifunanaya na Eziokwu* (brotherhood, love, and truth).

Pansophism is the idea that in reality all animate life is wise and rational. It affirms that human beings are not the only intelligent beings, for other animals exhibit traits of intelligence, wisdom, and rationality which help them to survive and overcome the exploits of humans. A revealing observation was made by C. S. Momoh, an Uchi elder and a renowned hunter, who explained that hunters had consistently changed their hunting skill and tactics, for they realized that animals were recognizing their strategies and therefore were avoiding being caught:

Traditionally, Uchi hunters used lampions made from pawpaw fruit to hunt at night … with them, it was easy to get close to an animal, so close as to be able to kill it with the butt of a gun, now, Uchi elders use modern hunting lamps which are always strapped to the forehead, with lamps, Uchi elders were initially very successful in their night hunting. After some time, however, it would seem that animals came to identify the lamp with danger. Animals also came to identify surface traps learnt to avoid them. Now, hunters have switched to setting underground traps and animals will soon catch up with the change.

(2000, p. 417)

A support for the rationality of nonhuman beings was discussed by Edward Evans-Pritchard in the report he got from the Azande about witchcraft. He explained that during initiation, the young one is reminded: "your relatives are animals, your father is an elephant, your father's elder brother is the red pig, your wives are cane-rats, your mother is a bush-buck, your maternal uncles are duickers, your grandfather is a rhinoceros" (1976, p. 1). All these analogies simply explain the ecological connection of human beings and other entities in reality. By acknowledging animals' intelligence, Africans are appreciating their worth, values, and rights, thereby recognizing the inevitable balance and sustainability. Momoh affirmed that:

pansophism tells us that man is not the only rational being in the universe and the African, therefore, within the context of Ancient African philosophy, holds that man cannot distinguish himself from the rest of nature by using that criterion … the African would also add that there would be peace among men on earth if man would learn to acknowledge and appreciate the help, the worth and the role played by others in his life. Everything has a place and a role in the universe hence it exists really, imaginarily, potentially, fictionally or conceptually.

(2000, p. 424)

This leads to another environmental value or principle: live and let live. This is a principle which affirms that all entities in reality must be accorded the right of existence and living through the necessity of appropriate environment. It recognizes that other animals aside from human beings have a need for growth and living that is compatible with the human need. The cliché affirming this necessity is expressed as a puzzle: each morning, as humans wake up, they will ask God for protection and a source of nourishment, as animals wake up each morning and petition God for protection and a source of nourishment; the question therefore is, "Who will God answer first?" It is in the answer to this that the Igbo have a name, *Ndubuisi* (life in all its manifestation is supreme). This belief is supported by rights and laws and hence is labelled a fundamental right. Africans will quickly state *ndu mmili, ndu azu*, meaning all life is as important to each other as water is to the existence of fish, therefore no one life ought to be abused or wasted for the other.

The principle of live and let live recognizes all entities in creation and argues for balance and justice through respect for one another. Live and let live recognizes the value of all entities within the environment and cautions the selfish to desist from waste, abuse, and plunder. The critical point in this universal affirmation is the connectedness of humans, animals, and the so-called inanimate world, the world of plants. All are accepted as existing entities in creation or evolution, and as such each must have the enabling environment to exist and live. It also affirms that the relationships of these entities is not one of higher-than or lower-than on the evolutionary scale. All are simply tenants of nature whose existence and living are such as to help in its realization, its metaphysical "beingness." Thus, there are necessary connections of all reality, an interchange and relationship in which the values of each is recognized and accepted for its role in creativity and development. This leads to another environmental value.

Existential gratitude

Existential value, according to Momoh, is simply an appreciation and acknowledgment of the worth and sometimes consequent expression of gratitude to an existent for its central and active roles in one's life or the community. He added:

it does not matter whether such things are natural, fabricated or acquired by man ... the question is not whether man is superior, inferior or equal to other things in nature ... but how dependent man is on other things in nature and how to express an appreciation for this dependency accordingly.

(2000, p. 425)

Depending on a people's economic, occupational orientation, they venerate or accord dignity and respect to such spaces or environment; and in some cases, appropriate rituals and ceremony are undertaken as signs of a people's deep appreciation of the salutary and positive role of that existent. The commonest is the recognition, acknowledgment, and reverence given to the primordial elements, namely fire, air, earth, and water. It is these ecological primaries which the early Greek philosophers rightly identified through the characters of Ionian philosophers. Among the Yorubas, for instance, there are *Sango* (deity of fire), *Olokun* (deity of water); for the Ibos, *Ani* (the earth deity) and water spirits. Francis Arinze explained:

the earth spirit, Ani (also written Ana, Ala) is the most important spirit after Chukwu, she is the Great Mother Spirit, the queen of the underworld, the owner of men and the custodian of public morality in conjunction with the ancestors. Rivers, rivulets and lakes are believed to have guardian spirits, examples are the Ezu of Agulu lake, the Idemili of Obosi, the Kisa of Ogbunike, the Orimili and Otumoye of Onitsha, et cetera ... and the water spirits have their particular laws.

(1970, pp. 14–15)

The values of pansophism, live and let live, and existential gratitude are the three environmental principles that showcase the thinking and action of the Africans with a view for sustainable development. With these they recognize and appreciate the symbiotic relationship of all entities in existence. Further, these values defend the ecological need for a qualitative and respectful usage of entities. These values are grounded in an ontological or metaphysical background principle which resolves everything on the thesis of force or spirits.

Metaphysics, epistemology, and ethics

African environmental values are derived from the belief that the natural environment, including humans, is composed of invisible energies, and it is their relationships and vibrations that result or manifest in one form of reality or another. Africans believe that nature, community, and humans are linked. D. E. Idoniboye explained the metaphysical ontology which begins first and foremost with the spirit:

> spirit is unembodied or disembodied in its pure state. As unembodied, spirit is not a thing, an entity or an aspect in the same way that a Spirit can be an entity, thing or aspect of reality. A spirit partakes of Spirit in its pure state. Spirit as unembodied (in its pure state) is the cosmic process that makes things be.
>
> (1973, p. 18)

Jim Unah explains that it is based on this fundamental reality of spirits that Africans developed environmental values and principles:

> Consequently, the way African metaphysics conceives reality as an ongo-ing process makes it a dynamic metaphysics. Unlike the static metaphysics of western philosophy which promotes an attitude of dominance, ven-geance and belligerence, the former cultivates in its adherents an attitude of tolerance and peaceful coexistence. It makes man more accommodat-ing of his fellow man and engenders a respectful approach to things and people.
>
> (1999, p. 230)

Herein lies the root of African environmental values. Malidonna Some gave a further explanation to the thesis of spirit:

> Beneath the material world that we can see and touch and feel is an ener-getic world, the world of spirit whose vitality enlivens not only all living things but the very geography of the world that holds life. In the indigenous view, the world of spirit and the material world co-exist, each needs the other because each feeds the other.
>
> (1998, p. 312)

Other philosophers like Alexis Kagame, Placid Tempels, and K. C. Anyanwu labeled the African primordial element of vital force. Kagame divided it into four categories: (1) *Muntu*: principle of intelligence (relating to God, gods, the living and the dead); (2) *Kintu*: relating to non-intelligent beings namely plants, minerals, tools, etc; (3) *Hantu*: refers to spirits that cause movement, change or motion; (4) *Kuntu*: refers to principles responsible for modalities such as beauty, laughter – all partaking in that universal dynamic energy from which all the principles emanate (Anyanwu, 1981).

Tempels in his Bantu ontology shares the thesis of an underlying force permeating all reality in African Philosophy: "there is no idea among the Bantu of being divorced from the idea of force, the concept, 'force' is bound to the concept being even in the most abstract thinking upon the notion of being" (cited in Unah, 1999, p. 227). Tempels categorized these forces into God, spiritualized beings, living beings, animals, plants, and animals, but explained that although some forces are stronger than the others, there is a bond among all forces. What all these defend is the relationship and interactions of energies in African environmental thought.

Anyanwu explains that the notion of life-force referring to Being in everything makes everything lively, full of power or energy. Nothing is lifeless or soul-less in African thought:

> life-force permeates the whole universe and matter and spirit are an inseparable reality. Behind the natural things and intimately co-existing with them is the non-material power and this life-force has existed from the beginning of the world. This force is active. Man, animals and plants share from this life-force and it can be communicated to things. Spirits and divinities or mythical beings possess this life-force. This life-force is impersonal and non-conscious yet constitutes the individuality of every living-force or individual. Every person has his own life-force and this can vary quantitatively as well as qualitatively. Life force is under the direction or guidance of the soul which is also a force, though it does not vary quantitatively or qualitatively.
>
> (1981, pp. 89–90)

The implication of the above quotation is that, according to Anyanwu, it is wrong to believe that Africans hold a hierarchical order of reality in which the lower beings are created ostensibly to serve the interest of the higher. Africans also do not believe that a human being is a special image of God who was charged with the lordship of nature. Rather, Africans believe in the unity of all forces, and a human being's special position is rather more that of a caretaker of the universe, a task which goes with appropriate responsibility and consequences.

With epistemology, we are looking at the principle of understanding and the logic of reasoning that informs Africans' view of reality and environmental consciousness or values. We want to know the basic assumptions, theories, and principles that underlie what they think, believe, and know. Thus, we start by stating that their beliefs and knowledge about reality are the product of human experience, which is arrived at through critical reasoning or reflection and usually couched in proverbs. Having an experience of some object means being involved with the object. There is therefore no distinction between subject and object, which from Africans' metaphysical notion of forces or spirit shows that it is the same principle exhibiting through various forms. Anyanwu continues his explanation:

> All contradictions which human beings face stem from the duality of experience and these include the one of One and Many, Individuality and universality, Time and Eternity, Freedom and necessity, Reason and Sentiment. Every culture faces this problem and all that we call cultural activities are responses to these basic contradictions in human experience. Consequently, the manner in which any culture consciously or unconsciously approaches these contradictory factors of experience determines its mode of thought, beliefs, values, activities and social norms.
>
> (1981, pp. 85–86)

For Africans, their epistemology is situated in complementary dualism in which there is no difference between the self and the world, subject and object. The African immerses himself in the object of experience, thereby ensuring a personal relationship with what he knows. According to Leopold Senghor, "the life-surge of the African, his self-abandonment to the other, is thus actuated by reason. But here, reason is not the eye-reason of the European; it is the reason-by-embrace which shares more the nature of logos than ratio" (1976, p. 33).

Anyanwu summarized his metaphysical and epistemological thesis by explaining that life-force, which we have already discussed, is what permeates everything in the Universe. For the Igbo, for example, although the life-force is divided into celestial entities, human beings, things incorporating animals, plants, and inanimate objects and elements, nevertheless they are rather different variations of the primeval energy or spirit, and the relationship between them is not one of superiority and differences. Complementary dualism emphasizes the relationship among entities in reality, the understanding being that they are in essence one.

Consequently, since life-force permeates everything, there is affinity with and among everything, and it is this very point that promotes sustainable development. Complementary dualism sees harmony and integration in all things, and by the spirit of accommodation and tolerance, positive growth is ensured; rather than having energy wasted in competition, possibilities are created and worked upon in thought and action. All these are translated into ethical principles.

The ethical and ecological implication is that there is respect for everything. This is expressed as the principles of *Nwanne, Ifunanaya na Eziokwu* (brotherhood, love, and truth). The concept of universal brotherhood enjoins humans to see all reality as one, irrespective of their placement. It is this that accounts for the value of pansophism discussed earlier. Love is an emotional response from humans that affects the way we relate to all entities, especially the ones that are not in a position to defend themselves, like the so-called inanimate. *Eziokwu* is a challenge to humans to walk on the pedestal of sincerity and right, a demand for justice. Among the Igbos this very demand amounts to a forceful demand in the realization and ritualization of *Ofo na Ogu* (Ekwealo, 2004, pp. 171–73), which are instruments of justice. The charge is on humans to refrain from abominable and antisocial human and natural activities because of the inevitable karmic consequences to one's self and one's family. What we called the principles of *Nwanne, Ifunanya na Eziokwu* is what we discussed earlier as the environmental value of live and let live, and it has its universal expression in the philosophy of Ubuntu, which simply teaches us that our beingness springs from the beingness of the other: we are because the other is. Whenever we harm the other, we are simply harming ourselves because of the great bonds between everything and everybody. J. S. Mbiti, the Kenyan theologian and philosopher, put it thus: "*umuntungumuntungabantu and mothokemothokabathoBabang,*" meaning, "I am because we are, and since we are, therefore, I am." It is also explained as "a person is a person through other persons." While some critics may argue to the contrary on Ubuntu's ecological spirit, since Mbiti's logic and theological stance appears to be defending the supremacy of the individual, the ethical implication of the message of Ubuntu can still be seen to have ecocentric implications. This is because the values it promotes when taken to their fullest cannot really be in defence of human beings alone. Regardless, by situating and linking it with *Nwanne, Ifunanaya na Eziokwu,* the argument is that it shares in the universal essence contained in the African metaphysical and epistemological meaning of force or spirit which links up huans, animals, plants, and the so-called inanimate. Edwin Etieyibo explains:

> because Ubuntu has these values, it fosters among other things the attitudes of a shared concern as well as collaboration and solidarity … because it is concerned with collective wellbeing, it does not commodify and monetize the natural environment … individuals basically think about communal wellbeing … Ubuntu's values of caring and sharing clearly encourage the development of a non-exploitative attitude towards the environment, an attitude that if cultivated by all will leave the world more sustainable than it currently is.
>
> (2011, pp. 125–27)

African environmental values borrowed from metaphysical, epistemological, and ethical principles and consciousness are biotic and generally ecocentric. Because of their theological bent, they see life as sacred and understand life to cover every aspect of reality. In order to ensure the preservation of values and principles and promote orderliness in the community and the world, Africans created elaborate rituals and ceremonies veiled with appropriate sanctions, mystical and mundane, which make people refrain from disobeying laws and values. In order to have universal understanding and for easy obedience, the values were equally encoded in their proverbs, the language of education and knowledge.

Proverbs as expressions of African environmental values

Proverbs are a medium for disseminating knowledge, worldview, and philosophy, especially in Africa. They are a condensed metaphysical system from which anything about reality could be alembicated. Thus, to be, especially in the ancient African system, is to be in proverbs. What the library is to western society, what the classroom, laboratory, church, and museum are to western society, so are the proverbs for ancient African consciousness. Explaining the importance of proverbs, C. Achebe stated that "among the Ibos, the art of conversation is regarded very highly and proverbs are the palm-oil with which words are eaten" (2008 [1958], p. 6).

Momoh quoted Achebe's observation that proverbs serve two important ends: "they enable the speaker to give universal status to a special and particular incident and they are used to soften the harshness of words and make them more palatable" (2000, p. 360). According to Professor Taiwo Oladele, proverbs for the Yoruba are "word's horse, word is proverb's horse. If a word is lost, we will use proverbs to search for it ... using proverbs to emphasize the words of the wise, use them to convey precious moral lessons, warnings and advices, since they make a great impact on the mind than ordinary words" (Oladele, 2000, p. 360).

Hillary Rodham Clinton, in giving a title to her book, *It Takes a Village and Other Lessons Children Teach Us*, acknowledged the influence of African proverbs: "I chose that African proverb to title this book because it offers a timeless reminder that children will thrive only if their families thrive and if the whole of society cares enough to provide for them" (1996, p. 12).

From proverbs are therefore derived ontology, metaphysics, epistemology, ethics, and, for our purposes, African environmental values. We have already introduced these values as pansophism, *Nwanne, Ifunanaya na Eziokwu*, and live and let live.

The first proverb that introduces this consciousness is the statement *Uwa mmadu na uwa mmuo bu ofu*, meaning that it is the same stream of life that encompasses the world of humans and the world of spirits. This cosmological emphasis serves as the background ecological wisdom that reminds everyone about the universality of all consciousness and the harmony of the universe, for it also introduces the relationship of the celestial and terrestrial worlds. In some situations, it is quoted as *Ala nmuo na Ala mmadu* (the land of the spirit-beings or departed and the land of the living human beings), referring to the entire cosmos of all reality, past and present.

The pansophist aspect of proverbs is shown in many stories that recount a dialogue between human beings, animals, and other entities and in which the wisdom of the other beings is celebrated. For example, an African proverb says that "Eneke the bird says that since men have learned to shoot without missing, he has learned to fly without perching." Another says that "the lizard that jumped from the high iroko tree to the ground said that he would praise himself if no one else did." A proverb in which plants are used says "those whose palm-kernel were cracked for them by a benevolent spirit should not forget to be humble," "God swats flies for a tailless cow." All these proverbs involving animals show that the relationship between the human and the animal worlds are normal affairs. The value of accommodation, live and let live, a necessary injunction for a world of sustainable development, is showcased in the proverbs shared by the Igbos in the breaking of kolanut, a necessary cultural ritual. It is usually started with an invocation and affirmation in which the belief in Almighty God is recognized, an appeal is made for the wellbeing of all entities, and the emphasis for justice and harmony is affirmed. The standard prayer always includes, "he who brings the kola nut brings life, You and yours (family) will live and I and mine will live. Let the eagle perch and let the dove perch, and if either decrees that the other not perch, it will not be well for him." In earlier times it would have read, "if either decrees that the other not perch, let its wings break off or let the former then show the latter where it will then perch," (Adichie, 2006, p. 164), which is a negation since the former had already resisted the perching of the latter.

However, the implication is that every existent must be accommodated and accorded right of place, and that no one has the right to deny the other its natural and fundamental environmental rights. It is these defences for space among entities in creation that ensure sustainable development.

Since we explained that proverbs have universal appeal, there are proverbs which argue for the selfish, exploitative, and anthropocentric nature of human beings, thereby justifying and encouraging the dehumanization of humans by fellow humans. Examples of such proverbs are listed below, drawn from various ethnic groups but really reflective of the entire African environment:

TIV PROVERB: "A person on top of a tree with ripe fruits will normally make sure that his brother gets the best fruit."
KUSUV PROVERB: "Nobody pulls a rope to an opponent's side."
YORUBA PROVERB: "A man who lives in the riverside does not wash his hand with spittle."
BENDEL PROVERB: "When the living has no woman, it will be unwise for the dead to dangle his penis."
HAUSA PROVERB: "It is God who swats flies for a tailless cow."
BENDEL PROVERB: "God can on occasion provide pounded yams without lumps."
YORUBA PROVERB: "Enjoy life now, tomorrow may be too late."
RIVERS PROVERB: "God caters for the bird who has no fish ponds."
IGBO PROVERB: "A cub does not chew grass."
YORUBA PROVERB: "Pocketing kola nuts from another person's farm is not stealing but carrying them (with a basket) is."

These proverbs are in defense of the naked capitalist, market-driven forces which characterize the postcolonial experience. The precolonial African cultures practiced a communalistic economy in which, as already said, everyone was a brother to the other, irrespective of whether one was a human being. Even when Africa entered the capitalist economy initiated by the guild system and the division of labour, it was one with a human face. It was therefore the contemporary African scene that fast witnessed this manipulative environment in which humans are expended for material acquisitions and glory. All these negative proverbs extolling the values of undue exploitation and marginalization are summarized in the Igbo proverb "a fish that does not eat the other does not grow." These kinds of proverbs that defend self-interest at the expense of the other represent the neocapitalist face in Africa, which has led to a corrupt, undeveloped, and polluted African environment. It has promoted personal development through unethical means at the expense of collective, qualitative development. It has equally destroyed green development, wasting environmental resources for the material acquisitions of the private few.

Although naturally everything has always depended on others for food and other physiological necessities, the African food chain was long based on the understanding that necessity occasions the use of the other. For example, among the Umueri in the Anambra Local Government Area, Anambra State, Nigeria, in ancient societies when you wanted to cut the bark or leaf of a tree, maybe for medicinal purposes, you would have first had to seek permission by appropriate incantation to the "spirit" of the tree. The spirit is always willing to yield its curative energy based on pansophist beliefs, but then humans must make the supplication. Here we are referring to the respect and recognition of the "rights" or "value" that is believed to be possessed by the trees (and other environmental realities). We just have to add that the food chain in which a being necessarily feeds on another in ancient African consciousness is not based on the inevitable "a fish not eating the other does not grow." Although the act is the same, the motive is not, for when one entity is feeding on the other, the background motive has always been necessity and inevitability, therefore a respectful acquisition of the other. In that case, there is a respect and dignity accorded to the possessions, not a forced possession.

Consequently, negative proverbs used to defend the wanton disregard for life and property in a bid for personal accumulation of wealth and possessions should be jettisoned, and the older principles already explained reinstituted.

Conclusion

African environmental values and principles are in support of biocentric and ecocentric views. They argue for the existence and survival of all entities, believing that healthy, respectful, and non-exploitative measures will promote qualitative, sustainable development. The thesis of African environmental values rests on the maxim from environmental sustainability to human peace and happiness; the point is that humans and the environment are joined in a necessary relation in which each must recognize the other for the wellbeing of all.

References

Achebe, C. 2008 [1958]. *Things Fall Apart.* 3rd edn. New York: W. W. Norton & Company.

Adichie, C. N. 2006. *Half of A Yellow Sun.* Lagos: Farafina.

Anyanwu, K. C. 1981. The African World-View and Theory of Knowledge. In *African Philosophy.* Eds. Omi E. A. Ruch, and K. C. Anyanwu. Rome: Catholic Book Agency.

Arinze, F. A. 1970. *Sacrifice in Ibo Religion.* Nigeria: Ibadan University Press.

Clinton, H. R. 1996. *It Takes a Village and Other Lessons Children Teach Us*. New York: Simon and Schuster.

Ekwealo, C. J. 2004. Truth in Governance in Traditional Igbo Society: A Philosophical Critique. *Ihafa: A Journal of African Studies* 5 (1), pp. 154–78.

——— 2008. *Traditional and Protracted Humanism and Ecocentricism: A Study of Environmental Philosophy*. PhD thesis. Lagos: University of Lagos.

Etieyibo, E. 2011. The Ethical Dimension of Ubuntu and Its Relationship to Environmental Sustainability. *Journal of African Environmental Ethics and Values* 1, pp. 116–30.

Evans-Pritchard, E. E. 1976. *Witchcraft, Oracles and Magic among the Azande*. Oxford: Clarendon.

Idoniboye, D. E. 1973. The Concept of Spirits in African Metaphysics. In *African Philosophy: Trends and Projections in Six Essays*. Ed. J. I. Unah. Lagos: Concept.

Momoh, C. S. 2000. Nature, Issues and Substance of African Philosophy; Pansophism and Ontological Placements in African Philosophy; Philosophy in African Proverbs. In *The Substance of African Philosophy*. C. S. Momoh. Auchi: African Philosophy Projects Publications.

Oladele, T. 2000. *Social Experience in African Literature*. Sacramento, Calif.: Fourth Dimension Publishing Co.

Senghor, L. S. 1976. *Prose and Poetry* Ed. and trans. J. Reed and C. Wake. London: Heinemann.

Some, M. P. 1998. *The Healing Wisdom of Africa, Finding Life Purpose Through Nature, Ritual, and Community*. New York: Jeremy P. Tarcher/Putnam.

Unah, J. I. 1999. *African Philosophy: Trends and Projections in Six Essays*. Lagos: Concept.

20 Achieving sustainability in Nigeria

Aina Thompson Adeboyejo and
David Victor Ogunkan

The theoretical underpinning of the Nigerian perspective to the human–environment relationship may be viewed and situated in African cosmology, which posits that human beings exist in relation to their environment. African environmental values recognize and accept the interdependency and peaceful coexistence between earth, plants, animals, and humans (Tangwa, 2004). It is the possibility of harnessing this underlying cultural milieu which provides hope and optimism that in Nigeria, despite the current state of its environment, sustainable environmental management is possible, and with it a sustainable future for its inhabitants.

In 1972, the United Nations (UN) Stockholm conference drew global attention to the human environment. The conference focused on the necessity of protecting the natural environment to ensure the sustainability of life on earth (Aghalino, 2009). The UN Stockholm conference changed the worldview on environmental issues. In the aftermath, the concern for environmental issues became a topical debate in academic, business, and political circles (Omiegbe, 1998; Omofonmwan and Osa-Edoh, 2008; Aghalino, 2009; Mwambazambi, 2010). This unprecedented attention to environmental questions is justifiable, considering that the physical, chemical, and biological integrity of the globe is being compromised daily.

Global environmental concern has been considered a prerequisite for global environmental sustainability both explicitly and implicitly (Beckmann *et al.*, 1997). It is however troubling that in spite of the high level of global concern for the environment, environmental degradation still advances at relatively high rates because those who express concern seldom influence environmentally responsible behavior (Maloney and Ward, 1973; Scott and Willits, 1994). The environmental crisis is a global phenomenon, and no society is immune to the threats and dangers which it poses to humanity and the planet. Even so, the situation as experienced in Africa is especially devastating, alarming, and worrisome (Ojomo 2011). Environmental problems currently constitute one of the key developmental challenges of the African continent. The African experience of environmental crisis is dreadful. The Nigerian environmental profile presents a particularly gloomy picture. The country has witnessed widespread environmental problems stemming from oil operations in the Niger Delta, and has the world's highest deforestation rate, having lost more than half of its primary forests in the last five years (Agagu, 2009). The combined effects of these and many other environmental features have resulted in a visible and alarming rate of degradation. The deplorable state of the environment in the country provides motivation to examine the environmental values ingrained in the diverse cultural landscape of Nigeria, with a view to harnessing them to achieve a sustainable environment.

Nigeria's environmental profile

The Nigerian environmental record has been ranked among the worst in the world (Butler, 2008). Its natural physical setting is uniquely fragile, and a number of threats related to human activities have further amplified the country's vulnerability to environmental degradation. The combined effects of these features have made Nigeria one of the world's most environmentally stressed regions. The environmental hazards in Nigeria vary according to geography (Mogbo, 1999). Deforestation is most pronounced in the southwest geopolitical zone. The United Nations Environment Programme (UNEP, 1995) estimated the rate of deforestation in Nigeria to be 663,000 hectares a year, one of the highest deforestation rates in the world, if not the highest. Increasing global demand for agricultural development, urban growth, industrial expansion, and pressure from an increasing population have ultimately reduced the extent, diversity, and stability of the Nigerian forest (Omiegbe, 1998; Agagu, 2009).

Desertification is an environmental problem that is peculiar to the northern part of the country. It is characterized by the covering of the greatest part of the northern frontier by heaps of sand from the Sahara (Mogbo, 1999). The states affected by desertification account for about 38 percent of the country's total land area (Agagu, 2009). Although the problem is mostly a result of drought and sand deposits caused by wind, it is aggravated by human-made factors, such as population pressure resulting in overgrazing and over-exploitation of sporadically distributed tress and gallery forest for fuel wood. The effects of desertification are grievous and are manifested in famine, disease, and the destruction of crops, livestock, and humans.

Municipal and industrial pollution is a major environmental problem in Nigeria, as most cities lack proper solid waste management schemes, and the monitoring and control of industrial waste are inefficient. The most devastating environmental problem is experienced in the southern region, where oil exploration has caused enormous environmental degradation and exacerbated a wide range of social, economic, and political problems to the inhabitants of the region. The petroleum industry contributes a significant share of Nigeria's environmental pollution, particularly a result of incessant vandalism of oil pipelines, corrosion of aged pipelines, malfunctioning equipment, and sabotage of installations by militants and oil thieves (Aghalino, 2009).

Erosion is another critical environmental problem, most visible in the southeastern region of the country and expressed in soil and coastal erosion. Soil erosion is particularly severe in those parts of Nigeria underlain by sandy formation. This problem is aggravated by such factors as increased agricultural activities, civil construction works, deforestation, bush burning, overgrazing, drainage blockage, poor waste management, urbanization, and increased population pressure.

Coastal erosion is highly visible in Nigeria, a serious ecological concern because a large proportion of Nigeria's population and economic activities is located within the coastal zone. Among the factors that influence coastal erosion in Nigeria, as identified by Olusegun Agagu (2009), are relatively flat coastal topography, which restrains proper drainage; climate change, leading to a rise in sea levels; reckless cutting of mangroves, which exposes the shoreline to increased erosion and reduces sediment stability; and sand mining and dredging around beaches, which depletes sand volume.

Conceptual and theoretical issues

The concept of sustainable development featured prominently, for the first time, in the UN Stockholm conference of 1972. The concept has a variety of definitions, but the most popularly employed definition, provided by the Brundtland Report (UNWCED, 1987), defines sustainable development as "development that meets the needs of the present without compromising the ability of future generations to meet their own needs."

The concept has traditionally been focused on an environmentalism framework that gives priority to the issues of ecological degradation (Nurse, 2006). Thus, it is logical to argue that the concept has been reinforced by a series of environmental disasters. As the concept of sustainability matured, further reflection led to a shift from a purely environmentalist perspective and toward a greater focus on the social and economic dimensions of development (Kadekodi, 1992; Nurse, 2006). The contemporary mainstream notion of sustainable development emphasizes the interface between environmental, economic, and social sustainability (Bell, 2003; Nurse, 2006; OECD, 2001). But whether we consider sustainable development a tridimensional concept or a strictly environmentalist one, the fact remains that a sustainable environment is a necessary prerequisite to other sustainable development indices. In discussing the relevance of environmental sustainability to the broader concept of sustainable development, John Morelli (2011) defines environmental sustainability as "a condition of balance, resilience and interconnectedness that allows human society to satisfy its needs while neither exceeding the capacity of its supporting ecosystems to continue to regenerate the services necessary to meet those needs nor by our actions diminishing biological diversity."

The concepts of culture and value are central to understanding cultural value as a concept. Unfortunately culture is a slippery and ubiquitous concept. Culture has been variously defined, but the classical definition, given by Edward Tylor (1871), is "the complex whole which include knowledge, belief, art, law, morals, customs and any other capabilities and habits acquired by man as a member of society." By contrast, "value" has been defined as a learned, relatively enduring, emotionally changed, epistemologically grounded, and represented moral conceptualization that assists us in making judgments and preparing to act (Frey, 1994). It has therefore been argued that cultural values represent the implicitly and explicitly shared abstract ideas about what is good, right, and desirable in a society.

Theoretical discourse on environmental ethics can be categorized into five perspectives: enlightened (weak) anthropocentrism; animal liberation and rights theory; biocentrism; ecocentrism; and ecofeminism (Ojomo, 2011). The enlightened (weak) anthropocentrism is a human-based argument for environmental policies which stems from the anthropocentric view that humans are sole bearers of intrinsic value and all living things are here to sustain humanity's existence (MacKinnon, 2007). This view of animal liberation and rights theory was expanded by Peter Singer (1975) to include all animals and all species in the universe. He opines that the pleasure and pain that animals experience are mentally relevant and therefore provide sufficient conditions for animals to receive moral consideration.

In a radical response to anthropocentrism, biocentrism accords moral worth to all organisms. The philosophers working within this tradition believe that the equal inherent worth of all lives warrants equal moral status, and therefore that we must respect all living organisms (Fadahunsi, 2007). Ecocentrism provides a more radical approach to ecological philosophy. It expands the biocentric view of "moral patient" (entities to which to accord moral consideration) to include nature as a whole (Ojomo, 2011). This ethical framework recognizes that all species including humans are the products of a long evolutionary process and are interrelated in their life processes (Lindenmeyer and Burgman, 2005). The ecocentric perspectives have been expressed in three different views: the land ethic, deep ecology, and the nature of theory's value (Yang, 2006).

Ecofeminism is a revolutionary feminist approach to environmental ethics. The ecofeminist theorists use a framework of gender and nature. They see the oppression of women and the dominance of nature as interconnected. Ecofeminism is revolutionary in that it promotes the overthrow of both types of dominance, since each type of dominance is oppressive (Abedi-Sarvestani and Shahvali, 2008).

According to Karen Warren (1994), there are important connections among systems of domination (e.g. historical, literary, political, empirical, and ethical connections), and any adequate feminism, environmentalism, or environmental policy must recognize these connections. Therefore, the ecofeminists believe that any feminist theory and any environmental ethic which fails to take seriously the twin and interconnected domination of woman and nature is at best incomplete and at worst simply inadequate (Warren, 2001).

Environmental ethics perspectives can be broadly classified into anthropocentric and non-anthropocentric. The enlightened (weak) anthropocentric and animal rights theories express the anthropocentric view, while biocentric, ecocentric, and ecofeminism express the non-anthropocentric view.

Environmental issues in Nigerian cultural landscapes

Living with nature as well as the preservation and conservation of natural ecosystems is an integral part of indigenous Nigerian traditions, culture, and values. Though largely without formal education, the traditional Nigerian societies' approaches to environmental conservation and planning are embedded in various cultural practices, festivals, oral traditions, folklore, and songs in different parts of the country. The rich Nigerian cultural heritage includes traditional environmental laws, rules, and regulations with in-built, self-enforcing mechanisms that ensure compliance and environmental sustainability.

In Nigeria, the environmental perspective emerges from the general cosmology found throughout Sub-Saharan Africa. Human beings live within a web of life, the spirits, and the environment, all of which are connected and interdependent. This state of coexistence implies a "dynamic relationship between God, deities, ancestors, human beings and nature" (Metuh, 1987). This metaphysical outlook underpins the ways, manner, and cosmic relationship between fellow humans (Ojomo, 2011) and between humans and the natural environment. It also explains why indigenous Africans are more cautious in their attitude to plants, animals, and inanimate things and the various invisible factors of the world than they are towards humans (Tangwa, 2004). Darrol Bryant (1992, pp.73, 76) succinctly states:

> It is essential that this wisdom be recovered if Africans were to address the environmental problems and other challenges facing the continent and its people. ... This is because, African traditions understood nature more than just matter for exploitation. Nature was a natural home. Being in harmony with nature meant living in close contact with deeper sources of divine life. ... It was necessary to listen to the voices from nature (implicit as they indeed were in) the rhythm of the seasons, the coming of the rain, the flowing of crops and the fruits of the earth.

True to this, the Yoruba in southwestern Nigeria recognize and acknowledge God's divine lordship over the whole earth and also believe that "man is a tenant on God's earth" (Idowu, 1978; Ogunade, 2009).

This belief provides a regular check on the way the Yoruba treat the environment (Ogunade, 2009). The Yoruba believe that creation is the wondrous work of God which must not be destroyed, so as not to incur God's wrath. This belief is reflected in their traditional folklore:

> *Tutu, tutu ni ni ni,*
> *Bee l'eweko igbe ri,*
> *Ije iwo ma wipe*
> *Ewa to wa lara won*
> *Lodo eleda lo ti wa*
>
> (The vegetation is fresh and evergreen, do you know
> that their beauty comes from God?)

That the natural environment is the work of God (Eledumare) is also acknowledged by Orunmila (a deity in Yorubaland):

> *Orunmila fehinti o wo titi*
> *Oni: Eyin ero okun,*
> *Eyin ero osa*
> *Eyin o mop e ise Olodumare tobi*
>
> (Orunmila leaned back, and gazing contemplatively, he said: "You travelers to the sea, you travelers to the lagoon, don't you perceive the wondrous work of God?")

The Yoruba believe that by respecting nature, they are respecting the wondrous work of God. Yoruba traditional religion is characterized by deities and ancestral worship. They believe that those deities and ancestors reside in hills, mountains, rivers, rocks, lakes, trees, brooks, and thick forests, which must be preserved and protected. Therefore, the aim of preserving the environment is not only to create a healthy and beautiful habitat for human beings but also an abode for a category of deities (Awolalu and Dopamu, 1979). The Osun groove in Osogbo (now a UN Educational, Scientific and Cultural Organization (UNESCO) cultural center), Oke'badan in Ibadan, and Olumo rock in Abeokuta are among the numerous shrines being preserved as tourists centers because they serve as an abode for some spiritual beings. Thus, the manifest function of preserving those special environments is rooted in the sacredness of those deities, while the latent function is to conserve and preserve the environment in a sustainable manner.

Yoruba religion also regards human beings, animals, plants, and nonliving things as cohabitants. Therefore, human beings must be careful not to maltreat nature in order to allow for a peaceful coexistence. It is believed that some environmental problems experienced in Nigeria have been due to people's disregard for nature (Ogunade, 2009).

In southeastern Nigeria, the environmental ethos among the Igbos has religious as well as social relevance. For instance, trees and forests have special significance in their religious and social worlds. Like the Yoruba, the Igbo have a high reverence for deities, which is profoundly influenced by nature, and they believe that certain parts of the environment are the abode of the deities. There is hardly any community in Igboland that exists without a sacred grove, evil forest, sacred pond, evil stream, or forbidden forest, where some parts of the environment are delineated for the worship of the gods (Tiwari *et al.*, 1998; Eneji *et al.*, 2009). The conservation strategy for those sacred parts of the environment is enshrined in taboos, totems, numerous cultural and religious rites and is maintained by revering gods and ancestral spirits (Eneji *et al.*, 2012). The fear and awe associated with those sacred environments have played a significant role in the conservation and management of natural resources in Igboland.

The Igbos also believe that the human community is related to the nonhuman community: the environment and human beings are coexistent, such that without human beings, the environment ceases to exist and vice versa (Nwosu, 2010).

The conceptualization of the complex web of interaction and interdependencies between human beings and nature on the one hand and among natural elements on the other is reflected in the Igbo wise saying, "*ife kwuru, ife akwudubuya*" ("if a thing stands, another stands near it"). In recognition of this fact, the Igbo hold the belief that the environment should be treated with dignity and respect. This belief is reflected in their strong cultural and religious tendency to encourage community participation in natural resources conservation and to sustain a positive awareness of nature and of the linkages between human beings and nature (Nwosu, 2010; Eneji *et al.*, 2012).

Apart from religious implications, Igbo environmental values also have sociocultural relevance. Traditional Igbo society recognizes and appreciates the beauty of nature as reflected in habits, practices, traditions, and values that enhance its purity and beauty (Nwosu, 2010). These habits, practices, and cultural values have been maintained through collective authority vested in a group of male elders and chiefs whose words and actions are laws in community matters and are much respected and obeyed (Eneji *et al.*, 2012). A typical example of these groups is the Okwonkwo society, which is of social and religious character, and has cultural resources that are directed toward conservation and effective use of the environment (Nwosu, 2010).

The traditional Hausa culture in the northern part of Nigeria has been significantly and permanently shaped by Islam since the ninth century AD (Sagagi, 1994), and the environmental values of the Hausa are derived from an Islamic environmental ethic. The Islamic worldview is theocentric in nature: Islam views the universe as God's creation.

> And whatever in the heavens and whatever is in the earth is Allah's and Allah encompasses all things.
>
> (Quran 4:126)

> Now surely they are in doubt as to the meeting of their Lord; now surely He encompasses all things.
>
> (Quran 41:54)

The Islamic worldview on environmental conservation is reinforced in a variety of ways: unity between human and nature, human responsibility toward nature, a guarantee to engage in righteous behavior, and comprehensiveness (Abedi-Sarvestani and Shahvali, 2008). Islam recognizes human beings and environment as having originated from the same source and coexisting in the universe. Just like human beings, nature is a creation of Allah: "There is not an animal (that lives) on the earth, or a being that flies on its wings, but (forms part of) communities like you. Nothing have we omitted from the Book and they (all) shall be gathered to their Lord in the end" (Quran 6:38).

It is therefore the responsibility of human beings to treat nature with respect and reverence as a co-tenant in the universe. However, humans are distinguished from animals by their capacity to reason and make moral choices. That is why they are entrusted and accountable as God's agents and stewards on earth. In other words, as part of God's creation the human being has a special position as God's vicegerent (*Khalifa*) on earth.

> Behold, thy Lord said to the angels: "I will create a vicegerent (*khalifa*) on earth." They said: "Wilt Thou place therein one who will make mischief therein and shed blood? Whilst we do celebrate Thy praises and glorify Thy holy name?" He said: "I know what ye know not."
>
> (Quran 2:30)

Although the human being has superiority over other creations, this mastery should be accompanied with worship. A good human being is one who follows God's commands and behaves toward God's creations righteously (Abedi-Sarvestani and Shahvali, 2008). Furthermore, the Glorious Quran made it known that God has made nature subservient (*sakhkhara*) to human beings. This by no means gave humans the power to abuse nature but was a means to test humans' gratitude toward God:

> It is Allah Who has subjected (*sakhkhara*) the sea to you, that ship may sail through it by His command, that ye may seek of His Bounty, and that ye may be grateful. And He has subjected to you, as from Him, all that is in the heavens and on earth: behold, in that are Signs indeed for those who reflect.
>
> (Quran 45:12–13)

From these Quranic verses it is evident that all creations are for the use of humankind. However, to show their gratitude to Almighty Allah, human beings must use these creations responsibly, with as much consideration and kindness as possible. The Hausas hold this environmental ethical value, which guides them in their daily interactions with the environment.

Recommendations and conclusion

The environmental crisis remains one of the most devastating problems confronting the African continent, especially Nigeria, which has come to be regarded as the most environmentally stressed region in the world (Agagu, 2009). To worsen the situation, the Nigerian environmental stakeholders are still grappling with developing an effective environmental management strategy to respond to threats in a sustainable manner.

Because the indigenous cultural values of Nigerians favor environmental conservation and preservation, the way to achieve a sustainable environment in Nigeria is to revitalize the indigenous environmental knowledge and cultural values. One way this can be done is by identifying and promoting cultural practices, folk traditions, and festivals that incorporate environmental education and conservation practices, by compiling such traditional folk practices of environmental management from different parts of the country, and by having the Federal Ministry of the Environment publish the resulting compilation for use in primary and secondary schools. The publication can be a resource book for media broadcasts and programs focused on environmental planning and management. Such a compendium of traditional environmental ethical approaches would provide the most viable and acceptable foundation for sustainable environmental management in Nigeria.

References

Abedi-Sarvestani, A., and M. Shahvali. 2008. Environmental Ethics: Toward an Islamic Perspective. *American-Eurasian Journal of Agricutural and Environmental Science* 3(4), pp. 609–17.

Agagu, O. K. 2009. *Threat to the Nigerian Environment: A Call for Positive Action.* Lecture delivered at the 7th Chief S. L. Edu Memorial Lecture, Victorial Island, Lagos.

Aghalino, S. O. 2009. Corporate Response to Environmental Deterioration in the Oil Bearing Area of the Niger-Delta, Nigeria, 1984–2002. *Jounal of Sustainable Development in Africa* 11(2).

Awolalu, J. O., and P. A. Dopamu. 1979. *West African Traditional Religion.* Ibadan: Onibonoje.

Beckmann, S. C., W. E. Kilbourne, Y. V. Dam, and M. Pardo. 1997. *Anthropocentrism, Value Systems, and Environmental Attitudes: A Multi-National Comparison.* Working Paper No. 10. Copenhagen: Department of Marketing, Copenhagen Business School.

Bell, S. 2003. *Measuring Sustainability: Learning by Doing.* London: Earthscan.

Bryant, D. M. 1992. God, Humanity and Mother Earth: African Wisdom and the Recovery of the Earth. In *God, Humanity and Mother Nature.* Ed. G. E. M. Ogutu. Nairobi: Masaki, pp. 73, 76.

Butler, J. 2008. *Nigerian Environmental Profile.* Retrieved on 20th December, 2012, from www.nigeriaworld.com.

Eneji, C. V. O., Q. I. Gubo Jian Xiaoying, S. N. Oden, and F. I. Okpiliya. 2009. A Review of the Dynamics of Forest Resources Valuation and Community Livelihood: Issues, Arguments and Concerns. *Journal of Agricultural Biotechnology and Ecology in China* 2(2), pp. 210–31.

Eneji, C. V. O, G. U. Ntamu, J. O. Ajor, C. B. Ben, J. E. Bassey, and J. J. Williams. 2012. Ethical Basis of African Traditional Religion and Sociocultural Practices in Natural Resources Conservation and Management in Cross River State. *Nigeria Journal of Research in Peace, Gender and Development* 22, pp. 34–43.

Fadahunsi, A. 2007. Challenging Africa's Environmental Crisis: The Ethical Imperative. Retrieved on 20th September, 2009, from http://www.utexas.edu/conferences/africa/2009/09abstracts_a-g.htm.

Frey, R. 1994. *Eye Juggling: Seeing the World through a Looking Glass and a Glass Pane: A Workbook for Clarifying and Interpreting Values.* Lanham, Md.: University Press of America.

Idowu, E. B. 1978. *African Traditional Religion: A Definition.* London: SCM.

Kadekodi, G. K. 1992. Paradigms of Sustainable Development. *Journal of SID* 3, pp. 72–76.

Lindenmeyer, D., and M. Burgman. 2005. *Practical Conservation Biology.* Collingwood, Victoria, Australia: CSIRO.

MacKinnon, B. 2007. *Ethics Theory and Contemporary Issues 5th Ed.* Belmont, Calif.: Wadsworth Publishing.

Maloney, M. P., and M. P. Ward. 1973. Ecology: Let's Hear from the People. *American Psychologist* 28, pp. 583–86.

Metuh, I. E. 1987. *Comparative Studies in African Traditional Religions*. Onitsha, Nigeria: IMICO.

Mogbo, T. C. 1999. An Integrative Approach to Environmental Reconstruction and Politics in Nigeria. *Journal of Environmental Sciences* 3(1), pp. 1–7.

Morelli, J. 2011. Environmental Sustainability: A Definition for Environmental Professionals. *Journal of Environmental Sustainability* 1, pp. 19–27.

Mwambazambi, K. 2010. Environmental Problems in Africa: A Theological Response. *Ethiopian Journal of Environmental Studies and Management* 3(2), pp. 54–64.

Nurse, K. 2006. *Culture as the Fourth Pillar of Sustainable Development*. Article prepared for the Commonwealth Secretariat. London: Malborough House.

Nwosu, P. U. 2010. The Role of Okonko Society in Preserving Igbo Environment. *Journal of Human Ecology* 311, pp. 59–64.

OECD (Organization for Economic Cooperation and Development). 2001. *Sustainable Development: Critical Issues*. Paris: O ECD.

Ogunade, R. 2009. Environmental Issues in Yoruba Religion. Retrieved on 22nd August, 2009, from www.unilorin.edu.ng.

Ojomo, P. A. 2011. Environmental Ethics: An African Understanding. *Journal of Pan African Studies* 4(3), pp. 101–13.

Omiegbe, O. 1998. Bush Burning and Its Effect in Africa: A Case Study of Nigeria. *Benin Journal of Environment Education* 11, pp. 10–20.

Omofonmwan, S. I., and G. I. Osa-Edoh. 2008. The Challenges of Environmental Problems in Nigeria. *Journal of Human Ecology* 23(1), pp. 53–57.

Sagagi, B. S. 1994. Culture and Islam in Hausa Land. *Barutiwa Newspaper* 3(2).

Scott, D, and F. K. Willits. 1994. Environmental Attitudes and Behavior: A Pennsylvania Survey. *Environment and Behavior* 26(2), pp. 239–60.

Singer, P. 1975. *Animal Liberation: A New Ethics for Our Treatment of Animals*. New York: Random House.

Tangwa, G. 2004. Some African Reflections on Biomedical and Environmental Ethics. In *A Companion to African Philosophy* Ed. K. Wiredu. Oxford: Blackwell, pp. 387–95.

Tiwari, B. K., S. K. Barik, and R. S. Tripathi. 1998. Biodiversity Value, Status, and Strategies for Conservation of Sacred Groves of Meghalaya, India. *Ecosystem Health* 4, pp. 20–32.

Tylor, E. B. 1871. *Primitive Culture*. London: J. Murray.

UNEP (United Nations Environment Programme). 1995. *The Marine and Coastal Environment of the West and Central African Region and Its State of Pollution*.Regional Seas Programmes (RSPS) 46. Nairobi: UNEP.

UNWCED (United Nations World Commission on Environment and Development). 1987. *Our Common Future (The Brundtland Report)*. Oxford: Oxford University Press.

Warren, K. 1994. The Power and Promise of Ecological Feminism. In *The Environmental Ethics and Policy Book*. Ed. D. Van DeVeer and C. Pierce. Belmont, Calif.: Wadsworth, pp. 267–81.

Warren, K. 2001. The Power and the Promise of Ecological Feminism. In *Environmental Ethics: Readings in Theory and Application*. Ed. L. Pojman. London: Thomson Learning, pp. 189–99.

Yang, T. 2006. Towards an Egalitarian Global Environmental Ethics. In *Environmental Ethics and International Policy*. UNESCO. Paris: UNESCO.

Introduction to Part III
Examples of values guiding behavior

Jack Appleton

While not statements of values, several of the chapters in Part III shed light on the values held by individuals throughout the world. The diversity and complexity of environmental values held by Chinese in Singapore is inferred in Chapter 28, with the discussion of Singapore's biodiversity and conservation efforts. In Chapter 27, Justus Kithiia and Anna Lyth describe how two cities in Africa are responding to their changes in circumstances within a sustainability framework. The chapters in Part III have been organized and selected to provide a sense of the possible, ranging from one's home and the plants that surround us on a daily basis, to the abstract and legal technical world of environmental diplomacy on a global scale. This part starts off with Michael Marder's essay in Chapter 21, which reminds us that it is the environment which sustains us, not human beings that sustain the environment. The planet is not a garden. In Chapter 22, Kathy Shearin focuses our attention on the environment in our homes and neighborhoods rather than on a global scale. She explicates the benefits not of gardening the planet, but of adopting natural landscaping to provide benefit for ourselves, our homes, our neighborhood, and to make a small, but significant difference which helps the planet sustain us. In Chapter 23, Nalini M. Nadkarni, Dan J. Pacholke, and Marc Bekoff take us from the comfort of our homes and neighborhoods into what for many of us is the frightening and unknown world of prisons. In so doing, they challenge our sense of the possible. If hardened criminals can care for the environment, the rest of us are left with few excuses. The success of the program is, for most of us, unimaginable, heartwarming and instructive. Blanca Fraijo-Sing, César Tapia-Fonllem, and Victor Corral-Verdugo provide some insight in Chapter 24 as to why Nadkarni *et al.* have been successful, and show us how such environmental education programs can be expanded and generalized to include all citizens. Kevin Halsey broadens the discussion in Chapter 25 to include our natural surroundings and he provides a concrete example of how both an ecosystem and a business venture can thrive and provide benefit to both. Halsey details cautionary tales in the hope that such insight will facilitate the expansion of co-consideratory thinking, at the business level of human organization. In Chapter 26, Mark E. Hillon further expands the discussion to the level of the organization, with another population not normally associated with environmental concern and sustainable development: corporate strategists. Hillon presents a sobering business worldview of the present and the possible. Ultimately, Hillon's message is optimistic and hopeful, as he explains how and why the business community will come to include sustainability values in its decisions. Kithiia and Lyth share Hillon's message in Chapter 27 and take it out of the realm of private corporate interests to the sphere of the community, with a discussion of municipal responses to climate change in two cities in East Africa. In Chapter 28, Kwek Yan Chong *et al.* take us beyond the level of the organization, to the level of the extended community: the national level and regional level. Taken together, these chapters explore the human impact on the environment, and the provisioning for nature from the micro level of daily life to the macro level of national economics and politics. Finally, Part III, and the book, end with an overview at the planetary level with Ambassador Amado S. Tolentino Jr's passionate insight and advocacy for global environmental protection in Chapter 29.

21 Sustainable perspectivalism
Who sustains whom?

Michael Marder

> The Ability to Be Small. One has still to be as close to the flowers, the grass, and the butterflies as a child, who is not so very much bigger than they are. We adults, on the other hand, have grown up high above them and have to condescend to them; I believe the grass *hates* us when we confess our love for it. – He who wants to partake of *all* good things must know how to be small at times.
>
> (Nietzsche, 1996)

The values implicit in sustainability discourses are broadly anthropocentric. From attempts to balance economic development and the health of ecosystems to concerns with the provision of sufficient natural resources to future generations, humanity remains the first and last point of reference, the unquestioned beneficiary of reformed environmental practices. One may argue, of course, that sustainability – a concept that is notoriously ambiguous (Bell and Morse, 2008, p. 10) – is not a zero-sum game, since diverse plant and animal species can flourish together under the human stewardship of the planet. But rather than provide a vital point of departure for the thinking of sustainable development, cross-species and cross-kingdom communities of interest are merely felicitous bonuses accompanying the relatively recent realization of the limits to our otherwise unbridled "mastery of nature." The existing sustainability discourses make adjustments in but do not abolish instrumental rationality, for which all organic and inorganic entities on Earth represented potentially usable resources and which was responsible for the onset of the environmental crisis. On the grounds of instrumental rationality itself, these sustainability discourses are more rational but hardly different qualitatively from the disastrous logic that has brought the planet to its current state.

Despite some of these problems, "sustainability" may prove indispensable – indeed, more so than deep ecology – for the revaluation of environmental values. To activate its hidden potential, we would need to resort to immanent criticism, not dismissing but interrogating its silent presuppositions.

Although sustainability discourses are quite heterogeneous, without exception they share the assumption that it is up to human beings to sustain – almost Atlas-like – the planet and to be its stewards. There is a grain of truth in this supposition, both reflecting and reacting to the fact that the activity of *Homo sapiens* has had by far the most widespread and devastating effect on its habitats. But it is also a piece of delusional arrogance to suggest that life on Earth is (or should be) sustained by humans. To be sure, the continuation of life is only negatively dependent on human beings, who can either render the planet empty and uninhabitable in a matter of seconds through the use of sophisticated weapons, or gradually drive it to exhaustion. Yet the positive conditions of possibility for life lie elsewhere, for instance in the photosynthetic activity of plants that ensure viable levels of oxygen in the atmosphere. Human stewardship, inspired by the disproportionate significance we attribute to our own role in the evolutionary and even cosmic processes, is superfluous in comparison to the indispensability of plants. And this occasions the question: Who, in fact, sustains whom?

If to sus-tain – *sub-tenere* – is literally to prop up or to hold up from below, then this word wields a definite spatial orientation and a differential valuation of the "higher" and the "lower." There is ineluctable inequality in the relation of the sustaining and the sustained, inequality that betokens the indebtedness of the latter before the former. Vegetal life, on which we depend both for nourishment and for oxygen, underpins animal and human lives and carries the weight of making them possible. We may term this potentiality of plants, put in the service of other living beings, *material sustainability*. At the same time, however, the most basic support that plants provide to non-vegetal organisms is debased and devalued, deemed to be low on the scale of value as well. From this vantage point, material sustainability does not usually merit discussion or critical consideration; instead, it is silently integrated into the strict teleology of the food chain, itself a reflection of the metaphysical hierarchy of beings. And conversely, the most superfluous creature, namely the human, proclaims itself the pinnacle of creation or evolution, as the case may be, and the *raison d'être* of the entire natural order (call it *ideal sustainability*). As those for the sake of whom the rest of the world presumably exists, human beings convert their supplementarity on the face of the planet into the most essential thing imaginable. Ideal sustainability obscures material sustainability behind the smokescreen of anthropocentrism and reconstructs a pale version of materiality itself on the basis of ideality, turning everything in the world into a material reserve for human use. The nihilistic inversion of values differentiation is complete, so that the highest becomes the lowest and the lowest becomes the highest.

When I mention nihilism and the inversion of values, I am making what are surely not-so-veiled references to the philosophy of Friedrich Nietzsche, who attributed these two phenomena to the entire history of western metaphysics, commencing with Plato. How do these Nietzschean concepts relate to environmental thinking in general and the sustainability discourses in particular? The common root of nihilism and the inversion of values is the prioritization of ideality – Plato's Ideas, Aristotle's unmoved mover, Augustine's God, Immanuel Kant's subject – over materiality. Not only is the true ground of existence said to lie elsewhere, in a realm inaccessible to our senses, but also the turn or the return to this ground demands that we forsake materiality and adopt a certain disembodied, indifferent perspective on the world where empirical multiplicities prevail. Such nihilistic indifference to the world, construed as an epiphenomenal expression of a more profound and stable reality, is absolutely detrimental to the environment: no matter how much we use and abuse living beings and their ecosystems, metaphysical ideality and truth will suffer no significant alterations.

Ideal sustainability, paving the way to the transcendent ground of existence, inevitably undermines material sustainability, which in turn props up and supports, unacknowledged, all metaphysical ventures. The world of western philosophy is constructed in such a way that it systematically distorts and weakens whatever is "useful" (Nietzsche's word) for life; it bestows the least value on the entities and processes that promote life and valorizes life-stunting abstractions in their stead (Nietzsche, 1997). While colloquially nihilism is associated with a valueless drift, in the aftermath of the destruction of value frameworks it would be more accurate to diagnose philosophical nihilism as the main effect of the metaphysical values themselves. The values of pure ideality are incredibly deadly for all aspects of empirical existence that stand in their way. Ideal sustainability is actually self-contradictory, in that its ideality militates against the very possibility of sustaining life.

The anti-environmental perspective of metaphysics is unsustainable for at least two reasons. First, it denies its own perspectivalism by claiming exclusive access to the truth. Its disembodied nature and self-professed indifference to the material world put it in a paradoxical position of a "perspective without perspective," a de-contextualized (and hence independent from the environment) objective description of what is. Perspectives necessarily entail a multiplicity of vantage points on and modes of accessing existence – something clearly incompatible with metaphysics. Second, metaphysical anti-environmentalism must obfuscate and repress the fact that it cannot but rely on materiality and on living beings for its ongoing survival. Incapable of acknowledging this "deeper" sense of sustainability, it indiscriminately utilizes and often physically obliterates its repressed support. In either case, various types of unsustainability will continue to haunt our thinking and praxis, so long as we do not call into question the potent remnants of metaphysics that motivate them, often unbeknown to us.

This, then, is the sense in which I would like to begin interpreting Nietzsche's aphorism "The ability to be small," extracted from *Human, All Too Human* (1996, p. 323). The "adulthood" Nietzsche derides there is an allusion to the Kantian ideal of Enlightenment, our emergence from "self-incurred immaturity," which depends in large part on our adoption of inverted metaphysical value systems and on a predilection to nihilism. Adults have "grown up high above" the grass and the flowers, though it is not primarily their physical size, as compared to that of children, that is at stake in this elevation but a self-aggrandizement on the scale of value and the concomitant diminution of the value of vegetation. What would it mean, in contrast to this ideal, "to be as close to the flowers, the grass, and the butterflies as a child"? Would it not imply a certain sympathy with the earthly perspective of the plants themselves, the sympathy that zealous and hyper-adult proponents of Enlightenment habitually dismiss as mythical, irrational, or animist? The ability to be small would be the fruit of human self-relativization, a self-evaluation, keeping the human place in the environment in perspective and mindful of other, nonhuman perspectives on the world. It is ontological – not ontic – smallness that Nietzsche has in mind, that is, not the bodily size of human beings, who are actually dwarfed by some trees such as sequoias, but our proximity to vegetal life, to which we are indebted for the very air we breathe and the food we consume.

How are the sustainability discourses complicit with the object of Nietzschean critique? They are doubtless more adult than the unsustainable metaphysics, with its teenage rebelliousness against the very world, on which it materially depends. The index for the maturity of sustainable thinking and practices is the responsibility they are willing to assume for the environment by imposing rational limits on its instrumentalization. While this strategy, against the backdrop of metaphysical excesses, is laudable, it does not evade criticism inspired by Nietzsche's aphorism. Rather than risk an all-encompassing revaluation of values, what goes on today under the title of sustainability has to do with a fine-tuning that leaves the self-aggrandizing image of humanity intact. Nietzsche would perhaps say that the desire animating sustainability discourses is even more condescending than that characteristic of metaphysical philosophy: our hubris is evident in our belief, our unwillingness to let go of the prejudice of ideal sustainability, that we could be the effective and benevolent managers of the planet which actually sustains us, physically and otherwise. The source of the problem, anthropocentrism, endeavors to reform itself so as to spin a possible solution on its own turf. That is why "the grass *hates* us when we confess our love for it" – when we are incapable of recognizing its intrinsic value, that is, what it is not only in itself but also for itself, from its unique vegetal perspective so dissimilar to and incomprehensible for the fully mature and enlightened humanity.

To begin shifting the focus from ideal to material sustainability, it will be necessary to admit nonhuman perspectives, including that of vegetal life, into the midst of environmental discourse. In what follows, I will point out the most decisive implication of this shift. For now, let me provisionally conclude the analysis of "sustainability" with a consideration of the suffix, -ability, which gives prominence not to what (or who) actually sustains life but to what (or who) could possibly sustain it. In line with material sustainability, -ability would denote the non-transcendental conditions of possibility for the persistence of living beings. Even the most conventional thinking of sustainability is future-oriented, in that it is driven by a justifiable worry that finite natural resources will at some point be depleted, prejudicing subsequent generations. But the possible is not confined to what may or may not occur in the future; it is also that which enables, makes possible, actively "possibilizes" the present. In keeping with this positive signification, material sustainability lies squarely on the side of plants, both now living and long dead, though still enriching the soil, in which they have decayed or transformed into "fossil fuels." Where plants already sustain life from below, from the literal and metaphorical ground wherein they are rooted, our chief worry should be with how to sustain sustainability, that is, how to let vegetal beings continue to do what they do best. In other words, our much more modest and oblique role would be to nurture and promote the material conditions of possibility *for* the possibility of life, rather than invest ourselves directly with the role of managers or stewards of the environment. Our acknowledgment of vegetal activity would then coincide with the kind of human receptivity, without which theories and practices of sustainability would continue to pose the masked original problem in the guise of a solution. And the sine qua non of environmental receptivity – not to be conflated with passivity or inaction – would be the interplay of human and nonhuman perspectives on the environment, an extended nonlinguistic dialogue whence a community of sustainable values could be forged.

The intrinsic value of vegetation: from the plant in itself to the plant for itself

Struggles against nihilism, either on the rational or on the affective front, tend to end in deadlock and a sense of futility. Nietzsche argues that humanity must first pass through an intense nihilistic phase, even if that takes hundreds of years and even if it is questionable whether anything or anyone would remain in its wake, before purging itself of this sentiment turned against life. The point is not to dismiss but to deepen nihilism, let it resonate in us and shake us with the yawn of nothingness threatening to devour us. To a large extent, this awakening is the effect of the environmental crisis, to which sustainability offers something of a response. Sustainability becomes a priority when firm ground shifts underneath our feet and when it seems that nothing sustains us – for instance, when we lose faith in the metanarrative of technological progress or realize that our power to control and dominate our environment threatens to destroy the controlled object altogether. When we learn about the accelerating disappearance of plant species, with (according to the most conservative of estimates) more than one-fifth of flora worldwide headed for extinction in the not-so-distant future, we perhaps imagine the near-absence of what so vitally sustains us and begin to value this inconspicuous substratum of life.

And yet, sustainability discourses cannot afford to undertake the revaluation of the human relation to the environment within the same productivist-progressivist paradigm that has been responsible for the dire situation of the planet today. Embedding sustainable development in the context of instrumental rationality is analogous to using more economical construction materials and more efficient architectural designs for a house built on the slopes of an active volcano. An obvious alternative to this is to insist on the intrinsic value of ecosystems and their members, as theorists associated with the deep ecology movement have done. It would appear that in the notion of intrinsic value, the thinking of sustainability would find an unsurpassable limit, something that would fall outside the scope of its logic and conceptual apparatus. Before dismissing the relevance of this notion, it is worth asking what exactly it implies and whether or not it may be harmonized with material sustainability.

Kant would argue that intrinsic value is the end-in-itself, which refers to the ethical status of human beings, who should not be used as means for externally imposed ends. Kant is not only highly anthropocentric in his moral philosophy, but also logocentric, since this ethical status is applicable, in general, to any rational being, and in particular to humans solely insofar as they are subjects of reason. For Kant, there is nothing respect-worthy in our animal, empirical, flesh-and-blood constitution; the body, in and of itself, does not deserve ethical protection as an end-in-itself. Needless to say, according to this philosophical system, neither animals nor plants nor the environment as a whole would be covered by the precepts of intrinsic value, simply because none participate in the community of rational beings who are ideally autonomous and whose individual actions are strictly in keeping with the ethical universality of pure practical reason that prompts them to will exactly the same in any given case.

The extension of intrinsic value to other-than-human beings will without a doubt interfere with Kant's sense of the end-in-itself, from which it will nonetheless retain an absolute resistance to the logic of means and ends – thus, to the possibility of instrumentalization. Furthermore, it will capitalize on Kant's radical conclusions: the philosophy of finitude, marked by an insistence on the self-limitation or self-critique of human reason. If plants, for instance, possess intrinsic value, it is because not everything in their mode of being turns toward us. As a non-object of knowledge and manipulation, the plant is, again in Kantian jargon, a thing-in-itself, which does not mean that it is simply mysterious but that it also exists and is of value for itself! After Kant, Georg Hegel dialectically transformed the thing-in-itself into the thing-for-itself, and hence into the subject who never finds anything but itself behind the curtain of phenomenal appearances. The same can be said of the plant endowed with intrinsic value that prompts its metamorphosis from "the plant in itself" into "the plant for itself," a living being with a uniquely vegetal perspective on the world. With this the plant exceeds everything measured from the human standpoint and appears to be incommensurable to us, even though its thriving is not at all contrary to our own.

Nietzsche's thinking was exquisitely attuned to the perspective of the plants themselves, inassimilable to the human view of the world. When he writes in one of his early notebooks that "*to the plant, the whole world is plant*; to us man" (Nietzsche, 2009, p. 138, emphasis added) or when in *The Will to Power* he explains Arthur Schopenhauer's "epistemological pessimism," with which he largely identifies, in terms of the understanding that there is no "absolute nature of things" and that reality is given through necessarily perspectival appearances (Nietzsche, 1968, pp. 14–15, 51), Nietzsche hints at what is behind the idea of the plant for itself. Above all, it leads us to believe that there is not one true world but multiple worlds of humans, animals, plants, and so forth, that only imperfectly overlap in the interactions of their inhabitants. Thanks to our faculty of imagination and our mimetic plasticity – the uncanny capacity to put ourselves in the shoes (and sometimes the skins and the roots) of others – it is possible to displace, if only for a short while, the habitual anthropocentric perspective that passes for an objective view of the world. As Nietzsche notes, "if we could only perceive now as a bird, now as a worm, now as a plant ... then nobody would talk about such a regularity of nature, but would understand it only a highly subjective construct" (2009, pp. 260–61). The intrinsic value of each kind of being is the perspective through which it relates to and, indeed, constructs its world. It is this multiplicity of biological species- and kingdom-specific approaches to what is that should capture the attention of those interested in sustainability.

The possibility of rapprochement between environmental theory and Nietzschean perspectivalism hinges upon the materiality at the core of both approaches. Since René Descartes, a multiplicity of perspectives was thought to be the feature of the human view of spatially extended things. Hegel maintained that perception dealt with the ever-changing manifold, empirically rich but empty and abstract from the standpoint of ideal Spirit. Edmund Husserl, in his phenomenology, conceived of everything that transcends our consciousness as given through adumbrations, the essentially incomplete and infinitely multiple surfaces that reveal certain sides of things at the price of occluding their other dimensions. Material sustainability, we may conclude, involves a multiplicity of species-relative perspectives as a necessary feature of its materiality. The more materially grounded an approach to the world is, the more perspectives it will welcome into its midst without narrowing the environment down to "objective reality." Material sustainability sustains, at bottom, this very multiplicity, according the highest value to the propagation of diverse worlds. To sustain sustainability is to enable the untamed self-proliferation of multiplicities outside and beyond any ideal forms, including the form of "diversity," that we might want to impose upon them. All this requires, in the first instance, not so much a change in practice but a change in attitude, in systems of valuation, and in the place we assign to ourselves vis-à-vis other beings, whether living or not.

Why situate plants at the forefront of perspectival environmentalism and material sustainability? Because aside from the aforementioned support they provide to the living, *their* perspective is much more material than that of humans and other animals: they live without resorting to the ideal powers of representation and without distancing themselves from the world, in the manner of animal sensorium. Already Nietzsche recognized this feature of "plant-thinking" in the exemplary non-imagistic, non-conscious, and wholly material memory of the mimosa (2009, pp. 39–40). Such proximity to materiality translates into vegetal hospitality to the multiplicity of other perspectives and modes of being, from which the plant does not ward itself off; free of an individuated, clearly demarcated self, its being in and for itself is, at the same time, its being for (better, the sustaining of) the other. Like the material substratum of life, to which it stays close, the plant subtends other forms of existence, even if this under-lying gets mistaken for its low position on the scales of being and value. So entrenched is this error that humans turn it into the basis for the teleological interpretation of plants as something destined for human and animal consumption. Again Nietzsche is insightful enough to point this out: "Do plants exist *in order* to be eaten by animals? There is *no purpose*. We *deceive* ourselves" (2009, p. 244, emphasis added). In conceiving the plant as a thing entirely available to us and existing for us, we fail to notice what or who it is – a being with its perspective on the world and with intrinsic value attached to this perspective. It is not enough merely to expose this deception as deception; its effects will not dissipate until plants regain the right of admission into the community of values, enriching it with their vegetal perspective.

Sustainable perspectivalism and the community of values

When debating the values of sustainability, one should not shy away from what in Aristotelian parlance is known as its "final causes," that is, that for the sake of which it may be valuable. The obvious answer to the Aristotelian question, tinged with a dose of anthropocentrism, is that the chief beneficiaries of sustainability are human beings, both those presently living and the future generations. But if we take seriously Nietzsche's claim that all valuation proceeds from a definite perspective (1968, p. 149), we would have to admit the incompletely conscious or the entirely nonconscious perspective of other-than-human beings into environmental practices aspiring to justice. It is non-anthropocentric perspectivalism alone that would be truly sustainable, as it would ensure the proliferation of nonhuman worlds neither as objects valuable for us nor even as things valuable in themselves but as values for themselves, from their unique perspectives.

Now, the propagation of disjointed multiplicities, not bound into a single whole, is precisely the principle of vegetal growth; Nietzsche's "to the plant the whole world is a plant" means that to the plant, the world is a growing being. In and of itself, a plant is already a community of beings, "an equivalent to an animal population," or a "metapopulation" (Hallé, 2002, p. 284). It spans distinct spatial perspectives, seeking water and minerals from the darkness of the soil and carbon dioxide along with solar energy from the open expanses above it. The plant in its singularity is thus a microcosm of multiple perspectives coexisting in the metapopulation that comprises it. Thanks to its specific world-creation, it sustains and exposes itself to a vast array of worlds without reducing them to elements of the same.

Precursors to sustainable perspectivalism

An important forerunner to sustainable perspectivalism is Aldo Leopold's "ethics of the land." As he puts it in *A Sand County Almanac*, "land ethic simply enlarges the boundaries of the community to include soils, waters, plants, and animals, or collectively: the land" (1968, p. 204). Citizenship in this community precludes human stewardship of the environment and affirms the "right to continued existence" of all its members, irreducible to natural resources (or to *nothing but* natural resources). Despite a difference in perspectives, the common value – material, not ideal –underpinning land ethic is one of existence, which is less homogeneous than that of life, understood objectively as dispersed into different modes: human, animal, plant, and so on. Existence is a predicate of soil as much as of animals, of water and of plants, but only when it is understood existentially does it entail an approach to the world from the perspective of each unique existent. Sustainable perspectivalism is sustainable non-anthropomorphic existentialism – the only approach that permits us to rescue other-than-human beings from their identification with manageable natural resources.

A more recent version of Leopold's land ethic has cropped up in *Temps des crises* by Michel Serres, who proposes the creation of a world parliament, where air and water, energy and soil, as well as the living species, would be represented (2009, p. 51). This "parliament of mutes" would be the political expression of land ethic, where the nonconscious intentionalities, nonsentient interests, and sheer existence of members would be promoted, along with the multiplicity of perspectives that they *are* or that they embody. The challenge is to imagine a transition from this dispersed multiplicity to a community of human and nonhuman – even inorganic – beings. Plants hold the key to this non-totalizing binding of water, solar energy, and the soil in which they grow and which they enrich by decaying in it. Plants hold the key to the living species that depend on them for nourishment, respiration, reproduction, or shelter; this is because plants grow in between and form living channels between the organic and the inorganic realms. Not only do they create microclimates propitious to the life of animals (Hallé, 2002, p. 291), they also sustain the conjunction of all these elements, without including them in an all-encompassing, immanent milieu, be it "place" or "land." In their singularity, they stand for the place of their growth while simultaneously interrelating the multiplicity of other perspectives by putting them in a "mute" dialogue and enhancing what I have termed *material sustainability*.

The emergent community of values, reflecting the distinct perspectives of its participants, is perhaps not altogether different from the bio-ontological community that is the plant, conceived as a meta-population. Plural in its very singularity, the plant also gathers around itself – magnet-like – the organic and the inorganic, the living and the dead, soil and air, minerals and animals. Sustainability discourses would benefit from learning this expanded version of value pluralism from the very beings whose continued existence they wish to sustain.

References

Bell, S., and S. Morse. 2008. *Sustainability Indicators: Measuring the Immeasurable?* London: Routledge.

Hallé, F. 2002. *In Praise of Plants*. Portland, Ore.: Timber.

Leopold, A. 1968. *A Sand County Almanac: With Other Essays on Conservation from "Round River."* Oxford: Oxford University Press.

Nietzsche, F. 1968. *The Will to Power*. New York: Random House.

Nietzsche, F. 1996. *Human, All Too Human: A Book for Free Spirits*. Cambridge: Cambridge University Press.

Nietzsche, F. 1997. On the Uses and Abuses of History for Life. In *Untimely Meditations*. Ed. D. Breazeale. Cambridge: Cambridge University Press.

Nietzsche, F. 2009. *Writings from the Early Notebooks*. Cambridge: Cambridge University Press.

Serres, M. 2009. *Temps des crises*. Paris: Le Pommier.

22 Landscaping with sustainability principles

Kathy Shearin

We all live within the landscape. In urban and suburban areas this may not be as apparent, with our buildings and streets obscuring our comprehension of how the land once looked and functioned. Many of us may have, or will someday have, a small piece of this landscape within our care. It may not seem significant, but collectively how we think about and manage these small pieces of land can have a big impact on the landscape, the region, and the world.

Caring for land entrusted to us

What happens when we need to care for a small piece of this larger landscape? Most of us have very little training or know-how. Where do we begin, and what should our goals be? It's a lot of responsibility. Caring for a landscape has the potential to cost money and be time-consuming, and then there is the learning curve if we are new to this sort of thing. There are expectations from our neighbors and from society in general, including some local ordinances that impose restrictions and may even dictate look and style. However, there are big benefits to both ourselves and the surrounding area if we take the time to incorporate some sustainability principles and native aspects back into the landscape.

Where might we start? What are the possibilities? Provided there are no restrictions preventing us, we have a number of routes to take. Our values guide our decisions. What do I want from this landscape? In what ways do I want or need this space to provide for me and my family? Examples may include a vegetable garden, a place for entertaining or relaxing, play areas, a dog run, privacy, etc. Then there is a question that we don't tend to ask ourselves enough: How do we want our landscape to function with and within the surrounding ecosystem?

We often forget that this landscape is but a small puzzle-piece of a larger picture. This larger picture comprises all the land, water, and species with which we humans share this planet. When we neglect to acknowledge the existence of these other pieces or view them only as commodities to be bought and sold, the result is often detrimental to long-term sustainability.

The biotic and abiotic components of nature not only provide valuable services to us, but the interactions and roles they play provide all the necessary ingredients for life on the planet. To simplify it, one can think of the natural environment as providing services. "Ecosystem services" is a concept that helps to describe the types of services provided by various components of an ecosystem. These services were defined by the United Nations Millennium Ecosystem Assessment of 2004. This group of scientists categorized four major types of ecosystem services: "*provisioning*, such as the production of food and water; *regulating*, such as the control of climate and disease; *supporting*, such as nutrient cycling and crop pollination; and *cultural*, such as spiritual and recreational benefits" (Corvalan *et al.*, 2005).

To protect as best we can the soil, water, and air quality on which we depend, it is important that we manage our landscapes in a less intensive and more conciliatory way. In doing so, we can perhaps prevent some of the long-term negative consequences that we are only recently beginning to experience.

It is possible for our small pieces of landscapes to have a less detrimental impact on the surrounding land, water, and air. To do this it is crucial to acknowledge that the decisions we make in our personal spaces have a rippling effect on the entire system upon which we (and countless other species) depend for food, clean water, fresh air, and resources. We *can* get closer to having landscapes that require less and offer more by acknowledging the interconnectedness of everything around us.

Sustainable landscaping: what does it mean?

Sustainability has become a widely and commonly used term. But what does it mean in regards to the landscape? Let us consider the root word *sustain*, with the meaning: "to give support or relief to." This is a great way to start thinking of our natural spaces. How can we give them support or relief? While a truly sustainable landscape is difficult or impossible to create in the sea of hardscape within our population centers, we can create functionally-cooperative landscapes. It is even possible to create ecological corridors consisting of contiguous landscaped yards to form a complex ecosystem that provides a myriad of ecosystem services. With an ecology-based perspective, we can provide "support" and "relief" to our natural areas in a more comprehensive way so that needs can continue to be met over the long term. This requires preserving a web of interconnections within the system, each piece relying upon another. It is important to consider all living creatures (macro and micro fauna and flora) and the interactions that they have with one another and to the nonliving (minerals), within their native climate. It is the natural biodiversity of a place that allows a landscape to be sustained over time.

The ultimate goal of landscaping with sustainable principles is to create a landscape where anthropogenic inputs would be minimal to nil once established, while providing the numerous ecological benefits indicative of a healthy ecosystem. The benefits of this type of landscaping to humans and the ecosystem are significant, including dramatic reductions in water use, synthetic chemicals, cost, and maintenance. A sustainable landscape also saves energy, improves air and water quality, and provides valuable habitat for countless other species, from the macro to the micro level.

Lawns

The dominant landscape within the USA is the turf lawn. According to a recent study, lawn covers 128,000 square kilometers (Over 31 million acres) across the USA. If irrigated, it is the single-largest irrigated crop in the USA, three times larger than corn (Milesi *et al.*, 2005).

Lawn (turf grass) is a great plant for some applications. However, when we begin to put lawn everywhere – even where it is not best suited or utilized (e.g. in parking strips, on steep slopes, and in dry, deep shade) – lawn begins to be more of an unsustainable detriment. To keep a lawn green, lush, and free of weeds there must be regular irrigation and consistent physical and chemical maintenance performed on it.

We are giving much to our lawn-dominated landscapes, and we are sacrificing for little gain. We are using more water and chemicals to keep a plant thriving where it just isn't best suited. Additionally, lawn-dominated landscapes do not offer us a sense of place, of local belonging. A lawn-based landscape could be almost anywhere, certainly anywhere within the USA; it does not connect us to our home. By valuing a different landscape model, we and our environment would benefit without the on-going sacrifice and effort. Lawn-based landscapes have a variety of deleterious impacts on our environment and our quality of life.

Lawn-based water issues, pollution and harm to biodiversity

By planting lawn-based landscapes and other plants not suited to a particular, local microclimate, it is necessary to water them and add nutrients to make them feel at home – away from home. In the USA watering our landscapes accounts for 30 to 60 percent (depending on the city) of our fresh, drinkable water-use. Much of this is to water our lawns (Bormann *et al.*, 2001).

Lawn-based landscapes are notorious consumers of petroleum-based pesticides, fertilizers, and fuels. In the USA, 30 million kilograms (67 million pounds) of synthetic, petroleum-based pesticides are used on lawns. Herbicides, insecticides, etc. are often employed to keep our traditional landscapes looking "perfect." However, pesticides often kill not only the harmful species but the beneficial ones as well (Bormann *et al.*, 2001). Pesticides inadvertently harm non-target species such as birds, fish, amphibians, people, and other species (Bormann *et al.*, 2001; IPM of NH, 2011). In addition to being harmful to many organisms, these chemicals do not always stay where we apply them. They flow off our landscapes into storm drains and into our waterways, causing water pollution (Bormann *et al.*, 2001).

The typical lawn is maintained with power tools. Each year in the USA, 580 million gallons (2626 million litres) of gasoline are used for lawnmowers each year (Bormann *et al.*, 2001). Of that, it is estimated that the few ounces spilled during each refueling of lawn and garden equipment add up to an estimated 17 million gallons (77 million litres) nationwide per year (Mariner *et al.*, 1997). The US Environmental Protection Agency estimates that "a gasoline powered lawn mower emits 11 times the air pollution of a new car for each hour of operation" (Mariner *et al.*, 1997); leaf blowers, especially gas-powered ones, in addition to the exhaust they emit (comparable to a mower), kick up dust and debris such as pesticides, fungi, chemicals, fecal matter, and street dust that can include heavy metals such as lead (Orange County, Calif., 2011). Some gas-powered leaf blowers are dangerously loud for the user and, along with lawn mowers, are significant noise polluters in our neighborhoods. Despite requiring a significant amount of water to remain green in the warmer months, lawn-based landscapes are able to absorb only a small fraction of the stormwater that falls on them compared to a forest plot of similar size. Add to that our abundance of impervious surface in urban areas, and the result is flooding and erosion.

According to the US Environmental Protection Administration, 50 to 74 percent of pesticide users don't store pesticides safely (Deinlein, 2011), 50 percent do not read or follow pesticide labels (Bormann *et al.*, 2001), and 110,000 people are sickened by pesticides every year in the USA and 3 million worldwide (IPM of NH, 2011). A study conducted by researchers at the Bloomberg School of Public Health at Johns Hopkins found that nearly 80,000 Americans each year require hospital treatment from injuries caused by lawn mowers (Costilla and Bishai, 2006).

Lawns, if kept a lush, green, and highly manicured monoculture, are a costly endeavor in terms of both time and money. Plants that are not native or well suited to a particular climate need more care and inputs: US$25 billion is spent per year for lawn care in the USA; US$5.25 billion is spent per year on fossil fuel-derived fertilizers; US$700 million is spent per year for pesticides (Bormann *et al.*, 2001).

Changing the paradigm: landscaping with sustainable principles

When we are determining how we might manage a landscape in a more sustainable way, it is helpful to start with an understanding of where we are geographically. Then consider the functions or ecosystem services that were once provided by the location and which ones can, realistically, be provided again. Look to healthy, functioning local natural areas for guidance. Within these healthy systems we can learn from the natural associations between the living creatures (plants and animals and micro-organisms) and their surroundings (climate, soils, topography, etc.). We likely cannot expect to reach this ecological state in its true form within our yards, but the result will be more stable if we use a local example as a guide. This is due primarily to the small scale within which we are working and to the often extreme conditions we have inflicted upon our landscapes. As builders and developers, we scrape the land of its vegetation, build our houses, garages, driveways, and roads, plant primarily lawn on the compacted soils that remain, and then ask ourselves why our communities are experiencing flooding, erosion, increased temperatures, pollution, and other negative side effects.

If we want our landscapes to function at a level beyond aesthetics and recreation, we need to think with a "value-added" framework; to look for ways to enhance our landscapes to include more ecosystem services. The following are good sustainable principles to utilize.

Ten sustainable landscaping principles

1. Build your soil

Compost and recycle all disease-free organic debris back into the landscape. Many urban and suburban soils are severely degraded by the construction and development process. It is therefore important that we add organic matter back into the soil. Composted organic matter helps with water infiltration and retention, will build up the population of beneficial soil microbes, and will provide your plants with the nutrients they need (Lowenfels and Lewis, 2006). Follow nature's example: let fallen dried leaves remain on the soil under trees and shrubs, where they will inhibit weeds, hold in moisture, and decay into nutrients the plants can use over the coming year. Compost your kitchen scraps and yard debris at home. You'll save on disposal fees, reduce landfill space and transportation impacts, while creating an organic soil amendment for your garden.

2. Plant with the "Right plant, right place" motto and tenets

Assess your site conditions: make note of where there is sun and moisture and select plants that thrive under those conditions. Select plants with the ultimate size and shape in mind that will fit the area and its needs: overcrowding can encourage diseases, while excessively sparse planting invites weeds. Avoid invasive plants and aggressive non-natives. Some plants, when removed from their native climate, lack the environmental or biological constraints that keep them from overrunning a landscape and creating swaths of monoculture. Don't plant plants that need to be replaced every year or that can't handle your climate and die every time the temperature or rainfall falls or rises out of their ideal range. This wastes resources.

3. Water conservation

Avoid ornamental plants that require long-term irrigation. Only irrigate to get plants established and during drought. Use drip irrigation to water efficiently and precisely. This will help you save water and minimize weeds. Use irrigation timers: they allow you to water at times that are better for the landscape, though inconvenient for you. They also keep you from accidentally leaving the water running. Water early in the day or in the middle of the night (with a timer, of course), when the air is still and the soil cooler. Use mulch to retain soil moisture and inhibit moisture- and nutrient-robbing weeds.

4. Retain stormwater on-site

When stormwater flows off the impermeable surfaces of our landscapes, it often heats up, and when flowing across asphalt to the nearest waterway it can pick up contaminants such as auto oil, heavy metal dust, pesticides, fertilizers, and other dirt and debris. This pollution-laden warm water can cause flooding and erosion and is often toxic to plant and animal life.

Instead of letting the water go, use it on your landscape – build a rain garden. A rain garden is a "sunken garden bed" planted with water-loving plants to which you can direct runoff from your roof, driveway, and other impervious surfaces. The rain can then soak into the ground naturally rather than running off. Other options include installing a vegetated roof (often called a "green-roof" or "eco-roof") or a vegetated "living wall." These features help slow the flow of stormwater coming off the roof of a building. Use permeable surfaces rather than concrete or other impermeable materials. These allow stormwater to soak through them rather than running off. If appropriate in your area, install a rainwater catchment system such as a cistern. You can then use the water to irrigate, flush toilets in your home, and in some areas, if it is treated, even for drinking.

5. Energy conservation

Plant more large trees and shrubs to shade buildings and cut cooling costs. Where feasible, use hand tools rather than power tools, electric or biodiesel tools rather than gas tools, and four-cycle rather than two-cycle gas engines. If you must use power tools, keep them well maintained – they will work more efficiently.

6. Encourage beneficial insects and micro-organisms

Choose plants that provide a larval food source, nectar, and cover. Avoid using synthetic, petroleum-based fertilizers and pesticides. They often harm the beneficial insects and micro-organisms in the soil. Both insects and micro-organisms break down organic matter that will then become fertilizer for our plants. Many insects pollinate our plants and help control some of our landscape "pests."

7. Don't use synthetic pesticides

Tolerate imperfections (and redefine perfection). Don't let a small infestation and a few notches in your leaves send you running for the spray. Let the beneficial insects build up their populations; they can be your biggest ally by eating some of the "pests" and bringing their populations down to a tolerable level. Then always use the least toxic solution – manual control is best and often most effective if done correctly. Pesticides are often not specific enough to kill just the pest you are targeting. We bring pesticides into our homes on our shoes, clothes, and pets. Pesticides escape our yards by water, wind, and leaf blowers and make their way to our streams and rivers and even into our air.

8. Don't use synthetic fertilizers

Synthetic fertilizers flow or are blown off our yards into the street and make their way to our waterways. Always use compost or other organic slow-release methods of adding nutrients to your plants. Compost, in addition to providing nutrients, improves the soil tilth (good structure and nutrient value).

9. Maintain a "sense of place"

Don't lose where you are. Find and revel in the uniqueness of wherever you are. Don't try to recreate the desert oasis of your previous residence in your current residence in a mild and moist maritime climate, or create a lush tropical paradise in the dry, harsh desert. Keep it local: choose locally native plants and locally produced soil amendments (compost, etc.).

10. Take your time

Sustainable landscapes are best installed a little at a time. Start with a small area of the yard and move inward. The goal is to have a landscape that will, when established, need very little maintenance.

The naturescaping program

Naturescaping emphasizes the use of native plants to create a landscape that reduces water use, stormwater runoff, and pollution, with the goal of making the environment safe and healthy for people, fish, and other wildlife. Naturescaping is beauty and function – ecological function. To landscape according to Naturescaping principles is to utilize clues from nature to create a landscape that provides some of the ecological functions and ecosystem services that were provided by this same land before development. Naturescaping emphasizes the use of native plants because they are adapted to the local weather cycles and the soils of the region, and are typically resistant to many pests of the region. They have also co-evolved with the macro and micro fauna of the particular eco-zone. If you plant a plant in an area where it is well suited (the correct soil moisture, sunlight, wind exposure, etc.), it can fare better against pests and other stressors and thus require fewer inputs (water, fertilizer, pest control, etc.). Other Naturescaping principles include water conservation, reduction or elimination of synthetic pesticides and fertilizers, retention of stormwater on-site, and wildlife-friendly design. Lawn reduction is emphasized because, as noted earlier, lawns require a high degree of inputs and have low ecological value compared to the biodiversity and varied layers of a Naturescaped yard.

Community-based Naturescaping

The Naturescaping Program works on the neighborhood scale to recruit volunteer hosts that will act as a liaison to their community by hosting these informational workshops. It is run by the East Multnomah County Soil and Water District, and funded by the US Department of Agriculture. By utilizing a volunteer community host, the program has a strengthened tie to the community. The host is asked to get the word out within the neighborhood, church, or group. As a result, the workshops typically include participants who would not have heard about, understood, or cared about sustainable landscaping had the workshop host not reached out to them. The program provides the workshops, taught by professional landscape designers, without charge to the neighborhoods, and asks that the host secure a location suitable for a workshop and provide refreshments and assistance in setting up and breaking down. The Naturescaping workshops show how to design and plan a Naturescape on private property or as part of a community project. The workshops walk attendees through the concepts of Naturescaping and the steps to consider when redesigning yards so that they provide not only for people but for the surrounding ecosystem as well.

The series starts out with a workshop on Naturescaping basics. This work-shop includes a discussion of watersheds and location, giving attendees a sense of place; a slideshow of Naturescaping before-and-after photos; a discussion of Naturescaping principles; a short field trip to a yard that demonstrates Naturescaping principles; an introduction to site planning and design; and a slideshow illustrating some of the region's native plants. Participants leave the workshop with a workbook and a free native plant to get them started. The second workshop, on site planning, is a more hands-on workshop that dives a bit deeper into Naturescaping site planning principles. It includes information on how to design a landscape that works with the location and the inhabitants. The third and final workshop of the series is the site plan feedback session. This is a smaller, more intimate workshop where graduates of the previous two workshops have the opportunity to bring in a draft site plan and get feedback from professional landscape designers.

As needs are identified, the program offers additional classes, workshops, and events on special topics to enhance the educational experience of the community. In the past these have included rain garden workshops that show participants how to create a beautiful landscape that will help them manage stormwater on-site; an annual bare-root native plant sale at which native plants can be purchased at very low cost; and workshops on native and invasive plants. This program has been immensely successful at showing the many benefits of landscaping with sustainable principles.

Our values guide us

As we work towards sustainability and the paradigm shift that must accompany it, we cannot overlook the longstanding messages that are entrenched in the human mind. We are socialized from our earliest years to believe the things we hold as truths. The attitudes that we hold about the natural world around us can predict the future that lies ahead for us in our elder years and for those who come after us. Humans and every other species with which we share this small planet are affected by our everyday decisions. For some species, a fish or a frog for example, the very fate of their existence might lie in these seemingly simple decisions that we make on our small properties. To underestimate the effect on the planet that each of us personally makes is perhaps one of our biggest downfalls as a species. This needn't be our fate.

References

Bormann, F. H., D. Balmori, and G. T. Geballe. 2001. *Redesigning the American Lawn: A Search for Environmental Harmony.* 2nd edn. New Haven, Conn.: Yale University Press.

Corvalan, C., S. Hales, and A. McMichael. 2005. *Ecosystems and Human Well-being: Health Synthesis : A Report of the Millennium Ecosystem Assessment.* Geneva, Switz.: World Health Organization. Retrieved on July 29th, 2011, from http://www.millenniumassessment. org/documents/document.357.aspx.pdf.

Costilla, V., and D. M. Bishai. 2006. Lawnmower Injuries in the United States: 1996 to 2004. Annals of Emergency Medicine. June. 47(6), pp. 567–73.

Deinlein, M. 2011. *When It Comes to Pesticides, Birds Are Sitting Ducks.* Fact sheet, Smithsonian National Zoo Migratory Bird Center. Retrieved on 26th July, 2011, from http://nationalzoo.si.edu/scbi/migratorybirds/fact_sheets/default.cfm?fxsht=8, 26-July 2011.

IPM of NH (Integrated Pest Management of New Hampshire). 2011. *What Is Integrated Pest Management?* Retrieved on July 28th, 2011, from http://www.ipmofnh.com/about_ us/faq/.Lowenfels, J., and W. Lewis. 2006. *Teaming with Microbes: A Gardener's Guide to the Soil Food Web.* Portland, Or.: Timber Press.

Mariner, R., D. Dreher, K. Huebner, and L. Hill. 1997. *Green Landscaping: Greenacres: A Source Book on Natural Landscaping for Public Officials.* Chicago, Ill.: Northeastern Illinois Planning Commission. Retrieved on July 22nd, 2011,from http://www.epa.gov/ greenacres/toolkit/chap2.html.

Milesi, C. S., W. Running, C. D. Elvidge, J. B. Dietz, B. T. R. Tuttle, and R. Nemani. 2005. Mapping and Modeling the Biogeochemical Cycling of Turf Grasses in the United States *Environmental Management* 36(3), pp. 426–38.

Orange County, Calif. 2011. *California Grand Jury. Leaf Blower Pollution Hazards in Orange County.* Retrieved on July 28th, 2011, from http://www.ocgrandjury.org/pdfs/ leafblow.pdf.

23 Bringing sustainability and science to the incarcerated

The Sustainable Prisons Project

Nalini M. Nadkarni and Dan J. Pacholke

Scientists and sustainability experts tend to seek answers to their questions through collaborations with people of similar background, culture, and education. They also tend to disseminate their work to audiences that hold similar values and have common vocabularies. Increasingly, there is a need for scientists and sustainability experts both to engage nonscientists in the practice of research, and to communicate their work to those who are outside the choir (Leshner, 2007).

Public engagement and involvement in sustainability efforts are typically viewed by the scientific community as at best a duty and at worst a burden, although certain activities that engage the public have also been viewed as a benefit to the scientist. For example, the growing field of citizen science and sustainability has demonstrated that untrained citizens can carry out aspects of data collection concerning reduced energy use with rigor if they have the guidance of an interested scientist or sustainability expert. However, citizen-implemented projects nearly always include those who are already interested in ecology, nature, or an aspect of conservation or sustainability, even if they do not hold advanced degrees in science. A great challenge for science and sustainability educators is to engage those who come from other backgrounds and ethnic groups, and who lack a previous interest in the scientific endeavor.

This chapter discusses the challenges and benefits of a collaborative project among scientists, sustainability experts, conservationists, prison administrators, and inmates. We discuss the goals, practices, and results of our efforts in Washington State to interact with one of the most underserved public groups in the USA – incarcerated men and women – to provide education, research, and conservation opportunities, and to guide sustainable practices by prisons. A program that has been successful in engaging inmates in five prisons in Washington State serves as a successful proof of the concept of these efforts. There has been strong interest in the program among ecologists, conservationists, corrections administrators, and inmates in other states. A proposed conference would draw together the people and institutions needed to bring this concept and these practices to a national level.

Incarceration, science, and sustainability

Locked away from contact with scientists and nature, incarcerated individuals are the most underserved and underutilized audience for science engagement in our country. Incarceration need not, however, preclude participation with science and sustainability. Since 2005, an innovative interdisciplinary project in Washington State – the Sustainable Prisons Project (SPP) – has shown that with minimal resources, scientists can raise the awareness of the importance of science, sustainability, and nature in the correctional population (www.sustainableprisons.org; Bhattacharjee, 2008;Ulrich and Nadkarni, 2009). They can also inspire inmates to consider and plan for a future profession or further education in science. With some notable exceptions, prisons offer limited educational opportunities. Yet many inmates wish to forge new lifestyles and professions after their release; they make excellent candidates for outreach and training in science and sustainability.

Where there is limited access to nature and the outside world, prisons and other institutions have noted the positive impact of working with plants and animals. Horticultural therapy and activities involving the training of guide dogs, for example, have been shown to reduce aggression, increase patience and social contacts, and enhance empathy for other living things (Grinde and Patil, 2009; Lee *et al.*, 2009; Weinstein *et al.*, 2009). These are exactly the characteristics that are valued by corrections administrators who wish to reduce violence, increase social interaction, and ultimately reduce recidivism.

To fulfill the multiple goals of bringing science to an underserved audience, reducing violence and recidivism, enhancing sustainability, and providing scientists with a new set of collaborators, scientists from Evergreen State College and administrators with the Washington State Department of Corrections (WDOC) forged the SPP. Its mission is to "bring science and nature into prisons. We conduct ecological research and conserve biodiversity by forging collaborations with scientists, inmates, prison staff, students, and community partners. We help reduce the environmental, economic, and human costs of prisons by inspiring and informing sustainable practices" (Sustainability in Prisons Project, 2013).

The effort began as a single ecology research project in 2004, funded by a small portion of a Communicating Research to Public Audience (CRPA) grant supplement from the National Science Foundation (NSF). The project, implemented in a single minimum-security prison, was intended to teach inmates how to grow moss *ex situ* to help reduce the need to collect moss from old-growth forests for the horticulture trade. The project engaged ten inmates to carry out moss horticulture experiments that taught them about botany, experimental design, and the scientific process. It also provided new scientific knowledge for the ecologist (about which species of mosses grew fastest under which watering regimes) and showed prison administrators that inmates involved in the program exhibited good behavior and had "different conversations" in the prison yard. One of these inmates was the co-author of a peer-reviewed paper, delivered a paper on the prison research at the annual meeting of the Ecological Society of America in 2008, and has since gone on to graduate school in molecular biology (Ulrich and Nadkarni, 2009).

Over the next three years, the SPP was funded by a contract with the WDOC to expand to four other prisons (both men's and women's, minimum to maximum security; see Table 23.1). Different educational, conservation, and sustainability projects have been placed under the general umbrella of the SPP, and a variety of collaborating partners have joined the project to create the mosaic of activities described below.

Education programs

The positive results of this preliminary collaboration led to the implementation of a monthly lecture series, "Sustainable Living, Sustainable Lives," which brought scientists and sustainability experts to the prison. Scientists, prison staff, and inmates sat side by side, learning about topics that ranged from recycling to brown bear ecology. In addition to educating inmates, the SPP has been responsible for the instruction and support of graduate students. Six students in the Masters of Environmental Studies Program, a two-year professional degree that emphasizes environmental policy, have been directly engaged with the SPP for internships and their thesis work. They have provided the logistical and educational support for the conservation projects, serving as critical intermediaries between collaborating scientists from partner agencies and the inmates. They also organize and implement the lecture series and workshops. The success of the moss-growing project inspired other scientists to work with inmates. Conservation biologists at the Washington State Department of Fish and Wildlife provided expertise and a framework for inmates to captive-rear the endangered Oregon Spotted Frog. Four other captive-rearing facilities in Washington State were raising these animals to restore their dwindling populations in the wild. Inmates received training from herpetologists, and their work resulted in the largest populations with the lowest mortality rates; they won the "Best Captive Rearing Facility Award" in 2009 and 2010.

Similarly, the SPP engaged a nonprofit conservation group, the Nature Conservancy, and biologists at the Joint Base Fort Lewis McChord, which promotes an effort to restore relict prairie communities. Inmates at another prison have grown about 500,000 plugs of 16 species of prairie plants each year for three years for outplanting in the prairies. Bird conservationists have benefited from a project in which inmates built 500 bird boxes for the Western Bluebird and the Purple Martin. The most recent project involves an effort by women at a minimum-security prison to rear the endangered Taylor's Checkerspot butterfly for release at Joint Base Fort Lewis McChord.

In 2009 and 2010, inmates successfully raised 149 frogs with a mean survivorship of 77 percent. Frogs raised in prisons were consistently larger than those

Table 23.1 Program facility locations, numbers, types, and activities

Facility	Number of inmates	Type of facility security	Sustainable activities
Cedar Creek Corrections Center	500 male	minimum	recycling, water conservation, gardening, beekeeping, tilapia farming, frogs
Stafford Creek Corrections Center	2,000 male	medium, maximum, supermax	recycling, gardening, beekeeping, lectures, prairie plants, bird boxes
McNeil Island Corrections Center	2,300 male	medium, maximum	gardening, lectures
Women's Correctional Center of Washington	1,700 female	medium, maximum, supermax	recycling, gardening, lectures
Mission Creek Corrections Center for Women	300 female	minimum,	gardening, lectures, butterfly biology

raised by local zoos. In 2011, field surveys revealed new frog egg masses, evidence that captive-reared frogs are reproducing. In addition, to reduce rearing and transportation costs, offenders raise crickets needed to raise frogs. In two years, inmates raised 515,000 native plants of 16 species for restoration of the South Sound prairie habitat.

The social climate of Washington State was conducive to instigating sustainable operations in all state agencies, including the Department of Corrections. The governor decreed that sustainability of water, energy, and materials was to be encouraged in all possible ways. Cost savings, always a goal of corrections departments, was also a driver in reducing the use of materials and shrinking the energy footprints of its facilities.

The initial sustainability lectures at the SPP prisons inspired a variety of sustainability projects: organic gardens; worm composting recycling sheds; water catchment containers; and beekeeping. By installing ultra-low-flow toilets, the Cedar Creek Corrections Center (CCCC) has saved over 11.2 million litres (250,000 gallons) of water each year. The CCCC recycles over 907 kilograms (2,000 pounds) of paper and 1,950 kilograms (4,300 pounds) of carton per month. Stafford Creek Corrections Center uses push-blade mowers to reduce gas use. Based on data from internal tracking by the Department of Corrections staff from 2005 to 2010, sustainable operations have increased diversion to recycling by 90 percent, food waste diversion to composting operations by 90 percent, and biodiesel use by 9 percent (from 2009 to 2010); they have reduced solid waste to landfills by 30 percent, facility heating and energy consumption by 8 percent, all transportation fuel consumption by 25 percent, and carbon emissions by 40 percent (from 2009 to 2010).

A wide range of institutions have collaborated with the project, including Amphibian Ark, the International Society for Arboriculture, Northwest Trek, the Center for Natural Lands Management, the Nature Conservancy, the Oregon Zoo, Point Defiance Zoo and Aquarium, Woodland Park Zoo, the US Fish and Wildlife Service, US Army Joint Base Lewis McChord, the Washington Department of Fish and Wildlife, and the Washington Department of Natural Resources.

The incarcerated men and women, though seemingly unreachable and unteachable, have proven to be interested, capable, and desirous of science education and sustainability practices. Scientists and sustainability experts see a number of important benefits: direct engagement and increased scientific awareness and appreciation in a hitherto underserved public audience (evaluations of prisoners showed significant integration of scientific content); potential new scientific insights gained from an audience approaching a topic with fresh eyes; much-needed restoration work for a large number of endangered plants and animals; fulfillment of broader impacts required for NSF grants in powerful and visible ways; and the possibility of recruiting new students to scientific study (some offenders expressed a keen desire to pursue scientific work after their release).

There are benefits for the corrections community as well: direct cost savings (e.g. from the cultivation of vegetables and honey); the chance to give inmates something to occupy their attention other than dissatisfaction with their condition; job skills for inmates after their release; and an improved image for prisons in the larger community because of positive media coverage, providing a sense of pride and accomplishment for a sector of society that rarely receives public approval.

Formal evaluation of the work to date was performed by a consultant, David Heil and Associates. Both types of programs, SPP lecture series and ERC Projects, appear to have resulted in increased awareness of the impact of their behaviors for participating offenders. For those who attend the lectures, this may simply mean that they better understand the impact of their personal choices on the environment. For those who participate in the more intensive ERC programs, this understanding of the impact of their behavior is also tied to a sense of ownership and responsibility for their work. These results suggest that the ties between environmental responsibility and personal and professional responsibility are an important element of the SPP. As the program moves forwards, efforts should be undertaken to enhance these outcomes and to further explore their implications.

The diverse perspectives reflected by the stakeholders in the SPP present a challenge to program development efforts to design a cohesive set of program activities. Nonetheless, the comprehensive program approach, including the lecture series, intensive ERC Projects, and efforts to support prison-wide sustainable practices, is already working to support these diverse goals, and focused program development efforts will help to ensure on-going success in these areas. Although the program must be deliberate in efforts for expansion, stakeholders universally agree that the SPP program should continue to expand. Both offenders and prison staff provided recommendations for expanding the lecture series and ERC Projects and developing additional SPPs. As SPP staff undertake these efforts, it will be essential to involve the stakeholders in these efforts to ensure that the program reflects their diverse interests.

The SPP has gained professional respect and visibility when members of the project have presented results of the work at professional meetings and conferences in the areas of ecology and corrections. For example, Nalini M. Nadkarni organized a well-received symposium at a meeting of the Ecological Society of America in 2009. One of the inmates who had been involved in the sustainability work gave a talk at this symposium. Dan J. Pacholke, the Director of Prisons of Washington State and co-leader of the SPP, and Nadkarni were invited to give a presentation on the SPP to the western regional meeting of Association for State Corrections Administrators. At the end of the presentation, when superintendents and directors were asked how many of them were interested in having a project like the SPP in their facilities, every hand in the room was raised. As the SPP has matured, members of the project staff have received numerous queries from 14 other states and 3 countries about how to implement similar collaborative programs. The inquiries have come from corrections administrators, corrections staff, inmates, families and friends of inmates, ecologists, and conservation biologists.

Case study: teaching wildlife conservation and sustainability behind bars

Marc Bekoff

For more than ten years I've been teaching animal behavior and conservation biology at the Boulder (Colorado) County Jail as part of the Jane Goodall Institute's Roots and Shoots Program (http://www.rootsandshoots.org). The course is one of the most popular in the jail. Students have to earn the right to enroll and they work hard to get in it.

Teaching animal behavior and conservation to inmates is very educational and rewarding. While there's student turnover, jail workers and I remain pleasantly surprised at how this course connects the inmates to various aspects of nature. Many of the students find it easier to connect with animals than with people. The major reasons they give are that animals don't judge them and that the animals trust them; many of the inmates had lived with dogs, cats, and other companions who were their best, and in some cases their only, friends, and for some they were family. Many of the inmates trust and empathize with animals in ways they don't with humans.

I also try to correct a prevailing and distorted view of how animals treat one another. At one of the first meetings someone was talking out of turn as I was setting up the video of the day. One of the guys yelled, "Hey, shut up, you're acting like an animal. This guy's here to help us." I immediately responded, "You've just paid him a compliment." I explained that animals are usually cooperative, kind, and empathic. While surely there is competition and aggression, there's also a lot of cooperation, empathy, and reciprocity observed during a number of social interactions, including social play. I explained that these "positive" or prosocial behaviors are examples of "wild justice" and this idea made them rethink what it means to be an animal (Pierce and Bekoff, 2009). They've had enough of nature red in tooth and claw, and many lament, "Look where that 'I'm behaving like an animal' excuse got me."

Topics we actively discuss include general aspects of animal behavior, the evolution of social behavior, evolution and creationism, biology and religion, sustainability, extinction, animal protection and environmental ethics, eugenics, environmental enrichment, balance in nature, complex webs of nature, cultural views of animals, and who we are in the grand scheme of things – anthropocentric influences on animals and the environment. When we discuss various aspects of wildlife conservation, almost all of the inmates have something to say. They're uniformly against killing wolves just because they kill livestock, and they get really upset when we discuss how destructive humans can be to animals and habitats. Our discussions about hunting are very interesting, and trophy and sport hunting are really frowned upon. Our exchanges rival those that I've had at university classes.

When we discuss environmental issues and sustainability, I frequently note a sensitivity rivaling that of former students at the University of Colorado. Most of the inmates have a working understanding of what it means to live sustainably, and all agree that the future of the planet relies on our living in such a way that we do not take more than we need. In fact, most of the men in the class note that what we think we need is more than we really do need, and that we need to change our ways so that we take less in the future.

Importantly, many of the students see the class as building community with animals and with people. They yearn to build healthy relationships. I use examples of the social behavior of group-living animals such as wolves as a model for developing and maintaining long-term friendships among individuals who must work together not only for their own good but also for the good of the group. The idea of a community working together fits in well with an attempt to live more sustainably in that the inmates realize that if we all take and use less, this will mean that we won't be as draining on limited resources. I believe that many of the guys are ready to make that change when they are released.

Occasionally, I ask the inmates what they get out of the class. Here are some of their responses:

- I've learned a lot about understanding and appreciating animals as individuals.
- The class gives us a sense of connection to webs of life.

Figure 23.1 Jane Goodall's Fifi. One of Jane Goodall's favorite chimpanzees drawn by Jeff, a student in Marc's Roots and Shoots class at the Boulder County Jail; presented with permission of Marc Bekoff

- The class helped me to think about how to live more sustainably.
- What I do counts. I now have a positive vision for the future.
- The class makes me feel better about myself.

It's clear that learning about animals inspires the students and gives them hope. I've been told that because of the class some of their kids are more likely to go into science. I know some students have gone back to school, while others have made contributions in time and money to conservation organizations. During the course, some have contributed to animal rescue programs, including one with which I work that's involved with rescuing and rehabilitating Asiatic moon bears. Some have gone on to work for humane societies. One student went back to school and received a master's degree in nature writing. When I ran into him in Boulder he was so proud of his accomplishments and incredibly enthusiastic, and he told me that he really considers how he's living so as not to take more than he really needs. He'd been able to stay out of jail and pursue his dreams.

My course has helped the inmates to connect with values that they otherwise wouldn't have. By discussing animal behavior and conservation, doors were opened so that understanding, trust, cooperation, community, individual and global sustainability, and hope could be developed and dreams pursued.

References

Bhattacharjee, K. 2008. Pathways into Science. *Science* 322, p. 1171.

Grinde, B., and G. P. Patil. 2009. Biophilia: Does Visual Contact with Nature Impact on Health and Well-Being? *International Journal of Environmental Research and Public Health* 6, pp. 2332–43.

Lee, J., B. Park, Y. Tsunetsugu, T. Kagawa, and Y. Miyazaki. 2009. Restorative Effects of Viewing Real Forest Landscapes, Based on a Comparison with Urban Landscapes. *Scandinavian Journal of Forest Research* 24(3), pp. 227–34.

Leshner, A. 2007. Outreach Training Needed. *Science* 315, p. 161.

Sustainability in Prisons Project. 2013. *Mission Statement*. Retrieved from http://sustainabilityinprisons.org/.

Ulrich, C., and N. M. Nadkarni. 2009. Sustainability Research in Enforced Residential Institutions: Collaborations of Ecologists and Prisoners. *Environment, Development, and Sustainability* 11, pp. 815–25.

Weinstein, N., A. K. Przybylski, and R. M. Ryan. 2009. Can Nature Make Us More Caring? Effects of Immersion in Nature on Intrinsic Aspirations and Generosity. *Personality and Social Psychology Bulletin* 35, pp. 13–15.

Case study references

Pierce, J., and Bekoff, M. 2009. Moral in Tooth and Claw. *The Chronicle of Higher Education* October 18th, 2009. Retrieved on July 15th, 2012, from http://chronicle.com/article/Moral-in-ToothClaw/48800/.

24 Designing environmental education programs
Modeling pro-environmental competency

*Blanca Fraijo-Sing, César Tapia-Fonllem,
and Victor Corral-Verdugo*

In order to cope successfully with increasing environmental degradation, every scientific branch is committed to investigate factors involved in environmental degradation and protection. Behavioral sciences address environmental problems mainly through two perspectives: environmental psychology (EP) and environmental education (EE).

EP studies the reciprocal relations between people's behavior and their socio-physical environment (Aragonés and Amérigo, 2010). The aims of this psychological field include the investigation of behavioral and dispositional traits that result in environmental conservation, and the study of human behavior within the framework of specific environmental topics or problems (Corral-Verdugo, 2001).

Since the 1970s, research has determined that human behavior is a causal factor in the alteration of the environmental balance. EP has provided theories, methods, and results making possible the implementation of preventive programs and behavioral interventions aimed at mitigating environmental problems (Fraijo, 2010).

In turn, EE is used as a strategy for developing a pro-sustainable citizenry, supporting the ideals of peace, freedom, social justice, and environmental conservation. Such a strategy is conceived as pursuing an essential function in the personal and collective development of individuals. This means that environmental education serves the purpose of promoting personal growth, social well-being, and ecological balance; therefore, EE has the potential to cope successfully with poverty, social exclusion and oppression, war, and environmental deterioration (Delors, 1996).

Educational systems are crucial in bringing about conditions for conceptual, attitudinal, and instrumental learning, including pro-environmental learning (Jensen, 2002; Tayci and Uysal, 2012). EE provides the means for acquiring knowledge, attitudes, and skills that allow a conservationist behavior. This implies the inclusion of instrumental sustainable actions, pro-environmental beliefs, and motives as aspects to develop in school curricula.

In 1970, the World Union for Conservation elaborated one of the most widely accepted EE definitions. EE was conceived as a process for promoting attitudes and skills needed to understand and accept the interrelations between humans, their culture, and the biophysical environment. During the 1980s, an interdisciplinary and holistic approach for the treatment of ecological issues was adopted, and the transition from a local focus toward a global one began in addressing environmental issues. Beginning in the 1990s, environmental education focused on the topic of sustainable development, acknowledging its importance to society, politics, and economics (De Castro, 2000).

According to José Antonio Collado and Silvia Corraliza (2012), EE is a set of formative and informative resources mobilized for the purpose of increasing human responsibility to face environmental problems. The EE concept may be identified as encompassing a series of dispositional (psychological) variables; for instance, UNESCO (United Nations Educational, Scientific and Cultural Organization) (2005, p. 2) defines EE as an action model in which "individuals and communities are aware of their environment, and acquire the knowledge, values, skills, experiences and the determination that allows them to individually and collectively act to solve current and future environmental problems." Based upon this EE conception, D. A. Simmons (1998) suggested that a program intended to induce pro-environmental behavior should include as programmatic objectives the acquisition of knowledge regarding environmental topics, knowledge of natural systems, problem-solving skills, pro-environmental attitudes, and self-esteem.

Decades earlier in 1969, William Stapp *et al.* had identified the EE goals, establishing that this discipline is aimed at "producing a citizenry that possesses knowledge regarding the socio-physical environment and their related problems, aware of how to help in solving those problems, and motivated to work in their solution" (1969, p. 31). Additionally, Holly Hungerford *et al.* (1994, p. 43) claimed that the fundamental aim of EE was "to help citizens to become environmentally informed, and above all, to be skilled and devoted citizens determined to work, individually and collectively, to achieve and maintain a dynamic balance between life quality and environmental quality." This definition emphasizes environmental knowledge and skills.

This brief review establishes the need for studying how the educational process helps in developing pro-environmental dispositions and actions and how these factors lead to environmental protection.

Goals of EE

The Tblisi Conference, organized by UNESCO (2005, 2009), defined the EE goals as follows:

- Acquiring awareness and sensitivity toward the environment and its problems; developing the ability to perceive and discriminate among stimuli; processing, refining, and extending these perceptions; and using such a new ability in a variety of contexts.
- Promoting a basic conception about how the environment works, how people interact with their milieu, and how environmental problems and topics emerge and can be solved.

- Developing a set of values and feelings of environmental concern, and also acquiring a motivation and commitment to participate in efforts to preserve and improve environmental conditions.
- Acquiring the skills needed to identify, investigate, and contribute to the solution of environmental problems.
- Generating experience, by using the acquired knowledge and skills, in developing reasoned and positive actions to solve environmental problems.

Knowledge

Knowledge of environmental problems and solutions is a basic aspect of any EE program. Thomas Kellaghan *et al.* (1993) define knowledge as all those behaviors and testing situations emphasizing the importance of remembering ideas, material, or phenomena, either as recognition or evocation. The behavior that is expected to be evocated in a situation is similar to the one that occurred during the original situation. Thomas Arcury (1990) defines environmental knowledge as factual information that people possess regarding the state of the environment and the influence of human actions on their milieu. He regards the knowledge of pro- and anti-environmental behaviors as a requisite for environmentally conscious acting. He also claims that although abundant information concerning environmental topics exists, the level of environmental knowledge among the population is low.

Florian Kaiser and Urs Fuhrer (2003) argue that before effectively acting, one should know what the problem is and what can be done to solve it; this might lead to a process of personal and social engagement in the solution of environmental problems. Such a process involves possessing declarative knowledge (information), followed by processual knowledge (knowing actions related to the solution of a problem), effective knowledge (problem-solving), and, finally, social knowledge (relations between community and its environment).

Although the relationship between knowledge and pro-environmental behavior seems obvious, it is not well documented or entirely supported by the existing literature. Ellen Matthies *et al.* (2012) report the results of an EE program involving the teaching of reuse and recycling practices in 10-year-old children. The authors found that recycling was more influenced by parents' models and sanctions than by children's environmental knowledge, while in the case of reuse, this behavior was affected by the way the communication concerning the advantages of reuse was delivered. Knowledge did not produce a significant influence in either case. Yet knowledge is necessary for the development of pro-environmental skills (Corral-Verdugo, 2012).

Skills

Skills are also considered an essential component of EE. They are defined as behaviors used by people to accomplish a task in an effective way (Ribes, 2007). In the case of environmental problems, a person is assumed to be skilled when he or she takes actions resulting in the protection of the socio-physical environment (De Young, 2000).

Nicholas Smith-Sebasto and Rosanne Fortner (1994) found a significant relationship between pro-ecological skills and environmentally protective behavior. Victor Corral-Verdugo (1996) reported that reuse and recycling skills were direct determinants of the practice of pro-environmental actions. In a related line of thinking, Raymond De Young (2000) suggested that pro-environmental skills promote the emergence and maintenance of intrinsic motivations, which in turn positively affect engagement in further sustainable behaviors.

Motives

Motives are the choices and preferences for objects, events, situations, and actions, including pro-environmental actions and its consequences (Corral-Verdugo, 1997). In addition to providing information to people, it is necessary to motivate them to conserve the environment through EE programs.

Lynnette Schultz and P. Wesley Zelezny (2003) conducted a study aimed at exploring different types of pro-environmental motivation. They found that pro-environmental motives can be classified into three types: egoistic, altruistic, and biospheric. These motives, along with the material benefits (money, comfort) and social benefits (reputation, social reinforcement) that someone obtains from his or her pro-environmental acting, are sources of extrinsic motivation. Moreover, some motives for behaving pro-environmentally come from intrinsic sources. Motivation usually emerges spontaneously when people face environmental problems, which lead them to understand that a pro-environmental behavior is needed (Oskamp, 2002). Additional intrinsic sources of motivation exist for pro-environmental actions, including the satisfaction a person experiences after his or her behavior is produced; sustainable actions also promote a state of competence motivation, produced by the perception of one's capacity, and by knowing that one has acted pro-environmentally; feelings of happiness and sensations of personal wellbeing are added to the list of intrinsic motives of sustainable actions, as Corral-Verdugo (2012) summarizes. He suggests that the very practice of sustainable behaviors within EE programs should be able to promote intrinsic motives sustaining further engagement in pro-environmental actions.

Beliefs

One more variable to include in an effective EE program is pro-environmental beliefs. Beliefs can be conceived as tendencies to associate or relate life situations and objects to make sense of life, people, and the environment. Beliefs can be instrumental (acquired through experience) or symbolic (transmitted through culture) (Carew and Mitchell, 2008; González-Gaudiano, 2005; Perfilova and Alizade, 2011). Riley Dunlap *et al.* (2000) argue that people might hold as a belief system the Dominant Social Paradigm (DSP) or the New Environmental Paradigm (NEP). The former constitutes an anthropocentric worldview conceiving humans as independent from nature, while the latter views humans as part of nature and subject to ecological laws. The NEP, being more pro-ecologically oriented, is a better instigator of pro-environmental behavior and disposition than the DSP (Dunlap *et al.*, 2000). Thus, EE programs include exposure of students to the tenets of the NEP, among other pro-ecological worldviews (Fraijo *et al.*, 2010).

Integrating pro-environmental variables

As mentioned before, EE goals include not only providing information, promoting ecological awareness, and developing pro-ecological skills as isolated actions. In addition, EE is aimed at integrating a set of dispositional variables (knowledge, attitudes, motives, values, skills, etc.) that predispose, guide, and make possible environmental conservation. A number of authors have elaborated theoretical models specifying factors necessary for an effective EE program (Alvarez-Suárezand and Vega-Marcote, 2010; Corraliza *et al.*, 2012; González-Gaudiano, 2005; Oskamp, 2002; Selma, 2012). Oskamp (2002), for instance, describes a perspective of behavioral change, integrating some of the above-exposed variables. This perspective offers three causal factors as elements of EE: (1) information, knowledge, or education; (2) motivation; and (3) behavioral skills. According to Stuart Oskamp, integrating these three factors results in behavioral change oriented to pro-environmentalism. Mat Duerden and Peter Witt (2010) establish a strong relationship between knowledge, attitudes, and pro-environmental behaviors; this relationship is favored by direct and indirect experiences with nature.

Competency

Since the 1990s, education within the framework of globalization and reforms in the educational system have focused on the need for human-resource formation. The use of notions such as equity, quality, innovation, development, efficacy, and efficiency characterize this framework, and the concept of competency makes sense as a primordial goal of EE (Popkewitz, 2000).

From a psychological perspective, competency is understood as a capacity to produce effective responses before problem-solving requirements (Corral-Verdugo, 2002). From an individual perspective, a competency could be understood as a capacity that a person holds; yet competencies should be studied while considering group processes that affect both individuals and their capacities. This makes sense, because environmental problems are not only individually but also collectively generated. Dominique Rychen and Laura Salganik define competency as "the ability to successfully meet complex demands in a particular context through the mobilization of psychological prerequisites (including both cognitive and non-cognitive aspects)" (2003, p. 43).

Pro-environmental competencies

Competency is a higher-order dispositional variable combining capacities to act (i.e. skills) with other types of variables such as beliefs, knowledge, attitudes, perceptions, and motives. Robert White initially defined competency as "an organism's capacity to effectively deal with the environment" (1959, p. 297). Therefore, a competent individual is – by definition – able to act in diverse ways. However, according to White, a competency includes skill components as much as motivational elements, meaning that skills are necessary but insufficient in shaping a competency. De Young agrees with this idea and introduces the notion of Competency Motivation (CM), applying it to pro-environmental behavior. CM is not the ability to deal effectively with the environment but "the motive people possess to develop and maintain their competency" (2000, p. 379). These two approaches and that of Corral-Verdugo (2002) conceive competency as a set of dispositions rather than a simple collection of skills. Corral-Verdugo also establishes that identifying pro-environmental skills is relatively easy: one should only observe how someone solves problems (like recycling, reusing products, or using water) in an effective manner. Yet identifying pro-environmental requirements is not as easy; and it is also not easy to identify a competency.

From the perspective of the EE goals, it can be concluded that skills and pro-environmental dispositions should be simultaneously produced, in a coordinated way, to generate a pro-environmental competency. Considering this, Corral-Verdugo (2002) tested a model of Pro-environmental Competency (PEC). He specified this factor from indicators of pro-environmental motives, beliefs, and perceptions (as pro-environmental requirements) and a set of skills for water conservation, expecting a significant relationship between them. His proposal was based on the EE goals, which stipulate the need to develop knowledge, skills, motives, and attitudes. Yet, according to Corral-Verdugo, those competency indicators should be interrelated in such a way so that they might predispose and lead someone to act pro-environmentally. In his study, PEC coherently emerged from the interrelations between all these indicators and also saliently and significantly influenced a measure of water conservation (Corral-Verdugo, 2002). Similar findings have been replicated by other authors (Baethge *et al.*, 2006; De Haan, 2006; Rychen and Salganik, 2003; Sleurs, 2008).

Blanca Fraijo *et al.* (2010) conducted a study of pro-environmental competency in elementary school students; in dispositional variables promoting water conservation and water consumption behaviors were studied. The conceptual framework of this investigation was based on the idea that pro-environmental competency emerges from high interrelations between environmentally protective skills (effective pro-environmental behaviors) and the demands (motives, need of knowledge) that the students impose on themselves or the requirements (social values, prescriptions, and beliefs) that their society and the educational system establish. This means that a competent individual should develop all these behaviors and requirements in a coordinated and interrelated way.

The diagnostic phase of the study revealed low levels of environmental knowledge and skills, moderate levels of biophilic motives, and a higher level of environmental beliefs. Water consumption behaviors did not correlate with water conservation requirements; the pro-environmental dispositional variables did not correlate with each other, or with water consumption behaviors. This would indicate that competency was absent in the studied children.

However, after conducting a 40-hour EE program that included providing information and training in motivation, attitudinal change, skills, and participation in pro-environmental actions, a significantly different picture emerged: pro-environmental skills and knowledge increased, as well as the children's engagement in pro-environmental practices. Skills and dispositional variables significantly correlated with each other, and this made possible the emergence of a pro-environmental competency factor influencing pro-environmental behavior, as the results of a structural equation model confirmed.

In addition to investigating levels of competency, EE research should study how educational processes contribute to the development of pro-environmental competency, integrating its components in a coherent way. Bjarne Jensen (2002) and Fatma Tayci and Fusun Uysal (2012) argue that EE is a key element for developing environmentally protective behavior, and pro-environmental competency is a direct antecedent of such behavior (Corral-Verdugo, 2002). Corral-Verdugo also stresses the importance of didactic aspects, program contents, infrastructure, and educators trained in the development of pro-environmental competency.

Sustainable competency

A recent review conducted by Corral-Verdugo and Rosario Domínguez (2011) indicates that although successful experiences are reported in the implementation of EE programs, these programs have focused on promoting the conservation of the physical environment, with no consideration for the social milieu. Duerden and Witt (2010), Elisabeth Kals and Heidi Ittner (2003), and Matthies et al. (2012) agree with this description. According to Corral-Verdugo (2012), sustainable behavior is indicated not only by pro-ecological and frugal behaviors, but also by altruistic and equitable conducts, which are especially aimed at protecting people (the social environment). Thus, a step that is usually missing in the implementation of EE programs based on pro-environmental competency is the incorporation of social protection in addition to conservation of the physical environmental.

Some authors (Chiu, 2003; Foladori, 2005; Godschalk, 2004) have highlighted the importance of the social dimension of sustainability, which is unattended in most EE programs and public policies. John Sinclair et al. (2008) and Suzanne Vallance et al. (2011) call this dimension "social sustainability." The inclusion of social sustainability elements in EE programs will imply studying and promoting the correspondence between requirements of conservation of the sociophysical environment and the skills that make possible the protection of natural resources and other persons. This is essential because sustainability requires the simultaneous effort of conserving both natural and human capital (Bonnes and Bonaiuto, 2002). Of course, as with pro-environmental competency, sustainable competency should lead to conservationist behaviors; thus, Corral-Verdugo (2012) defines sustainable competency as the exhibition of behavioral capacities in response to requirements of natural and social protection. This means that sustainably competent people should demonstrate the ability to solve ecological and

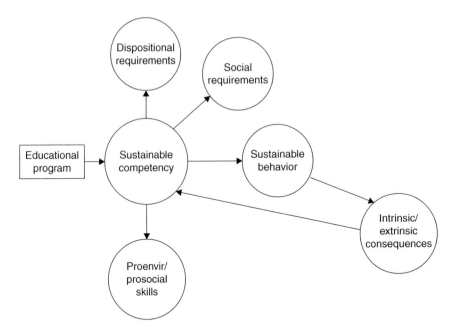

Figure 24.1 A model of sustainable competency promoted by EE programs

social problems, adapting their abilities to the challenges, problems, and requirements that they or society presents.

Conclusion: sketching an EE program based on sustainable competencies

The model illustrated in Figure 24.1 is proposed to guide the design of educational strategies for a formal environmental education.

According to the model, pro-environmental and pro-social skills co-variating with dispositional requirements (knowledge, beliefs, attitudes), and also social requirements (values, norms) inculcated through EE programs, will constitute a sustainable competency. This in turn will influence sustainable behavior. This behavior would be indicated by pro-ecological, frugal, altruistic, and equitable actions. The design of EE programs should consider strategies that promote, in a balanced way, actions encouraging the display of environmentally protective behaviors, at both physical and social levels. This means that pro-social (altruistic, equitable) and pro-environmental (biophilic, frugal) skills have to be taught as effective actions to practice in educational and natural scenarios. The model includes the provision of extrinsic consequences (incentives) to the display of sustainable behavior (i.e. social reinforcement, grades, etc.) but also anticipates intrinsic consequences (satisfaction, competence motivation, wellbeing) that should be recorded and reported by students participating in the program, as Corral-Verdugo and Domínguez (2011) suggest. This motivational factor would provide a source of influence for maintaining the sustainable competency.

The empirical evidence of studies concerning EE involving children (Fraijo 2010; Fraijo *et al.*, 2010; Fraijo *et al.*, in press) and adults (Corral-Verdugo, 2012) suggests that interventional programs based on competencies are able to generate pro-environmental dispositions and behaviors. The new challenge is to design EE strategies that generate sustainable competency, while simultaneously paying attention to both the social and the physical levels of environmental protection (Corral-Verdugo, 2012; Vallance *et al.*, 2011), as well as providing strategies aimed at evaluating the social and environmental impact of the educational programs (Carleton-Hug and Hug, 2010).

References

Alvarez-Suárez, P., and P. Vega-Marcote. 2010. Developing Sustainable Environmental Behavior in Secondary Education Students 12–16: Analysis of a Didactic Strategy. *Procedia: Social and Behavioral Sciences* 2, pp. 3568–74.

Aragonés, J., and M. Amérigo. 2010. *Psicología ambiental*. Madrid: Pirámide.

Arcury, T. 1990. Environmental Attitude and Environmental Knowledge. *Human Organization* 49, pp. 300–304.

Baethge, M., F. Achtenhagen, L. Arends, E. Babic, V. Baethge-Kinsky, and S. Weber. 2006. *PISA-VET: A Feasibility-Study*. Stuttgart: Franz Steiner.

Bonnes, M., and M. Bonaiuto. 2002. Environmental Psychology: From Spatial Physical Environment to Sustainable Development. In *Handbook of Environmental Psychology*. Eds. R. B. Bechtel, and A. Churchman. Thousand Oaks, Calif.: Sage.

Carew, A. L., and C. A. Mitchell. 2008. Teaching Sustainability as a Contested Concept: Capitalizing on Variation in Engineering Educators' Conceptions of Environmental, Social and Economic Sustainability. *Journal of Cleaner Production* 16, pp. 105–15.

Carleton-Hug, A., and J. W. Hug. 2010. Challenges and Opportunities for Evaluating Environmental Education Programs. *Evaluation and Program Planning* 33, pp. 159–64.

Chiu, R. 2003. Social Sustainability and Sustainable Housing. In *Housing and Social Change: East, West Perspectives*. Eds. R. Forrest, and J. Lee. London: Routledge, pp. 221–39.

Collado, S., and J. A. Corraliza. 2012. Perceived Restoration and Environmental Orientation in a Sample of Spanish Children. *Procedia: Social and Behavioral Sciences* 38, pp. 264–74.

Corraliza, J. A., S. Collado, and L. Bethelmy. 2012. Nature as a Moderator of Stress in Urban Children. *Procedia: Social and Behavioral Sciences* 38, pp. 253–63.

Corral-Verdugo, V. 1996. A Structural Model of Reuse and Recycling in Mexico. *Environment and Behavior* 28, pp. 665–96.

Corral-Verdugo, V. 1997. Environmental Psychology in Latin America: Efforts in Critical Situations. *Environment and Behavior* 29, pp. 163–68.

Corral-Verdugo, V. 2001. *Comportamiento Proambiental: una introducción al estudio de las conductas protectoras del ambiente*. Tenerife: Resma.

Corral-Verdugo, V. 2002. A Structural Model of Pro-environmental Competency. *Environment and Behavior* 34, pp. 531–49.

Corral-Verdugo, V. 2012. The Positive Psychology of Sustainability. *Environment, Development and Sustainability* 14, pp. 651–66.

Corral-Verdugo, V., and R. Domínguez. 2011. El rol de los eventos antecedentes y consecuentes en la conducta sustentable. *Revista Mexicana de Análisis de la Conducta* 37, pp. 9–29.

De Castro, R. 2000. Educación ambiental. In *Psicología Ambiental*. Eds. J. I. Aragonés, and M. Amérigo.Madrid: Pirámide.

De Haan, G. 2006. The BLK "21" Programme in Germany: A "Gestaltungskompetenz"-Based Model for Education for Sustainable Development. *Environmental Education Research* 12, pp. 19–32.

Delors, J. 1996. *La Educación Encierra un Tesoro*. París: UNESCO.

De Young, R. 2000. New Ways to Promote Pro-environmentalBehavior: Expanding and Evaluating Motives for Environmentally Responsible Behavior. *Journal of Social Issues* 56, pp. 509–26.

Duerden, M. D., and P. A. Witt. 2010. The Impact of Direct andIndirect Experiences on the Development of Environmental Knowledge, Attitudes, and Behavior. *Journal of Environmental of Psychology* 30, pp. 379–92.

Dunlap, R. E., K. D. Van Liere, A. G. Mertig, and R. E. Jones. 2000. New Trends in Measuring Environmental Attitudes: Measuring Endorsement of the New Ecological Paradigm: A Revised NEP Scale. *Journal of Social Issues* 56, pp. 425–42.

Foladori, G. 2005. Advances and Limits of Social Sustainability as an Evolving Concept. *Canadian Journal of Development Studies/Revue canadienne D'études du développement* 26, pp. 501–10.

Fraijo, B. 2010. La educación proambiental basada en competencias proecológicas: unestudio diagnóstico de requerimientos y acciones proambientales en niños. In *Conductas protectoras del ambiente*. Ed. V. Corral-Verdugo. Mexico City: Plaza y Valdez.

Fraijo, B., V. Corral-Verdugo, C. Tapia, and F. García. In press. Adaptación y prueba de una escala de orientación hacia la sustentabilidad en niños de sexto año de educación básica. *Revista Mexicana de Investigación Educativa*.

Fraijo-Sing, B., Corral-Verdugo, V., Tapia-Fonllem, C., and González-Lomeli, D. 2010. Promoting Pro-environmental Competency. In*Psychological Approaches to Sustainability: Current Trends in Theory, Research and Applications*. Eds. V. Corral-Verdugo, C. García, and M. Frías. New York: Nova Sciences, pp. 225–47.

Godschalk, D. R. 2004. Land Use Planning Challenges: Coping with Conflicts in Visions of Sustainable Development and Livable Communities. *Journal of the American Planning Association* 70, pp. 5–13.

González-Gaudiano, E. 2005. Education for Sustainable Development: Configuration and Meaning. *Policy Futures in Education* 3, pp. 243–50.

Hungerford, H., R. Peyton, and R. Wilke.1994. *Estrategias para la formación del profesorado en educación ambiental. Programa Internacional de educación ambiental UNESCO-PNUMA*. Madrid: Los libros de la catarata.

Jensen, B. B. 2002. *Knowledge, Action and Pro-environmental Behaviour*. London: Routledge.

Kaiser, F., and U. Fuhrer. 2003. Ecological Behavior's Dependency on Different Forms of Knowledge. *Applied Psychology: An International Review* 52, pp. 598–613.

Kals, E., and H. Ittner. 2003. Children's Environmental Identity: Indicators and Behavioral Impacts. In *Identity and the Natural Environment*. Eds. S. Clayton, and S. Opotow. Cambridge, Mass.: MIT Press, pp. 135–57.

Kellaghan,T., K. Sloane, B. Álvarez, and S. B. Bloom. 1993. *The Home Environment and School Learning*. San Francisco: Jossey Bass.

Matthies, E., S. Selge, and C. A. Klöckner. 2012. The Role of Parental Behavior for the Development of Behavior Specific Environmental Norms: The Example of Recycling and Re-use Behavior. *Journal of Environmental Psychology* 31, pp. 277–84.

Oskamp, S. 2002. Environmentally Responsible Behavior: Teaching and Promoting It Effectively. *Analyses of Social Issues and Public Policy* 2, pp. 173–82.

Perfilova, O., and Y.Alizade. 2011. The Role of Ecological Competence in Manager's Professional Education. *Procedia: Social and Behavioral Sciences* 15, pp. 2293–98.

Popkewitz, T. 2000. *Sociología política de las reformas educativas*. Madrid: Morata.

Ribes, E. 2007. *Psicología General*. Mexico City: Trillas.

Rychen, D. S., and L. K. Salganik. 2003. *Key Competencies for a Successful Life and a Well-Functioning Society*. Göttingen: Hogrefeand Huber.

Schultz, P. W., and L. Zelezny. 2003. Reframing Environmental Messages to Be Congruent with American Values. *Human Ecology Review*10, pp. 126–36.

Selma, A. B. 2012. On the Role of IntrinsicValue in Terms of Environmental Education. *Procedia: Social and Behavioral Sciences* 47, pp. 1087–91.

Simmons, D. A. 1998. Epilogue, or Some Future Thoughts on: "Are We Meeting the Goal of Responsible Environmental Behavior?"An Examination of Nature and Environmental Education Center Goals. In *Essential Readings in Environmental Education*. Eds. H. R. Hungerford, W. J. Bluhm, T. L. Volk,and J. M. Ramsey. Champaign, Ill.: Stipes, p. 319.

Sinclair, A. J., A. Diduck, and P. Fitzpatrick. 2008. Conceptualizing Learning for Sustainability through Environmental Assessment: Critical Reflections on 15 Years of Research. *Environmental Impact Assessment Review* 28, pp. 415–28.

Sleurs, W. 2008. *Competencies for ESD Education for Sustainable Development Teachers: A Framework to Integrate ESD in the Curriculum of Teacher Training Institutes*. Comenius 2, no. 1, project 118277-CP-1–2004-BE-Comenius-C2.1. Brussels: Environments and Schools Initiative. Retrieved on July 15th, 2012, from http://www.unece.org/fileadmin/DAM/env/esd/inf.meeting.docs/EGonInd/8mtg/CSCT%20Handbook_Extract.pdf.

Smith-Sebasto, N. J., and R. W. Fortner. 1994. The Environmental Action Internal Control Index. *Journal of Environmental Education* 25, pp. 23–29.

Stapp, W. B., D. Bennett, W. Bryan Jr, J. Fulton, J. MacGregor, P. Nowak, J. Swan, R. Wall, and S. Havlick. 1969. The Concept of Environmental Education. *Journal of Environmental Education* 1, pp. 30–31.

Tayci, F., and F. Uysal. 2012. A Study Determining the Elementary School Students' Environmental Knowledge and Environmental Attitude Level. *Procedia: Social and Behavioral Sciences* 46, pp. 5718–22.

UNESCO (United Nations Educational, Scientific and Cultural Organization). 2005. *United Nations Decade of Education for Sustainable Development (January 2005–December 2014): Framework for a Draft International Implementation Scheme*. Paris: UNESCO.

UNESCO (United Nations Educational, Scientific and Cultural Organization). 2009. *Policy Dialogue 1: ESD and Development Policy: Education and the Search for a Sustainable Future*. Paris: UNESCO.

Vallance, S., H. C. Perkins, and J. E. Dixon. 2011. What Is Social Sustainability? A Clarification of Concepts.*Geoforum* 42, pp. 342–48.

White, R. V. 1959. Motivation Reconsidered: The Concept of Competence. *Psychological Review* 66, pp. 279–333.

25 Avoiding wrong turns on the road to ecosystem services valuation

Kevin Halsey

A friend recently forwarded to me an exchange from a local planning listserv that she likes to follow. The exchange was about the merits of using ecosystem services as part of the decision-making process in land use planning. The participants sought to be balanced, acknowledging that there certainly could be some benefits to using ecosystem services approaches, but ultimately the dialogue focused on the detrimental and "immoral" aspects of the ecosystem services concept.

Those who took part in the exchange expressed concern that ecosystem services analysis was based on the premise that "nature is here to serve us," and that this had scary ramifications. Some of those ramifications were described as "overuse of a few high performance species" (presumably plant species used in planting plans), the importation of invasive species as "infrastructure," limited biodiversity, and habitat impacts. The commentators concluded that it was wrong to think that the ecosystem served us – that thinking of this sort led to a view of nature as a collection of commodities and was arrogant and morally corrupt.

Somehow, the very intelligent participants in the listserv dialogue accepted as a fundamental and undisputed premise that ecosystem services is the study of how "nature is here to serve us." Believing in ecosystem services was even compared to espousing manifest destiny (Anonymous, 2011). I could not read the dialogue without seeing it as writing on the wall: a sign that there are serious issues in how ecosystem services concepts are being communicated. But more important is the fear that when it comes to implementing the concept, the perception on the listserv may not be as far from the truth as we would like. Certainly our efforts to implement the concept do not always reflect the theoretical basis from which ecosystem services originated.

The ecosystem services concept expresses human dependence on ecological processes (Costanza and Folke, 1997). The idea of ecosystem services is that while many in society are unwilling or unable to accept the entirety of this dependence, failure to do so inevitably has economic and social consequences. Placing a value on natural processes is not an effort to assert dominance or even necessarily to commoditize natural processes. It is an effort to understand and quantify the ramifications of failing to properly respect those ecological dependencies. The ecosystem services concept suggests that nature can sustainably support us only if we respect and understand how it functions.

There is an ongoing debate within the world of ecosystem services practitioners – many maintain that the term "ecosystem services" does not adequately convey the concept to a broader public. The Nature Conservancy hired a polling firm to get a better feel for how the public responds to the concepts and the language we use to describe the concept. According to the Nature Conservancy, it turns out that ecosystem services is one of the terms least likely to resonate with the public. Dumbing down language to connect with the least common denominator creates the danger of stripping out so much nuance and detail that the communication does as much harm as good (Metz, 2010). However, given the potential for the word "services" to be so easily misconstrued, there may be good reason to think about using a term that better describes the concept. In the survey results, the terms "nature's value" and "nature's benefits" scored highest. These terms may not convey the entirety of the concept in a short, pithy title, but what will? At least these terms are not as misleading as "ecosystem services." In the formative years of the ecosystem services discipline, conversations like the one that unfolded on the listserv could have undue influence over the final shape of the discipline.

People will be exposed to ecosystem services from similar listserv conversations, blogs, and tweets, etc. Given the potential for quickly spreading misinformed conversations on ecosystem services, we need to ask ourselves whether we are communicating the concept in a misleading or overly simplistic manner. If doing so leads to widespread misunderstanding, then moving the ecosystem services concept forward will be much harder. Even more important, as the discipline expands, are ecosystem services practitioners going to continue to understand the underlying fundamental principles and reflecting them in their ecosystem services valuation efforts? Are we in danger of having the description from the listserv dialogue become an accurate reflection of how ecosystem services approaches are actually being implemented? The necessary wake-up call from the listserv conversation described above is not just that we need better language. The important question it raises is this: When we value ecosystem services, how true to the concept are we being?

There is a fundamental underpinning which supports a clear purpose and need expressed in the theory underlying ecosystem services, and reflexive awareness of that purpose is needed as ecosystem services valuations are performed. Further, to ensure that valuations are true to the purpose and need for the ecosystem services concept, the following elements should be considered for all ecosystem services valuation: seek a clear means of connecting ecological performance to value determination; make appropriate choices for when to use economic versus noneconomic metrics; practice ecosystem services holistically and systematically (the use of the term ecosystem instead of ecological value extraction is not accidental); make use of multiscale approaches to the valuation process – value at one flow rate within the system is not a constant at all flow rates within the system. Incorporating these considerations will ensure that valuing exercises stay true to the intent concept of the ecosystem services.

Admittedly some of these concepts are difficult, and some will be impractical in certain contexts. However, as a community we can and should be moving toward measurement practices that incorporate these concepts. If we do not, then we should consider whether the use of ecosystem services approaches will really provide the benefits that we expect.

Starting at the beginning: what is the intent of the ecosystem services concept?

"Nature has value" – that is often the shorthand explanation used to describe ecosystem services. Nature has value – a true statement from an ecosystem services perspective and certainly a fundamental conclusion that ecosystem services practitioners have asked people to accept. Unfortunately, too many people currently being exposed to ecosystem services develop a superficial and misguided understanding of the concept by launching from this basic statement and never digging deeper into its underpinnings. Rest assured, the listserv conversation described above is not unique. It actually encapsulates many of the criticisms that are commonly leveled at ecosystem services as a concept.

However, these criticisms are largely based on a fundamental misunderstanding of the premise upon which ecosystem services concepts are based. The starting point is not nature has value. Regrettably, this leads some to believe that the discipline of ecosystem services is premised on commoditizing nature, which leads to the conclusion that nature is here to serve us. In fact, that is exactly the opposite of the fundamental premise underlying ecosystem services analysis. The ecosystem services concept is premised on the belief that humans have a level of dependency on ecological processes that we have been unwilling, or unable, to admit. The logical conclusion of this premise is not that nature serves us, but that we exist at the sufferance of nature, and that failure to recognize this will have economic and social consequences. The important corollary is that the recognition of the economic and social value of nature will lead humanity to preserve it. The most important part of that logical sequence is arguably that humans rely on properly functioning ecosystems for their survival and quality of life. That is the fundamental premise upon which ecosystem services concepts are based. The intent of the ecosystem services concept is not about dominating nature, it is about understanding the relationships between our ecology, society, and economy.

Do the conceptual models for sustainability not suggest the same thing? Ultimately, ecosystem services analysis is a mechanism for measuring ecological, social, and economic relationships in the manner that sustainability models suggest is appropriate – if done correctly, ecosystem services analysis is a means of bringing sustainability considerations into decision-making processes.

The starting point for a proper ecosystem services analysis is that properly functioning ecosystems provide benefits which humans rely on for their survival and quality of life. Accordingly, the first question to ask with regard to the importation of an invasive species to develop infrastructure is whether the action will improve or diminish the system's ecological functions. In the case of invasive species, the analysis typically shows that a few functions may in fact improve: for instance, fast-growing invasive species often provide increased erosion control. However, a complete analysis usually indicates that monoculture diminishes species support – which could mean reduced pollination, pest control, and other important functions and services. In this instance, the long-term effect of losing species support for songbirds and pollinators would be severe.

There is generally very limited regulatory protection against species transplantation in the USA. Erosion control, a common reason for transplantation, is typically regulated through the Clean Water Act (40 CFR Part 122). The appropriate application of ecosystem services concepts would lead the decision maker to conclude that intentionally planting an invasive species was a bad idea. Any planner who is using the economic benefits of planting invasive species as a justification is clearly missing the ecosystem component of ecosystem services.

The necessary next step in the analysis is: How do we ensure that ecosystem services valuations are leading to the intended outcomes?

Connecting ecological performance to value determination

The example of whether to use invasive species to provide "natural" infrastructure presumes that the ecosystem services analysis is actually based on ecological performance. Basing ecosystem services analysis on ecological performance is an important principle that needs to be applied to ecosystem services valuations. When calculating the potential social and economic costs associated with the loss of ecosystem services, that loss should be understood to the best of our ability in terms of change to the ecological performance that is responsible for the ecosystem services in the first place. The feasibility and need to incorporate ecological condition information increases as the geographic scale of analysis decreases. At a site level it is imperative that decisions be made based on a good understanding of the ecological implications for the site. Nevertheless, if we are asking what the economic value is of the world's forests, then our ability to incorporate ecological condition information will be significantly reduced, and because of the general nature of the question the need to do so will be commensurately lower as well. That does not mean that we can ignore ecological condition whenever we are operating at larger landscape scales. However, it does mean that we need to be realistic about the quality and extent of the information we will be able to use.

Parametrix, a consulting firm based in the Pacific Northwest, has developed a framework for thinking about ecosystem services (see Figure 25.1). The framework suggests that to measure ecosystem services a series of steps must be followed.

First, it is necessary to understand the attributes of the landscape being evaluated: the soil conditions, vegetative structure and composition, topography, and water regime are contributing to the performance of ecological functions (both biotic and abiotic). Second, the ecological functions combine to provide the benefits that we need for survival and quality of life. Third, by understanding how these various functions combine to provide the ecosystem services, it is possible to measure the amount of benefit (i.e. ecosystem services) provided by the landscape being analyzed. Fourth, consider the flow of benefits from the

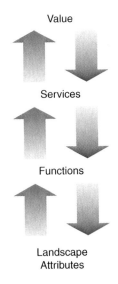

Value

Services

Functions

Landscape
Attributes

Figure 25.1 Ecosystems steps framework

landscape, and then apply context considerations (scarcity, proximity, relative need, replacement cost, avoided cost, etc.) to determine the societal value of the benefits being produced. This is the level of understanding we should be striving for when we perform ecosystem services valuations. If we do not incorporate these steps in our analysis, then what are we actually measuring?

Capturing economic and noneconomic value

The term "ecosystem services" means figuring out how much people are willing to pay for nature. The apparent assumption is that once we know how much they are willing to pay for it, we are going to go ahead and sell it to them. The berating typically starts with a question: "Don't ecosystem services just limit nature to those who can afford it?" How do you respond to such a philosophical non sequitur? After a few of these experiences it is clear that individuals have a hard time distinguishing environmental capitalism (the belief that market forces should determine environmental protection decisions) from ecosystem services. Many of the ecosystem services measuring tools are more focused on measuring and understanding the flow of benefits from the landscape than on monetizing those benefits. Even when the desire is to understand the "value" of those ecosystem services, that does not necessarily mean monetary value. There are ecosystem services that cannot be replaced and that many would deem priceless. The Grand Canyon, for example, is a natural wonder and a place that provides spiritual, cultural, and aesthetic benefits that are beyond strict monetary quantification. For instance, if we conduct a contingency valuation (willingness to pay) study to determine how much the Grand Canyon is worth, we will likely get dollar figures that exceed what the respondents can really afford.

This does not mean that we cannot value the Grand Canyon. It means that to do so we must use a different unit of measurement. Focusing on preferences or setting priorities is a much better way of talking about priceless resources. This noneconomic approach still describes how we value the resource, but it does so in a less deterministic manner. Essentially, the output of this valuation process is a prioritization of societal desires. This noneconomic value provides a more meaningful input into decision-making processes. It forces the evaluation of trade-offs between potential resources or outcomes in the emotional terms necessary for nondeterministic resources.

For the most part, practitioners are doing a good job of recognizing the importance of thinking beyond mere dollar equivalencies. The Business for Social Responsibility (BSR) Ecosystem Services, Tools and Markets Working Group, which vets ecosystem services decision-support tools, evaluated seven tools in its Tool Developers Round Table in 2010; five of the seven tools did not include an economic value output. One of the tools specifically focused on determining noneconomic value, while only one of the tools has economic valuing as a primary purpose. All ecosystem services provide multiple values at multiple levels; ultimately, there is no one way to properly value all ecosystem services. It is important to use the right approach in the right context.

The dangers of reductionism

The ecosystem services concept represents a departure from the way we have analyzed ecological issues over the past 50 years. Science and industrial technology specialists tend to analyze a given problem by determining its factors and components, isolating them, then reconfiguring them with the expectation that the initial problem will have been solved; such an approach has been encouraged because it has been successful. However, there is a second edge to the specialization sword. With specialization has come a tendency toward reductionism. Such reductionism suggests that complex systems are nothing more than the sum of their parts. The corollary is that we can just focus on those parts. Given the complexity of looking beyond the components, it is not surprising that over time planners and policy makers opt for reductionism. It is easy to see evidence of reductionism in our environmental laws. Most countries, and the USA is a prime example, have developed environmental laws that focus on regulating very narrow aspects of our natural system. The USA has a law that protects wetlands, a law that protects endangered species, a law that protects water quality and another that protects air quality. However, environmental scientists and environmental economists do not have any ecosystem laws.

The potential exception to this rule is the National Environmental Policy Act (NEPA), which in fact provides a tragic case in point. While NEPA as drafted was a landmark and visionary piece of legislation, it fell victim to reductionism in its application. NEPA requires federal agencies to consider the "environmental consequences" of their actions. Its language is quite the opposite of reductionism: "all agencies of the federal government shall: (A) utilize a systematic, interdisciplinary approach which will insure the integrated use of the natural and social sciences and the environmental design arts in planning and in decision making which may have an impact on man's environment" (NEPA, 42 USC § 4332 (2) (A)). However, in application compliance with the NEPA translates to the production of a series of technical papers on a few of the systems' component parts. Most federal agencies have made the reductionist approach even easier by identifying in advance the specific component parts that they want analyzed.

Focusing on a few of the parts within the system does not equal focusing on all of the necessary parts. The US regulatory structure can be seen as representing the lowest common denominator of public belief. Regulations reflect only those issues so pressing as to be accepted as problems by enough people and so the political process addresses them. Regulatory silos not only epitomize society's tendency toward reductionism: they institutionalize the practice. That may be one reason that the concept of ecosystem services is confusing. A reductionist perspective is fundamentally the opposite of ecosystem services analysis.

Ecosystem-based management is increasingly being promoted and advocated as a better way to understand the natural environment than the methods used in the past. This type of systems thinking focuses not just on the component parts of the system but on the relationships between these parts. Systems thinking takes the perspective that there are important cause-and-effect issues embedded within those relationships. Without understanding the important relationships, the actions taken to address ecological issues are too likely to be directed at symptoms of a problem rather than the root cause of the problem.

However, even when systems-based analysis approaches are being used, their application is still limited. For example, with ecosystem-based analysis, there is seldom consideration of how changes to ecosystems relate to social or economic systems. In contrast, ecosystem services analysis is a systems thinking approach at many levels. First, ecosystems services analysis requires adopting a holistic ecosystem approach as an initial step. The focus is on broad ecosystem performance, considering the contribution of many ecosystem attributes toward overall ecological performance. Second, the extent to which this ecological performance relates to social and economic concerns moves the analysis from considering a single system to assessing the interrelationship of multiple systems. It is within the relationships between these multiple systems that we derive a more meaningful understanding of the consequences of our activities. Ecosystem services analysis helps us to get at the interrelationships between our ecosystem and our economic and social systems.

Ecosystem services analysis requires the meshing of many different experts. Economists, ecologists, anthropologists, hydrologists, climatologists, and as many other "ologists" as you can think of are all necessary parts of understanding the many relationships captured by ecosystem services analysis. Our understanding of ecosystem services and the tools that we develop to measure and value them need to have the input of all these "ologists."

Understanding ecological processes at multiple scales

To really understand ecological processes, and thereby ecosystem services, it is necessary to understand those processes at multiple scales across the landscape. Many ecosystem services are best understood in the context of their performance over large areas, that is, at an ecoregional, watershed, or other landscape scale. Water provisioning, water regulation, and climate regulation are all examples of services that can only truly be understood in a regional context. However, many decisions that change the landscape and affect service production are made at the site scale, project by project.

Accordingly, it is important to be able to measure performance at multiple scales and to understand what the outputs at one scale mean for measurements at the other scale. At both landscape and site levels, our understanding is vastly improved by first measuring the performance of the functions that provide a particular ecosystem service, then determining the value associated with that service in a subsequent step. A good landscape-level evaluation provides important information about ecosystem performance and answers questions such as these: Which ecosystem functions (e.g. specific species support, or physical processes such as infiltration, interception, or evaporation) are in good condition and which ones have been impaired? Are there important ecosystem processes (i.e. dynamic physical processes) that are currently limited? Are there specific habitats or functions that should be prioritized for preservation or recovery?

Understanding the answers to these questions creates a context for and adds meaning to the measurements that occur at the site scale. If the context is properly understood, then it is possible to use weighting or other tools to reflect the greater value of certain locations, habitats, or functions on the landscape, thereby incentivizing meaningful conservation actions.

Likewise, conducting the site-level assessment in a manner that allows direct comparison with the landscape assessment gives decision makers a clearer understanding of the effects of their decisions. The potential impact is no longer an abstract harm or benefit to something we feel is probably important. Instead, it is a quantified, concrete effect with consequences that are defined and tangible. When these consequences are quantified, they can be tracked over time. This means decision makers do not just understand the consequences of their individual decisions, but also the cumulative effect of those decisions over time. Relating the landscape and site measurement outputs in this way provides the information necessary to improve market transaction outcomes. For instance, if an ecosystem priority is given greater weight within the system, then the impacts to the resource become costlier and the rewards for restoring and protecting the resource become greater. This will directly benefit project siting and design decisions, and it will create revenue-generating opportunities for restoration actions.

Conclusion

Ecosystem services analysis can be used in a variety of ways. While the philosophical underpinnings of the concept lie with Henry David Thoreau and

Aldo Leopold, there is no guarantee that the concept, as it evolves and is applied over time, won't warp into something unrecognizable to those great writers. The study of ecosystem services is a relatively new discipline and accordingly it is not a standardized, narrowly prescribed field of study. In this nascent stage it is particularly important that we pay attention to the purpose underlying the concept. By adopting some basic guidelines early on to protect the intent of the concept, we can hopefully keep it from becoming the misrepresented concept described in the listserv conversation.

References

Anonymous. 2011. Conversation from August11th–12th, August. Oregon Planners Network Listserv, University of Oregon.

Costanza, R., and Folke, C. 1997. Valuing Ecosystem Services with Efficiency, Fairness, and Sustainability as Goals. In *Nature's Services: Societal Dependence on Natural Ecosystems*. Ed. G. C. Daily. Washington, DC: Island Press.

Metz, D. 2010. *Key Findings: National Voter Survey on Ecosystem Services. Missoula Mt.: Nature Conservancy*. April 25th. Retrieved on July 15th, 2012, from http://api.ning. com/files/9NcL1yGUl*8qMHIFxHZ6yg5WdBnhUu7XJ8vSwJUeczYam3MMTAzgay2 w7I6BWOeaddR6LwcRTmQ5GF85GBtdYVYHv7QxH7Og/NationalOpinionResearchonEcosystemServices.pdf.

26 Values and strategies for the environment and sustainable development

Mark E. Hillon

The difficulty of strategy and planning is in uncovering and aligning the hidden objectives of each stakeholder. The three principal stakeholder groups in sustainability (shareholders; environmentalists; economic community) present the same conundrum because economic, social, and environmental objectives – even when transparent – are often at odds with each other on multiple dimensions. We also suffer from unrealistic assumptions about the worlds of all three stakeholders. Even though we know better, it is easier to assume an inherent knowable order in all human interactions, to assume that rational choice guides all decisions, and that capabilities will be put to intended uses (Kurtz and Snowden, 2003).

The triple bottom line approach to sustainability proposes a decision-making balance of financial, social, and environmental needs. However, sustainability tends to be approached separately by stakeholders of these three perspectives even though they constitute a single shared human social ecology. Sustainability is meant to preserve a human ecology, which requires coexistence with a reasonably healthy natural world. The financial element is firmly rooted in the firm's concerns, while the social/community and environmental elements tend to reside beyond the incorporated boundaries of the enterprise. The function of a firm is to increase shareholder returns as fast as possible, not to improve the global social ecology for all humanity. This is why the financial line of the triple bottom line will always trump the other lines.

Life cycle analysis, ecosystem services, and other research into sustainability often begins with the naïve belief that all we need is some applied thought and calculation to arrive at a total or more complete cost of economic activity. A mass energy balance approach could conceivably anchor all three disparate elements of the triple bottom line and allow one organization or enterprise to simultaneously view the financial, social, and environmental ramifications of their choices. For instance, Peter Gleick and Heather Cooley (2009) demonstrated a straightforward procedure for calculating the energy embodied in the materials, manufacture, and transport of bottled water. Their procedure could easily be extended a step or two forward to the landfill or recycler to capture the entire life cycle of the product. Add in a modest cost for externalities – pollution, depletion of natural resources, marketing noise to encourage consumption – and we can put a realistic total cost on all major aspects of the life cycle. Calculating a total cost of ownership is relatively easy, even if it spans years. However, it is foolish optimism to think that putting an irrefutably more accurate price on our economic actions will lead smoothly into behavioral change. Asking someone to pay the net present value of the total cost cash flow at the point of sale is extremely unrealistic (Pitcher, 1999). In the quest to increase shareholder returns, denial of environmental responsibility effectively externalizes the cost of preserving the planet.

Dissociation from sustainable systems

Tension in future planning is always present in decisions concerning sustainability because everything we do today will undoubtedly affect how the now-quiet future voices cope with the world they inherit. Human ecological systems are artificial constructions (Faber *et al.*, 2005) and can be modeled adequately as socio-psychological and technical-economic systems (Savall and Zardet, 2008). The environments of human ecological systems – everything beyond an arbitrary pervious boundary – have causal textures, and the entire system-environment map has dimensions of context, scale, and time that must figure into any strategic planning for the shared future of all stakeholders (Emery and Trist, 1973). In practice though, the technical-economic voices within a business generally dominate the future dialogue. Therefore, maladaptive and socially dysfunctional organizations are the norm rather than the exception.

The time dimension is perhaps the greatest obstacle to effective planning, as economic concerns operate within extremely short time horizons compared with social and environmental timelines. Market economics also treats the many environments of the scattered human ecological systems around the globe as one big source for natural capital and disposal of waste. Economic analysis of resource allocation based on efficient use and marginal utility is inadequate when trying to determine a fair division of natural resources between present and future generations. In a dialogical sense, the future voice cannot be anticipated with clarity because needs and preferences change along with techniques for extracting and utilizing resources.

The Brundtland definition of sustainable development does not challenge the necessity of economic growth (Common, 1998), nor does it offer any practical advice on how to balance the needs of the future against our present wants and desires: "meeting the needs of the present generation without compromising the ability of future generations to meet their own needs" (UNWCED, 1987). Subhabrata Banerjee characterizes the Brundtland definition as a slogan instead of a theory that can be operationalized and measured. In the "Brundtland report, development is accorded a priority over the environment [and] sustainable development uses the logic of markets and capitalist accumulation to determine the future of nature" (Banerjee, 2003, p. 153). Julianne Newton and Eric Freyfogle (2005) reach the hidden heart of the sustainability debate in highlighting that the vagueness of the term allows it to be easily co-opted and redefined by the goals of whatever field or discipline adopts it. They add that the concept of sustainability now in fashion does not differ from the resource conservation movement of the early twentieth century, which "assured people that they could have it all. They merely needed to use better science and economics to get nature's resources flowing in perpetuity" (2005, p. 25).

Crawford Holling spent five years on the Resilience Project, funded by the MacArthur Foundation, working under the apparently hidden assumption that humans are both the sustainers and the sustained. Rather than abandon a term that meant the opposite of what they intended, the members of his team simply redefined sustainable development to mean "the goal of fostering adaptive capabilities while simultaneously creating opportunities" (2001, p. 399). This bit of creative writing is all the more ironic in light of the Resilience Project's finding that the three features that distinguish the tremendous potential of human systems: 1) foresight and intentionality; 2) communication; and 3) technology are also the keys to sustaining a maladaptive system. The anti-heroic plot of the sustainability narrative is that humans all too often either cannot understand or do not believe that their actions are destructive. "Our environmental problems are ultimately caused by bad human conduct. Our Earth is not a defective or sub-par planet; we have problems with the earth because we do not live well on it" (Newton and Freyfogle, 2005, p.25). If the accepted meaning of sustainability is so individualized and the heart of the concept refers to resource depletion rather than maintaining the health of the natural ecological system, then the strategist must either discard the term as useless or expand the concept to encompass a broader human ecological systems perspective.

The status quo is maintained by dissociating individual goals from the larger context of a functioning interdependent social system. These dissociated goals follow from the dominance of a market economy, a normative force that reorients societies to fit its needs. A market is part of the extended network of social institutions and cultural practices that facilitates private economic activity, but dissociated individualism allows only a financial monologue. Economic activity is a form of social dialogue that cannot be sustained in a dissociated context. Michael Cernea notes the importance of social interdependence to economic relations:

> People's economic activities are embedded in a structure of social relations … When public investment in technical infrastructures proceeds alongside disinvestment in the social, cultural, and institutional structures within which the former are embedded, the sustainability of the technical advancement itself is undermined.
>
> (1985, p. 9)

Trade within a society based on reciprocity or redistribution does not require the additional institutional arrangement for a market, which is based on exchange (e.g. barter or buying and selling). However, trade with external parties – people who do not share the same cultural exchange assumptions – requires separate market institutions to make transactions possible. As external trade increases, the market emerges from its origins in the network of social relations to become a separate and independent institution. As it further develops, the market gains the power to reorganize society around external commercial activity (Polanyi,

1944). In the context of sustainability, destructive effects spread to more and more external markets and to future stakeholders. Because the underlying integrative norm driving the expanding global market is individual, private, and unequal exchange, the economic subsystem undermines the social aspects of the system. Globalization "objectively places finance above the control of national governments" (Perez, 2009, p 802), and community and environmental concerns can be ignored. "The economy is not the subsystem, it is the total system; the 'environment' is the subsystem, a sector of the economy to which resources can be allocated just like any other sector" (Daly, 1999, p. 48).

Strategy for sustainable development

Stephen Marglin (2008) stresses the importance of reciprocal community relationships in resilient economic systems. He emphasizes that reality strongly conflicts with the tenets of mainstream economics:

> It is highly misleading about how society actually works … you have to separate individuals, focus on the individual, and leave out of the analysis the connections between individuals … as soon as they are not self-interested anymore – even if that non-self-interest takes the benign form of altruism – then the theorems about Pareto optimality, the efficiency of markets, break down.
>
> (2008, p. 17)

Frederick Emery and Eric Trist anticipated that people would recognize the complexity of human interactions and work together to improve their shared ecosystem (1973). Economic success requires us to become ever more like the imaginary individualistic agents that cannot belong to a supportive community, and happiness declines with prosperity in social isolation (Speth, 2008).

Just as future stakeholders lack a voice in the present, so too does the natural world. Yet, human interests offer voices for whatever natural subsystems they find important. As a result, it is unambiguously clear that the question of sustainability is a question of competing human interests. However, we have attempted to maximize human well-being without a clear understanding of how our actions will affect the earth's ability to continue to sustain us (Raudsepp-Hearne *et al.*, 2010). "The object of preserving biodiversity is not to increase economic activity, but to be able to continue it into the future at some constant sustainable level" (Daly, 1999, p. 51). If we are to make progress toward a sustainable human ecology, we will ultimately need to return the economy to its place as a subsystem entangled within a complexly interrelated social system. Doing so will merge the separate triple bottom line interests of finance, community, and environment so that the needs of each can be balanced systemically.

The reality of human existence shows eras of progress interspersed with localized civil calamities. Jared Diamond (2005) studied the collapse of selected complex societies throughout history and traced the general cause to their failure to manage natural resources. Diamond's students repeatedly asked, after he detailed the series of events and circumstances of each society's self-destruction, why they continued to deplete essential resources until the ecological damage sealed their fate. The simplest answer is a conflict of individual versus group interests. Mark Whitehead (2007, p. 187) observes that "all forms of sustainability are ultimately local sustainabilities," meaning that our actions are felt most directly by those closest to us, in the communities in which we exercise our rights and responsibilities as citizens. Confined to a relatively small area, ecological devastation rationally follows when people realize "that they can advance their own interests by behavior harmful to other people" (Diamond, 2005, p. 427). Harmful industries can in turn become so crucial to the local economy that they are mistaken for core values, immune to regulation and change.

A more complex explanation for catastrophic resource depletion is that human societies destroy their own social and natural ecologies because humans live in artificial complex systems that lack "equilibrium-restoring capabilities, which can cause them to stay in a non-sustainable situation until they collapse" (Faber *et al.*, 2005, p. 6). Individual choice allows us to continue along with the momentum of our past and our current way of life toward collapse instead of pursuing the gentler rebalancing common to nonhuman complex adaptive systems. Collapse allows the artificial system to restructure toward a new, but different, equilibrium without learning how to avoid a repeat performance. It is ironic that we have identified the symptoms of societal decline and the characteristics of failing states, yet we are often unable to remedy the human condition or turn the momentum in time. Uneven accumulation of wealth, the inability of governments to deliver basic services, food insecurity, crumbling infrastructure, and environmental degradation are slow-moving harbingers of collapse (Brown, 2006). Planning for sustainability is difficult if individual goals cannot be aligned toward common human ecological needs. Assuming that effective financial and governmental incentives could be created, we would still need to determine what constitutes good individual behavior for the long-term sustenance of our ecosystem. Dietrich Dorner attributes our inability to think in systems for long-range planning to the fact that our prehistoric ancestors did not "need to see a problem embedded in the context of other problems ... For us, however, this is the rule, not the exception" (Dorner, 1996, p. 6).

Systems thinking helps to conceptualize the relevant participants and contextual factors that are necessary for planning and causal awareness. An effective strategist must begin with an accurate portrayal of each stakeholder's motives, assumptions, and expectations. Given the current state of social and resource inequity, sustainability must include development if resilience is a goal for all of humanity. However, Milton Friedman market economics is currently the dominant frame of postindustrial capitalism. The needs of multiple stakeholders working within the same time horizon will likely force the frame to expand and break into a more accommodating context for dialogue.

To create a strategic confluence of timelines, the financial stakeholders must have incentives to begin to recapture negative externalities. The externalization of costs means the taking of costs that should be or should have been the responsibility of a corporation, and eliminating them by making them someone else's responsibility (e.g. the covering of bank losses by a government); so the recapture of negative externalities would mean that the bank takes responsibility and accounts for the expenses that are currently external to its accounting, thus increasing its costs. There are two main reasons for them to accept this: greater efficiency and a change in societal values that makes sustainable business practices desirable to customers. Although lessons from publicly traded companies dominate business school curricula, it is encouraging for an ecological strategist to remember that privately owned and managed companies account for roughly half of the American workforce and gross domestic product (GDP). Therefore, the sustainability dialogue could find receptive ears among the silent half of our economy. A simple profit motive through waste reduction might provide the spark to push lean manufacturing principles toward a systems perspective of sustainability. Beyond lean waste reduction, sustainability requires a look at energy consumption and environmental impact (Gustashaw and Hall, 2008). A more efficient industrial process can offer savings in the material and energy costs of production, as well as reductions in environmental harm and other negative life cycle externalities (Fishman, 2007). Efficiency improvements can easily move an organization one-third of the way toward carbon neutrality at no net cost (Carlson, 2008).

Concerning changing customer values, reduction of environmental harm can be captured as a benefit to the organization in the form of an improved public image. Disclosure of environmental performance – even greenwashing – tends to improve the public perception of companies in industries known for poor ecological stewardship (Cho *et al.*, 2012). Research also shows improved financial performance for companies that espouse environmental and social values while serving a broader group of stakeholder interests over a longer time horizon (Eccles *et al.*, 2011). These benefits offer real financial incentives for recapturing negative externalities. Diamond (2005) cites an example of an oil company planning for the estimated 30-year life cycle of an oil field. Over such a long time horizon, the managers knew from experience that the costs to keep neighbors happy were minimal compared to the cost of lost production.

"From a policy perspective, ... sustainability no longer is perceived as an achievable goal, but as a continuing process of improvement, requiring constant effort ... and a relative, dynamic perspective ... with continuous learning" (Faber *et al.*, 2005, p. 28). However, policy can also inhibit adoption of sustainable practices. Industry researchers note that good design and engineering should produce energy- and resource-efficient results, but capital budgeting decisions for sustainability initiatives often do not consider life cycle costs (Brown, 2011). Hence, long-term planning might refer to anything beyond two to three years. Additionally, cost neutrality is no longer sufficient, as companies are increasingly demanding that environmental sustainability must have an ROI (return on investment) (Blaeser and Whiting, 2012). Such constraints reinforce the dependent link between profitability and negative externalities, while imposing a higher threshold for decisions that might produce social and environmental benefits.

Our interaction with the social and natural environments creates a human ecology characterized by contradictory needs and expectations. The false unity and equality implied by the sustainability triple bottom line hides the antagonism embedded in stakeholder relations. It would be more productive to recognize that people do not like to be forced to experience the novelty of change. Rather, they need to have the free will to explore problems and unfamiliar perspectives by choice (Grandin and Johnson, 2009). Forced solutions also present a competency threat to stakeholders, in that people are naturally reluctant to stretch beyond the safety of their knowledge and capabilities to solve complex and unfamiliar problems (Ramnarayan et al., 1997). Shared purposeful or goal-directed action gains momentum when all stakeholders co-create strategies. People require compelling reasons to shed free market individualism in favor of interdependent communities. Emery and Trist note that "adaptation to complex environments is possible by appropriate value transformations" (1973, p. xiv). However, the transformation begins with current values. We cannot ask a culture or society to jump from comfort to a new value paradigm, even if the jump represents a return to previously held values.

We find ourselves in a difficult spot, between the general expectations for socially responsible work and a corporate structure that has been legally constructed to avoid responsibility for any harm done. Our "efforts to maximize one species necessarily diminish the habitats and populations of many others" (Newton and Freyfogle, 2005, p. 26). Today, human beings are the pre-eminent species and we hold the capability to cause mass extinctions just like the meteor strikes, volcanic eruptions, and ice ages of past epochs. Extinction is an unavoidable consequence of failure to adapt fast enough to a changing environment. The main difference today is that human beings can select and sustain the most useful and interesting species. Yet, such unnatural selection tends to be due to the actions of individual actors pursuing their own self-interest and not the result of strategic planning from an ecological systems perspective. Human beings can choose not to passively adapt and suffer significant tragic consequences, but a sustainable human ecology requires active adaptation in order to survive and thrive. A strategist planning for action and accountability with regard to our shared ecological futures must approach the task from a systems perspective, with emphasis on local individualized action over a multi-generational time horizon. There will necessarily be an accompanying transformation of values as we change from independent economic agents to interrelated human beings and attempt to create an intentionally healthy ecosystem, a "vibrant, fertile, self-perpetuating community of life that includes people, other life forms, soils, rocks, and waters" (Newton and Freyfogle, 2005, p. 29).

References

Banerjee, S. B. 2003. Who Sustains Whose Development? Sustainable Development and the Reinvention of Nature. *Organization Studies* 24(1), pp. 143–80.

Blaeser, J. and Whiting, G. 2012. *Environmental Sustainability Benchmark Study: Leaders Find 'Green' ROI*. Retrieved onJune 18th, 2012, from http://www.americanshipper.com/Main/Reports.aspx.

Brown, A. S. 2011. *Sustainability: ASME's Third Annual Survey Finds That Engineers Are Still Trying to Understand How Sustainability Fits into Their Workflow*. Retrieved on January 3rd, 2012, from http://memagazine.asme.org/Articles/2011/November/Sustainability.cfm.

Brown, L. R. 2006. *Plan B 2.0*. New York: W.W. Norton.

Carlson, S. 2008. Small Colleges Worry about Cost of Sustainability. *Chronicle of Higher Education* 54(19), pp. 14.

Cernea, M. M. 1985. Knowledge from Social Science for Development Policies and Projects. In*Putting People First*. Ed. M. M. Cernea. New York: Oxford University Press. pp. 1–41.

Cho, C. H., R. P. Guidry, A. M. Hageman, and D. M Patten. 2012. Do Actions Speak Louder Than Words? An Empirical Investigation of Corporate Environmental Reputation. *Accounting, Organizations and Society* 37(1), pp. 14–25.

Common, M. 1998. Economics and the Natural Environment: A Review Article. *Journal of Economic Studies* 25(1), pp. 57–73.

Daly, H. E. 1999. *Ecological Economics and the Ecology of Economics*. Cheltenham: Edward Elgar.

Diamond, J. 2005. *Collapse: How Societies Choose to Fail or Succeed*. New York: Penguin.

Dorner, D. 1996. *The Logic of Failure*. Cambridge, Mass.: Perseus.

Eccles, R. G., I. Ioannou, and G. Serafeim. 2011. *The Impact of a CorporateCulture of Sustainability on Corporate Behavior and Performance*. Working Paper 12–035. Retrieved on June 18th, 2012, from http://hbswk.hbs.edu/item/6865.htm.

Emery, F. E., and E. L. Trist. 1973. *Towards a Social Ecology*. London: Plenum.

Faber, N., R. Jorna, and J. Engelen. 2005. The Sustainability of "Sustainability": A Study into the Conceptual Foundations of the Notion of "Sustainability." *Journal of Environmental Assessment Policy and Management* 7(1), pp. 1–33.

Fishman, C. 2007. *Sustainable Growth – Interface, Inc*. Fast Company, December 18th. Retrieved on June 14th, 2011, from http://www.fastcompany.com/magazine/14/sustain.html.

Gleick, P. H., and H. S. Cooley. 2009. Energy Implications of Bottled Water. *Environmental Research Letters* 4, pp. 1–6.

Grandin, T., and C. Johnson. 2009. *Animals Make Us Human*. Boston, Mass.: Mariner.

Gustashaw, D., and R. Hall. 2008. From Lean to Green: Interface, Inc. *Association for Manufacturing Excellence Target Magazine* 24(5), pp. 6–14.

Holling, C. S. 2001. Understanding the Complexity of Economic, Ecological, and Social Systems. *Ecosystems* 4(5), pp. 390–405.

Kurtz, C. F., and D. J. Snowden. 2003. The New Dynamics of Strategy: Sense-Making in a Complex and Complicated World. *IBM Systems Journal* 42(3) pp. 462–83.

Marglin, S. 2008. Why Thinking like an Economist Can Be Harmful to the Community: Interview with Stephen Marglin. *Challenge* 51(2), pp. 13–26.

Newton, J. L., and E. T. Freyfogle. 2005. Sustainability: A Dissent. *Conservation Biology* 19(1). pp. 23–32.

Perez, C. 2009. The Double Bubble at the Turn of the Century: Technological Roots and Structural Implications. *Cambridge Journal of Economics* 33, pp. 779–805.

Pitcher, P. 1999. Artists, Craftsmen, and Technocrats. *Training and Development* July. pp. 30–33.

Polanyi, K. 1944. *The Great Transformation: The Political and Economic Origins of Our Time*. Boston, Mass.: Beacon.

Ramnarayan, S., S. Strohschneider, and H. Schaub. 1997. Trappings of Expertise and the Pursuit of Failure. *Simulation and Gaming* 28(1), pp. 28–44.

Raudsepp-Hearne, C., C. Raudsepp-Hearne, G. D. Peterson, M. Tengö, E. M. Bennett, T. Holland, K. Benessaiah, G. K. MacDonald, and L. Pfeifer. 2010. Untangling the Environmentalist's Paradox: Why Is Human Well-being Increasing as Ecosystem Services Degrade? *BioScience* 60(8), pp. 576–89.

Savall, H., and V. Zardet. 2008. *Mastering Hidden Costs and Socio-economic Performance*. Charlotte, NC: Information Age.

Speth, J. G. 2008. *The Bridge at the Edge of the World*. New Haven, Conn.: Yale University Press.

UNWCED: United Nations World Commission on Environment and Development. 1987. *Our Common Future (The Brundtland Report)*. Oxford: Oxford University Press.

Whitehead, M. 2007. *Spaces of Sustainability: Geographical Perspectives on the Sustainable Society*. London: Routledge.

27 Building resilience in East African cities: the spirit of "harambee"

Adaptive capacity: the nexus between sustainability and climate change response

Justus Kithiia and Anna Lyth

Introduction

Climate change presents one of the greatest challenges to sustainable urban futures in low income countries and is likely to significantly increase current vulnerabilities and the capacity of urban administrations to continue providing opportunities and services to their ever increasing number of inhabitants. For example, in the East African cities of Mombasa (Kenya) and Dar es Salaam (Tanzania), rapidly growing urban populations and the urbanization of poverty have caused huge intra-urban social inequalities, and present an enormous challenge for economic development and the delivery of adequate infrastructure. The impact of climate change will further compound the issues of urban poverty, and local economic development, as well as affecting local natural resources and landscapes. The degree of vulnerability faced by these cities is dependent on the degree of exposure to a range of critical climate change pressures and threats (from sea level rise through to changes in the frequency and magnitude of extreme weather events), and the cities' sensitivity to the pressure caused by the specific events that they experience. The degree of successful adaptation is linked to the degree of sensitivity of a number of subsystems within the urban environments: socio-economic, institutional, physical and ecological. The other factor will be the temporal aspect of the change; if the changes are gradual or abrupt, this will greatly impact these cities' ability to adapt.

In East African cities, the infrastructure to cope with a myriad of day to day pressures, ranging from the provision of adequate housing, clean water supply, reliable energy, transportation and opportunities for work, is already near or lacking in capacity. The impact of climate change will further complicate the challenges associated with these basic urban requirements and the provision and consumption of these in a sustainable way. For example, it will also impact on long-term patterns of material and energy consumption, water supply and demand, infrastructure design and maintenance requirements, and accessibility to and demand for public services.

Linking sustainable urban development to climate change adaptation response and the need to build resilient cities

More than 25 years after the World Commission on Environment and Development (WCED) presented the definition of sustainability or sustainable development in 1987, its meaning is still debated. Nevertheless, there are some broadly agreed principles. These include sustainable development being a process of change in which the exploitation of resources, the direction of investments, the orientation of technological development and institutional changes are made consistent with the future as well as with present needs (WCED, 1987, p. 46); the process of change being a dynamic, balanced and adaptive evolutionary one, where the stock of natural resources should not be depleted beyond its regenerative capacity. The implication of the latter is that the environmental utilisation of space has not only to be related to social and economic factors, but the carrying capacity should also be dynamic (Camagni et al., 1998). The concepts of dynamic carrying capacities and development that considers future as well as present needs are particularly pertinent to sustainable development that is viewed through the lens of climate change.

As sustainable development needs to embrace the challenges of climate change so too should climate change adaptation approaches embed sustainability principles, as each separate objective will be undermined if they fail to comprise the other. In order to demonstrate this link, the meaning of the key terminology surrounding climate change adaptation needs further explanation, specifically adaptive capacity. The sensitivity of places to climate change and vulnerability that is determined by socio-economic, ecological, physical and institutional contexts has already been mentioned. Adaptive capacity has been defined as the ability of countries, communities, households and individuals to adjust in order to reduce vulnerability to climate change, cope with and recover from its consequences (Tyndall Centre for Climate Change Research, 2006), as well as the ability of systems to evolve in order to accommodate environmental hazards or policy changes and to expand the range of variability with which they can cope (Lim, 2005; Adger, 2006). The ecological literature has moved from using the term resilience to the use of adaptive capacity to refer to the ability to reconfigure or to retain the same controls and functions (Holling and Walker, 2003, p. 1) or the ability to 'bend without breaking' when disasters occur.

The rate and character of urban development will influence the adaptive capacity of a city and vice versa. For example, climate change adaptation measures can be designed to reduce vulnerabilities and risks by enhancing the adaptive capacities of communities and economies, in turn building the capacity of the urban system to cope with a myriad of other urban pressures. Indeed, one of the core climate change adaptation options of promoting the building of community and institutional resilience to a range of pressures is also an overarching goal in sustainable development, since more resilient communities tend to have a higher adaptive capacity (Dale et al., 2001; Spittlehouse and Stewart, 2003). Quintessentially, sustainable development serves to increase adaptive capacity thus creating resilient communities, environments and economies, while resilience is also seen as a necessary precondition for sustainability (Folke *et al.*, 2004; Walker and Salt, 2006; Mäler, 2008).

In East Africa and indeed Africa as a whole, development remains far from sustainable despite many years of international summitry and local discourse about it. The sets of commitments, plans and tools remain incoherent and the concept is yet to find its way from rhetoric and policy statements into tangible reality in everyday life. The major cities in the region seem to have been locked in what Keiner *et al.* (2005) describe as environmental agenda transitions (brown, grey and green agenda issues), with time- and space-related impacts transforming the timing, speed and sequencing of these transitions. Consequently, challenges are appearing sooner, growing faster and emerging more simultaneously. Progress in improving the quality of life of the people continues to be slow, and the services that ecosystems provide humanity are critically degraded. Furthermore, municipal authorities lack financial, knowledge, skill and institutional capacities to provide most everyday urban services. However, while everyday problems rarely cause major policy changes, real actions are mainly induced by shocks or crisis, such as the climate change case, which will require urgent actions in order to avoid catastrophic outcomes. It is these response actions, including adaptation and mitigation measures, that will contribute to the immediate goal of reducing vulnerability as well as providing a wide range of complementary sustainability services.

The East African coastal cities in context

The East African coastal cities of Mombasa and Dar es Salaam are located along the coasts of Kenya and Tanzania respectively. The two cities are faced with similar climate change effects and have similar physical and structural characteristics. They occupy low-lying often flood-prone coastal locations and lack adequate protection from extreme weather events. Consequently, they are deemed to be vulnerable to the impacts of climate change, especially global sea level rise, with severe consequences for coastal infrastructure, resources and livelihoods (Kithiia, 2010). Apart from their pervasive external contexts and dependency and shared postcolonial statuses, the two cities are also home to an undifferentiated yet ethically heterogeneous social structure (Oosterveer, 2009), with Swahili being the most commonly spoken language. Furthermore, the cities are characterised by substantial and growing social-economic and environmental problems, including those associated with pressures of population growth, housing quality, air pollution, water and sanitation, among others. Similar to other coastal locations around the world, climate change is expected to exacerbate these problems, contributing to heightened risk of flooding, coastal storm damage and seashore erosion, as well as vulnerability to diseases associated with climatic conditions and land use such as malaria, typhoid fever and other vector borne diseases.

It is also important to note that despite the shared status of the two cities, post-independent Kenya and Tanzania have followed radically different sets of policy histories, levels of market penetration and property rights. Dar es Salaam, Tanzania's largest city, has been experiencing rapid urbanisation under conditions of poverty. It carries the largest proportion of Tanzania's coastal population (26 per cent), with most households deriving their incomes from in and around the city, and often linked to coastal tourism (Chaggu *et al.*, 2002). Due to lack of effective urban planning, about 75 per cent of the population resides in unplanned settlements which lack essential municipal services (Kiunsi *et al.*, 2009). However, being a port city and a major conduit of commerce between the interior regions and the rest of the world, Dar es Salaam remains a major economic powerhouse accounting for a big proportion of Tanzania's gross domestic product (GDP).

Similar to Dar es Salaam, Mombasa city has the largest seaport in East Africa and plays an important role in both the country's and regional economies. The city facilitates external trade for the landlocked countries of Uganda, Burundi, Southern Sudan, Congo and Rwanda, and therefore the sensitivity and adaptive capacity of its transport infrastructure and port facilities is equally important to the vulnerability of these other countries. Its unique physiographic features, which include fringing coral reefs, creeks, tidal flats, mangrove forests, glamorous sand beaches, and international cuisine, all contribute to make the city an important tourist destination (Republic of Kenya, 2002; Kithiia and Dowling, 2010). Most household incomes are derived from maritime trade and the fishing and tourism industries. As in Dar es Salaam, urbanisation of poverty in Mombasa is evident, with the number of urban poor reported to have increased by 38.2 per cent between 1994 and 1997 (Republic of Kenya, 2002). In addition, the urban poor tend to inhabit places of highest environmental risks, such as flood-prone areas, and lack the most basic services thus exposing themselves to catastrophic events. Therefore, the effects of climate change are likely to fall disproportionately on this category of urban residents.

Climate change impacts and the need for action

Predictions by the Intergovernmental Panel on Climate Change (IPCC) indicate that developing countries and their cities are among those regions at greatest risk to the impacts of climate change (Parry *et al.*, 2007, pp. 433–67). Due to their low lying coastal locations, Mombasa and Dar es Salaam cities are expected to be impacted by climate change in numerous ways. Despite insufficient regional and local data, by 2100 the East African region is predicted to warm by 2–4°C, while in the coastal areas rainfall is predicted to increase by 30–50 per cent. This increased rainfall coupled with its cyclical variations is likely to result in more frequent and severe flooding. Sea level is predicted to rise by 0.01–0.90 m and this is expected to further aggravate flooding with the adaptation bill rising to 10 per cent of the GDP (Hulme *et al.*, 2001; Dodman *et al.*, 2010; Kithiia, 2010). In Mombasa city, it has been predicted that an area of 4–6 sq. km (4,600 ha), or 17 per cent of the land area of Mombasa island, will be submerged in the event of a 0.3 m rise in sea level (Republic of Kenya, 2002), resulting in the destruction or damage of human settlements, cultural monuments, shipping ports and industries as well as interfering with water supply and sewage systems. Rose Sallema and Godliving Mtui (2008) attributes the 1978 submergence of Maziwa Island (an important nesting ground for endangered marine turtles located 8 km from Dar es Salaam) to sea level rise. Reported damage to coastal reefs arising from unknown coral fungal diseases and harmful algae blooms have also been attributed to the changing climate.

These two East African coastal cities are interesting places with regards to discussing adaptive capacity for long-term sustainability. First, these cities are already struggling to meet challenges posed by existing socio-economic and biophysical problems, including rapidly growing populations, the loss of coastal ecological systems such as mangroves, coastal erosion, housing and sanitation, vector borne disease and so on. Second, climate change comes with increased livelihood challenges to the residents as the resources on which they depend for a living (e.g. fisheries and tourism) and key coastal infrastructure will be impacted. These cities are important centres of commerce and industry for Kenya and Tanzania, and climate change presents another pressure on their already struggling economies. Third, although the East African region is the least urbanised in the world, it is urbanising rapidly and now has the world's shortest population doubling time with the population expected to hit 106.7 million by 2017 (UN HABITAT, 2008). The preference for humans to settle in coastal areas is a global phenomenon with more than half of the world's population living within 60 km of the coast and half of the world's industries and commerce situated within 1 km of the coast (Hardly, 2009). On this account, and based on trends to date, a great proportion of the growing population in East Africa is expected to settle in coastal urban areas. This will place greater stress on social-economic and biophysical systems, in addition to intensifying the vulnerability associated with climate change and capacity for more sustainable development. Fourth, recent events have exposed the inherent vulnerability of some of the socio-ecological, economic and biophysical systems in the two cities, implying the need for action. During our field work in Dar es Salaam we heard of how farmers in Pemba, Pangani and Rufiji areas in greater Dar es Salaam were abandoning their farming activities due to increased water salinity. In addition, accelerated marine erosion and flooding in the past is reported to have uprooted settlements and resulted in the abandonment of luxury beaches (Ibe and Awoski, 1991). In 2007 and 2008, strong winds ripped off several roofs and the ensuing floods submerged houses leading to deaths and displacements in Mombasa city (Kenya Television Network, 2007; Nation News, 2008). Given the above situation, measures geared towards building adaptive capacity are crucial for at least three main reasons: helping 'climate proof' the cities; facilitating more sustainable development; and ensuring prudent use of both financial and human resources in a region which experiences enormous economic and skill capacity deficiencies.

Opportunities and prospects for building adaptive capacity

There is an increasing body of literature on developing countries which shows that there are few differences between initiatives that can be considered good development, and climate change response initiatives which are geared towards building resilience (adaptive capacity) (see McGray *et al.*, 2007). Therefore, even if the sustainability agenda per se remains a peripheral issue, there are opportunities to address it through actions geared towards reducing the impacts of climate change, for example rethinking traditional approaches to infrastructure design and engineering to better consider risk management and future climatic conditions rather than relying on historical climatic data. Given the magnitude of the impacts of uncertain climate change explained above, this 'predict and prevent' paradigm as described by Anna Brown and Sam Kernaghan (2011) is no longer tenable. In East African cities this planning paradigm seems to have led to what Stephen Putnam (1983) describes as premature obsolescence: the infrastructure was designed in the 1960s and 1970s, constructed in the 1980s with the aim of serving until the twenty-first century, but it was already over-congested and a cause of public annoyance by the late 1990s. For instance, the storm water drains and the sewage systems in the cities of Dar es Salaam, Kampala and Mombasa were constructed in late 1950s (Dodman *et al.*, 2010; Kithiia and Dowling, 2010) and are now largely dysfunctional. Engineers and planners now have the opportunity to design additional or new infrastructure based not on forecasts that assume linearity from historical data, but on future climate risk models.

Although adaptation planning frameworks have been developed and applied internationally, they have had very limited application in urban areas in Africa, although they are now becoming more prevalent, both nationally and region-ally. Currently, under the United Nations Framework Convention on Climate Change (UNFCCC), Least Developed Countries (LCDs), such as Tanzania, are required to formulate National Adaptations Programmes of Actions (NAPAs), while developing countries prepare National Climate Change Communication reports outlining their adaptation agenda. This has started to bring the adapta-tion planning frameworks to the fore but, generally, the region is a 'late comer' in adaptation. Cities in the region can take advantage of this position and ben-efit from best practices in other parts of the developed world, 'leapfrogging' to more sustainable practices and outcomes, and circumventing some of the worst urban problems faced by those in high income countries. With the pressure of rapid urbanisation and significant backlogs in basic infrastructure provision, East African cities have the opportunity to ensure that future infrastructure designs take account of the effects of climate change. While the process of leapfrogging to sustainable futures is not new, the extent of leapfrogging for climate change adap-tation and capacity building in developing countries may still be limited by tech-nological, financial and skill capacities. Consequently, the success of leapfrogging is likely to depend on the ability to devise effective strategies to surmount these barriers and may include alternative governance models, investments in educa-tion and training, and the involvement of a range of stakeholders.

The traditional role of urban centres in East Africa as trading, commercial or administrative is gradually changing. Ambitious blueprints, such as *Vision 2025* and *Vision 2030* in Tanzania and Kenya respectively, are strategies geared towards transforming their economies to improve the quality of life of citizens (The United Republic of Tanzania, n.d.; Republic of Kenya, National Economic and Social Council of Kenya, 2007). The implementation of the provisions of these vision documents, especially those involving the development of manufacturing and high end service economies, offers a window of opportunity to build resilient and carbon free cities. For example, aiming at low carbon trajectories is likely to ensure that the envisaged future growth avoids spillover into high emission pathways, thus making it possible for the economies to benefit from low carbon financing opportunities. A recent study by the Stockholm Environmental Institute (SEI) on the economics of climate change in Kenya concludes that there are significant economic, environmental and social benefits in following a low carbon development pathway (SEI, 2009). Innovative strategies such as pro-poor low carbon energy access and carbon capture could have the twin objectives of mitigating climate change and poverty alleviation. For example, in Dar es Salaam a local resident group is working closely with the private sector to address issues of gas capture and landfill as an income generating activity.

Certain climate change response strategies can exacerbate vulnerability, resulting in unintended consequences. Take for example the adaptation actions needed to respond to food insecurity of the urban poor living in the coastal cities of Mombasa and Dar es Salaam. If the adaptation actions involve some dependency on credit schemes (access micro-credits) to undertake income generating activities, such as mariculture, aquaculture, fishing etc., in the event of coastal flooding this will not only leave the people without sources of income but they will also be in debt. Therefore, if not linked to a more comprehensive resilience building strategy for the city, many response measures may weaken instead of strengthen the capacity of the city as a whole to respond to the spectrum of challenges happening now and in the future.

Capacity of East African governance systems to respond

The municipal authorities in East African cities lack both capacity and robust frameworks to respond to the enormous implications of climate change. It is unimaginable for successful policy and response actions to emerge amidst current technological, financial, institutional and skill challenges facing both local and national governments. Authorities have limited resources to invest in climate change response initiatives, such as those requiring huge investments in protective infrastructure. For example, the cost of protecting the 100 km coastline of Dar es Salaam by building a sea wall has been estimated to be US$270 billion (Kithiia, 2011, p. 19), while associated costs for coastal flooding arising from sea level rise in and around Mombasa are estimated to be US$7–58 million per year in 2030 increasing to US$31–313 million per year in 2050 (SEI, 2009). This is beyond the affordability of local and national economies in these countries. The lack of financial capability is also an impediment for authorities to offer protection to slum dwellers, yet the quality of housing and overall infrastructure is an important determinant of people's vulnerability to flooding, storms and extreme heat (Kithiia, 2010).

Notwithstanding the above shortcomings, urban residents and businesses continue to exhibit exceptional resilience in adopting survival strategies and transforming every opportunity into positive action. It may therefore be useful to view response actions along a continuum from discrete adaptation measures undertaken by various individuals geared towards building adaptive capacity to highly visible, large-scale formal public works projects undertaken by the government and/or external quasi-governmental agencies (the United Nations (UN), World Bank, etc.). At the same time, these sets of adaptation actions are stimulated by policy influences and experiences originating from many sectors. This is where municipal authorities as regulators of local development come in; that is, their regulatory mandates, including powers to control development can be leveraged to facilitate integrated planning that looks at the full set of required actions. The authorities then take the leading role in facilitating climate change responsive planning. According to Harriet Bulkeley *et al.*, (2009), provided climate change is considered as an additional source of stress, response action can take place within the overall municipal development planning framework and be implemented using existing institutions and structures.

In the case of East Africa, treating climate change within the purview of municipal planning systems can help tailor the existing resources to value adding sustainable development, but it is an undertaking that requires leadership from municipal authorities. The authorities can facilitate the understanding and identification of various citywide programmes/projects or policies and the determination of areas that may be candidates for effective response. This is especially important for sectors where planning and implementation cycles are long, involve heavy financial investments and plans that are difficult to adjust once in place. A key consideration in formulating integrated plans, however, is the involvement of stakeholders and ensuring that participation and collaborative roll-out runs across sectors, institutions, agency, sections and disciplines.

Stakeholder involvement and the spirit of 'harambee'

The IPCC and literature on vulnerability to climate change have emphasized the importance of stakeholder involvement in planning and implementation processes (Burton *et al.*, 2002; IPCC, 2007). An important characteristic of well engaged stakeholders would be their ability to function as enablers that avoid static bureaucratic conceptions of administrative scale and sector, to indicate the importance of various players acting across boundaries to build local adaptive capacities or coping mechanisms. Similarly, as Charles Eyong and I. I. Foy (2006) point out, if sustainable development is viewed as a planned cultural, economic, social, environmental and political change for the better, then clearly this will require cooperation at all levels by all the stakeholders in order to achieve the well-being of the masses, by the masses and for the masses. Furthermore, both adaptive capacity and sustainability are societal goods and so a range of social actors should be involved in the pursuit of these. Adaptive capacity has the twin advantage of providing legitimacy to various interventions as well as helping to utilise local innovativeness. It is this transmission of ideas and local innovations from bottom-up that will permit the flexibility necessary to build adaptive capacity and to help communities to define sustainability for their local perspective.

In East Africa, the spirit of facilitative collaboration in the national context, whereby the state is able to forge effective partnerships with citizens, has been in existence for a long time, albeit with various degrees of success. In Kenya, immediately after independence from Britain in 1963, stakeholder participation was strongly encouraged by the state and incorporated into national movements, strategies and development known as *harambee* (a Swahili slogan which means 'let's pull together'), which worked as a catalyst for the development of the countryside (Schafer, 2005; Kithiia and Lyth, 2011). In Tanzania, the founding president, Mwalimu Julius Nyerere, was emphatic on the need to value people's culture and to include them in local decision making (Lipnack and Stamps, 1986).

When governing authorities fail to involve people, they risk facing hurdles in policy implementation. This was evident during our recent research in Mombasa. A coast fishermen's umbrella organisation rejected a new fisheries policy, stating that the document did not address vital issues affecting them. They viewed the policy with skepticism, describing it as elitist and threatening to draw a parallel one since the government had failed to involve them. This is not an uncommon story but it reminds us that certain climate change and/ or sustainability measures are likely to face resistance from politicians, private developers, community members and other interested parties if they are not genuinely engaged. Therefore, the development of a strong local opinion based on common stakeholder understandings via their participation in the development of visions, planning and management objectives can help the effective opposition of inappropriate development, mobilise for policy change or even enact behavioural changes.

There are many examples of local resident groups who are involved in discrete mutually beneficial measures as well as large organisations undertaking projects geared towards building adaptive capacity in Mombasa and Dar es Salaam. The relationships resulting from these collective actions are not only primary sources of residents' own risk management and vulnerability reduction, but are also assets which can be used to improve urban socio-economic and environmental conditions. For example, in one of the suburbs in Mombasa, the degradation of mangrove forests continued unabated despite the presence of government forest guards. According to local residents, forest guards were unable to prevent logging as they were not only few in number, but they were also compromised and received bribes from private loggers.

However, when a local resident group was formed to protect this resource, the situation changed as group members took turns to keep a 24-hour vigil. This curtailed opportunities to free ride and the forest is gaining its integrity, and fish species which had disappeared are beginning to reappear. Among other initiatives, the group has set out to educate other residents on the importance of preserving this key ecosystem. It was interesting to learn that this particular group has also shattered the long-held myth that mangroves can only grow naturally. The group has established nurseries of various mangrove species which are growing very well, to the amazement of the local mangrove experts. In addition, some group members who were initially jobless became engaged and are no longer seeking employment, as they can now derive their livelihoods from a silvo fisheries project which they started. In Dar es Salaam, a turtle conservation group, operating around the Kigamboni area, has succeeded in preventing the destruction of turtles' nesting sites. Prior to the establishment of the group, it was rare for marine turtle nests to survive exploitation, which endangered some marine turtles including Olive Ridley, Green and Hawksbill turtles (Kithiia, 2010).

The Lafarge Eco-Systems programme in Mombasa is a good example of how, through corporate social response, private businesses can contribute to resilience building and long-term sustainability. The programme has rehabilitated 220 ha of quarry mines, turning the desolate wasteland north of Mombasa into an 'urban wilderness'. As we have outlined in our paper on the Larfage Eco-systems case study (Kithiia, and Lyth, 2011), the provision of urban greenspaces and landscapes is a viable climate change response measure capable of yielding multiple benefits for both climate change mitigation and adaptation.

Through self-organization to take charge of their local resources, the above local actors continue to provide a platform for social learning, develop local ecological knowledge, and create and reshape management practices, rules and organisational structure (Olsson and Folke, 2004), all of which are necessary in responding to environmental feedback. In other words, the groups have enacted behavioural changes that are consistent with sustainable resource use and management. And in the face of climate change, which is characterised by uncertainty and a plurality of legitimate perspectives and risks, the opportunity to catalyse and harness synergies found in such groups offers a valuable resource for the enhancement of adaptive governance approaches in cities in low income countries.

Undeniably, there are instances when local groups (collective endeavours) do not achieve the desired outcomes. Our research showed that clientelism, rent seeking, and conflicts had developed among some of the coastal resource-users in Mombasa and Dar es Salaam. Indeed, some critics have argued that claims of success for bottom-up initiatives contain an over-romanticised view of local residents, as it ignores the presence of tensions in community boundaries, intra-community and intra-households relationship and in representation (Oosterveer, 2009). However, while local residents may reflect power differences based on social hierarchy, ethnicity, gender, and political affiliation etc., they also exhibit relationships of trust, cooperation, altruism and reciprocity. These relationships can reinforce normative behaviour and facilitate collective actions for the benefit of the environment, economic pursuits, and social well-being. Besides, the unintended outcomes could provide opportunities for differences to be openly debated, compromises negotiated and trade-offs understood.

Conclusion

The discussion in this chapter has reiterated the fact that climate change sensitivities are always related to socio-economic and biophysical sensitivities that exist at various levels. In view of this fact, at the urban scale, it is important for climate change to be understood within the context of potential constraints to the well-being of the present and future generations. Consequently, actions geared towards adaptive capacity should be planned and implemented as wider processes of sustainable urban development. This way, climate change becomes not just another problem to be solved, but an opportunity for urban communities to respond to changes to their livelihood and conditions. At the same time, stakeholder engagement in building adaptive capacity in the face of climate change will serve to provide legitimacy to various interventions and help to utilise local innovativeness. Furthermore, building adaptive capacity for long-term sustainability will require measures that fall outside the neo-liberal planning paradigm of economic efficiency and rationalisation or 'conservation at all costs' to embrace integrated municipal planning frameworks and collaborative multi-stakeholder approaches.

For East African coastal cities, the technological and financial knowledge, and skill constraints combined with operational weaknesses, such as the absence of proactive initiatives in identifying and addressing problems, and the lack of analytical capacity to advocate for requisite changes among key decision makers, constitute serious impediments to climate change response actions. However, it is also clear that in practice in developing countries, there are few differences between initiatives that can be considered good development and adaptation initiatives. This presents opportunities to build capacity by addressing other developmental problems, such as housing, infrastructure, energy, public health education and other poverty reduction initiatives, as well as forging partnerships with local residents in the spirit of facilitative collaboration. Furthermore, decision makers can take advantage of the topical nature and elevated status of climate change to incorporate vulnerability reducing measures within the overall sustainable municipal development.

References

Brown, A., and S. Kernaghan. 2011. Beyond Climate Proofing: Taking an Integrated Approach to Building Climate Resilience in Asian Cities. *Urbanization and Global Environmental Change Viewpoints* 6, pp 4–7. Retrieved on August 17th, 2012, from http://www.ugec.org/docs/ViewpointsVI%20Nov2011.pdf.

Bulkeley, H., H. Schroeder, K. Janda, J. Z. Zhao, A. Armstrong, Y. S. Chu, and S. Ghosh. 2009. *Cities and Climate Change: The Role of Institutions, Governance and Urban Planning: A Report prepared for the World Bank Symposium on Climate Change.* Washington, DC: World Bank.

Burton, I., S. Huq, B. Lim, O. Pilifosova, and L. E. Schipper. 2002. From Impact Assessment to Adaptation Priorities: The Shaping of Adaptation Policy. *Climate Policy* 2, pp. 145–59.

Camagni, R., R. Capello, P. Nijkamp. 1998. Towards Sustainable City Policy: An Economy-environment Technology Nexus. *Ecological economics* 24(1), pp. 103–18.

Chaggu, E., D. Mashauri, J. van Buuren, W. Sanders, and G. Lettinga. 2002. Excreta Disposal in Dar es Salaam. *Environmental Management* 30(5), pp. 609–20.

Dale, V. H., L. A. Joyce, S. McNulty, and R. P. Neilson. 2001. Climate Change and Forest Disturbances. *Biosciences* pp.723–24.

Dodman, D., E. Kibona, and L. Kiluma. 2010. *Tomorrow is Too Late: Responding to Social and Climate Vulnerability in Dar es Salaam, Tanzania: Case Study Prepared for Cities and Climate Change: Global Reports on Human Settlements 2011*. Retrieved on August 15th, 2012, from http://www.unhabitat.org/downloads/docs/GRHS2011/GRHS2011CaseStudyChapter06DaresSalaam.pdf.

Eyong, C.T, and I. I. Foy. 2006. Towards Alternative Strategies for Sustainable Development in Africa. *International Journal of Sustainable Development Planning* 1(2), pp. 133–56.

IPCC. 2007. *Climate Change: Synthesis Report. Contribution of Working Groups I, II and III to the Fourth Assessment*. Eds. R. K. Pachauri, and A. Reisinger. Geneva, Switzerland: IPCC.

Folke, C., S. R. Carpenter, B. H. Walker, M. Scheffer, T. Elmqvist, L. H. Gunderson, C. S. Holling. 2004. Regime Shifts, Resilience and Biodiversity in Ecosystem Management. *Annual Review of Ecology, Evolution and Systematics* 35, pp. 557–81.

Hardly, D. 2009. Land Use and Coastal Zone. *Land Use Policy* 26, pp. 198–203

Holling, C. S., and B. H. Walker. 2003. Resilience Defined. *Internet Encyclopedia of Ecological Economics*. Retrieved on August 27th, 2012, from www.ecoeco.org/pdf/resilience.pdf .

Hulme, M., R. Doherty, T. Ngara, M. New, and D. Lister. 2001. African Climate Change: 1900–2100. *Climate Research* 17, pp.145–68.

Ibe, A. C., and L. F. Awoski. 1991. Sea-level Rise Impact in African Coastal Zones. *A Change of Weather: African Perspective on Climate Change* pp. 105–12.

Keiner, M., M. Koll-Schretzenmayr, and W. A. Schmidt, eds. 2005. *Managing Urban Future: Sustainability and Urban Growth in Developing Countries*. Hampshire, UK: Ashgate Publishing Company.

Kenya Television Network (KTN). 2007. News, May.

Kithiia, J. 2010. Old Notion-new Relevance: Setting the Stage for the use of Social Capital Resource in Adapting East African Coastal Cities to Climate Change. *International Journal of Urban sustainable Development* 1, pp. 17–32.

Kithiia, J. 2011. Climate Change Adaptation and Mitigation in East African Coastal Cities: Need, Barriers and Opportunities. In *Megacities and the Coast: Transformation for Resilience*. Ed. M. Pelling. Geesthacht, Germany: LOICZ, pp. 18–23. Retrieved on August 15th, 2012, from http://www.ferrybox.eu/imperia/md/content/loicz/hotspots/urbanization/Megacities_and_the_coast_report_4_6_2011.pdf.

Kithiia, J., and R. Dowling. 2010. An Integrated City-level Planning Process to Address the Impacts of Climate Change in Kenya: The Case of Mombasa. *Cities* 27, pp. 466–75.

Kithiia, J., and A. Lyth.2011. Urban Wildscapes and Greenscapes in Mombasa and their Potential Contribution to Climate Change Adaptation and Mitigation. *Environment and Urbanization* 23(1), pp. 251–65.

Kiunsi, R. B., J. Lupala, F. Lerise, M. Meshack, B. Malele, A. Namangaya, and E. Mchome. 2009. Building Disaster-Resilient Communities: Dar es Salaam, Tanzania. In *Disaster Risk Reduction: Cases from Urban Africa*. Eds. M. Pelling, and B. Wisner. London: Earthscan.

Lim, B., ed. 2005. *Adaptation Policy and Frameworks for Climate Change: Developing Strategies, Policies and Measures.* Cambridge: Cambridge University Press.

Lipnack, J., and J. Stamps. 1986. The Networking Book; People Connecting with People. In *Local Actors in Development: A Case of Mwanga District.*Ed. C. K. Omari. New York: Routledge and Kegan Paul.

Mäler, K.-G. 2008. Sustainable Development and Resilience in Ecosystems. *Environmental and Resource Economics* 39(1), pp. 17–24.

McGray, H., A. Hammill, and R. Bradley. 2007. *Weathering the Storm: Options for Framing Adaptation and Development.* Washington, DC: World Resource Institute.

Nation News. 2008. *Man Dies as Heavy Rain Pounds Coast.* Nationmedia. June. Retrieved on June 17th, 2008, from http://allafrica.com/stories/2008006170166.html.

Olsson, P. and C. Folke, 2004. Adaptive comanagement for building resilience in social-ecological systems. *Environmental management,* 34(1), pp. 75–90.

Oosterveer, P. 2009. Urban environmental services and the state in East Africa; between neo-developmental and network governance approaches. *Geoforum.* 40, pp. 1061–1068.

Parry, M. L., O. F. Canciani, J. P. van der Linden, and C. E. Hanson, eds. 2007. *Climate Change 2007: Impacts, Adaptation and Vulnerability. Contribution of Working Group II to the Fourth Assessment Report of the Intergovernmental Panel on Climate Change. Assessment Report of the International Panel on Climate Change.* Cambridge: Cambridge University Press.

Putnam, S. H. 1983. *Integrated Urban Models: Policy Analysis of Transportation and Land Use.* London: Pion Ltd.

Republic of Kenya, Ministry of Planning and National Development. 2002. *Mombasa District Development Plan.* Nairobi: Republic of Kenya.

Republic of Kenya, National Economic and Social Council of Kenya. 2007. *Kenya Vision 2030.* Nairobi: Republic of Kenya.

Sallema, R. E., and Mtui, G Y. S. 2008. Adaptation Technologies and Legal Instruments to Address Climate Change Impacts to Coastal and Marine Resources in Tanzania. *African Journal of Science and Technology* 2(9), pp. 239–48.

Schafer, M. J. 2005. Family Contributions to Self-help Schooling in Malawi and Kenya. *Rural Sociology* 70, pp. 70–93.

SEI (Stockholm Environmental Institute). 2009. *Project Report. Economics of Climate Change in Kenya. Final Report Submitted in Advance of COP15.* Stockholm: Stockholm Environmental Institute.

Spittlehouse, D. L., and R. B. Stewart. 2003. Adaptation to Climate Change in Forest Management. *BC Journal of Ecosystems and Management* 4, pp. 1–11.

The United Republic of Tanzania. *Tanzania Development Vision 2025.* Dar es Salaam, Planning Commission.

Tyndall Centre for Climate Change Research. 2006. *Research Strategy 2006–2009.* Norwich, England: University of East Anglia.

UN HABITAT. 2008. *The State of African Cities.* Nairobi: United Nations Human Settlements Programme.

Walker, B. H., and D. Salt. 2006. *Resilience Thinking Sustainable Ecosystems and People in a Changing World.* Washington, DC: Islands Press.

WCED (World Commission on Environment and Development). 1987. *Our Common Future.* London: Oxford University Press.

28 The impact of development on biodiversity in Singapore

Kwek Yan Chong, Marcus Aik Hwee Chua, Mei Lin Neo, Daniel Jia Jun Ng, Siti Maryam Yaakub, Tai Chong Toh, Alison Kim Shan Wee, and Ding Li Yong

Singapore is home to diverse groups of flora and fauna found in a variety of marine and terrestrial habitats. In the last five decades, since the 1970s, these habitats have undergone considerable changes due to Singapore's industrial, commercial, and residential development.

Singapore's coral reefs and seagrass habitats

Coral reefs in Singapore consist in both fringing and patch reefs (Chuang, 1977) and are primarily found in the Southern Islands (Tan et al., 2010). Currently, coral reefs in Singapore stand at less than 50 square kilometers (UNEP/COBSEA, 2010) with 255 species of hard corals (Huang et al., 2009) and 111 species of marine fish (Chou et al., 2004). Singapore has lost approximately 60–65 percent of coral reefs (Chua et al., 2003) due to extensive coastal developments and reclamation projects which have increased the marine turbidity. Increased turbidity has reduced light penetration to the point where remaining reefs are found in waters no more than 6 meters deep (Chou et al., 1997).

With large-scale reclamation and coastal development in Singapore, visibility in coastal waters is reported to have decreased from 10 meters in the 1960s to 2 meters in the 1990s (Chua and Chou, 1992), with sedimentation rates of up to 44.64 g/cm^2 per day (Low and Chou, 1994). These impacts have resulted in a decline of the coral reefs' biodiversity (Chou et al., 2004; Chou, 2008). Sediment pollution continues to be a contributing factor to the decline of coral reefs and the steady loss of remaining marine biodiversity (Dikou and van Woesik, 2006).

Seagrasses were previously common on reef-flats and in the intertidal zones of the southeastern coasts around Tanah Merah and Changi (den Hartog, 1970) and at Kranji and the West Johor Straits (Chuang, 1961). Today, they are widely dispersed in the coastal marine environments of Singapore and offshore islands (McKenzie et al., 2007), with an estimated cover of less than 1 square kilometer (UNEP/COBSEA, 2010). Currently, they occur in isolated patches in the marine environments surrounding offshore islands, such as Pulau Ubin and Semakau, as well as in patch reefs such as Cyrene Reef.

A total of 12 species of seagrasses are present in Singapore waters, the most recent discovery being the deepwater seagrass *Halophila decipiens* (McKenzie et al.,

2007). Globally, one species, *Halophila beccarii*, has been listed as vulnerable on the IUCN Red List (Short *et al.*, 2011), but seagrasses in Singapore are threatened at the local scale, as they are subject to the same stressors as the coral reef in the same environments. Seagrass communities support a large group of animals, particularly the Dugongs, *Dugong dugon* (Heinsohn *et al.*, 1977). Dugongs feed preferentially on the spoon seagrass, *Halophila ovalis*, and feeding trails have been sighted at Chek Jawa.

The impact of local scale losses in marine habitats cannot be underestimated, as they contribute to the fragmentation of the marine environment. Such fragmentation has far-reaching implications for marine habitats in neighboring areas. Some dugong populations, for example, have been shown to be highly migratory, visiting several seagrass meadows along their migratory route to feed and shelter (Sheppard *et al.*, 2006). Destruction of one or two of these feeding grounds can be devastating to migratory dugongs, as they have to travel further between feedings. Likewise, connectivity is also important for coral reef organisms, as the recruitment of juvenile corals and fish is partly dependent on inputs from nearby reefs (Cowen *et al.*, 2000; Levin, 2006).

Mangroves

Currently, patches of mangroves can be found in small pockets along the northern mainland coast (e.g. Sungei Buloh Wetland Reserve and Lim Chu Kang), as well as on offshore islands (e.g. Pulau Ubin and Pulau Tekong) (Chou *et al.*, 1997). The largest areas are on Pulau Ubin, which is perhaps the most significant site for mangrove birds. On the mainland, a stretch of mangroves along the northwest coast of Singapore was gazetted as a Wetland Reserve in 2002 (Chan *et al.*, 2011). This area, named Sungei Buloh Wetland Reserve (SBWR), and its neighboring mangrove patches at Kranji and Lim Chu Kang form a significant tract of mangroves. At the time of writing, only the mangroves within the SBWR boundary are protected by law (Bird *et al.* 2004), although there are plans to include the adjacent mangrove areas in Kranji in the new SBWR master plan in 2013.

Singapore harbours a diverse assemblage of thirty-two mangrove plant species, two of which are included in the IUCN Red List: *Avicennia rumphiana* and *Bruguiera hainesii* (Polidoro *et al.*, 2010). Mangrove-associated mudflats host important wintering populations of migratory waders but have seen continuous declines since the mid-1990s. With the destruction of several key sites, many formerly common waders, such as the rufous-necked stint, *Calidris ruficollis*, are now uncommon or rare (Lim, 2009). Mangrove specialist birds have experienced less avian extinctions than inland forest birds because of the species-poor climax bird community; however, a number of species are now extinct on Singapore's mainland and only occur in small populations on the satellite islands, such as the mangrove blue-flycatcher, *Cyornis rufigastra*, on Pulau Tekong (Lim, 2009).

The fate of mangrove habitats outside SBWR is uncertain at the moment, with possible losses occurring through scheduled damming and land reclamation projects. There are heartening efforts to restore mangroves, such as the replanting exercise at Pulau Semakau after reclamation destroyed part of the original mangroves of the area, and the incorporation of mangroves into existing recreation parks, such as Pasir Ris Park, which has a mangrove boardwalk. Perhaps the mangrove species that best represents conservation efforts would be *Bruguiera hainesii*, which is currently listed as critically endangered under the IUCN Red List. This rare species was first reported in Singapore in 2003 (Sheue *et al.*, 2005), with two individuals recorded at Sungei Loyang (mainland) and Sungei Jelutong (Pulau Ubin). *Bruguiera hainesii* was planted in SBWR in conjunction with its tenth anniversary celebration, signifying Singapore's commitment to mangrove conservation.

Terrestrial flora and fauna

Singapore's primary lowland rain forest was almost completely lost during British colony rule (Corlett, 1992). At the time of writing, just over half of Singapore's land area is under green cover (Tee *et al.*, 2009) – a fact lauded by the authorities as an accomplishment given the highly urbanized landscape. Much of this green cover, however, consists of managed vegetation, followed by open scrub and woodland on waste ground and reclaimed land, which are mostly dominated by exotic species (Tan *et al.*, 2010). As of 2011, only 5 percent of the land area consists of native-dominated, closed-canopy forest (Yee *et al.*, 2011), the bulk of which is protected in the Bukit Timah Nature Reserve (BTNR) and the Central Catchment Nature Reserves (CCNR), including Singapore's tiny remaining fragments of primary forests.

The near complete loss of the original forest cover has brought with it the loss of many species (Brook *et al.*, 2003). The extant forest bird community, for example, is now relatively depauperate with the extinction of entire families, such as the trogons, *Trogonidae*, and a large proportion of other families such as the woodpeckers, *Picidae* (Castelletta *et al.*, 2000; Castelletta *et al.*, 2005). Some 637 of 2,150 plant species have been presumed locally extinct from the lack of recent sightings or collections, including two species endemic to Singapore (Chong *et al.*, 2009). The loss of endemic species is significant and has global implications, because these species are restricted in their distribution outside Singapore; their loss therefore contributes to the global decline in species diversity. Singapore also supports a surprisingly large number of butterfly species: 415, or over one-third of the entire butterfly diversity of the Malay Peninsula (Corbet and Pendlebury, 1992). There are 143 locally extinct species of butterflies (Koh *et al.*, 2004a), most of which are forest-dwelling species whose extinctions can be attributed to the destruction of native forests.

An estimated 71 percent of the original mammal species in Singapore are considered locally extinct (Brook *et al.*, 2003). The 59 species of mammals that still exist (Chua and Lim, 2011) are small- to medium-sized and are mostly able to live in secondary and cultivated vegetation (Corlett, 1992). Of these, a large proportion is listed in the national Red List as threatened, and many are nationally critically endangered (Lim *et al.*, 2008) such as the greater mousedeer, *Tragulus napu*. Other critically endangered species, such as the Malayan porcupine, *Hyxtrix brachyura*, on Pulau Tekong, do not receive the same level of legal protection as species in nature reserves (Lim *et al.*, 2008).

Of the 25 native amphibian species found locally, only one species – the endemic Singapore black caecilian, *Ichthyophis singaporensis*, has not been recorded since the type specimen was obtained in the eighteenth century; it is believed to be extinct. A few species, such as the Saint Andrew's cross toadlet, *Pelophryne signata*, blue-legged tree frog, *Rhacophorus cyanopunctatus*, and the thorny tree frog, *Theloderma horridum*, are critically endangered and restricted to small fragments of suitable habitat within the nature reserves (Lim and Leong, 2008).

It remains to be seen how these extinctions may affect local mutualisms such as dispersal and pollination. For example, the close relationships between butterflies and their host plants – the primary food source for their larvae – implies that the distribution and persistence of many species are limited by their corresponding host plants; more importantly, local extinctions of these plants may result in the co-extinction of their butterfly dependants (Koh *et al.*, 2004b).

Forest reserves

Nature conservation had an early start during the colonial period in the 1840s (Logan, 1848). Bukit Timah and Central Catchment Area were among the first areas to receive protection under the Nature Reserves Ordinance in 1951 (Tan *et al.*, 2010). Nature reserves receive the highest level of legal protection in Singapore under the Parks & Trees Act of 2005. The central forest reserves, BTNR and CCNR, are the largest and most important conservation sites for the remaining plants and animals, the majority of which are confined to primary and tall secondary forests.

Despite the relatively high level of legal protection, biodiversity in the reserves still faces several threats. The forest reserves are small and have a combined primary forest area of only 279 hectares (Turner *et al.*, 1996; Corlett, 1997). Fragmentation of the forest habitat is further aggravated by the six-lane Bukit Timah Expressway (BKE), which bisects the two reserves, disrupting movement and gene flow between the forest patches. Mammals such as the globally endangered Sunda pangol, *Manis javanica*, that try to make the crossing often end up as road kill. Fragmentation of the reserves also reduces the actual extent of habitat available, allows urban and open country species to invade, and increases access to human users including poachers. High visitorship and shared use of the reserves for recreation have caused trail degradation in BTNR and may result in human disturbance of wildlife (Chatterjea, 2007). To mitigate habitat fragmentation and promote connectivity, the National Parks Board (NParks) has proposed the Eco-link, a planted wildlife corridor that will be constructed across the BKE to connect the two forest reserves by 2013 (Goh, 2010). Since the majority of native species are confined to the central forest reserves, threats to biodiversity need to be taken seriously, as extirpation from the forest reserves also means national extinction for many of the species (Corlett, 1995). In the face of encroaching urban sprawl on the already small reserves, some positive steps have been taken to reduce the combined threat of small size and the increasing edge effect, which increases isolation and heightens the risk of extinction (MacKinnon, 1997). The size of BTNR has since increased from 81 hectares in 1995 to 164 hectares in 2011, and an additional 63 hectares of land surrounding the reserves was demarcated as buffer areas where recreational activities can take place (NParks, 2009a).

Urbanization and the invasion of exotics

Species loss through local extinction is not the only alteration to Singapore's biota; the introduction of exotic species from far-flung areas is the next biggest threat. After deforestation, a wave of agricultural introductions followed. Those exotics that could survive and reproduce became integrated into the landscape. Economic development and political independence brought a second wave of introduced species. With the early establishment of a botanical garden in the nineteenth century, a significant number of horticultural species were introduced during Singapore's colonial days. With a post-independence political vision of a "Garden City," landscaping efforts included the importation of a massive number of ornamentals from places such as South America and Africa (Corlett, 1988).

For animals, the pet trade remains a continual source of alien species, some of which are now locally established, like the white-crested laughing-thrush, *Garrulax leucolophus*, and spreading throughout the island (Lim *et al.*, 2003; Lim, 2009). The deliberate release of the American bullfrog, *Lithobates catesbeiana*, for religious practices has resulted in its presence throughout Singapore, even in the nature reserves. Its impact on native biodiversity has not been investigated but is of important concern, as it is a known vector of the chytrid fungus, *Batrachochytrium dendrobatidis*, responsible for the widespread decline in amphibians worldwide. The direct impact of exotic species on native biodiversity warrants urgent conservation attention. Established birds may be able to out compete native birds, thus driving further extinctions (Lim *et al.*, 2003; Yap and Sodhi, 2004). Naturalized plant species are not locally known to have directly resulted in the decline of native species in the nature reserves, but this may not hold true in the future if exotic plants continue to be introduced (Lok, Chong, Tan, and Tan, 2010).

Increased urbanization has carved out habitat niches for some open country mangrove, and introduced species which are able to take advantage of extensive parkland and park connectors island wide (Ward 1968; Sodhi *et al.*, 1999), and even of highly built-up areas (Lim *et al.*, 2003). Extensive land reclamation, for example, has also created large areas of coastal scrub, and this development has been linked to the spread of the tawny coster, *Acraea violae*, previously unknown in Singapore. Commensals, such as the Asian toad, *Duttaphrynus melanostictus*, and the Common tree frog, *Polypedates leucomystax*, have benefited from the extensive forest loss and are very common in open country areas throughout the island, but are relatively rare in forests. The black-naped oriole, *Oriolus chinensis*, formerly a relatively rare species, is now common (Ward, 1968; Lim, 2009) and has clearly benefited from the widespread planting of ornamental plants which provide nesting and feeding resources (Sodhi *et al.*, 1999). The widespread creation of manicured parkland, some of which contains patches of secondary forest (e.g. various town parks), has benefited a large number of butterflies, including even locally threatened species such as the common birdwing, *Troides helena*, especially where host plants are deliberately planted (Koh and Sodhi 2004; Khew, 2008). The cultivation of host plant species can potentially mitigate further butterfly extinctions, and will be key to the future conservation of butterfly communities (Koh and Sodhi, 2004). Human-animal conflicts are on the rise because of rapid urban development, with altercations between the long-tailed macaques, *Macaca fascicularis*, and common palm civets, *Paradoxurus hermaphroditus*, in residential areas, causing the animals to be trapped and sometimes euthanized (Ang, 2009). Public education and outreach efforts are being implemented to help resolve human-animal conflicts (Ang, 2010).

One of the main challenges is the general paucity of knowledge and research about the basic ecology of species in Singapore when relevant conservation and management decisions are made. This situation has improved in recent years. For example, faunal surveys in BTNR and CCNR have produced a new record and rediscovered a bat species thought to have been extinct in Singapore (Leong and Lim, 2009), and several "locally extinct" plant species have been rediscovered with the increased exploration of lesser-known areas such as a patch of freshwater swamp forest in the central catchment reserves (Ang, Lok and Tan, 2010; Ang, Lok, Yeo, Tan and Tan, 2010; Lok, Ang, Chong and Tan, 2010).

Biodiversity conservation

Currently, biodiversity conservation and sustainable development are administered by two statutory boards belonging to two parent ministries. In January 2008, the Inter-Ministerial Committee on Sustainable Development (IMCSD) was formed to develop a national strategy for Singapore's sustainable development needs. In the IMCSD's Sustainable Development Blueprint (MEWR and MND, 2009), one key recommendation was to implement a National Biodiversity Strategy and Action Plan (NBSAP).

The NBSAP now outlines Singapore's approach to nature conservation and biodiversity. It contains plans and strategies that can be applied to nationwide conservation efforts, while keeping track of ongoing programs and identifying major gaps in knowledge (Chan *et al.*, 2011). Among the key strategies of the NBSAP are to safeguard biodiversity by implementing species conservation plans, to incorporate biodiversity conservation considerations into administrative processes, and to improve knowledge on biodiversity by facilitating research, engaging in regular monitoring, and maintaining a species list and conservation status (NParks, 2009b). While some of these strategies have been met, such as the maintenance of a Red Data List (Davison *et al.*, 2008), the implementation of other strategies has not been as successful: for example, mandatory environmental impact assessment prior to development has not yet been legislated (Lye, 2008). The interagency approach to developing a roadmap for sustainable development and the adoption of strategies to approach biodiversity conservation from a variety of angles are big steps in the right direction and bode well for conservation in Singapore.

Citizen action and nongovernmental organizations

Civic groups and nongovernmental organizations (NGOs) have also proved to be a force in conservation in Singapore. Nature Society (Singapore) (NSS), Singapore's oldest environmental NGO, has been an active local advocate for conservation. It has its roots in the Singapore branch of the Malayan Nature Society, founded in 1954. This branch split from its parent body in 1991 and has operated under its present name since (Lum, 2011).

The role of the society as a lobby group and watchdog came into prominence in the 1980s, when it lobbied for the retention of Sungei Buloh as a nature area, a move that would later see the area established as a nature park in 1989 and a reserve in 2002. Over the years, the society has successfully pushed for several local conservation milestones, such as the government's initiation of the Singapore Green Plan: a master plan for managing nature in Singapore that followed the society's *Master Plan for the Conservation of Nature in Singapore* (Briffett, 1990). The society's members include many professional biologists, some of whom took the lead in the conservation of a plot of nature reserve land in 1992 after the society conducted and presented its own environmental impact assessment (EIA) on the proposal of a golf course to be developed over the land. NSS also published the first edition of the *Singapore Red Data Book* in 1994 (Ng, 1994), highlighting threatened species in Singapore that need conservation action.

Other nature groups and NGOs have also contributed to biodiversity conservation, especially in raising public awareness and engaging the public in citizen conservation and volunteerism. One example is the International Coastal Cleanup Singapore (ICCS), an annual effort to remove and collect information on debris in coastal habitats. It is one of the largest environmental conservation programs in Singapore, with an annual participation of over 1,500 volunteers and an average collection of 60,000 pieces of litter.

Singapore's remaining coral reefs are being lost to coastal development; they continue to be assaulted by heavy sedimentation and anthropogenic activities. The intensified loss of Singapore's marine flora and fauna has alarmed many marine enthusiasts, though at the time of writing Blue Water Volunteers and Hantu Bloggers are the only two marine-related NGOs actively promoting the protection of coral reefs. Local interest groups have also provided an avenue for Singaporeans to appreciate this unique natural heritage and promote reef conservation. In 2008, NGOs and interest groups came together to celebrate the International Year of the Reef (IYOR) 2008. One of the highlights of the meetings was the *Singapore Blue Plan 2009* that was submitted on May 23rd, 2009, to Mah Bow Tan, then minister of national development, and Yaacob Ibrahim, then minister of environment and water resources (Civil Society for Integrated and Balanced Conservation of Singapore's Marine Heritage, 2009). The IYOR exemplifies the passion and appreciation of local marine enthusiasts to push forth the conservation of coral reefs in Singapore.

To prevent the loss of even more corals, various groups have initiated marine projects on coral relocation before initiating reclamation projects, putting out artificial reef units, transplanting coral, and building a coral nursery. Although these projects have shown improvements in coral rehabilitation and recruitment on the local reefs, the limited scale and continued coastal impacts have hindered progress on increasing coral reef density. The nationwide Mega Marine Survey, launched in December 2010 and funded by the NParks, the Hongkong and Shanghai Banking Corporation, and Shell, aims to conduct comprehensive surveys of Singapore's marine environment.

Conclusion

Although much of the damage to the native biodiversity has been attributed to the massive loss of primary habitat under the British administration in Singapore's early days, the country's independence after a brief merger with neighbouring Malaysia brought about a second wave of impacts. Coastal habitats were reclaimed and estuaries were dammed for reservoirs. Inland, primary habitat loss during the colonial era was followed decades later by secondary deforestation to make way for a modern economy. A common denominator underlies most of these impacts: the need for more space in a land-starved country. There is little denying that both periods of development resulted in the extinction of some species and the decline of many others. Yet there can also be no illusions that Singapore could have progressed from a third-world fishing village to a first-world metropolis without such sacrifices.

Even within biological groups, not all species are dealt the same hand by development. A handful of native species have adapted to the highly urbanized environment. A significant number of exotic species have likewise become established over the years and are increasing in number, which has generated concerns that an invasion meltdown is brewing, although as yet there is little evidence of wide-scale negative impacts on native biodiversity.

In the everyday experience of the average urban resident, what is seen and heard about is an impoverished subset of the biodiversity of Singapore, much of which is considered exotic. A fuller picture of the remnants of the original ecosystems is limited to the nature lover who frequently embarks on trips into the old-growth forest fragments or the volunteer working on dive trips and intertidal surveys.

On the administrative front, several positive changes have been made to address the concerns of an increasingly aware public and the need to balance conservation with the continued growth of a resource-scarce nation. Concerned people involved in nature and the environment, together with credible nature groups, are making their presence felt in Singapore. With increasing recognition by the government of the importance of sustainable development and the preservation of a rich ecological heritage, nature in Singapore may have some hope yet.

Acknowledgments

We are indebted to Professors Peter Ng, Richard Corlett, and Chou Loke Ming and Assistant Professors Peter Todd and Koh Lian Pin for providing helpful comments on the manuscript. We also need to thank Paul Chen, Teo Siyang, and Chung Yi Fei for their input, and Jack Appleton for inviting this submission.

Conservation groups in Singapore

Name	*Website address*
Nature Society Singapore	www.nss.org.sg
Blue Waters Volunteers	www.bluewatervolunteers.org
Hantu Bloggers	www.pulauhantu.org
Conservation International Singapore	www.conservation.org
World Wide Fund for Nature	www.wwf.sg
Wild Singapore	www.wildsingapore.com
Naked Hermit Crabs	http://nakedhermitcrabs.blogspot.com/
Team Seagrass	teamseagrass.blogspot.com
Butterfly Circle	www.butterflycircle.com
Environmental Biology Research Group	www.nus.edu.sg
Raffles Museum of Biodiversity Research	http://rmbr.nus.edu.sg
Tropical Marine Science Institute	www.tmsi.nus.edu.sg
Nanyang Technological University	www.ntu.edu.sg
DHI Water & Environment Singapore	www.dhi.com.sg
National Parks Board Singapore	www.nparks.gov.sg
Singapore Tourism Board	www.stb.com.sg
National Environmental Agency	www.nea.gov.sg
Underwater World Singapore	www.underwaterworld.com.sg/

References

Ang, Y. 2009. The Great Musang "Stakeout." *Straits Times* November 30th, 2009, B1–2.

Ang, Y. 2010. Don't Turn Tail, Get to Know Them Instead. *Straits Times* October 21st, 2010.

Ang, W. F., A. F. S. L. Lok, and H. T. W. Tan. 2010. Rediscovery in Singapore of *Pinanga Simplicifrons (Miq.) Becc. (Arecaceae)*. *Nature in Singapore*. 3, pp. 83–86.

Ang, W. F., A. F. S. L. Lok, C. K. Yeo, S. Y. Tan, and H. T. W. Tan. 2010. Rediscovery of *Dendrobium Aloifolium (Blume) Rchb.f. (Orchidaceae)* in Singapore. *Nature in Singapore* 3, pp. 321–25.

Bird, M. S., K. Chua, T. S. Fifield, and J. Lai. 2004. Evolution of the Sungei Buloh–Kranji Mangrove Coast, Singapore. *Applied Geography* 24, pp. 181–98.

Briffett, C., ed. 1990. *Master Plan for the Conservation of Nature in Singapore*. Singapore: Malayan Nature Society.

Brook, B. W., N. S. Sodhi, and P. K. L. Ng. 2003. Catastrophic Extinctions Follow Deforestation in Singapore. *Nature* 424, pp. 420–23.

Castelletta, M., N. S. Sodhi, and S. Rajathurai. 2000. Heavy Extinctions of Forest Avifauna in Singapore: Lessons for Biodiversity Conservation in Southeast Asia. *Conservation Biology* 14, pp. 1870–80.

Castelletta, M., J.-M. Thiollay, and N. S. Sodhi. 2005. The Effects of Extreme Forest Fragmentation on the Bird Community of Singapore Island. *Biological Conservation* 121, pp. 135–55.

Chan, L., L. Tan, G. W. H. Thiollay, and W. Yap. 2011. Public Policy and Strategy. In *Singapore Biodiversity: An Encyclopedia of the Natural Environment and Sustainable Development*. Eds. K. L. Ng, R. T. Corlett, and H. T. W. Tan. Singapore: Didier Millet, pp. 148–53.

Chatterjea, K. 2007. Assessment and Demarcation of Trail Degradation in a Nature Reserve, Using GIS: Case of Bukit Timah Nature Reserve. *Land Degradation and Development* 18, pp. 500–18.

Chong, K. Y., H. T. W. Tan, and R. T. Corlett. 2009. *A Checklist of the Total Vascular Plant Flora of Singapore: Native, Naturalised and Cultivated Species*. Singapore: Raffles Museum of Biodiversity Research, National University of Singapore.

Chou, L. M. 2008. Nature and Sustainability of the Marine Environment. In *Spatial Planning for a Sustainable Singapore*. Eds. T-C. Wong, B. Yuen, and C. Goldblum. New York: Springer Science and Business Media, pp. 169–82.

Chou, L. M., B. P. L. Goh, and T. J. Lam. 1997. *Environmental Protection and Biodiversity Conservation in Singapore*. Workshop on Environmental Issues and Regional Needs, July 17th–19th, 1997, Sarawak, Malaysia.

Chou, L. M., J. Y. Yu, and T. L. Loh. 2004. Impacts of Dedimentation on Soft-Bottom Benthic Communities in the Southern Islands of Singapore. *Hydrobiologia* 515, pp. 91–106.

Chua, C. Y. Y., and L. M. Chou. 1992. Coral Reef Conservation in Singapore: A Case Study for Coastal Area Management. In *Third ASEAN Science and Technology Week Conference Proceedings*. Eds. L. M. Chou, and C. R. Wilkinson (6), pp. 437–45. Singapore: Department of Zoology, National University of Singapore/National Science and Technology. Conference: Marine Science: Living Coastal Resources, held September 21st–23rd, 1992, in Singapore.

Chua, M. A. H., and K. K. P. Lim. 2011. Mammals. In *Singapore Biodiversity: An Encyclopedia of the Natural Environment and Sustainable Development*. Eds. K. L. Ng, R. T. Corlett, and H. T. W. Tan. Singapore: Didier Millet, p. 372.

Chua, S. C., J. Low, and, L. Gouw-Iwata, and K. Lee, eds. 2003. *Singapore Waters: Unveiling*. Singapore: Nature Society, Marine Conservation Group.

Chuang, S. H. 1961. *On Malayan Shores*. Singapore: Muwa Shosa.

Chuang, S. H. 1977. *Ecology of Singapore and Malayan Coral Reefs: Preliminary Classification*. Proceedings of Third International Coral Reef Symposium, Miami, Florida, pp. 55–61.

Civil Society for Integrated and Balanced Conservation of Singapore's Marine Heritage. 2009. *Singapore Blue Plan 2009*. April. Singapore: Civil Society for Integrated and Balanced Conservation of Singapore's Marine Heritage.

Corbet, A. S., and H. M. Pendlebury. 1992. *The Butterflies of the Malay Peninsula*. 4th edn. Kuala Lumpur: Malayan Nature Society.

Corlett, R. T. 1988. The Naturalized Flora of Singapore. *Journal of Biogeography* 15, pp. 657–63.

Corlett, R. T. 1992. The Ecological Transformation of Singapore, 1819–1990. *Journal of Biogeography* 19, pp. 411–20.

Corlett, R. T. 1995. The History of Bukit Timah Nature Reserve. In Rain Forest in the City: Bukit Timah Nature Reserve, Singapore. Eds. S. C. Chin, R. T. Corlett, Y. C. Wee, and S. Y. Geh. *Gardens' Bulletin, Singapore supplement* 3, pp. 7–10.

Corlett, R. T. 1997. The Vegetation in the Nature Reserves of Singapore. *Gardens' Bulletin, Singapore* 49, pp. 147–59.

Cowen, R. K., K. M. M. Lwiza, S. Sponaugle, C. B. Paris, and D. B. Olson. 2000. Connectivity of Marine Populations: Open or Closed? *Science* 287(5454), pp. 857–59.

Davison, W. H., P. K. L. Ng, and H. H. Chew, eds. 2008. *The Singapore Red Data Book: Threatened Plants and Animals of Singapore*. Singapore: Nature Society, pp. 81–94.

den Hartog, C. 1970. Seagrasses of the World. *Verhandl. der Koninklijke Nederlandse Akademie van Wetenschappen, Afd. Natuurkunde* 59, pp. 1–275.

Dikou, A., and R. van Woesik. 2006. Survival under Chronic Stress from Sediment Load: Spatial Pattern of Hard Coral Communities in Southern Islands of Singapore. *Marine Pollution Bulletin* 52(11), pp. 1340–54.

Goh, C. Y. 2010. Singapore: Bukit Timah Eco-bridge to Link Nature Reserves on Its Way. *Straits Times* December 11th.

Heinsohn, G. E., J. Wake, H. Marsh, and A. V. Spain. 1977. The Dugong Dugong Dugon Müller in the Seagrass System. *Aquaculture* 12(3), pp. 235–48.

Huang, D., K. P. P. Tun, L. M. Chou, and P. A. Todd. 2009. An Inventory of Zooxanthellate Scleractinian Corals in Singapore: Including 33 New Records. *Raffles Bulletin of Zoology Supplement* 22, pp. 69–80.

Khew, S. K. 2008. Butterflies. In *The Singapore Red Data Book: Threatened Plants and Animals of Singapore*. Eds.W. H. Davison, P. K. L. Ng, and H. H. Chew. Singapore: Nature Society, pp. 81–94.

Koh, L. P., and N. S. Sodhi. 2004. Importance of Reserves, Fragments, and Parks for Butterfly Conservation in a Tropical Urban Landscape. *Ecological Applications* 14, pp. 1695–708.

Koh, L. P., N. S. Sodhi, and B. W. Brook. 2004a. Ecological Correlates of Extinction Proneness in Tropical Butterflies. *Conservation Biology* 18, pp. 1571–78.

Koh, L. P., N. S. Sodhi, and B. W. Brook. 2004b. Co-extinctions of Tropical Butterflies and Their Hostplants. *Biotropica* 36, pp. 272–74.

Leong, T. M., and K. P. P. Lim. 2009. Noteworthy Microchiropteran Records from the Bukit Timah and Central Catchment Nature Reserves, Singapore. *Nature in Singapore* 2, pp. 83–90.

Levin, L. 2006. Recent Progress in Understanding Larval Dispersal: New Direction and Digressions. *Integrative and Comparative Biology* 46(3), pp. 282–97.

Lim, H. C., N. S. Sodhi, B. A. Brook, and M. C. K. Soh. 2003. Undesirable Aliens: Factors Determining the Distribution of Three Invasive Bird Species in Singapore. *Journal of Tropical Ecology* 19, pp. 685–95.

Lim, K. K. P., and T. M. Leong. 2008. Amphibians. In *The Singapore Red Data Book: Threatened Plants and Animals of Singapore*. W. H.Davison, P. K. L. Ng, and H. H. Chew. Eds. Singapore: Nature Society, pp. 155–59.

Lim, K. K. P, R. Subaraj, S. H. Yeo, N. Lim, D. Lane, and B. Y. H. Lee. 2008. Mammals. In *The Singapore Red Data Book: Threatened Plants and Animals of Singapore*. W. H.Davison, P. K. L. Ng, and H. H. Chew. Eds. Singapore: Nature Society, pp. 190–207.

Lim, K. S. 2009. *The Avifauna of Singapore*. Singapore: Nature Society.

Logan, J. R. 1848. The Probable Effects on the Climate of Pinang of the Continued Destruction of the Hill Jungle. *Journal of the Indian Archipelago and East Asia* 2, pp. 534–36.

Lok, A. F. S. L., W. F. K. Ang, Y. Chong, and H. T. W. Tan. 2010. Rediscovery of *Liparis barbata Lindl.* (*Orchidaceae*) in Singapore. *Nature in Singapore* 3, pp. 277–81.

Lok, A. F. S. L., K. Y. Chong, K.-x. Tan, and H. T. W. Tan 2010. A Checklist of the Spontaneous Exotic Vascular Plant Flora of Singapore. *COSMOS* 6, pp. 57–83.

Low, J. K. Y., and L. M. Chou, 1994. Sedimentation Rates in Singapore Waters. In*Proceedings, Third ASEAN-Australia Symposium on Living Coastal Resources, vol. 2, Research Papers*. Eds. S. Sudara, C. R. Wilkinson, and L. M. Chou. Bangkok: Chulalongkorn University, pp. 697–701.

Lum, S. K. Y. 2011. Non-governmental Organisations and the Nature Community. In *Singapore Biodiversity: An Encyclopedia of the Natural Environment and Sustainable Development*.Eds. P. K. L. Ng, R. T. Corlett, and H. T. W. Tan. Singapore: Didier Millet, pp. 156–61.

Lye, L. H. 2008. Nature Conservation Laws: The Legal Protection of Flora and Fauna in Singapore. In *The Singapore Red Data Book: Threatened Plants and Animals of Singapore*. Eds. W. H.Davison, P. K. L. Ng, and H. H. Chew. Singapore: Nature Society, pp. 5–13.

MacKinnon, J. R. 1997. *Protected Areas Systems Review of the Indo-Malayan Realm*. Canterbury: Asian Bureau for Conservation.

McKenzie, L. J., S. M. Yaakub, and R. L. Yoshida. 2007. *Seagrass-Watch: Guidelines for Team Seagrass Singapore Participants*. Proceedings of a training workshop, National Parks Board, Biodiversity Centre, Singapore, March 24th–25th (DPI&F, Cairns, Australia).

MEWR and MND. 2009. *A Lively and Liveable Singapore: Strategies for Sustainable Growth*. Singapore: Ministry of the Environment and Water Resources and Ministry of National Development.

Ng, P. K. L. 1994. *The Singapore Red Data Book: Threatened Plants and Animals of Singapore; a Community Service Project by Asia Pacific Breweries*. Singapore: Nature Society

NParks. 2009a. *New Dairy Farm Nature Park Officially Opens*. 5th September. Retrieved on August 1st, 2012, from http://www.nparks.gov.sg/cms/index.php?option=com_news &task=view&id=165&Itemid=50.

NParks. 2009b. *Conserving Our Biodiversity: Singapore's National Biodiversity Strategy and Action Plan*. Singapore: National Parks Board.

Polidoro, B. A., K. E. Carpenter, S. R. Livingstone, J. C. Sanciangco, L. Collins, N. C. Duke, S. G. Salmo III, A. M. Ellison, J. C. Ellison, E. J. Farnsworth, E. S. Fernando, K. Kathiresan, N. E. Koedam, T. Miyagi, G. E. Moore, V. N. Nam, J. E. Ong, J. H. Primavera, S. Sukardjo, Y. Wang, and J. W. H. Yong. 2010. The Loss of Species, Mangrove Extinction Risk and Geographic Areas of Global Concern. *PLoS ONE* 5, e10095.

Sheppard, J. K., A. R. Preen, H. Marsh, I. R. Lawler, S. D. Whiting, and R. E. Jones,. 2006. Movement Heterogeneity of Dugongs, Dugong Dugon (Müller), over Large Spatial Scales. *Journal of Experimental Marine Biology and Ecology* 334(1), pp. 64–83.

Sheue, C. R., W. H. J. Yong, and Y. P. Yang. 2005. The Bruguiera Rhizophoraceae Species in the Mangroves of Singapore, Especially on the New Record and the Rediscovery. *Taiwania* 50, pp. 251–60.

Short, F. T., B. Polidoro, S. R. Livingstone, K. E. Carpenter, S. Bandeira, J. S. Bujang, H. P. Calumpong, T. J. B. Carruthers, R. G. Coles, W. C. Dennison, P. L.A. Erftemeijer, M. D. Fortes, A. S. Freeman, T. G. Jagtap, A. H. M. Kamal, G. A. Kendrick, W. J. Kenworthy, Y. A. La Nafie, I. M. Nasution, R. J. Orth, A. Prathep, J. C. Sanciangco, B. van Tussenbroek, S. G. Vergara, M. Waycott, and J. C. Zieman. 2011. Extinction Risk Assessment of the World's Seagrass Species. *Biological Conservation* 144, pp. 1961–71.

Sodhi, N. S., C. Briffett, L. Kong, and B. Yuen. 1999. Bird Use of Linear Areas of a Tropical City: Implications for Park Connector Design and Management. *Landscape and Urban Planning* 45, pp. 123–30.

Tan, H. T. W., L. M. Chou, D. C. J. Yeo, and P. K. L. Ng. 2010. *The Natural Heritage of Singapore*. Singapore: Pearson Education South Asia.

Tee, S. P., W. K. Yong, J. S. C. Ng, and Z. M. Ong. 2009. *Trees of Our Garden City: A Guide to the Common Trees of Singapore*. Singapore: National Parks Board.

Turner, I. T., Y. K. Wong, P. T. Chew, and A. Ibrahim. 1996. Rapid Assessment of Tropical Rain Forest Successional Status Using Aerial Photographs. *Biological Conservation* 77, pp. 177–83.

UNEP/COBSEA. L. M. Chou, ed. 2010. *State of the Marine Environment Report for the East Asian Seas 2009*. Bangkok: COBSEA Secretariat.

Ward, P. 1968. Origin of the Avifauna of Urban and Suburban Singapore. *Ibis* 110, pp. 239–55.

Yap, C. A. M., and N. S. Sodhi. 2004. Southeast Asian Invasive Birds: Ecology, Impact and Management. *Ornithological Science* 3, pp. 57–67.

Yee, A. T. K., R. T. Corlett, S. C. Liew, and H. T. W. Tan. 2011. The Vegetation of Singapore: An Updated Map. *Gardens Bulletin Singapore* 63, pp. 205–12.

29 Environmental law as a foundation for sustainable development

Ambassador Amado S. Tolentino Jr

Currently, there are many environmental challenges for human beings to consider: population, food security, loss of species and ecosystems, energy, climate change, carrying capacity, land use, etc. How humans handle the challenges and provide a better world for the next generation is a burning issue. The main concern of environmental law is to govern the relationship of humans with their natural surroundings. In the past, humans viewed nature and its resources as available for unlimited exploitation. Little thought was given to the future or for the harms being done.

As a custodian, human beings must also conserve resources and not merely exploit them. Considering the trend toward industrial development, this task extends to planning and creating an environment of our choice. We should strive to strike a harmonious balance between development and environmental protection for human beings' survival and well-being. More so because of the recognized unity of nature and humanity, and the fact that the earth's resources are finite. The guiding cautionary principle should be, respect and preserve nature in its present or prior condition, and if possible restore it while maintaining its beneficial characteristics. This is presently construed alongside the concept of sustainable development or "development without destruction." It is a wise use of the environment which implies sustainable utilization for the benefit of humankind in a way that is compatible with the maintenance of natural elements of the ecosystem.

Law is an essential tool for the sound management of the environment and its resources. The development and application of legal structures is of vital importance with regard to the preservation, conservation, restoration, and rehabilitation of the environment as well as sustainable utilization of its natural resources. The effectiveness of government development policies depends on the use of law as an instrument of social change as well as social control. Environmental law, as a set of legal rules addressed specifically to activities which potentially affect the quality of the environment whether natural or human-made, involves laws at every level: international, transnational, national, and local. It consists of both "hard law" (e.g. international treaties and national legislations) and "soft law" (e.g. guidelines and standards). Its elements are derived from sectoral areas (e.g. air, marine and inland water, soil, energy, biological diversity) and functional tasks such as environmental impact assessment, natural resources accounting, and environmental auditing (Craig *et al.*, 2002). It is only one component of environmental protection techniques and should be complemented by other functional tasks, such as development and financial plans, conservation strategies and institutional arrangements, and technical support, in order to establish a comprehensive approach to the protection of the environment.

Environmental law: a new field of law

Environmental law has emerged relatively recently as a field of law. Historically, other branches of law were used to remedy environmental problems. In the common law system, tort law (which provides remedies for harm caused by one party to another) provided the necessary legal foundation in early cases. Nuisance suits were the most popular because they allow a successful plaintiff-litigant to receive not only compensation from the other party but also an order from the court abating the nuisance.

The inadequacies and sometimes inefficiency of tort and property law convinced governments to create a new body of law to tackle the most pressing environmental problems. Environmental laws have traditionally been formulated around specific themes such as the conservation of nature and protection of the principal areas of environmental concern: air, water, and land. This specificity of focus allowed the elaboration of rules with limited application that have been relatively easy to manage and enforce, but did not acknowledge the importance of a holistic approach to deal with significant natural relationships such as the effect of air pollution on water quality and land use.

In the area of environmental law, specific legislation preceded the adoption of general or organic laws. There were instances when legislation addressing specific issues developed gradually, or when laws were amended to include the environmental dimensions. This was the situation in many developing countries during the early 1970s when virtually all countries had laws prohibiting pollution, protecting forests, and regulating the exploitation of mineral resources (UNESCAP, 2006). However, for the most part these laws have proven inadequate. Often, what was originally labeled environmental legislation was actually a set of natural resources laws that were "use-oriented," or designed for the maximum exploitation and development of natural resources. Environmental legislation that is "resource-oriented," or designed for the rational management and conservation of natural resources to prevent their depletion or degradation is needed to fill a void.

Environmental law has evolved into a complex field. It now covers preventive and remedial measures relating to all aspects of resource use: the regulation of predominantly quantitative aspects of natural resource use (e.g. water, wildlife, forestry, and fishery legislation); the regulation of predominantly qualitative aspects of resource use (e.g. anti-pollution legislation); and the regulation of the general framework for resource use through the deployment of development, land use planning, and other environmental planning tools. These sub-fields are very much interlinked. Thus, optimal environmental legislation embraces not only the necessary and appropriate sectoral mechanisms but also inter-sectoral ones. Moreover, environmental legislation increasingly explicitly takes into account the uncertainties associated with development: changing technology, resource availability, pollution changes, and the probability of damage from natural phenomena.

Sustainable development and environmental law

The United Nations (UN) Stockholm Conference on the Human Environment (1972), the Rio Summit on Environment and Development (1992), and the Johannesburg Summit on Sustainable Development (2002) all exhorted governments to establish effective legal regulatory frameworks. The 2012 UN Rio + 20 Conference on Sustainable Development is expected to call on governments for further action toward effective implementation of environmental legislations.

There have been significant changes in environmental legislation since the historic environmental summits. Among the emerging trends are:

- crystallization of environmental issues in constitutional and policy documents (e.g. the right to a healthy environment; sustainable use of natural resources);
- more comprehensive coverage of environmental issues (e.g. biodiversity conservation; management of hazardous wastes);
- the establishment of environmental standards and norms (e.g. national air and water quality standards; maximum emission levels for airborne pollutants; maximum noise levels);
- use of economic instruments for environmental management (e.g. tax incentives for installation of anti-pollution devices not locally available; natural resource user-pays and polluter-pays schemes; environment funds);
- recognition of international environmental norms (e.g. legislative and institutional arrangements to give effect to multilateral environmental agreements (MEAs); financial obligations required under some conventions or treaties); environmental impact assessments (EIAs);
- effective coordination of environmental management (e.g. ministries responsible for the environment; high level advisory councils responsible for environment and development issues);
- the development of coherent legislative frameworks (e.g. institutional mechanisms like inter-agency committees for cross-sectoral coordination and harmonization of policies and programs);
- mechanisms for facilitating compliance with environmental regulations and for more effective implementation, compliance and enforcement of environmental law (e.g. environmental law compliance guidelines; enforcement procedures);
- provisions for public participation and review (e.g. public consultation in the EIA process; recognition of legal standing to sue and public interest litigation) (Wilson *et al.*, 2000).

With many countries emphasizing economic development, it is often nec-essary to make the case for MEAs which have taken into consideration the socioeconomic dimension, and that is what sustainable development is all about. Examples are the UN Convention on Biological Diversity and the UN Framework Convention on Climate Change which not only define rights and obligations for environmental protection, but also takes into account the asso-ciated developmental concerns. Furthermore, ways have been found to develop international legal instruments that are sufficiently flexible and capable of accom-modating change as scientific evidence becomes clearer. For instance, the con-cept of common but differentiated responsibilities, according to which each state acts according to its own capability and capacity, is embodied in the Climate Change Convention and the Montreal Protocol (in addition to the 1985 Vienna Convention for the Protection of the Ozone Layer) on Substances that Deplete the Ozone Layer. The differentiation of obligation is an important factor in the development of sustainable development law.

While the key benefits of MEAs are usually environmental and, of late, eco-nomic, they may also be socio-political (e.g. empowering the public to become involved) and administrative. The clearest benefits of any particular MEA usu-ally relate to its specific goals. Thus, CITES (Convention on International Trade in Endangered Species of Wild Flora and Fauna) seeks to ensure that no wild-life species becomes or remains subject to unsustainable exploitation through international trade, but it also allows legitimate trade and scientific research; and the Basel Convention (Convention on Control of Transboundary Movements of Hazardous Wastes and their Disposal) seeks to protect human health and the environment from illegal transboundary movements. Additionally, even if the priority of many countries is on development, participation in MEAs can enhance the long-term sustainability of development initiatives. To the extent that they contribute to the country's ability to address environmental issues ear-lier rather than later, the result may be a cost reduction in the long term, since it is often less expensive to prevent international harm than to address that harm after the fact.

With regard to the unique nature of the implementation process of interna-tional law in the field of sustainable development, there is a history of introduc-ing innovative means and mechanisms of implementation. What can be seen in recent environmental treaties is not only the setting of ambitious goals but also the provision of supportive means for achieving those goals, including finan-cial mechanisms and provisions for transferring resources and technology. These facilitating and supportive means of environmental law will continue to develop, complementing the prohibitive mechanisms that have so long characterized legal regimes (UNDP/UNESCAP, 2002).

Indeed, the number and scope of international environmental agreements have grown at a fast pace since 1985. It is estimated that there are about 700 different international agreements that govern some aspect of the environment and several more being negotiated at the bilateral, regional and global levels. In this regard, the UN Environment Programme (UNEP) has published guidelines to facilitate the implementation of MEAs (UNEP, 1995). Expanding upon the guidelines, the manual provides ideas, approaches, and experiences that governments and other stakeholders may consider when seeking to improve compliance and enforcement (UNEP, 1995) (updated information is available at http://www.unep.org/delc/). Governments have expressed particular interest in approaches designed to simplify the implementation of MEAs in countries with limited resources such as priority setting and MEA clustering.

Be that as it may, apart from establishing appropriate legal and institutional frameworks, effective implementation and enforcement of national environmental legislation remains a daunting challenge, especially for developing countries. How the matter is resolved will largely determine the capacity of the legal arrangements to effectively contribute toward realizing the objectives of sustainable development. For, in the final analysis, ineffective law may be worse than no law at all. Its existence may satisfy political and administrative conscience, or a formal international obligation, but it will have no impact on the problems which it is supposed to solve. It may have some initial deterring effect but this will disappear as soon as it becomes evident that the law will not be enforced. The law gives the impression that something is being done, whereas the existing legal arrangements are contributing little in terms of practical environmental management. In fact, the lack of ability to enforce the legislation will have promoted in its continued breach an undesirable disrespect toward an important state policy.

Priorities for effective environmental law implementation

From its beginning as natural resources law to its transformation into environmental law, this branch of law is fast becoming referred to as the law of sustainable development. This enlarged nomenclature reflects the understanding that environmental law has to integrate environmental protection into economic development and vice versa. The goal of this integration is to raise living standards while preserving the environmental potential of the future; in short, to bring about sustainable development. For developing countries in particular, a sound economy is a social and environmental precondition to environmental commitment.

The transition of environmental law to a law of sustainable development can best be made by organizing the reform agenda around human activities, thus infusing the main body of development law with ecological principles. This requires a re-examination of property rights principles, banking operations, the tax code, and a sector-by-sector revision of the laws governing agriculture, energy, transportation, and manufacture of goods. By tailoring environmental law more closely to patterns of human behavior, the administration and enforcement of environmental law will be more efficient and, ultimately, environmental law will blend with other areas of law, thus strengthening the effectiveness of environmental law as well as the respect it deserves.

All the efforts made in the recent past to protect the environment under command-and-control regulation produced legal activity focused almost exclusively either on pollution control laws or on resource management laws but seldom on the interface between the two. Pollution control laws focus primarily on processing and recovering resources for disposal while natural resources laws focus primarily on resource extraction. The law concentrates on consequences but not on causes: on water purification but not on pollution prevention; on saving protected areas but not on checking soil erosion; on protecting endangered species but not on biological diversity. This piecemeal reaction in lawmaking even resulted in piecemeal emergency responses to industrial incidences such as chemical accidents, oil spills, etc. Emergency response should be integrated into a coherent environmental management system that is held accountable within a legal structure. The worst manifestation of this problem is the regulation of the same activity by many government agencies: pollution from mining by the mining agency; pollution from industry by the environment agency; coastal pollution by the coast guard, etc. (Futrell, 1994). In short, the law on environment and development has not been purposefully integrated.

To illustrate how environmental laws could be better integrated with development regulations, let us take as an example of the human activity associated with forestry. Formulation of sustainable development legislation would require an analysis of the life cycle of forestry and each stage's impact on the environment from extraction to processing to disposal, showing how economic activity at each stage affects the environment. Using a resource-to-recovery analysis centered on forest products would start with the natural resource laws and regulations affecting timber harvesting, proceed through regulation of air and water pollution, and waste regulation as it affects milling operations, and end with laws relating to the manufacture, recycling, and ultimate disposal of wood products.

Such a resource-to-recovery analysis would identify the pollution control and natural resources laws that must be integrated with property tax and other development laws to create a system that promotes sustainability. It would expose those areas where development and environmental regulation clash and it would help modify the provisions that undermine sustainability. Let us take as another example a resource threatened by overuse anywhere in the world: groundwater. In developing countries, in particular, groundwater is being withdrawn for irrigation much faster than it is being recharged, and whole watersheds either are or will soon face shortages. The need to control groundwater pollution and conserve groundwater is an intricate policy and regulatory challenge to which the revision of agricultural law could be a solution. Most often, agricultural law works at cross-purposes with pollution control, resource and tax laws. Reform should be aimed at achieving an integrated scheme compatible with a sustainable economy and a sustainable ecology.

A simpler example is offered by the land use laws as they relate to pollution control legislation. Command-and-control regulation might be lighter on industry if land use laws effectively directed factory location to more easily achieve sustainable development. In other words, land use planning should balance environmental and developmental interests by incorporating air and water pollution control at the outset. The transition to sustainable development law will require a move beyond the command-and-control regulation to the use of all available legal tools.

Assessing how these laws promote or impede sustainability will require a review of the "non-environmental laws" in the realms of agriculture, banking, public works, taxation, and transportation. Examination of the laws should proceed natural resource by natural resource, industry sector by industry sector, taking into account the total resource-to-recovery cycle and being careful to keep the basic structure of the law in place. As the transition to sustainable development law progresses, the pollution control laws can be simplified and the burden of command-and-control regulation will ease. Furthermore, the integration of development and environmental law can lead to increased use of more effective tools such as planning, process changes for pollution prevention, and economic incentives, all encouraging sustainability. This will in turn lead to better law by infusing the environmental movement with economic realism and a commitment to social justice.

Conclusion

Environmental law has become a foundation for sustainable development. One could view sustainable utilization of a natural resource as framed and reinforced by an effective and efficient legal structure from which other legal structures will emerge. The overall result will be actions which are legal and, at the same time, sustainable. As changes are made through environmental law, sustainable development will define the path which preserves the dignity of nature and the dignity of humanity.

References

Craig D., N. Robinson and K. L. Koh. 2002. *Capacity Building for Environmental Law in the Asian and Pacific Region*. Manila: Asian Development Bank.

Futrell, W. 1994. *The Transition to Sustainable Development Law*. Washington, DC: Environmental Law Institute.

UNDP/UNESCAP (United Nations Development Program/United Nations Economic and Social Commission for Asia and the Pacific). 2002. *Environmental Governance for Sustainable Development in Asia and Pacific*. New York: UNDP.

UNDP/UNESCAP 2006. *Manual on Compliance with and Enforcement of Multilateral Environmental Agreements*. Nairobi: UNEP. http://www.unep.org/delc/.

Wilson, P. et al. 2000. *Emerging Trends in National Environmental Legislation in Developing Countries*. Nairobi: UNEP.

Further reading

Part I: Methods for understanding individuals' values

Aiken, L. R. 2002. *Attitudes and Related Psychosocial Constructs: Theories, Assessment, and Research*. Thousand Oaks, Calif.: Sage.

Allport, G. 1954. *The Nature of Prejudice*. New York: Addison-Wesley.

Appiah, K. A. 2005. *The Ethnics of Identity*. Princeton, NJ: Princeton University Press.

Argyris, C. 1985. *Strategy, Change, and Defensive Routines*. New York: Pitman.

Bakhtin, M. M., M. Holquist, ed., V. Liapunov, ed., trans., K. Brostrom, trans. *The Dialogic Imagination: Four Essays*. Austin, Tex.: University of Texas Press.

Boje, D. 2011. *Storytelling and the Future of Organizations: An Antenarrative Handbook*. Oxford: Routledge.

Burger, P., and T. Luckman. 1967. *The Social Construction of Reality*. Garden City, NY: Doubleday Anchor.

Condon, P. M. 2007. *Design Charrettes for Sustainable Communities*. Washington, DC: Island Press.

Fairclough, N., and I. Ietcu-Fairclough. 2012. *Analysing Discourse*. Oxford: Routledge.

Gable, R. K., and M. B. Wolf. 1993. *Instrument Development in the Affective Domain: Measuring Attitudes and Values in Corporate and School Settings*. Norwell, Mass.: Kluwer Academic.

Geertz, C. 1973. *The Interpretation of Cultures*. New York: Basic Books.

Goffman, E. 1959. *The Presentation of Self in Everyday Life*. Garden City, NY: Doubleday Anchor.

Goffman, E. 1982. *Interaction Ritual*. New York: Pantheon.

Hofstede, G. 2001. *Culture's Consequences*. Thousand Oaks, Calif.: Sage.

Huesmann, M., and J. Huesmann. 2011. *Techno-Fix: Why Technology Won't Save Us Or the Environment*. Gabriola Island, BC: New Society Publishers.

Kahane, A. 2012. *Transformative Scenario Planning: Working Together to Change the Future*. San Francisco: Berrett-Koehler Publishers.

Lennertz, B., and A. Lutzenhiser. 2006. *The Charrette Handbook*. Washington, DC: American Planning Association.

Liamputtong, P. 2011. *Focus Group Methodology: Principle and Practice*. Thousand Oaks, Calif.: Sage.

Loorbach, D. 2007. *Transition Management: New Mode of Governance for Sustainable Development*. Dublin: International Books.

Loorbach, D. 2010. *Transitions to Sustainable Development: New Directions in the Study of Long Term Transformative Change*. Oxford: Routledge.

McNamee, S., and J. K. Gergen. 1998. *Relational Responsibility: Resources for Sustainable Dialogue*. Thousand Oaks, Calif.: Sage.

McNamee, S., and D. M. Hosking. 2011. *Research and Social Change: A Relational Constructionist Approach.* Oxford: Routledge.

Nellemann, C., and E. Corcoran. 2010. *Dead Planet, Living Planet – Biodiversity and Ecosystem Restoration for Sustainable Development.* Arendal, Norway: UNEP.

Patnaik, U., and S. Mayo. 2011. *The Agrarian Question in the Neoliberal Era: Primitive Accumulation and the Peasantry.* Oxford: Pambazuka Press.

Polanyi, K. 2012. *The Great Transformation: The Political and Economic Origins of Our Times.* Mattituck, NY: Amereon Ltd.

Rees, W. E., M. Wackernagel, and P. Testemale. 1998. *Our Ecological Footprint: Reducing Human Impact on the Earth.* Gabriola Island, BC: New Society Publishers.

Rokeach, M. 1979. *Understanding Human Values.* New York: Free Press.

Schiffrin, D., D.Tannen, and H. E. Hamilton, eds. 2003. *The Handbook of Discourse Analysis.* Oxford: Blackwell.

Scollon, R. 2001. *Mediated Discourse: The Nexus of Practice.* Oxford: Routledge.

Secretariat of the Convention on Biological Diversity. 2010. *Global Biodiversity Outlook 3.* Montréal, Quebec, Canada: Secretariat of the Convention on Biological Diversity.

Shiva, V. 2005. *Earth Democracy: Justice, Sustainability, and Peace.* Cambridge, Mass.: South End Press.

Shiva, V. 2010. *Staying Alive: Women, Ecology, and Development.* Cambridge, Mass.: South End Press.

Tannen, D. 2005. *Conversational Style: Analyzing Talk among Friends.* Oxford: Oxford University Press.

Triandis, H. C. 1971. *Attitude and Attitude Change.* New York: John Wiley and Sons.

Verbong, G. and D. Loorbach, eds. 2012. *Governing the Energy Transition: Reality, Illusion or Necessity?* Oxford: Routledge.

Part II: Religious and ethnically based environmental values

Asquith, P. and A. Kalland. 2004.*Japanese Images of Nature.* Oxford: Routledge.

Bellah, R. N. 2011. *Religion in Human Evolution: From the Paleolithic to the Axial Age.* Cambridge, Mass.: Harvard University Press.

Brecher, W. 2000. *An Investigation of Japan's Relationship to Nature and the Environment.* Lampeter, Ceredigion, UK: Edwin Mellen Press.

Cajete, G. 2000. *Native Science.* Santa Fe, NM: Clear Light.

Chappel, C. K., and M. E. Tucker, eds. 2000. *Hinduism and Ecology.* Cambridge, Mass.: Harvard University Press.

Corral-Verdugo, V., C. H. Garcia-cadena, and M. Frias-armenta, eds. 2010. *Psychological Approaches to Sustainability: Current Trends in Theory, Research and Applications.* New York: Nova Science.

Economy, E. 2004. *The River Runs Black.* London: Cornell University Press.

Edmunds, R. L. 2004. *Managing the Chinese Environment.* Oxford: Oxford University Press.

Elvin, M. 2004. *The Retreat of the Elephants.* New Haven, Conn.: Yale University Press.

Foltz, R. C., F. M. Denny, and A. Baharuddin, eds. 2003. *Islam and Ecology.* Cambridge, Mass.: Harvard University Press.

Glave, D., and M. Stoll. 2005. *To Love the Wind and the Rain: African Americans and Environmental History.* Pittsburgh, Pa.: University of Pittsburgh Press.

Harris, P. 2011. *China's Responsibility for Climate Change: Ethics, Fairness and Environmental Policy.* Bristol, UK: Policy Press.

Harris, P. 2012. *Environmental Policy and Sustainable Development in China: Hong Kong in Global Context.* Bristol, UK: Policy Press.

Hendry, J. 2012. *Understanding Japanese Society*. Oxford: Routledge.

Kalof, L., and T. Satterfield. 2005. *Environmental Values*. London: Earthscan.

Kirby, P. W. 2010. *Troubled Nature*. Hawaii: University of Hawaii Press.

Knight, J. 2006. *Waiting for Wolves in Japan*. Hawaii: University of Hawaii Press.

Lebra, T. S. 1976. *Japanese Patterns of Behavior*. Hawaii: University of Hawaii Press.

Lee, O. 1982. *Smaller is Better*. Tokyo: Kodansha.

McGrath, A. 2003. *The Reenchantment of Nature: The Denial of Religion and the Ecological Crisis*. London: Galilee Trade.

Nakane, C. 1972. *Japanese Society*. Berkeley, Calif.: University of California Press.

Nelson, M. 2008. *Original Instructions*. Rochester, Vt.: Bear & Co.

Selin, H. 2003. *Nature Across Cultures*. London: Kluwer Academic.

Smil, V. 2004. *China's Past, China's Future*. Oxford: Routledge.

Tirosh-Samuelson, H. *Judaism and Ecology*. Cambridge, Mass.: Harvard University Press.

Tucker, M. E. and D. R. Williams, eds. 1997. *Buddhism and Ecology*. Cambridge, Mass.: Harvard University Press.

Van Dyke, F. 1996. *Redeeming Creation: The Biblical Basis for Environmental Stewardship*. Downers Grove, Ill.: IVP Academic.

Van Dyke, F. 2010. *Between Heaven and Earth: Christian Perspectives on Environmental Protection*. New York: Praeger.

Wharton, V. 1947. *The Negro in Mississippi 1865–1890*. Chapel Hill, NC: UNC Press.

Yaffe, M. 2001. *Judaism and Environmental Ethics*. Oxford: Lexington Books.

Part III: Examples of values guiding behavior

Balmford, A. 2012. *Wild Hope: On the Front Lines of Conservation Success*. Chicago, Ill.: University Of Chicago Press.

Bekoff, M., and J. Goodall. 2008.*The Emotional Lives of Animals: A Leading Scientist Explores Animal Joy, Sorrow, and Empathy – and Why They Matter*. New York: New World Library.

Beyerlin, U., and T. Marauhn. 2011. *International Environmental Law*. Oxford: Beck/Hart.

Briffett, C., ed. 1990. *Master Plan for the Conservation of Nature in Singapore*. Singapore: Malayan Nature Society.

Jorgensen, S. E., F. Xu, and R. Costanza. 2010. *Handbook of Ecological Indicators for Assessment of Ecosystem Health*.New York: CRC Press.

Landscaping. www.emswcd.org/naturescaping.

Managi, S. 2012. *The Economics of Biodiversity and Ecosystem Services*. Oxford: Routledge.

Nadkarni, N. 2009. *Between Earth and Sky: Our Intimate Connections to Trees*. Berkeley, Calif.: University of California.

Redekop, B. W. 2011. *Leadership for Environmental Sustainability*. Oxford: Routledge.

Reynolds, J. 2011. *Only the Mountains Do Not Move: A Maasai Story of Culture and Conservation*. New York: Lee & Low Books.

Ruhl, J. B., S. E. Kraft, and C. Lant. 2007. *The Law and Policy of Ecosystem Services*. Washington, DC: Island Press.

Van Dyke, F. 2010. *Conservation Biology: Foundations, Concepts, Applications*. New York: Springer.

Index

Figures and illustrations are in italics. Tables are in bold.

DATE DUE

PRINTED IN U.S.A.